More True Ghost Stories

More True Ghost Stories

Hans Holzer

DORSET PRESS
NEW YORK

2002 Dorset Press

ISBN 0-7607-3415-1

Printed and bound in the United States of America

02 03 04 05 MP 9 8 7 6 5 4 3 2 1

Table of Contents

Introduction

Are There Such Things As "Living" Ghosts?

As my investigations of psychic phenomena mounted in number and importance, it became increasingly clear to me that ghosts and spirits and human beings must all have something in common: if a living person can turn into a "dead" spirit or ghost, then that which survives must already have been contained within mortal man. We are as much spirit in our lifetime as we'll ever be.

I also noticed an amazing analogy between certain sleep and dream states and death—as reported by those claiming to be surviving entities speaking through entranced mediums.

The seat of personality seems encased within a temporary frame called the physical body. Under certain conditions, the personality (or soul, if you want to be religious-minded) can emerge from the "box" and behave independently of it. This is called astral travel, or out-of-the-body experience. Here the separation is temporary and still under the control of the traveler—the sleeper. At death the separation is permanent and the personality, the inner self, leaves the "box" behind, rising to a new and freer existence in what Dr. Joseph Rhine of Duke University has called the world of the mind and what I prefer calling the non-physical world.

But there are cases where a ghost appears and on checking it is found that the one whose ghost it is is still alive and kicking.

Are there such things as "living ghosts"?

In 1920 Mrs. L. lived in a small oil town in Oklahoma. Her husband was a drilling contractor and their lives were ordinary lives with-

1

out a trace of the uncanny. One morning Mrs. L. awoke to the sound of a buzzer that preceded the sounding of the hour on her alarm clock. She opened her eyes and noticed it was 7 A.M., or rather five minutes before the hour. In direct line between her eyes and the wall was a chest of drawers. Between the chest and the window there was some space, and as her eyes fastened themselves on that area, she became aware of a figure standing there. It was her husband, staring straight at her. However, she noticed that the apparition ended at the knees where the figure faded out. He wore his usual tan pants, but she also noticed a white shirt with purple stripes. What puzzled her about this shirt was the fact that it was at this moment neatly tucked away inside the chest of drawers.

Now the figure of her husband started to fade away, slowly, from the bottom on up. By the time the apparition had fully dissolved, the clock chimed the hour—seven o'clock.

Mrs. L. got up quickly and opened the chest of drawers; there was the shirt. Before she realized what she was doing she had torn the shirt to bits!

A short time after, Mr. L. was involved in an explosion at the oil rig where he worked. He was blown into a wheelhouse and knocked unconscious. Everything around him was on fire, but he came to just in time to grab a plank and kick it out of the wheelhouse, and thus make his escape.

At the time she saw her husband's "ghost," Mrs. L. was sure he was alive. She was equally convinced that it was a kind of warning. If she hadn't destroyed the telltale shirt and if he had worn it that fatal day, would he have been able to save himself?

A tantalizing question.

"Haven't seen a ghost now for about two years," confided the lady from New Britain, Connecticut, who had come to hear my lecture at the college.

It turned out she had seen ghosts galore before that date, however. Mrs. Lillian Dorval had a husband, a daughter, and a lot of common sense. But she is very psychic, like it or not.

The first time anything unusual happened was in 1957. She had just fed the baby her bottle and fallen asleep, around midnight. Suddenly she awoke to see what she thought was her husband standing beside her bed. It was 2 A.M. When she asked him what he was doing, standing there like that, he did not answer. So Mrs. Dorval reached over and switched on the light. There in bed beside her was her husband, sleeping peacefully.

When she explained that she had just seen him standing near her bed, he thought she had had a nightmare. But she had no doubt about it—she knew she had been awake. What she did not know at the time was that she had just undergone an experience of bi-location. Mrs. Dorval encountered the "living ghosts" again, some time after her husband had passed away unexpectedly. A friend of hers had left her and she had gone to bed. In the middle of the night she saw his apparition standing by her bed. He was very much alive at the moment she saw him, perhaps still thinking of their evening together.

In November 1966 she saw an apparition of a man she could not recognize at the time. Again it was in the very heart of the night, around 1 A.M.

Several months later she met this man and became friendly with him. Obviously he had been alive at the time she saw his apparition—but how could one explain this link, since she had not yet encountered him, nor he her, except by prevision on her part.

"Regular" ghosts—that is, of dead people—are nothing new to her, of course.

Take her favorite uncle, Harry, for instance. Five days after the family had buried him, there he stood on the right side of her bed. All the "living ghosts," projections of people still in the body, had always appeared on her *left* side. Moreover, the living ones were in color while Uncle Harry wore a plain white suit. When she switched the lights on, he melted away like the others.

Mrs. Dorval fears ridicule so she has not seen fit to talk about her experiences. She also has had out-of-the-body experiences of her own when she found herself soaring out onto rooftops and trees. And the incident she remembers most vividly was her neighbor's funeral which she attended. While the proceedings went forward in the customary manner, she noticed the neighbor sitting on a wall near the casket, laughing and looking over the mourners.

Projections of living people, or "Phantasms of the Living," as the author Sidgwick has called them, occur when a person's thoughts are so strongly engaged at a distance that part of their personality travels with them. If the person on the other end of the "line" happens to be receptive, that is, a psychic person "in tune" with the sender, reception of an image or even a voice may result. And yet, by nature, the ghosts of the living and the ghosts of the dead have much in common. Both prove by the sheer weight of the evidence—numerous as these cases are—that man possesses an indestructible inner self which is capable of breaking through the conventional limits of time and space.

But apparitions of the living and ghosts of the dead have a common frontier in the type of ghost that refuses to accept the facts of afterlife. These people are aware that they are not what they used to be but persist in their habits in what was formerly their world. In a way, they too are psychotic in the sense every ghost is disturbed, but their aberration is more refined, more sophisticated than that of the "run of the mill" specter unable to recognize its own demise.

A young lady by the name of Shaaron Kennett, in an eastern New England city, has lived with her psychic experiences without too much concern. So what if several relatives have dropped in on her at the precise moment of their deaths? Distance has no bearing on these visitations. Miss Kennett was in Rhode Island once and the dead left this world in Philadelphia, but the twain met in Miss Kennett's bedroom at the very instance of death.

In 1962 the young lady moved into an old house in town, along with her parents and a brother. Two weeks after they had installed themselves Miss Kennett was startled to find another person in the house, a person who could not be accounted for as a visitor or otherwise. The woman was clearly visible in the downstairs bedroom, so clearly, in fact, that Miss Kennett had a good chance to look at her carefully. Her stern face was what struck her strongly, and she wore a plain, dark dress with high neck and a thin strip of lace at the throat. Her steel-gray hair was pulled back severely from her face. The woman was of medium height, very slight build, and seemed elderly.

After this initial experience when Miss Kennett saw the woman for several seconds before she disappeared, the ghostly occupant of the house returned a number of times. Soon she would show up all over the house, day or night, meeting the family at the top of the stairs and always looking them over before "allowing" them to pass, then descending the stairs herself. Miss Kennett's mother also saw her, so much so that it became a daily routine for her to see the ghost woman in her kitchen first thing every morning.

The stern expression on her face never changed and though the family accepted their "house ghost," the dogs and cats did not and kept out of her way.

Miss Kennett made some discreet inquiries about their house. She was able to trace the apparition to a former owner of their house, a Mrs. Frances F. The lady evidently felt the house was still hers, and the downstairs bedroom in which she first appeared to Shaaron Kennett was indeed her former bedroom. What were strangers doing in *her* house? What sort of people are going up *her* staircase? Look at it from the ghost's point of view, if you please.

I daresay that at least one percent of all those who die either unhappily or with some unfinished business on their minds may stay behind in what was for so long their proper home.

Ghosts are always the personalities of people who died tragically, it is true, but this death need not be sudden.

Lingering suffering, mental or physical, can result in the same type of phenomenon.

My files are bulging with such cases, verified properly and containing the eyewitness—or sometimes ear witness—reports of reputable people.

Neither are the ones clinging to their former abodes spirits in the sense that all of us turn spirit at death, if death occurs normally and is accepted by us as such.

The natural order of things is to leave one's physical surroundings at the time the physical body is left behind.

Those refusing to leave are therefore in violation of this rule and become like fish out of water: of spirit "matter," yet within the physical world, they are part of neither one.

The stay-behinds are a real problem only when they become so filled with hatred for those succeeding them in their former homes that they attempt to drive them out, by whatever means are at their command.

Thus the *Poltergeist* or physical phenomena stage is reached, when frightening movements of objects, noises and other manifestations occur and convince the living that theirs is not a safe place to be. Unfortunately people are filled with fears of the Unknown. They often do give in and move out, leaving the stay-behind dead in command. In so doing, they condemn the stay-behinds to a far worse existence than being dead—an in-between state where no progress is possible.

Until people became used to my ideas of contacting the stay-behinds through trance mediums, there was really little they could do: either stay and endure the shenanigans, or leave and let the stay-behinds have the house, or perhaps rent it to some other tenant with thicker skin.

Not everybody is psychic in the same degree. The majority of people are so insensitive they may not even notice a stay-behind. But a substantial minority do get impressions of them ranging all the way from a mere "uneasy feeling of a presence" to full sight of the dead one. This is why not everybody experiences the presences by merely walking into a place plagued by stay-behinds. One cannot request a command performance by the stay-behind just so one can prove that he or she is always there. They are, having no other place to go to.

Often enough, they frequent a certain room or even a favorite piece of furniture.

Having imparted much of their personal aura or magnetism to the object through long years of bodily contact with it, they naturally are drawn to it both by sentimental memory and by automatic attraction. If a stranger sits in their favorite chair, quite rightly the stay-behind will deeply resent the intrusion. To the stay-behind the living are the intruders in *his* world, not the other way round. He neither comprehends nor cares to know that things have changed through his death.

It is futile to walk into an old house in the hope of encountering a "ghost," just because the house has been lived in for a long time and perhaps has seen many and varied emotional scenes, or even violent death or struggle.

What the sensitive person might feel in such a place would be an impression of past events rather than participants in them.

On the other hand, some such houses do have ghosts or stay-behinds in them. But then one should rather expect someone among the living, sooner or later, to have an experience of an objective kind, an experience of either seeing or hearing the stay-behind. I, for one, would never investigate a house unless and until several reputable people reported to me that they had indeed had an unusual firsthand experience in the house in question.

Miss Kennett and her family have long accepted the former owner as one of their people. They are not overjoyed with her, but they understand why she is there. And if she looks out for them and the safety of their house—as Mary Wallace's ghost still does for the Ocean-born Mary House in Henniker, New Hampshire—then having Mrs. F. around isn't so bad after all!

Because the people involved in the following story are all prominent in present-day society in New England, I will not mention their names. Suffice it to say that I have them, and the story, to the best of my knowledge, is absolutely true.

Miss S. has a winter home on New York's East Side and a summer home in Massachusetts. All her life she had partaken of the supernatural, be it in little warnings or larger incursions from the so-called dead.

Once she was shopping at Bloomingdale's when she felt a sudden and inexplicable urge to visit her aged uncle in Washington Square. She tried to reason it out, saying to herself that the time of day was already too late for such a visit and that she should go the next morning, but the urge within her got the upper hand.

When she reached her uncle she found him happily smoking his pipe and in good spirits. He was an elderly gent and almost blind. Miss S. was sure that she had given in to a foolish impulse, but she went to take her coat off and hang it in the nurse's room. When she returned to her uncle, she saw that the bowl of his pipe had just caught fire and was blazing away, and he was not at all aware of it. Within moments, she managed to put out the fire. Had she not been there at the time, surely the uncle would have perished.

In 1940 Miss S. moved into her present summer home in Massachusetts. Seventeen years later she bought it from the friend who had owned it at the time. Built originally in 1904, the house had had a total of four owners prior to herself.

Her friend, a Mrs. R., had only owned the house for about a year when Miss S. moved in. Neither lady recalls anything unusual until one day in 1944, when they experienced something they could not explain by ordinary means. The house has a rear piazza in back of the living room, in direct line with the front door and the steps leading up to it. That day, they and some friends clearly heard some heavy footsteps coming up the front steps. Miss S. got up and hurried to see who it was, but found no one.

At first Miss S. dismissed it as some sort of practical joke, but she soon learned differently. Over the years, the steps would return, mainly in July and August, and always between noon and 3 P.M. Other phenomena included banging noises coming from an empty workshop once used by a former owner, and the clicking sound of a light switch being turned—but no light.

It became difficult to "explain" these happenings to the maid and various visitors, but Miss S. steadfastly refused to accept the supernatural explanation, although she knew at heart what it was.

Finally, the matter came to a head. Miss S. had been ill and her doctor was coming to see her. Since she was expecting him, she was sitting on the back piazza facing the front door. The doctor happened to be a cousin, and when she heard footsteps coming up the front steps she rose to greet him.

To her horror it was not her cousin who appeared now before her, but a strange man she had never seen before. He was a thin, elderly man in a Palm Beach suit and a panama hat.

Miss S. rushed to the door as fast as her feet would carry her, but he stepped sideways and just disappeared. She looked everywhere but there was no trace of the stranger. This experience so unnerved her she decided to discuss the apparition with her neighbors. It was then that she learned the story of her house. The man she had seen was indeed well know in the community. It was Mr. B., who had died in 1940. Up to 1939 the house had been owned by the P.'s, husband and wife. Mr. P. was an economist at one of the leading eastern universities. At the time, it was common knowledge in the community that a love affair had been going on between Mr. P. and Mrs. B., also dead now. The ghostly visitor was the husband, looking, apparently, for his wife at his neighbor's house.

What convinced Miss S. that this was indeed the case, was her friend's experience when she bought the house from the economist's wife. Overly anxious to sell the house, Mrs. P. took a sum below its actual value, and left everything in the house behind—even personal items such as the family Bible. Surely the house must have had bad memories for her and she wanted to get out as quickly as possible.

Well, Miss S. was not one bit amused. The prospect of having the ghost of the deceived husband dropping in on her unannounced did not please her at all. She took her Bible and said a few prayers in the firm New England manner that is part of her character. She followed this up with a request that Mr. B. should get his rest and not drop around again.

Either Mr. B. realized that the family scandal had better be forgotten now that he didn't have a ghost of a chance to do anything about his rival, or Miss S.'s direct approach worked.

Except for some tapping at her bedroom window in the summer of 1966, she did not hear any unusual noises again. And the tapping might have been *someone else*. After all, Miss S. is a receptive person.

New England

Country House Ghosts

In May of 1964, I received a telephone call from a lady who identified herself as Doris Armfield. She had read my book *Ghost Hunter*, and wanted to invite me to a house at Rehoboth, Massachusetts, where a poltergeist had taken up residence.

I asked her to give me a detailed account of her experiences.

"My husband and I purchased the house sometime around 1940. It was purported to be more than 200 years old. We have never heard that it was haunted or that any violent death had occurred in it, but the legend has persisted that this was the house that had a fortune buried somewhere in a stone wall, and we treated this story as an old-time tale.

"We have had many odd happenings at the house during the years, but the noises heard in the kitchen are what concern me. The original house was a regular Cape Cod consisting of four rooms downstairs and an attic upstairs. One hundred years after the original house was built, a kitchen ell was added, consisting of the kitchen, a small room off the kitchen, and a large back hall. Our current postmaster in town lived in the house at one time and he added dormers upstairs. We put a porch along the ell. There is also a small barn used as a garage. These constitute the physical plan of the house. We own about 100 acres on both sides of the street.

"Shortly after we moved in, the first event happened. My husband and I were eating supper in the kitchen when a sound like an explosion made us both bound from our chairs. We found that a glass dish in the kitchen cupboard on the top shelf had shattered. We decided that maybe a change of temperature had made the dish break and left it at that. However, this particular noise has been the only one where we found physical evidence of breakage.

"About two years after this, my husband joined the Navy in World War II and his aunt came to stay with me for a week or two. The first night as we sat down to supper in the kitchen, my dog Dusty sat beside my chair, and all of a sudden he started to growl very deeply. The hackles rose on his back, he bared his teeth, and scared me half to death, because I had never seen him do this unless he thought my husband or I was threatened. He was *staring at an empty chair* to my left, but I thought his growl meant someone was around the house. I went out and looked around, but no one was there.

"My aunt went home to her own house after a week or so and I lived alone in the house with the dog and some assorted cats. One night I was reading in bed, with the dog at my feet. I reached up to put off the bed lamp when I heard a tremendous crash and the sound of dishes banging, crashing, and shattering. I knew immediately that the dish cupboard in the kitchen had fallen loose from the wall and that it had hit the counter beneath it and just spewed all the hundreds of dishes across the floor and smashed them to smithereens. The dog and I flew into the kitchen only to find everything was intact. I took a flashlight and went all over the house from cellar to attic, knowing all the while that the only big quantity of dishes were in that kitchen cupboard.

"We decided to make a three-room apartment upstairs for a girlfriend of ours who had lost her husband a few years before. She moved in, and the years went by, eighteen years, in fact.

"One evening at 5 P.M., she came home from work, and walked upstairs to her apartment. She had her foot on the last step when she just stood there unable to believe that horrible crashing and clattering of dishes being broken.

"Naturally, she expected to see the three-shelved kitchen cupboard torn away from the wall, figured it had hit the counter beneath it, and that every dish had fallen, breaking and rolling along the floor. She stood there in amazement when she found nothing was disturbed.

"We went home the next weekend, and as we compared noises, we found we had both had the same impression of what had happened, and the noises were identical. This happened about two years ago.

"About two months ago, a neighbor and myself were singing, and also playing the piano in the dining room, and were also tape recording our efforts. My husband was in the room behind the kitchen, and my sister was reading in the living room. At the end of a song we heard a crash of dishes or glasses and we all converged on the kitchen. I thought our Siamese cat had climbed onto a shelf on the hutch and possibly knocked off three or four plates that had then broken. Once again we all looked at each other and couldn't believe that nothing was broken. I then thought of the fact that the crash was on the tape, and we played it back and sure enough, we heard it loud and clear."

Immediately after I received Mrs. Armfield's report, I telephoned her at her weekday residence in Connecticut. The house at Rehoboth, Massachusetts, where the uncanny phenomena had taken place, was a weekend retreat.

I offered to come out to have a look at the house on my next trip to Boston.

"Everything is quiet for the moment," she replied, "but you're welcome any time."

Somehow the trip never occurred, and it was not until April, 1965, when I finally got around to reaching the Armfields again. I have no staff to help me, and cases just pile up until I can get around to them myself. This time my note was answered by Doris' husband, Richard Armfield. His wife had passed away in January of 1965. Under the circumstances, I decided not to trouble him, hoping that Mrs. Armfield herself might have discovered what or who it was who caused the uncanny noises in the Rehoboth house—from her side of the veil.

*   *   *

Charles Demers, who described himself as a combat veteran and unafraid of anything, lived with his family in an old house in Hampstead, New Hampshire. He bought the house in 1959. His two older girls—he had three children—slept upstairs in a finished room at the rear of the attic. Right away, they complained about noises in the attic. When he went to investigate, he himself heard the footsteps of a heavy person walking across the floor, night after night, at 10 P.M. The two children were moved downstairs, and Demers himself took the room in the attic.

"I have stared death in the eye many times, Mr. Holzer," Demers said, "and I was not afraid. I listened hard and sure enough, *it* was coming to the door of the bedroom. I gently slid out of bed and turned on the light, waiting. The ghost was just outside the door. I looked at the door knob, and *it was being turned slowly.* I did not panic, but nothing further was heard."

No footsteps going down, for instance.

*   *   *

Another New Hampshire case concerned a certain Mrs. V., who had been subject to the uncanny all her life. On more than one occasion she had seen an apparition of her own father, especially when she was in some sort of difficulty. The house she and her second husband occupied in a small town in New Hampshire was very old. There was a little door leading up to the attic. A narrow staircase ascended to the attic, and for no apparent reason, the door kept opening by itself. Someone walking about in the attic, softly, as if in stocking feet, had become an almost daily occurrence. Finally, she asked around, and found out that the house had once belonged to an old man who had been abused and put into the attic. The man finally cut his throat, and was buried in the family cemetery nearby. It was his house once, but his people apparently took it away. And now he was back in command once more.

*　　　*　　　*

Mae Ramirez was a widow in her late thirties, with three children, who lived in a small town in the Cape Cod area. I talked to her on the telephone at length and she struck me as pretty level-headed, although she seemed scared of ghostly visitations. Small wonder, with the ones she had.

There was a certain young man her father disliked very much. She stopped seeing him when she got married, but after her divorce many years later, she took up with him again.

Her father had died in 1945, and Mrs. Ramirez left Massachusetts soon after, only to return in 1954. Shortly after she had placed some flowers on her father's grave after her return to Cape Cod, she woke one night from deep sleep with the fearful feeling that she was not alone in the room. Groping for some matches she had put under the pillow, she was unable to find them. In the semi-darkness her eyes fell upon the left side of her pillow where she distinguished the outline of a man. Finally she overcame her fears, and sat up in bed. Before her stood her late father, dressed in dark clothes, looking directly at her. Without saying a word, he left slowly and quietly.

"I heard the steps," Mrs. Ramirez said, "but when he reached the stairs, he did not go down, *but through the wall.* Afterwards I went downstairs, and checked the doors, looked in closets, and there was no one there."

After she stopped seeing the young man her father had disapproved of, the ghost of her father never returned.

*　　　*　　　*

Jane Morgan had a house in Kennebunkport, Maine, that was full of ghosts. I had talked to her time and again, offering my services and those of Sybil Leek to help her get relief. But she didn't want to free her house from its ghosts. To begin with, her brother, who shared ownership in the house with the talented singer, had for years insisted that there was nothing to the story.

"You may have discussed the hauntings in my house with my sister," he said cheerily, "but I live here and I assure you there ain't none!"

I thanked Mr. Currier—Currier is Jane Morgan's real name—and forgot all about it, for, let's face it: I've got more unsolved hauntings to take care of than an army of parapsychologists could handle. But the whole controversy—was there or wasn't there a ghost at Jane Morgan's place—was brought to mind again when the *New York Daily News*, November 16, 1964, quoted the singer as saying:

"I don't want to have them exorcised. That would be cruel. They might have no other place to go . . . and besides, I'd miss these friendly spirits."

Having read *Ghost Hunter*, Miss Morgan knew perfectly well what happens to a freed ghost, and that the "place" they are helped to reach is infinitely more joyous than a musty New England mansion.

Because of an exciting séance I held with Ethel Johnson Meyers in a New York apartment, a piece appeared in the *New York World Telegram* in which columnist Norton Mockridge described the procedure we used. He was swamped with mail from people with similar problems, he says, although I never saw the letters. But he did manage to follow up his first piece with an interview with Jane Morgan in which she unburdened herself of the whole story of her ghosts.

Ned, a revolutionary soldier, had killed his girlfriend Nellie's other lover, and since that time, he and his lady-love had cavorted in the old house, kept there, presumably, by their guilt feelings. Their laughing and moaning had been heard by many. Doors opened and closed by themselves at night and spectral figures had been seen flitting from room to room. Visitors, it was alleged, had spoken of a "lady in gray" in the hall who did not return their greetings, and there was a sealed coffin in the cellar of the house.

"I had a medium at the house," Miss Morgan told me, but when she mentioned her name, I confessed I had never heard of her.

"She refused to stay at the house," Jane Morgan continued, and explained that for that reason anyone else would not be likely to succeed either. I patiently explained the rather considerable difference between a successful parapsychologist and a timid medium who runs at the first chilly sign of a *real* ghost!

All the same, Jane Morgan refused to allow us to have a go at it. Meanwhile, Norton Mockridge reported that playgoers at the nearby Kennebunkport Playhouse frequently saw a man in Colonial uniform and a woman framed in the window of the haunted house across the road. They usually took them for actors rehearsing for the next week's play.

The Curriers have, however, abandoned the house for another place not far away. The new tenants didn't complain about any ghostly visitations. But then Ned and Nellie may have needed some time to get used to their new keepers.

*   *   *

The John Jay House near Bedford Village, Westchester, New York, was a museum maintained by the county. Restored exactly as it was when one of America's founding fathers, Chief Justice John Jay, lived in it, it had the reputation of being haunted. "Was there anything to it?" I asked the curator, Lewis Rubenstein.

"According to family tradition," the curator explained, "Mrs. William Jay, wife of the second of the Jays to live permanently at Bedford, saw the ghost of her mother-in-law in one of the bedrooms.

Two guests at widely spaced intervals are also reported to have seen the apparition.

Although he personally did not put stock in such stories, Mr. Rubenstein extended a cordial invitation for me to visit the house.

"We know that discovery of a ghost would be good for business," he said, "but we would prefer that people came to see the site for its real historic value rather than for its other somewhat tenuous merit."

When I finally got around to making an appointment to see the house in the company of a good medium, Mr. Rubenstein got cold feet, it seems. Retracting his invitation, he referred the decision to the trustees. Otto Koegel, board chairman, informed me curtly that I was not welcome. Maybe the ghostly mother-in-law was afraid I'd dislodge her.

"Ocean-Born" Mary

A mong the ghostly legends of the United States, that of "Ocean-Born" Mary and her fascinating house at Henniker, New Hampshire, is probably one of the best known. To the average literate person who has heard about the colorful tale of Mary Wallace, or the New Englander who knows of it because he lives "Down East," it is, of course, a legend not to be taken too seriously.

I had a vague idea of its substance when I received a note from a lady named Corinne Russell, who together with her husband, David, had bought the Henniker house and wanted me to know that it was still haunted.

That was in October of 1963. It so happens that Halloween is the traditional date on which the ghost of six-foot Mary Wallace is supposed to "return" to her house in a coach drawn by six horses. On many a Halloween, youngsters from all around Henniker have come and sat around the grounds waiting for Mary to ride in. The local press had done its share of Halloween ghost hunting, so much so that the Russells had come to fear that date as one of the major nuisance days of their year.

After all, Halloween visitors do not pay the usual fee to be shown about the house, but they do leave behind them destruction and litter at times. Needless to say, nobody has ever seen Mary ride in her coach on Halloween. Why should she when she lives there *all year round*?

To explain this last statement, I shall have to take you back to the year 1720, when a group of Scottish and Irish immigrants was approaching the New World aboard a ship called the *Wolf,* from

Londonderry, Ireland. The ship's captain, Wilson, had just become the father of a daughter, who was actually born at sea. Within sight of land, the ship was boarded by pirates under the command of a buccaneer named Don Pedro. As the pirates removed all valuables from their prize, Don Pedro went below to the captain's cabin. Instead of gold, he found Mrs. Wilson and her newborn baby girl.

"What's her name?" he demanded.

Unafraid, the mother replied that the child had not yet been baptized, having been recently born.

"If you will name her after my mother, Mary," the pirate said, overcome with an emotion few pirates ever allow into their lives, "I will spare everybody aboard this ship."

Joyously, the mother made the bargain, and "Ocean-Born" Mary received her name. Don Pedro ordered his men to hand back what they had already taken from their prisoners, to set them free, and to leave the captured ship. The vicious-looking crew grumbled and withdrew to their own ship.

Minutes later, however, Don Pedro returned alone. He handed Mrs. Wilson a bundle of silk.

"For Mary's wedding gown," he said simply, and left again.

As soon as the pirate ship was out of sight, the *Wolf* continued her voyage for Boston. Thence Captain and Mrs. Wilson went on to their new home in Londonderry, New Hampshire, where they settled down, and where Mary grew up.

When she was 18, she married a man named Wallace, and over the years they had four sons. However, shortly after the birth of the fourth son, her husband died and Mary found herself a widow.

Meanwhile, Don Pedro—allegedly an Englishman using the Spanish nom *de pirate* to disguise his noble ancestry—had kept in touch with the Wilsons. Despite the hazards of pirate life, he survived to an old age when thoughts of retirement filled his mind. Somehow he managed to acquire a land grant of 6,000 acres in what is now Henniker, New Hampshire, far away from the sea. On this land, Pedro built himself a stately house. He employed his ship's carpenters, as can be seen in the way the beams are joined. Ship's carpenters have a special way of building, and "Ocean-Born" Mary's house, as it later became known, is an example of this.

The house was barely finished when the aging pirate heard of Mary Wallace's loss of her husband, and he asked Mary and her children to come live with him. She accepted his invitation, and soon became his housekeeper.

The house was then in a rather isolated part of New England, and few callers, if any, came to interrupt the long stillness of the many cold winter nights. Mary took up painting and with her own hands created the eagle that can still be seen gracing the house.

The years went by peacefully, until one night someone attacked Don Pedro and killed him. Whether one of his men had come to challenge the pirate captain for part of the booty, or whether the reputation of a retired pirate had put ideas of treasure in the mind of some local thief, we may never know. All we know is that by the time Mary Wallace got out into the grove at the rear of the house, Don Pedro was dying with a pirate cutlass in his chest. He asked her to bury him under the hearthstone in the kitchen, which is in the rear of the house.

Mary herself inherited the house and what went with it, treasure, buried pirate, and all. She herself passed on in 1814, and ever since then the house had been changing hands.

Unfortunately, we cannot interview the earlier owners of the house, but during the 1930s, it belonged to one Louis Roy, retired and disabled and a permanent guest in what used to be his home. He said the house to the Russells in the early sixties.

During the great hurricane of 1935, Roy claims that Mary Wallace's ghost saved his life 19 times. Trapped outside the house by falling trees, he somehow was able to get back into the house. His very psychic mother, Mrs. Roy, informed him that she had actually seen the tall, stately figure of "Ocean-Born" Mary moving behind him, as if to help him get through. In the 1950s, *Life* told this story in an illustrated article on famous ghost-haunted houses in America. Mrs. Roy claimed she had seen the ghost of Mary time and again, but since she herself passed on in 1948, I could not get any details from *her*.

Then there were two state troopers who saw the ghost, but again I could not interview them, as they, too, were also on the other side of the veil.

A number of visitors claimed to have felt "special vibrations" when touching the hearthstone, where Don Pedro allegedly was buried. There was, for instance, Mrs. James Nisula of Londonderry, who visited the house several times. She said that she and her "group" of ghost buffs had "felt the vibrations" around the kitchen. Mrs. David Russell, the owner who contacted me, felt nothing.

I promised to look into the "Ocean-Born" Mary haunting the first chance I got. Halloween or about that time would be all right with me, and I wouldn't wait around for any coach!

"There is a lady medium I think you should know," Mrs. Russell said when I spoke of bringing a psychic with me." "She saw Mary the very first time she came here."

My curiosity aroused, I communicated with the lady. She asked that I not use her married name, although she was not so shy several months after our visit to the house, when she gave a two-part interview to a Boston newspaper columnist. (Needless to say, the interview was not authorized by me, since I never allow mediums I work with to talk about their cases for publication. Thus Lorrie shall remain without a family name and anyone wishing to reach this medium will have to do so without my help.)

Lorrie wrote me she would be happy to serve the cause of truth, and I could count on her. There was nothing she wanted in return.

We did not get up to New Hampshire that Halloween. Mr. Russell had to have an operation, the house was unheated in the winter except for Mr. Roy's room, and New England winters are cold enough to freeze any ghost.

Although there was a caretaker at the time to look after the house and Mr. Roy upstairs, the Russells did not stay at the house in the winter, but made their home in nearby Chelmsford, Massachusetts.

I wrote Mrs. Russell postponing the investigation until spring. Mrs. Russell accepted my decision with some disappointment, but she was willing to wait. After all, the ghost at "Ocean-Born" Mary's house is not a malicious type. Mary Wallace just lived there, ever since she died in 1814, and you can't call a lady who likes to hold on to what is hers an intruder.

"We don't want to drive her out," Mrs. Russell repeatedly said to me. "After all, it is her house!"

Not many haunted-house owners make statements like that.

But something had happened at the house since our last conversation.

"Our caretaker dropped a space heater all the way down the stairs at the 'Ocean-Born' Mary house, and when it reached the bottom, the kerosene and the flames started to burn the stairs and climb the wall. There was no water in the house, so my husband went out after snow. While I stood there looking at the fire and powerless to do anything about it, the fire went right out all by itself right in front of my eyes; when my husband got back with the snow it was out. It was just as if someone *had smothered it with a blanket.*"

This was in December of 1963. I tried to set a new date, as soon as possible, and February 22 seemed possible. This time I would bring Bob Kennedy of WBZ, Boston, and the "Contact" producer Squire Rushnell with me to record my investigation.

Lorrie was willing, asking only that her name not be mentioned.

"I don't want anyone to know about my being different from them," she explained. "When I was young my family used to accuse me of spying because I knew things from the pictures I saw when I touched objects."

Psychometry, I explained, is very common among psychics, and nothing to be ashamed of.

I thought it was time to find out more about Lorrie's experiences at the haunted house.

"I first saw the house in September of 1961," she began. "It was on a misty, humid day, and there was a haze over the fields."

Strange, I thought, I always get my best psychic results when the atmosphere is moist

Lorrie, who was in her early forties, was Vermont born and raised; she was married and had one daughter, Pauline. She was a tall redhead with sparkling eyes, and, come to think of it, not unlike the accepted picture of the ghostly Mary Wallace. Coincidence?

A friend of Lorrie's had seen the eerie house and suggested she go and see it also. That was all Lorrie knew about it, and she did not really expect anything uncanny to occur. Mr. Roy showed Lorrie and her daughter through the house and nothing startling happened. They left and started to walk down the entrance steps, crossing the garden in front of the house, and had reached the gate when Pauline clutched at her mother's arm and said:

"Mamma, what is that?"

Lorrie turned to look back at the house. In the upstairs window, a woman stood and looked out at them. Lorrie's husband was busy with the family car. Eventually, she called out to him, but as he turned to look, the apparition was gone.

She did not think of it again, and the weeks went by. But the house kept intruding itself into her thoughts more and more. Finally she could not restrain herself any longer, and returned to the house—even though it was 120 miles from her home in Weymouth, Massachusetts.

She confessed her extraordinary experience to the owner, and together they examined the house from top to bottom. She finally returned home.

She promised Roy she would return on All Hallow's Eve to see if the legend of Mary Wallace had any basis of fact. Unfortunately, word of her intentions got out, and when she finally arrived at the house, she had to sneak in the back to avoid the sensation-hungry press outside. During the days between her second visit and Halloween, the urge to go to Henniker kept getting stronger, as if someone were possessing her.

By that time the Russells were negotiating to buy the house, and Lorrie came up with them. Nothing happened to her that Halloween night. Perhaps she was torn between fear and a desire to fight the influence that had brought her out to Henniker to begin with.

Mediums, to be successful, must learn to relax and not allow their own notions to rule them. All through the following winter and summer, Lorrie fought the desire to return to "Ocean-Born" Mary's house. To no avail. She returned time and again, sometimes alone and sometimes with a friend.

Things got out of hand one summer night when she was home alone.

Exhausted from her last visit—the visits always left her an emotional wreck—she went to bed around 9:30 P.M.

"What happened that night?" I interjected. She seemed shaken even now.

"At 11 P.M., Mr. Holzer," Lorrie replied, "I found myself driving on the expressway, wearing my pajamas and robe, with no shoes or slippers, or money, or even a handkerchief. I was ten miles from my home and heading for Henniker. Terrified, I turned around and returned home, only to find my house ablaze with light, the doors open as I had left them, and the garage lights on. I must have left in an awful hurry."

"Have you found out why you are being pulled back to that house?" She shook her head.

"No idea. But I've been back twice, even after that. I just can't seem to stay away from that house."

I persuaded her that perhaps there was a job to be done in that house, and the ghost wanted her to do it.

We did not go to Henniker in February, because of bad weather. We tried to set a date in May, 1964. The people from WBZ decided Henniker was too far away from Boston and dropped out of the planning.

Summer came around, and I went to Europe instead of Henniker. However, the prospect of a visit in the fall was very much in my mind.

It seemed as if someone were keeping me away from the house very much in the same way someone was pulling Lorrie toward it!

Come October, and we were really on our way, at last. Owen Lake, a public relations man who dabbles in psychic matters, introduced himself as "a friend" of mine and told Lorrie he'd come along, too. I had never met the gentleman, but in the end he could not make it anyway. So just four of us—my wife Catherine and I, Lorrie, and her nice, even-tempered husband, who had volunteered to drive us up to New Hampshire—started out from Boston. It was close to Halloween, all right, only two days before. If Mary Wallace were out haunting the countryside in her coach, we might very well run into her. The coach is out of old Irish folktales; it appears in numerous ghost stories of the Ould Sod. I'm sure that in the telling and retelling of the tale of Mary and her pirate, the coach got added. The countryside is beautiful in a New England fall. As we rolled toward the New Hampshire state line, I asked Lorrie some more questions.

"When you first saw the ghost of 'Ocean-Born' Mary at the window of the house, Lorrie," I said, "what did she look like?"

"A lovely lady in her thirties, with auburn-colored hair, smiling rather intensely and thoughtfully. She stayed there for maybe three minutes, and then suddenly, *she just wasn't there.*"

"What about her dress?"

"It was a white dress."

Lorrie never saw an apparition of Mary again, but whenever she touched anything in the Henniker house, she received an impression of what the house was like when Mary had it, and she had felt her near the big fireplace several times.

Did she ever get an impression of what it was Mary wanted?

"She was a quick-tempered woman; I sensed that very strongly," Lorrie replied. "I have been to the house maybe twenty times altogether, and still don't know why. She just keeps pulling me there."

Lorrie had always felt the ghost's presence on these visits.

"One day I was walking among the bushes in the back of the house. I was wearing shorts, but I never got a scratch on my legs, because I kept feeling heavy skirts covering my legs. I could feel the brambles pulling at this invisible skirt I had on. I felt enveloped by something, or someone."

Mrs. Roy, the former owner's mother, had told of seeing the apparition many times, Lorrie stated.

"As a matter of fact, I have sensed her ghost in the house, too, but it is not a friendly wraith like Mary is."

Had she ever encountered this other ghost?

"Yes, my arm was grabbed one time by a malevolent enricy," Lorrie said emphatically. "It was two years ago, and I was standing in what is now the living room, and my arm was taken by the elbow and pulled.

"I snatched my arm back, because I felt she was not friendly."

"What were you doing at the time that she might have objected to?"

"I really don't know."

Did she know of anyone else who had had an uncanny experience at the house?

"A strange thing happened to Mrs. Roy," Lorrie said. "A woman came to the house and said to her, 'What do you mean, the *rest* of the house?' The woman replied, 'Well, I was here yesterday, and a tall woman let me in and only showed me half of the house.' But, of course, there was nobody at the house that day."

What about the two state troopers? Could she elaborate on their experience?

"They met her walking down the road that leads to the house. She was wearing a Colonial-type costume, and they found that odd. Later they realized they had seen a ghost, especially as no one of her description lived in the house at the time."

Rudi D., Lorrie's husband, was a hospital technician. He was with her on two or three occasions when she visited the house. Did he ever feel anything special?

"The only thing unusual I ever felt at the house was that I wanted to get out of there fast," he said.

"The very first time we went up," Lorrie added, "something kept pulling me toward it, but my husband insisted we go back. There was an argument about our continuing the trip, when suddenly the door of the car flew open of its own volition. Somehow we decided to continue on to the house."

An hour later, we drove up a thickly overgrown hill and along a winding road at the end of which the "Ocean-Born" Mary house stood in solitary stateliness, a rectangular building of gray stone and brown trim, very well preserved.

We parked the car and walked across the garden that sets the house well back from the road. There was peace and autumn in the air. We were made welcome by Corinne Russell, her husband David, and two relatives who happened to be with them that day. Entering the main door beneath a magnificent early American eagle, we admired the fine wooden staircase leading to the upstairs—the staircase on which the mysterious fire had taken place—and then entered the room to the left of it, where the family had assembled around an old New England stove.

During the three years the Russells had lived at the house, nothing uncanny had happened to Mrs. Russell, except for the incident with the fire. David Russell, a man almost typical of the shrewd New England Yankee who weighs his every word, was willing to tell me about *his* experiences, however.

"The first night I ever slept in what we call the Lafayette room, upstairs, there was quite a thundershower on, and my dog and I were upstairs. I always keep my dog with me, on account of the boys coming around to do damage to the property.

"Just as I lay down in bed, I heard very heavy footsteps. They sounded to me to be in the two rooms which we had just restored, on the same floor. I was quite annoyed, almost frightened, and I went into the rooms, but there was nobody there or anywhere else in the house."

"Interesting," I said. "Was there more?"

"Now this happened only last summer. A few weeks later, when was in that same room, I was getting undressed when I suddenly heard somebody pound on my door. I said to myself, "Oh, it's only the house settling," and I got into bed. A few minutes later, the door knob turned back and forth. I jumped out of bed, opened the door, and there was absolutely nobody there. The only other people in the house at the time were the invalid Mr. Roy, locked in his room, and my wife downstairs."

What about visual experiences?

"No, but I went to the cellar not long ago with my dog, about four in the afternoon, or rather tried to—this dog never leaves me, but on this particular occasion, something kept her from going with me into the cellar. Her hair stood up and she would not budge."

The Lafayette room, by the way, is the very room in which the pirate, Don Pedro, is supposed to have lived. The Russells did nothing to change the house structurally, only restored it as it had been and generally cleaned it up.

I now turned to Florence Harmon, an elderly neighbor of the Russells, who had some recollections about the house. Mrs. Harmon recalls the house when she herself was very young, long before the Russells came to live in it.

"Years later, I returned to the house and Mrs. Roy asked me whether I could help her locate 'the treasure' since I was reputed to be psychic."

Was there really a treasure?

"If there was, I think it was found," Mrs. Harmon said. "At the time Mrs. Roy talked to me, she also pointed out that there were two elm trees on the grounds—the only two elm trees around. They looked like some sort of markers to her. But before the Roys had the house, a Mrs. Morrow lived here. I know this from my uncle, who was a stone mason, and who built a vault for her."

I didn't think Mrs. Harmon had added anything material to knowledge of the treasure, so I thanked her and turned my attention to the other large room, on the right hand side of the staircase. Nicely furnished with period pieces, it boasted a fireplace flanked by sofas, and had a rectangular piano in the corner. The high windows were curtained on the sides, and one could see the New England landscape through them.

We seated ourselves around the fireplace and hoped that Mary would honor us with a visit. Earlier I had inspected the entire house, the hearthstone under which Don Pedro allegedly lay buried, and the small bedrooms upstairs where David Russell had heard the footsteps. Each of us had stood at the window in the corridor upstairs and stared out of it, very much the way the ghost must have done when she was observed by Lorrie and her daughter.

And now it was Mary's turn.

"This was her room," Lorrie explained, "and I do feel her presence." But she refused to go into trance, afraid to "let go." Communication would have to be via clairvoyance, with Lorrie as the interpreter. This was not what I had hoped for. Nevertheless we would try to evaluate whatever material we could obtain.

"Sheet and quill," Lorrie said now, and a piece of paper was handed her along with a pencil. Holding it on her lap, Lorrie was poised to write, if Mary wanted to use her hand, so to speak. The pencil suddenly jumped from Lorrie's hand with considerable force.

"Proper quill," the ghost demanded.

I explained about the shape of quills these days, and handed Lorrie my own pencil.

"Look, lady," Lorrie explained to the ghost. "I'll show you it writes. I'll write my name."

And she wrote in her own, smallish, rounded hand, "Lorrie."

There was a moment of silence. Evidently, the ghost was thinking it over. Then Lorrie's hand, seemingly not under her own control, wrote with a great deal of flourish "Mary Wallace." The "M" and "W" had curves and ornamentation typical of eighteenth-century calligraphy. It was not at all like Lorrie's own handwriting.

"Tell her to write some more. The quill is working," I commanded.

Lorrie seemed to be upset by something the ghost told her.

"No," she said. "I can't do that. No."

"What does she want?" I asked.

"She wants me to sleep, but I won't do it."

Trance, I thought—even the ghost demands it. It would have been so interesting to have Mary speak directly to us through Lorrie's entranced lips. You can lead a medium to the ghost, but you can't make her go under if she's scared.

Lorrie instead told the ghost to tell *her*, or to write through her. But no trance, thank you. Evidently, the ghost did not like to be told how to communicate. We waited. Then I suggested that Lorrie be very relaxed and it would be " like sleep" so the ghost could talk to us directly.

"She's very much like me, but not so well trimmed," the ghost said of Lorrie. Had she picked her to carry her message because of physical resemblance, I wondered.

"She's waiting for Young John," Lorrie now said. Not young John. The stress was on young. Perhaps it was one name—Young john.

"It happened in the north pasture," Mary said through Lorrie now. "He killed Warren Langerford. The Frazier boys found the last bone."

I asked why it concerned her. Was she involved? But there was no reply.

Then the ghost of Mary introduced someone else standing next to her.

"Mrs. Roy is with her, because she killed her daughter," Lorrie said, hesitatingly, and added, on her own, "but I don't believe she did." Later we found out that the ghost was perhaps not lying, but of course nobody had any proof of such a crime if it were indeed a crime.

"Why do you stay on in this house?" I asked.

"This house is my house, h-o-u-s-e!" "Ocean-Born" Mary reminded me.

"Do you realize you are what is commonly called dead." I demanded. As so often with ghosts, the question brought on resistance to face reality. Mary seemed insulted and withdrew.

I addressed the ghost openly, offering to help her, and at the same time explaining her present position to her. This was her chance to speak up.

"She's very capricious," Lorrie said. "When you said you'd bring her peace, she started to laugh."

But Mary was gone, for the present anyway.

We waited, and tried again a little later. This time Lorrie said she heard a voice telling her to come back tonight.

"We can't," I decided. "If she wants to be helped, it will have to be now."

Philip Babb, the pirate's real name (as I discovered later), allegedly had built a secret passage under the house. The Russells were still looking for it. There were indeed discrepancies in the thickness of some of the walls, and there were a number of secret holes that didn't lead anywhere. But no passage. Had the pirate taken his secrets to his grave?

I found our experience at Henniker singularly unsatisfactory since no real evidence had been forthcoming from the ghost herself. No doubt another visit would have to be made, but I didn't mind that at all. "Ocean-Born" Mary's place was a place one can easily visit time and again. The rural charm of the place and the timeless atmosphere of the old house made it a first-rate tourist attraction. Thousands of people came to the house every year.

We returned to New York and I thought no more about it until received a letter from James Caron, who had heard me discuss the house on the "Contact" program in Boston. He had been to the house in quest of pirate lore and found it very much haunted.

James Caron was in the garage business at Bridgewater, Massachusetts. He had a high school and trade school education, and was married, with two children. Searching for stories of buried treasure and pirates was a hobby of his, and he sometimes lectured on it. He had met Gus Roy about six years before. Roy complained that his deceased mother was trying to contact him for some reason. Her picture kept falling off the wall where it was hung, and he constantly felt "a presence." Would Mr. Caron know of a good medium?

In August of 1959, James Caron brought a spiritualist named Paul Amsdent to the "Ocean-Born" Mary house. Present at the ensuing séance were Harold Peters, a furniture salesman; Hugh Blanchard, a lawyer; Ernest Walbourne, a fireman, and brother-in-law of Caron; Gus Roy; and Mr. Caron himself. Tape recording the séance, Caron had trouble with his equipment. Strange sounds kept intruding. Unfortunately, there was among those present someone with hostility toward psychic work, and Gus Roy's mother did not manifest. However, something else did happen.

"There appear to be people buried somewhere around or in the house," the medium Amsdent said, "enclosed by a stone wall of some sort."

I thought of the hearthstone and of Mrs. Harmon's vault. Coincidence?

Mr. Caron used metal detectors all over the place to satisfy Gus Roy that there was no "pirate treasure" buried in or near the house.

A little later, James Caron visited the house again. This time he was accompanied by Mrs. Caron and Mr. and Mrs. Walbourne. Both ladies were frightened by the sound of a heavy door opening and closing with no one around and no air current in the house.

Mrs. Caron had a strong urge to go to the attic, but Mr. Caron stopped her. Ernest Walbourne, a skeptic, was alone in the so-called "death" room upstairs, looking at some pictures stacked in a corner. Suddenly, he clearly heard a female voice telling him to get out of the house. He looked around, but there was nobody upstairs. Frightened, he left the house at once and later required medication for a nervous condition!

Again, things quieted down as far as "Ocean-Born" Mary was concerned, until I saw a lengthy story—two parts, in fact—in the *Boston Record-American*, in which my erstwhile medium Lorrie had let her hair down to columnist Harold Banks.

It seemed that Lorrie could not forget Henniker, after all. With publicist Owen Lake, she returned to the house in November, 1964, bringing with her some oil of wintergreen, which she claimed Mary

Wallace asked her to bring along.

Two weeks later, the report went on, Lorrie felt Mary Wallace in her home in Weymouth near Boston. Lorrie was afraid that Mary Wallace might "get into my body and use it for whatever purpose she wants to. I might wake up some day and *be* Mary Wallace."

That's the danger of being a medium without proper safeguards. They tend to identify with a personality that has come through them. Especially when they read all there is in print about them.

I decided to take someone to the house who knew nothing about it, someone who was not likely to succumb to the wiles of amateur "ESP experts," inquisitive columnists and such, someone who would do exactly what I required of her: Sybil Leek, famed British psychic.

It was a glorious day late in spring when we arrived at "Ocean Born" Mary's house in a Volkswagen station wagon driven by two alert young students from Goddard College in Vermont: Jerry Weener and Jay Lawrence. They had come to Boston to fetch us and take us all the way up to their campus, where I was to address the students and faculty. I proposed that they drive us by way of Henniker, and the two young students of parapsychology agreed enthusiastically. It was their first experience with an actual séance and they brought with them a lively dose of curiosity.

Sybil Leek brought with her something else: "Mr. Sasha," a healthy four-foot boa constrictor someone had given her for a pet. At first I thought she was kidding when she spoke with tender care of her snake, coiled peacefully in his little basket. But practical Sybil, author of some nine books, saw still another possibility in "Life with Sasha" and for that reason kept the snake on with her. On the way to Henniker, the car had a flat tire and we took this opportunity to get acquainted with Sasha, as Sybil gave him a run around the New Hampshire countryside.

Although I have always had a deep-seated dislike for anything reptilian, snakes, serpents, and other slitherers, terrestrial or maritime, I must confess that I found this critter less repulsive than I had thought he would be. At any rate, "Mr. Sasha" was collected once more and carefully replaced in his basket and the journey continued to Henniker, where the Russells were expecting us with great anticipation.

After a delightful buffet luncheon—"Mr. Sasha" had his the week before, as snakes are slow digesters—we proceeded to the large room upstairs to the right of the entrance door, commonly called the Lafayette room, and Sybil took the chair near the fireplace. The rest of us—the Russells, a minister friend of theirs, two neighbors, my wife Catherine and I, and our two student friends—gathered around her in a circle.

It was early afternoon. The sun was bright and clear. It didn't seem like it would be a good day for ghosts. Still, we had come to have a talk with the elusive Mary Wallace in her own domain, and if I knew Sybil, she would not disappoint us. Sybil is a very powerful medium, and something *always* happens.

Sybil knew nothing about the house since I had told our hosts not to discuss it with her before the trance session. I asked her if she had any clairvoyant impressions about the house.

"My main impressions were outside," Sybil replied, "near where the irises are. I was drawn to that spot and felt very strange. There is something outside this house which means more than things inside!"

"What about inside the house? What do you feel here?"

"The most impressive room I think is the loom room," Sybil said, and I thought, that's where Ernest Walbourne heard the voice telling him to get out, in the area that's also called the "death" room.

"They don't want us here . . . there is a conflict between two people . . . somebody wants something he can't have . . ."

Presently, Sybil was in trance. There was a moment of silence as I waited anxiously for the ghost of Mary Wallace to manifest itself through Sybil. The first words coming from the lips of the entranced medium were almost unintelligible.

Gradually, the voice became clearer and I had her repeat the words until I could be sure of them.

"Say-mon go to the lion's head," she said now. "To the lion's head. Be careful."

"Why should I be careful?"

"In case he catches you."

"Who are you?"

"Mary Degan."

"What are you doing here?"

"Waiting. Someone fetch me."

She said "*Witing*" with a strong cockney accent, and sudenly I realized that the "*say-mon*" was probably a seaman.

"Whose house is this?" I inquired.

"Daniel Burn's." (Perhaps it was "Birch.")

"What year is this?"

"1798."

"Who built this house?"

"Burn . . ."

"How did you get here?"

"All the time, come and go . . . to hide . . . I have to wait. He wants the money. Burn. Daniel Burn."

I began to wonder what had happened to Mary Wallace. Who was this new member of the ghostly cast? Sybil knew nothing whatever of a pirate or a pirate treasure connected by legend to this house. Yet her very first trance words concerned a *seaman and money.* Did Mary Degan have someone else with her, I hinted. Maybe this was only the first act and the lady of the house was being coy in time for a second act appearance.

But the ghost insisted that she was Mary Degan and that she lived here, "with the old idiot."

"Who was the old idiot?" I demanded.

"Mary," the Degan girl replied.

"What is Mary's family name?"

"Birch," she replied without hesitation.

I looked at Mrs. Russell, who shook her head. Nobody knew of Mary Wallace by any other name. Had she had another husband we did not know about?

Was there anyone else with her, I asked.

"Mary Birch, Daniel, and Jonathan," she replied.

"Who is Jonathan?"

"Jonathan Harrison Flood," the ghostly girl said.

A week or so later, I checked with my good friend Robert Nesmith, expert in pirate lore. Was there a pirate by that name? There had been, but his date is given as 1610, far too early for our man. But then Flood was a very common name. Also, this Flood might have used another name as his *nom de pirate* and Flood might have been his real, civilian name.

"What are they doing in this house?" I demanded.

"They come to look for their money," Sybil in trance replied. "The old idiot took it."

"What sort of money was it?"

"Dutch money," came the reply. "Very long ago."

"Who brought the money to this house?"

"Mary. Not me."

"Whose money was it?"

"Johnny's."

"How did he get it?"

"Very funny. . . he helped himself . . . so we did."

"What profession did he have?"

"Went down to the sea. Had a lot of funny business. Then he got caught, you know. So they did him in."

"Who did him in?"

"The runners. In the bay."

"What year was that?"

"Ninety-nine."

"What happened to the money after that?"

"She hid it. Outside. Near the lion's head."

"Where is the lion's head?"

"You go down past the little rocks, in the middle of the rocks, a little bit like a lion's head."

"If I left this house by the front entrance, which way would I turn?"

"The right, down past the little rock on the right. Through the trees, down the little . . ."

"How far from the house?"

"Three minutes."

"Is it under the rock?"

"Lion's head."

"How far below?"

"As big as a boy."

"What will I find there?"

"The gold. Dutch gold."

"Anything else?"

"No, unless she put it there."

"Why did she put it there?"

"Because he came back for it."

"What did she do?"

"She said it was hers. Then he went away. Then they caught him, a good thing, too. He never came back and she went off, too."

"When did she leave here?"

"Eighteen three."

"What was she like? Describe her."

"Round, not as big as me, dumpy thing, she thought she owned everything."

"How was Jonathan related to Daniel?"

"Daniel stayed here when Johnny went away and then they would divide the money, but they didn't because of Mary. She took it."

"Did you see the money?"

"I got some money. Gold. It says 1747."

"Is anyone buried in this ground?"

"Sometimes they brought them back here when they got killed down by the river."

"Who is buried in the house?"

"I think Johnny."

I now told Mary Degan to fetch me the other Mary, the lady of the house. But the girl demurred. The other Mary did not like to talk to strangers.

"What do you look like?" I asked. I still was not sure if Mary Wallace was not masquerading as her own servant girl to fool us.

"Skinny and tall."

"What do you wear?"

"A gray dress."

"What is your favorite spot in this house?"

"The little loom room. Peaceful."

"Do you always stay there?"

"No." The voice was proud now. "I go where I want."

"Whose house is this?" Perhaps I could trap her if she was indeed Mary Wallace.

"Mary Birch."

"Has she got a husband?"

"They come and go. There's always company here that's why I go to the loom room."

I tried to send her away, but she wouldn't go.

"Nobody speaks to me," she complained. "Johnny. . . she won't let him speak to me. Nobody is going to send me away."

"Is there a sea captain in this house?" I asked.

She almost shouted the reply.

"Johnny!"

"Where is he from?"

"Johnny is from the island."

She then explained that the trouble with Johnny and Mary was about the sea. Especially about the money the captain had.

"Will the money be found?" I asked.

"Not until I let it."

I asked Mary Degan to find me Mary Wallace. No dice. The lady wanted to be coaxed. Did she want some presents, I asked. That hit a happier note.

"Brandy. . . some clothes," she said. "She needs some hair . . . hasn't got much hair."

"Ask her if she could do with some oil of wintergreen," I said, sending up a trial balloon.

"She's got a bad back," the ghost said, and I could tell from the surprised expression on Mrs. Russell's face that Mary Wallace had indeed had a bad back.

"She makes it . . . people bring her things . . . rub her back . . . back's bad . . . she won't let you get the money . . . not yet . . . may want to build another house, in the garden . . . in case she needs it . . . sell it . . . she knows she is not what she used to be because her back's bad . . . she'll never go. Not now."

I assured her that the Russells wanted her to stay as long as she liked. After all, it was her house, too.

"Where is Johnny's body buried?" I now asked.

"Johnny's body," she murmured, "is under the fireplace."

Nobody had told Sybil about the persistent rumors that the old pirate lay under the hearthstone.

"Don't tell anyone," she whispered.

"How deep?"

"Had to be deep."

"Who put him there?"

"I shan't tell you."

"Did you bury anything with him?"

"I shan't tell. He is no trouble now. Poor Johnny."

"How did Johnny meet Mary?"

"I think they met on a ship."

"Ocean-Born" Mary, I thought. Sybil did not even know the name of the house, much less the story of how it got that name.

"All right," I said. "Did Mary have any children?"

"Four . . . in the garden. You can never tell with her."

"Did anyone kill anyone in this house at any time?"

"Johnny was killed, you know. Near the money. The runners chased him and he was very sick, we thought he was dead, and then he came here. I think she pushed him when he hurt his leg. We both brought him back here and put him under the fireplace. I didn't think he was dead."

"But you buried him anyway?" I said.

"She did," the ghost servant replied. "Better gone, she said. He's only come back for the money."

"Then Mary and Johnny weren't exactly friendly?"

"They were once."

"What changed things?"

"The money. She took his money. The money he fought for. Fighting money."

Suddenly, the tone of voice of the servant girl changed.

"I want to go outside," she begged. "She watches me. I can go out because her back is bad today. Can't get up, you see. So I can go out."

I promised to help her.

Suspiciously, she asked, "What do you want?"

44

"Go outside. You are free to go," I intoned.

"Sit on the rocks," the voice said. "If she calls out? She can get very angry."

"I will protect you," I promised.

"She says there are other places under the floor . . ." the girl ghost added, suddenly.

"Any secret passages?" I asked.

"Yes. Near the old nursery. First floor. Up the stairs, the loom room, the right hand wall. You can get out in the smoke room!"

Mr. Russell had told me of his suspicions that on structural evidence alone there was a hidden passage behind the smoke room. How would Sybil know this? Nobody had discussed it with her or showed her the spot.

I waited for more. But she did not know of any other passages, except one leading to the rear of the house.

"What about the well?"

"She did not like that either, because she thought he put his money there."

"Did he?"

"Perhaps he did. She used to put money in one place, he into another, and I think he put some money into the smoke room. He was always around there. Always watching each other. Watch me, too. Back of the house used to be where he could hide. People always looking for Johnny. Runners."

"Who was Mr. Birch?"

"Johnny had a lot to do with his house, but he was away a lot and so there was always some man here while he was away."

"Who paid for the house originally?"

"I think Johnny."

"Why did he want this house?"

"When he got enough money, he would come here and stay forever. He could not stay long ever, went back to the sea, and she came."

I tried another tack.

"Who was Don Pedro?" That was the name given the pirate in the popular tale.

She had heard the name, but could not place it.

"What about Mary Wallace?"

"Mary Wallace was Mary Birch," the ghost said, as if correcting me. "She had several names."

"Why?"

"Because she had several husbands."

Logical enough, if true.

"Wallace lived here a little while, I think," she added.

"Who was first, Wallace or Birch?"

"Birch. Mary Wallace, Mary Birch, is good enough."

Did the name Philip Babb mean anything to her? That allegedly was the pirate's real name.

"She had a little boy named Philip," the ghost said, and I thought, why not? After all, they had named Mary for the pirate's mother, why not reciprocate and name *her* son for the old man? Especially with all that loot around.

"If I don't go now, she'll wake up," the girl said. "Philip Babb, Philip Babb, he was somewhere in the back room. That was his room. I remember him."

How did Philip get on with Johnny? I wanted to know if they were one and the same person or not.

"Not so good," the ghost said. "Johnny did not like men here, you know."

I promised to watch out for Mary, and sent the girl on her way.

I then brought Sybil out of trance.

A few moments later, we decided to start our treasure hunt in the garden, following the instructions given us by Mary Degan, girl ghost.

Sybil was told nothing more than to go outside and let her intuition lead her toward any spot she thought important. The rest of us followed her like spectators at the National Open Golf Tournament.

We did not have to walk far. About twenty yards from the house, near some beautiful iris in bloom, we located the three stones. The one in the middle looked indeed somewhat like a lion's head, when viewed at a distance. I asked the others in the group to look at it. There was no doubt about it. If there was a lion's head on the grounds, this was it. What lay underneath? What indeed was underneath the hearthstone in the house itself?

The Russells promised to get a mine detector to examine the areas involved. If there was metal in the ground, the instrument would show it. Meanwhile, the lore about "Ocean-Born" Mary had been enriched by the presence in the nether world of Mary Degan, servant girl, and the intriguing picture of two pirates—Johnny and Philip Babb. Much of this is very difficult to trace. But the fact is that Sybil Leek, who came to Henniker a total stranger, was able, in trance, to tell about a man at sea, a Mary, a pirate treasure, hidden passages, a child named Philip, four children of Mary, and the presence of a ghost in the loom room upstairs. All of this had been checked.

Why should not the rest be true also? Including, perhaps, the elusive treasure?

Only time will tell.

Proper Bostonian Ghosts

The proper Bostonian ghosts here are not the political skeletons rattling in many a Back Bay closet. In Boston, a ghost is a ghost. But make no mistake, something of their English forebears has rubbed off on many a Bostonian. They take their specters with grim pride and a matter of nature—it is part of the regional scenery, so to speak, and really all terribly chic, but the Bostonian prefers to pretend it's nothing much. Far from it. New England ghosts can be pretty exciting stuff.

Sometimes New Englanders take the memories of their ghosts with them even when they move to other states. A Mrs. C. E. Foster once wrote me from Indianapolis about her grandmother, who seems to have been buried alive. At the time her grandmother, Louisa Wallace, was lowered into her grave in Revere, Massachusetts, Mrs. Foster had a vision of her in the casket . . . and heard her cough. The dead don't do that, and Mrs. Foster thinks her grandmother tried to tell her that she wasn't quite ready yet. Unfortunately, nothing was done about it at the time, so she went, ready or not.

*   *   *

Many of my contacts have been made through a Boston radio program called "Contact," with Bob Kennedy, on Station WBZ. I appeared on it many times and always found it most rewarding. After one of my radio stints in the fall of 1963, I was approached by a young lady with the appealing name of Aimee Violante, a nurse who had a most interesting and rather touching experience she wanted to tell me about.

"In 1957, my boyfriend took me to Lake Quannapowette outside of Boston. We rented a rowboat and rowed to the other side of the lake to go swimming, as swimming was prohibited there.

"In the boat, I sat facing the opposite shore. We were heading for a strip of beach with a few benches on it. There were three benches. It was nearing dusk. Sitting on these benches were elderly people all dressed in white. The ladies were dressed in silky dresses, wearing big picture hats and gloves. The men wore white suits. They were just sitting watching us. They weren't frightening, so I didn't pay too much attention to them, but I was angry that my boyfriend was pulling in there, as I thought they would say something about us going swimming. He didn't see them, as his back was toward them, and when we pulled up, they were gone.

"When we rowed back, I was wondering where they all went to, so I asked him. When I told him about the people I saw, he got frightened and hurried me back to the car. There he told me that on the side we were on was a cemetery, and there was no way any people could get to the benches once the gates were closed."

*   *   *

The Peter Hofmann family consisted of husband, wife Pennie, and baby—then about three or four years old. The parents were articulate, well-educated people making their home in Harvard. Not Harvard University, but Harvard near Ayer, Massachusetts, about an hour's ride from the university.

An automobile accident in 1956 had left Mrs. Hofmann partially paralyzed, but her keen gift of observation was not impaired. She had always had a peculiar liking for graveyards, and her first psychic experience, in 1951, consisted of a vision of a horse-drawn hearse that had passed near a cemetery. One could argue that lots of such hearses used to pull into cemeteries, but the fact remains that Mrs. Hofmann's was not a real one.

Their house stands next to a house built by Mrs. Hofmann's father, a well-known physician, and it seemed that both houses were haunted. The larger house, owned by Mrs. Hofmann's father, was built in 1721 "on the bounty received from an Indian scalp."

From the first moment she saw it, Pennie Hofmann had odd sensations about it. In 1960 or 1961, she and her husband were spending the night there, when at about two in the morning they both woke up for no apparent reason.

"I spoke to what I thought was Pete," she said, "as I could see someone by the front window, but it turned out that Pete was *behind* me. Needless to say, we left right away."

Peter Hofmann nodded and added: "I myself have been in the house at night a few times alone, and I've always had the feeling I was being watched."

Then in late October, 1963, Pennie Hofmann phoned me in New York. Could I please come to Boston and tell her if she was *seeing things*?

What sort of things, I asked.

"Well," she replied, somewhat upset, "we'd been staying over in my father's house again a week ago. I saw a soldier in the bedroom. He was dark and had a noose around the neck; the rope was cut and his face seemed almost luminous. I swear I saw him."

I hurried to Boston and they met me at radio station WBZ.

What about the ghostly soldier? Any clues?

Both Hofmanns nodded.

"We've checked in Nourse's *History of the Town of Harvard*," Mrs. Hoffman said gravely, "and there was a Colonial drummer named Hill who was hanged in this area . . . for some misdeeds."

I remembered her telling me of a ghost in their own house on Poor Farm Road, and Mrs. Hofmann filed me in on this far gentler wraith.

"During the summer months," she explained, "there is what appears to be a Quaker lady that walks across our front lawn, usually during the afternoon. This person often appears many times a day."

Her husband added that she had given him many details of the ghost's dress, which he checked for authenticity. He found that they were indeed worn by the Quaker women of the eighteenth century.

Why a member of so gentle a persuasion as the Quakers would turn into a ghost we may never know, but perhaps someday the Quaker lady will walk again for me.

*   *   *

There is said to be the ghost of a pirate near the water's edge in old Boston, where so many secret passages existed in the days when Massachusetts was British. The *Black Lady of Warren Island*, out in the bay, has been seen by a number of people. She was executed during the Civil War for helping her husband, a Yankee prisoner, break out of prison.

Boston's emotional climate is fine for special activities. There may not be any medieval castles, but Beacon Hill can look pretty forbidding, too—especially on a chilly November night when the fog drifts in from the sea.

In September of 1963 I appeared on WBZ-TV on Mike Douglas's television show, discussing my ever-present interest in haunted houses. As a consequence, there was an avalanche of letters, many of which contained leads to new cases.

One came from a Mrs. Anne Valukis, of South Natick, near Boston, Massachusetts. She wrote me of an old house she lived in where the stairs creaked unaccountably at odd times, as if someone were walking up and down them; of the strange behavior her little boy showed whenever he was in a certain room of the house; and of an over-all atmosphere of the uncanny prevailing throughout the house, as if an unseen force were always present.

I wrote for additional data about herself and the background of the house. Meanwhile, the public television station in Boston, Channel 2, took an interest in my work, and the station and I decided to join forces for an expedition to the haunted house in South Natick. Fred Barzyk, the director, undertook the preliminary task of additional research. My visit was scheduled for the last week of October. Mrs. Valukis wasn't long in answering me.

"The stairs haven't creaked for over a week, but my four year old woke Saturday night four times, and was really scared, so much so he would not go back upstairs to his room . . . Years ago this house was kind of a speakeasy, connected to a dance hall that was on the Charles River. Probably anything could have happened here. Who knows?"

Not because of the spooky stairs, but for other reasons, the Valukis family decided to move to Anne's parents' house. This made our visit problematical, until Fred Barzyk discovered that the house belonging to Mrs. Valukis' parents was even more haunted than Anne Valukis' place.

Mrs. Rose Josselyn, Anne's mother, was a Canadian Indian, and, like many of her people, had had psychic experiences all her life.

About 39 years before I met her, Mrs. Josselyn was living in Annapolis Royal, Canada, in what was purported to be a haunted house. Frequently she awoke in the middle of the night and found it difficult to breathe. Her arms seemed to be pinned down by an unseen force and she was unable to move even so much as a finger!

"It felt as if someone were choking me," she said to me later. "I tried to scream, but could not move my lips."

This had gone on for about a year. Finally Rose told her mother, who was mediumistic herself, and Rose was forbidden ever to sleep again in "that room." Twenty years later, Mrs. Josselyn still remembered the stark terror of those nights in Canada, but nothing like it had happened to her since—nothing, that is, until she moved into this house.

The house itself was a gray-white, medium-sized early American house, built in the stately manner of early Georgian architecture and very well preserved. It was set back from the road a bit, framed by tall, shady trees, and one had the feeling of being far from the bustle of the big city. Built about 150 years before, the house had an upper story and a total of eight rooms. Bordering on the lawn of the house was a cemetery, separated from the Josselyn house by an iron gate and fence.

When the Josselyns moved in with their family, Mrs. Josselyn had no thoughts of anything psychic or uneanny. She soon learned differently.

Upstairs, there were two bedrooms separated only by a thin wall. The larger one belonged to Mrs. Josselyn; the smaller one, to the rear of the house, to her husband Roy. It was in her bedroom that Mrs. Josselyn had another attack of the terrible feeling she had experienced in her Canadian youth. Pinned down on her bed, it was as if someone were upon her, holding her.

"Whose bedroom was this before you took it?" I inquired.

"Well, my daughter-in-law slept here for awhile," Mrs. Josselyn confided, "that is, before she died."

I asked further questions about this girl. At the age of 21, she had fallen ill and suffered her last agonies in this very room, before being taken off to a hospital, never to return. Her only child, to whom she was naturally very attached, was reared by Mrs. Josselyn and Mrs. Valukis.

I walked across the floor to a small room belonging to David Josselyn, 17, the brother of Mrs. Valukis. Here I was shown a handmade wooden chair that was said to creak at odd moments, as if someone were sitting in it. David himself had been awakened many times by this unearthly behavior of his chair, and Anne had also observed the noise. I tried the chair. It was sturdy enough, and only strong efforts on my part produced any kind of noise. It could not have creaked by itself.

"Who gave you this chair?" I asked.

"The same man who made our clock downstairs," David said. I

recalled seeing a beautiful wooden grandfather clock in the corner of the downstairs room. The odd thing about that clock was it sometimes ticked and the hands moved, even though it no longer had any works or pendulum!

The clock, chair, and a desk in David's room were the work of a skilled craftsman named Thomas Council, who was a well-liked house guest of the Josselyns and gave them these things to show his gratitude for their hospitality. He was a lonely bachelor and the Josselyns were his only close friends. David in particular was the apple of his eye. Thomas Council's body rested comfortably, it is hoped, across the way in the cemetery, and the Josselyns made sure there were always fresh flowers on his grave.

I decided to return to Mrs. Josselyn's room.

"Outside of your nightmarish experiences here and in Canada, " said, "have you had any other psychic incidents?"

Mrs. Josselyn, a serious, quiet woman of about 59, thought for a moment.

"Yes, frequently. Whenever my children are in some sort of trouble, I just know it. No matter how trifling. You might say we have telepathic contact."

"Did you also hear those stairs creak at your daughrer's house across the road?"

"Yes, many times."

"Was that after or before your daughrer-in-law passed away?"

"After."

"I clearly heard those steps upstairs, and there wasn't anyone but me and the baby in the house," added Anne Valukis for corroboration.

They all had been visited, it seemed to me, except the father, Roy Josselyn. It was time I turned my attention in his direction.

Mr. Josselyn sat on the bed in his room, quietly smoking a pipe. I had been warned by Fred Barzyk that the man of the house was no particular believer in the supernatural. To my relief, I discovered Mr. Josselyn at least had an open mind. I also discovered that a great-aunt of his in Vermont had been a spiritualistic medium.

I asked if he had seen or heard anything unusual.

"Well," he said, "about a year ago I started to hear some moans and groans around here . . ." he pointed toward the wall adjoining the bedroom occupied by his wife. "At first I thought it was my wife, but there was no one in her room at the time. I looked."

"This moaning . . . was it a human voice?"

"Oh yes, very human. Couldn't sleep a wink while it lasted."

"When did you last hear it?"

"Yesterday," he said laconically.

"How did you and your daughter-in-law get along?" I suddenly felt compelled to ask.

"Very well," he said. "As a matter of fact, she took more to me than to anyone else. You know how women are—a bit jealous. She was a little on the possessive side as far as her baby was concerned. I mean, she was very much worried about the child."

"But she wasn't jealous of you?"

"No, not of me. We were very close."

I thought of the 21-year-old girl taken by death without being ready for it, and the thoughts of fear for her child that must have gone through her mind those dreadful last hours when her moaning filled the air of the room next to Roy Josselyn's.

I also thought about Mrs. Roy Josselyn's background—the fact that she was Princess of the Micmac Indian Tribe. I remembered how frequent psychic experiences were among Indians, who are so much closer to nature than we city-dwellers.

Perhaps the restless spirit of the 21-year-old girl wanted some attention. Perhaps her final moments had only impressed themselves on the atmosphere of the upstairs room and were relived by the psychically sensitive members of the family. Perhaps, too, Thomas Council, the family friend, roamed the house now and then to make sure everything was all right with his favorite family.

When we drove back to Boston late that night, I felt sure I had met a haunted family, for better or worse.

The Ghost Clock

New England is full of ghosts. A young woman with the improbable first name of Dixie-Lee, and the acquired-by-marriage second name of Danforth, lived in the small town of Milford, just over the border in New Hampshire. She chanced to hear me on a Boston radio program, and presto, there was a note in the mail about something pretty eerie that had happened to her.

In 1954, when Dixie-Lee was 17, she took on a two-week job as companion to an elderly lady by the name of Mrs. William Collar. Mrs. Collar, then 82 years old, had been a fine artist, and had lived a happy life all over the world. Dixie-Lee found being a companion an easy way to make some extra money. Mrs. Collar's housekeeper went home nights, and the elderly lady wanted someone with her in the large, rambling house, at least until she could find a full-time housekeeper who would sleep in.

The Collars had met in France, both studying there, and though they married against the wishes of their parents, they had a wonderful and happy life together. When Mr. William Collar died, things were never the same. They had occupied a large double room on the second floor, with a bed on either side, and a wash basin for each. They truly lived close together.

After her husband's death, Mrs. Collar moved out of the room, and never slept in it again. She left everything as it was, including a big grandfather clock, which was never wound again after Mr. Collar's passing. Finally, in 1958, she joined her Bill. She may have been able to prepare herself for it, for she was often heard talking to "her Bill" when no one else could be seen in the room.

There was a fight over the will. The Collars had had no children, and a niece inherited the house.

But let me get back to Dixie-Lee and 1954. The young girl had moved into Mrs. Collar's imposing white house at New Ipswich, as the section was called, and given a room on the second floor next to the large bedroom once occupied by Mr. and Mrs. Collar. She had barely enough time to admire the expensive antique furniture around the house, when it was time to retire for the night.

Mrs. Dixie-Lee Danforth had come to Boston to meet me, and I questioned her about what happened then.

"I went to bed," she said, "and in the wee hours of the morning I awoke to the faint sound of footsteps and ticking of a clock. The sound of both kept getting louder—louder—till it seemed to beat against my brain."

At first she thought she was dreaming, but, biting her own hand, she realized she was fully awake. Cold sweat stood on her forehead when she realized that Mrs. Collar was an invalid *who could not walk*. What was more, the big clock had not worked for years. Suddenly, just as suddenly as it had come, it ceased. Dixie-Lee lay still for a while in sheer terror, then she turned on the light. Her bedroom door was firmly closed, just as she had left it before going to bed. She checked the door leading to what was once the Collars' big bedroom. It was shut tight, too. She ventured out onto the narrow landing of the staircase leading to the lower floor. It was shut off from the downstairs part of the house by a hall door. That, too, was shut. She retraced her steps and suddenly noticed a rope and pulley. She pulled it and another door appeared.

"I opened it, heart in my mouth," Dixie-Lee said, "and was relieved to find a pretty, light bedroom behind it. It was furnished with modern furniture, and seemed to me much gayer and more peaceful than the rest of the house. The room was empty."

"What did you do then?" I wondered.

"First, I checked the big clock in my room. It was not going. Just as dead as it had been all those years. I looked around the house for other clocks. The only one in going condition was downstairs in the room occupied by Mrs. Collar, and I'd have to have had superhearing to hear that one tick all the way up to the second floor through three sets of closed doors and a heavy wooden floor!"

I readily agreed that was not very likely, and wondered if she had told anyone of her frightening experience that night.

"I told the daytime housekeeper, with whom I was friendly, and she laughed. But I refused to stay another moment unless someone else stayed with me. She and her young daughter moved in with me upstairs, and stayed the full two weeks. I never heard the footsteps or the ticking of the clock again while they were with me. But after I left, housekeepers came and went. Nobody seemed to stay very long at the big white house in New Ipswich. Possibly they, too, heard the uncanny noises.

I nodded and asked about Mrs. Collar. Could she have gotten out of bed somehow?

"Not a chance," Dixie-Lee replied. "She was a total invalid. I checked on her in the morning. She had never left her bed. She couldn't have. Besides, the footsteps I heard weren't those of a frail old woman. *They were a man's heavy footfalls.* I never told Mrs. Collar about my experience though. Why frighten her to death?"

"Quite so," I agreed, and we talked about Dixie-Lee now. Was she psychic to any degree?

Dixie-Lee came from a most unusual family. Her great-grandmother knew how 'to work the table.' Her grandfather saw the ghost of his sister, and Dixie-Lee herself had felt her late grandfather in his house whenever she visited, and she had numerous premonitions of impending danger.

On at least one such occasion she had a feeling she should not go on a certain trip, and insisted on stopping the car. On investigation, she found the wheels damaged. She might have been killed had she not heeded the warning!

We parted. Mrs. Danforth returned to her somewhat-more-than skeptical husband in Milford, and I took the next plane back to New York.

But the haunted house in New Ipswich never left my mind. I was due back in New England around Halloween, 1963, and decided to join Mrs. Danforth in a little trip up to the New Hampshire border country. A friend of hers, their children, a Boston-teacher friend of ours named Carol Bowman, and my wife and I completed the party that drove up to New Ipswich on that warm fall day. We weren't exactly expected, since I did not know the name of the present owner of the house. But Mrs. Danforth had sent word of our coming ahead. It turned out the word was never received, and we actually were lucky to find anyone in, luckier yet to be as cordially welcomed as we were by the lady of the house, whom we shall call Mrs. F.

Mrs. Jeanette F. was a sophisticated, well-educated lady whose husband was a psychiatrist, who was once also interested in parapsychology. She asked that I not use her full name here. A strange "feeling" of expecting us made her bid us a cordial welcome. I wasn't surprised to hear this—in this business, nothing surprises me anymore.

The F.'s had only had the house for a year when we visited them. They had not intended to buy the house, although they were on the lookout for a home in New England. But they passed it in their car, and fell in love with it . . . or rather were somehow made to buy the place. They discovered it was built in 1789. That wasn't all they discovered after they moved in.

"I always had the feeling," Mrs. F. said, "that we were only *allowed* to live here . . . but never really alone. Mrs. Collar's bedroom, for instance. I had the distinct feeling something was buried there under the floorboards. My sister-in-law slept upstairs. The next morning she told me she had 'heard things.' Right after we moved in, I heard footsteps upstairs."

"You too?" marveled Dixie-Lee, shooting a triumphant side glance at me, as if I had doubted her story.

"Last winter at dusk one day, I heard a woman scream. Both of us heard it, but we thought—or rather, *liked* to think—that it was a bobcat. Soon thereafter, we heard it again, only now it sounded more like a *child crying*. We heard it on several occasions and it gave us the willies."

On another occasion, there had been five people in the house when they heard the scream, followed by a growl. They went out to look for a bobcat . . . but there were absolutely no traces in the fresh snow, of either animal or human. There had also been all sorts of noises in the basement.

"Something strange about this child crying," Mrs. F. continued. "When we moved in, a neighbor came to see us and said when they saw we had a child, 'You've brought life back to the Collar house.'"

Dixie-Lee broke in.

"I seem to recall there was something about a child. I mean that they had a child."

"And it died?" I asked.

"I don't know," Mrs. F. said. "But there were diaries—they were almost lost, but one of Bill Collar's best friends, Archie Eaton, saved them. Here they are."

Mrs. F. showed us the remarkable books, all written in longhand. On cursory examination I did not uncover the secret of the child.

There is a hollow area in the basement. We went down to get "impressions," and Dixie-Lee felt very uneasy all of a sudden, and didn't feel like joining us downstairs, even though moments before she had been the spirit of adventure personified.

We returned to the ground floor and had some coffee.

I decided to return with a medium, and hold a séance next to the chimney down in the basement, underneath the room where Mrs. F. felt the floorboards held a secret.

But somehow we were thwarted in this effort.

In December of 1963, we were told that our visit would have to be postponed, and Mrs. F. asked us to come later in the winter. Too many living relatives in the house were making it difficult to listen for the dead.

"Something happened yesterday," she added, "that will interest you. My housekeeper is a very bright and trusted woman. She has never mentioned anything strange about the house. Yesterday I was telling her about our plans to sell the house. As I spoke, she was looking in the room next to me—I was standing in the kitchen. She was looking into the dining room, when she turned pale and interrupted me. She had seen a short, old woman in a long gray dress walk through the dining room. Now I questioned her about anything she might have seen in the past. She admitted she had seen figures on several occasions, but was afraid to be ridiculed. Strangely enough, she wants to buy the house despite these experiences. She calls it 'the house that watches,' because she always feels she is being observed while she cares for the children, even when she has them in the garden."

In February, 1964, we tried to fix a new date to visit the house. My letters remained unanswered. Had the house changed hands again?

But no matter who actually *lived* there. It seemed the *real* owner was still Mrs. Collar.

The Ghost Who Would Not Leave

Hardly had I finished investigating the rather colorful haunting in the New York State home of *Newsday* columnist Jack Altschul, which resulted in my name appearing in his column as a man who goes around chasing ghosts, than I heard from a gentleman, now deceased, who was the public relations director of the Sperry Company and a man not ordinarily connected with specters.

Ken Brigham wanted me to know that he had a resident ghost at his summer home in Maine, and what was I to do about it. He assured me that while the lady ghost he was reporting was not at all frightening to him and his family, he would, nevertheless, prefer she went elsewhere. This is a sentiment I have found pervasive with most owners of haunted property, and while it shows a certain lack of sentimentality, it is a sound point of view even from the ghost's perspective because being an earthbound spirit really has no future, so to speak.

All this happened in January of 1967. I was keenly interested. At the time, I was working closely with the late Ethel Johnson Meyers, one of the finest trance mediums ever, and it occurred to me immediately that, if the case warranted it, I would get her involved in it.

I asked Mr. Brigham, as is my custom, to put his report in writing, so I could get a better idea as to the nature of the haunting. He did this with the precision expected from a public relations man representing a major instrument manufacturer. Here then is his initial report:

As a member of the public relation/advertising profession, I've always been considered a cynical, phlegmatic individual and so considered myself. I'm not superstitious, I walk under ladders, have never thought about the "spirit world," am not a deeply religious person, etc., but . . .

Eight years ago, my wife and I purchased, for a summer home, a nonworking farm in South Waterford, Maine. The ten-room farmhouse had been unoccupied for two years prior to our acquisition. Its former owners were an elderly couple who left no direct heirs and who had been virtually recluses in their latter years. The house apparently was built in two stages; the front part about 1840, and the ell sometime around 1800. The ell contains the original kitchen and family bedroom; a loft overhead was used during the nineteenth century for farm help and children. The former owners for many years occupied only a sitting room, the kitchen, and a dining room; all other rooms being closed and shuttered. The so-called sitting room was the daily and nightly abode. We never met the Bells, both of whom died of old age in nursing homes in the area, several years before we purchased the farm. They left it to relatives; all the furniture was auctioned off.

The first summer my wife and I set about restoring the farmhouse. The old kitchen became our living room; the Bell's sitting room became another bedroom; the old dining room, our kitchen. One bright noontime, I was painting in the new living room. All the doors were open in the house. Aware that someone was looking at me, I turned toward the bedroom door and there, standing in bright sunlight, was an elderly woman; she was staring at me. Dressed in a matronly housedress, her arms were folded in the stance common to many housewives. I was startled, thinking she must have entered the house via the open front door and had walked through the front sitting room to the now-bedroom. Behind her eyeglasses, she maintained a passive, inquisitive expression. For a moment or two, we stared at each other. I thought, What do you say to a native who has walked through your house, without sounding unneighborly? and was about to say something like What can I do for you? when she disappeared. She was there and then she wasn't. I hurried through the bedrooms and, of course, there was no one.

Once or twice that summer I was awakened by a sudden, chill draft passing through the second-floor room we used as a master bedroom. One early evening, while I was taking a shower, my wife called me from the living room with near-panic in her voice. I hurried downstairs as quickly as possible only to have her ask if I intended to remain downstairs.

Before closing the house up for the winter, I casually described the apparition to local friends without disclosing my reasons, excusing the inquiry from a standpoint I was interested in the previous owners. Apparently my description was accurate, for our friends wanted to know where I'd seen Mrs. Bell; I had difficulty passing it off.

My wife wasn't put off, however, and later that evening we compared notes for the first time. The night she called me, she explained, she had felt a cold draft pass behind her and had looked up toward the door of the former sitting room (which was well lighted). There, in the door, was the clear and full shadow of a small woman. My wife then cried out to me. The chill breeze went through the room and the shadow disappeared. My wife reported, however, that surprisingly enough she felt a sense of calm. No feeling of vindictiveness.

Over the years, we've both awakened spontaneously to the chill draft and on more than one occasion have watched a pinpoint light dance across the room. The house is isolated and on a private road, discounting any possible headlights, etc. After a moment or so, the chill vanishes.

A couple of times, guests have queried us on hearing the house creak or on hearing footsteps, but we pass these off.

The summer before last, however, our guests' reaction was different.

A couple with two small children stayed with us. The couple occupied the former sitting room, which now is furnished as a Victorian-style bedroom with a tremendous brass bed. Their daughter occupied another first-floor bedroom, and their son shared our son's bedroom on the second floor. A night light was left on in the latter bedroom and in the bathroom, thereby illuminating the upper hallway, and, dimly, the lower hallway. My wife and I occupied another bedroom on the second floor that is our custom.

During the early hours of the morning, we were awakened by footsteps coming down the upper hallway.

They passed our door, went into the master bedroom, paused, continued into our room and after a few minutes, passed on and down the staircase. My wife called out, thinking it was one of the boys, possibly ill. No answer. The chill breeze was present, and my wife again saw the woman's shadow against the bedroom wall. The children were sound asleep.

In the morning, our adult guests were quiet during breakfast, and it wasn't until later that the woman asked if we'd been up during the night and had come downstairs. She'd been awakened by the footsteps and by someone touching her arm and her hair. Thinking it was her husband, she found him soundly sleeping. In the moonlight, she glanced toward a rocking chair in the bedroom and said she was certain someone had moved it and the clothes left on it. She tried to return to sleep, but again was awakened, certain someone was in the room, and felt someone move the blanket and touch her arm.

My wife and I finally acknowledged our "ghost," but our woman guest assured us that she felt no fright, to her own surprise, and ordinarily wouldn't have believed such "nonsense," except that I, her host, was too "worldly" to be a spiritualist.

At least one other guest volunteered a similar experience.

Finally I admitted my story to our local friends, asking them not to divulge the story in case people thought we were "kooks." But I asked them if they would locate a photograph of the Bell family. Needless to say, the photograph they located was identical with my apparition. An enlargement now is given a prominent place in our living room.

Although this experience hasn't frightened us with the house, it has left us puzzled. My wife and I both share the feeling that "whatever [it is] is more curious than unpleasant; more interested than destructive."

I was impressed and replied we would indeed venture Down East. It so happened that Catherine, whom I was married to at the time, and I were doing some traveling in upper New Hampshire that August, and Ethel Johnson Meyers was vacationing at Lake Sebago. All that needed to be done was coordinate our travel plans and set the date.

Mr. Brigham, who then lived in Great Neck, New York, was delighted and gave us explicit instructions on how to traverse New Hampshire from Pike, New Hampshire, where I was lecturing at the Lake Tarleton Club, to our intended rendezvous with Ethel in Bridgton, Maine, at the Cumberland Hotel. The date we picked was August 14, 1967. Ken and Doris Brigham then suggested we could stay over at the haunted house, if necessary, and I assured them that I doubted the need for it, being a bit cocksure of getting through to, and rid of, the ghost all in the same day.

*   *   *

Crossing the almost untouched forests from New Hampshire to Maine on a road called the Kancamagus Highway was quite an experience for us: we rode for a very, very long time without ever seeing a human habitation, or, for that matter, a gas station. But then the Indians whose land this was never worried about such amenities.

Before we left, we had received a brief note from Ken Brigham about the existence of this road cutting through the White Mountains. He also informed me that some of the witnesses to the phenomena at the house would be there for our visit, and I would have a chance to meet them, including Mrs. Mildred Haynes Noyes, a neighbor who was able to identify the ghostly apparition for the Brighams. Most of the phenomena had occurred in the living room, downstairs in the house, as well as in the long central hall, and in one upper-story front bedroom as well, Mr. Brigham added.

At the time I had thought of bringing a television documentary crew along to record the investigations, but it never worked out that way, and in the end I did some filming myself and sound recorded the interviews, and, of course, Ethel Meyers's trance.

When we finally arrived at the house in question in Waterford, Maine, Ethel had no idea where she was exactly or why. She never asked questions when I called on her skills. Directly on arrival she began pacing up and down in the grounds adjacent to the house as if to gather up her bearings. She often did that, and I followed her around with my tape recorder like a dog follows its master.

"I see a woman at the window, crying," she suddenly said and pointed to an upstairs window. "She wears a yellow hat and dress. There is a dog with her. Not from this period. Looking out, staring at something."

We then proceeded to enter the house and found ourselves in a very well appointed living room downstairs; a fire in the fireplace gave it warmth, even though this was the middle of August. The house and all its furnishings were kept as much as possible in the Federal period style, and one had the feeling of having suddenly stepped back into a living past.

When we entered the adjacent dining room, Ethel pointed at one of the tall windows and informed us that the lady was still standing there.

"Dark brown eyes, high cheekbones, smallish nose, now she has pushed back the bonnet hat, dark reddish-brown hair," Ethel intoned. I kept taking photographs pointing the camera toward the area where Ethel said the ghost was standing. The pictures did not show anything special, but then Ethel was not a photography medium, someone who has that particular phase of mediumship. I asked Ethel to assure the woman we had come in friendship and peace, to help her resolve whatever conflict might still keep her here. I asked Ethel to try to get the woman's name. Ethel seemed to listen, then said, "I like to call her Isabelle, Isabelle . . ."

"How is she connected to the house?"

"Lived here."

I suggested that Ethel inform the woman we wanted to talk to her. Earnestly, Ethel then addressed the ghost, assuring her of no harm. Instead of being comforted, Ethel reported, the woman just kept on crying.

We asked the ghost to come with us as we continued the tour of the house; we would try and have her communicate through Ethel in trance somewhere in the house where she could be comfortable. Meanwhile Ethel gathered further psychic impressions as we went from room to room.

"Many layers here . . . three layers . . . men fighting and dying here . . ." she said. "Strong Indian influence also . . . then there is a small child here . . . later period . . . the men have guns, bleeding . . . no shoes . . .

69

pretty far back . . . Adam . . . Joseph . . . Balthazar . . . war victims . . .
house looks different . . . they're lying around on the floor, in pain . . .
some kind of skirmish has gone on here."

I decided to chase the lady ghost again. We returned to the living
room. Ethel picked a comfortable chair and prepared herself for the
trance that would follow.

"I get the names Hattie . . . and Martin . . . not the woman at the
window. . . early period . . . connected with the men fighting . . . not in
house, outside . . . Golay? Go-something . . . it is their house. They are
not disturbed but they give their energy to the other woman. Someone
by the name of Luther comes around. Someone is called Marygold . . .
Mary . . . someone says, the house is all different."

I decided to stop Ethel recounting what may well have been psychic impressions from the past rather than true ghosts, though one cannot always be sure of that distinction. But my experience has taught me
that the kind of material she had picked up sounded more diffuse, more
fractional than an earthbound spirit would be.

"Abraham . . .," Ethel mumbled and slowly went into deep trance
as we watched. The next voice we would hear might be her guide,
Albert's, who usually introduces other entities to follow, or it might be
a stranger—but it certainly would not be Ethel's.

"It's a man. Abram . . . Ibram . . ., " she said, breathing heavily. I
requested her guide Albert's assistance in calming the atmosphere.

Ethel's normally placid face was now totally distorted as if in great
pain and her hands were at her throat, indicating some sort of choking
sensation; with this came unintelligible sounds of ah's and o's. I continued to try and calm the transition.

I kept asking who the communicator was, but the moaning continued, at the same time the entity now controlling Ethel indicated that
the neck or throat had been injured as if by hanging or strangulation.
Nevertheless, I kept up my request for identification, as I always do in

such cases, using a quiet, gentle vocal approach and reassurances that the pain was of the past and only a memory now.

Finally, the entity said his name was Abraham and that he was in much pain.

"Abraham . . . Eben . . . my tongue!" the entity said, and indeed he sounded as if he could not use his tongue properly. Clearly, his tongue had been cut out, and I kept telling him that he was using the medium's now and therefore should be able to speak clearly. But he continued in a way that all I could make out was "my house."

"Is this your house?"

"Yes . . . why do you want to know. . . who are you?"

"I am a friend come to help you. Is this your house?"

"I live here . . ."

"How old are you?"

No answer.

"What year is this?"

"Seventy-eight . . . going on . . . seventy-nine . . ."

"How old are you?"

"Old man . . . fifty-two . . ."

"Where were you born?"

"Massachusetts . . . Lowell . . ."

"Who was it who hurt you?"

Immediately he became agitated again, and the voice became unintelligible, the symptoms of a cutout tongue returned. Once again, I calmed him down.

"What church did you go to?" I asked, changing the subject.

"Don't go to church much . . .," he replied.

"Where were you baptized?"

"St. Francis . . . Episcopal."

I suggested the entity should rest now, seeing that he was getting agitated again, and I also feared for the medium.

"I want justice . . . justice . . .," he said.

I assured him, in order to calm him down, that those who had done him wrong had been punished. But he would have none of it.

"They fight every night out there . . ."

Again, I began to exorcise him, but he was not quite ready.

"My daughter. . . Lisa . . . Elizabeth . . ."

"How old is she?"

"Thirteen . . . she cries for me, she cries for me, she weeps . . . all the blood . . . they take her, too . . ."

"Where is your wife?"

"She left us in misery. Johanna . . . don't mention her . . . she left us in misery."

"What year was that?"

"This year. NOW. . ."

"Why did she leave you?"

"I don't know."

"Where did she go?"

"I don't know."

And he added, "I will go to find her . . . I never see her . . ."

"What about your father and mother? Are they alive?"

"Oh no . . ."

"When did they die."

"1776."

The voice showed a definite brogue now.

"Where are they buried?"

"Over the water . . . Atlantic Ocean . . . home . . ."

"Where did your people come from?"

"Wales . . . Greenough . . ."

Further questioning brought out he was a captain in the 5th regiment.

"Did you serve the king or the government of the colonies?" I asked. Proudly the answer came.

"The king."

When I asked him for the name of the commanding officer of the regiment he served in, he became agitated and hissed at me . . .

"I am an American citizen . . . I'll have you know!"

"Are you a patriot or a Tory?"

"I will not have you use that word," he replied, meaning he was not a Tory.

I went on to explain that time had passed, but he called me mad; then I suggested I had come as a friend, which elicited a bitter reply.

"What are friends in time of war?"

I explained that the war had long been over.

"The war is not over . . . I am an American . . . don't tempt me again . . ."

Once again I pressed him for the name of his commanding officer and this time we received a clear reply: Broderick. He was not infantry, but horse. We were finally getting some answers. I then asked him for the names of some of his fellow officers in the 5th regiment.

"All dead . . ." he intoned, and when I insisted on some names, he added, "Anthony . . . Murdoch . . . Surgeon . . . my head hurts!"

"Any officers you can remember?"

"Matthew . . ."

I asked, what battles was he involved in.

"Champlain . . . Saint Lawrence . . . it's bad, it's bad . . ."

He was showing signs of getting agitated again, and time was fleeting.

I decided to release the poor tortured soul, asking him whether he was ready to join his loved ones now. Once again he relived the wars.

"He won't come home again . . . Hatteras . . . fire . . . I'm weary."

I began to exorcise him, suggesting he leave the house where he had suffered so much.

"My house . . . my tongue . . . Indians," he kept repeating.

But finally with the help of Ethel's spirit guide (and first husband) Albert, I was able to help him across. Albert, in his crisp voice, explained that one of the female presences in the house, a daughter of the spirit we had just released, might be able to communicate now. But what I was wondering was whether a disturbed earthbound spirit was in the house also, not necessarily a relative of this man. Albert understood, and withdrew, and after a while, a faint, definitely female voice began to come from the medium's still entranced lips.

"Ella . . ." the voice said, faintly at first.

Then she added that she was very happy and had a baby with her. The baby's name was Lily. She was Ella, she repeated. When I asked as to who she was in relation to the house, she said, "He always came . . . every day . . . William . . . my house . . ."

"Where is he? You know where he went?"

There was anxiety in her voice now. She said he left St. Valentine's Day, this year . . . and she had no idea what year that was.

Who was Willie? Was he her husband?

This caused her to panic.

"Don't tell them!" she implored me. The story began to look ominous. Willie, Ella, the baby . . . and not her husband?

She began to cry uncontrollably now. "Willie isn't coming anymore . . . where is he?"

What was she doing in the house?

"Wait for Willie . . . by the window . . . always by the window. I wait for him and take care of Lily, she is so sweet. What I can do to find Willie?"

I began to exorcise her, seeing she could not tell me anything further about herself. Her memory was evidently limited by the ancient grief. As I did so, she began to notice spirits. "There is my Papa . . . he will be very angry . . . don't tell anyone . . . take me now . . . my Papa thinks we are married . . . but we have no marriage . . . Willie must marry me . . ."

She cried even harder now.

"Andrew. . . my husband . . ."

Once again I asked Albert, the guide, to lead her outside, from the house. It wasn't easy. It was noisy. But it worked.

"She is out," Albert reported immediately following this emotional outburst, "but her father did find out."

"What period are we in now?"

"The eighteen-something."

"Is there anything in the way of a disturbance from the more recent past?"

"Yes, that is true. An older lady . . . she does not want to give up the home."

Albert then went on to explain that the woman at the window who had been seen had actually been used in her lifetime by the earlier entities to manifest through, which created confusion in her own mind as to who she was. Albert regretted that he could not have her speak to us directly. Andrew, he explained, was that more recent woman's father. Both women died in this house, and since the earlier woman would not let go, the later woman could not go on either, Albert explained.

"We have them both on our side, but they are closer to you because their thoughts are on the earth plane, you can reach them, as you are doing."

After assuring us and the owners of the house that all was peaceful now and that the disturbed entities had been released, Albert withdrew, and Ethel returned to herself as usual blissfully ignorant of what had come through her mediumship.

Two of the ladies mentioned earlier, who had been connected with the house and the phenomena therein, had meanwhile joined us. Mrs. Anthony Brooks, a lady who had been sleeping in one of the bedrooms with her husband two years prior to our visit had this to say.

"I had been asleep, when I was awakened by ruffling at the back of my head. I first thought it was my husband and turned over. But next thing I felt was pressure on my stomach, very annoying, and I turned and realized that my husband had been sound asleep. Next, my cover was being pulled from the bed, and there was a light, a very pale light for which there was no source. I was very frightened. I went upstairs to go to the bathroom and as I was on the stairs I felt I was being pushed and held on tightly to the banister."

I next talked to Mrs. Mildred Haynes Noyes, who had been able to identify the ghostly lady at the window as being the former resident, Mrs. Bell. Everything she had told the Brighams was being reiterated. Then Ken Brigham himself spoke, and we went over his experiences once more in greater detail.

"I was standing in front of the fireplace, painting, and at that time there was a door to that bedroom over there which has since been closed up. It was a bright morning, about eleven o'clock, the doors were open, windows were open, my wife Doris was upstairs at the time, I was alone, and as I stood there painting, I glanced out and there, standing in the doorway, *was a woman.* As I was glancing at her I thought it peculiar that the neighbors would simply walk through my house without knocking.

"She stood there simply looking at me, with her arms folded, a woman who was rather short, not too heavy, dressed in a flowerprint housedress, cotton, she had on glasses and wore flat-heel Oxford shoes, all of this in plain daylight. I did not know what to say to this woman who had walked into my house. I was about to say to her, What can I do for you? thinking of nothing more to say than that, and with that— she was gone. I raced back to the hall, thinking this little old lady had moved awfully fast, but needless to say, there was no one there. I said nothing to anyone, but several weeks later, during the summer, both my wife and I were awakened several times during the night by a very chilly breeze coming into the bedroom. That was one of the bedrooms upstairs. Neither of us said anything but we both sat up in bed and as we did so, we watched a little light dance across the wall! We are very isolated here, and there is no light from the outside whatsoever. This continued for the next year.

At this point it was decided that Mrs. Brigham would tell her part of the story.

"The first summer that we had the house," Mrs. Doris Brigham began, "I was sitting here, about five in the afternoon, my husband was upstairs, and my son was outside somewhere. I was alone and I was aware that someone was here, and on this white doorway, there was a solid black shadow. It was the profile of a woman from top to bottom, I could see the sharp features, the outline of the glasses, the pug in the back of her head, the long dress and shoes—all of a sudden, the shadow disappeared, and a cold breeze came toward me, and it came around and stood in back of my chair, and all of a sudden I had this feeling of peace and contentment, and all was right with the world. Then, all of a sudden, the cold air around my chair, I could feel it moving off. Then, practically every night in the room upstairs, I was awakened for several years in the middle of the night, by a feeling of someone coming into the room. But many times there would be the dancing lights. We moved into another bedroom, but even there we would be awakened by someone running their fingers up my hair! Someone was pressing against me, and the same night, a neighbor was in the house, and she told us the same story. Footsteps of someone coming up the stairs. A feeling of movement of air. A black shadow on the ceiling, and then it disappeared. Often when the children were sick, we felt her around. It was always strong when there were children in the house."

I wondered whether she ever felt another presence in the house, apart from this woman.

Mrs. Brigham replied that one time, when she did not feel the woman around, she came into the house and felt very angry. That was someone else, she felt.

I decided it was time to verify, if possible, some of the material that had come through Mrs. Meyers in trance, and I turned to Ken Brigham for his comments.

"It has been one of the most astounding experiences I have ever had," he began. "There are several points which no one could know but my wife and myself. We did a considerable amount of research back through the deeds of the house. This only transpired a few weeks ago. I had been excavating up out front, preparing some drains, when I came across some foreign bricks, indicating that there had been an extension to the house. This is not the original house, the room we are in; there was a cottage here built for Continental soldiers, at the end of the revolutionary war.

These cottages were given to Massachusetts soldiers, in lieu of pay, and they got some acres up here. This house has been remodeled many times, the most recent around 1870. The town here was formed around 1775; the deeds we have are around 1800. Several things about the house are lost in legend. For example, down there is a brook called Mutiny Brook. There was a mutiny here, and there was bloodshed. There were Indians, yes, this was definitely Indian territory. At one time this was a very well settled area; as recently as 1900 there were houses around here."

I realized, of course, that this was no longer the case: the house we were in was totally isolated within the countryside now.

"The original town was built on this hill, but it has disappeared," Mr. Brigham continued, and then disclosed a strange coincidence (if there be such a thing!) of an actual ancestor of his having lived here generations ago, and then moving on to Canada.

"We only just discovered that at one time two brothers with their families decided to share the house and remodel it," Brigham continued his account. "But one of them died before they could move in. Much of what Mrs. Meyers spoke of in trance is known only locally."

"What about the two women Mrs. Meyers described?" I asked. "She mentioned a short, dark-haired woman."

"She was short, but had gray hair when I saw her," Mr. Brigham said. "A perfectly solid human being—I did not see her as something elusive. We only told our son about this recently, and he told us that he had heard footsteps of a man and a woman on the third floor."

"Anything else you care to comment on?"

"Well, we have the names of some of the owners over a period of time. There were many, and some of the names in the record match those given by Ethel Meyers, like Eben."

"When Mrs. Meyers mentioned the name Isabelle," Mrs. Brigham interjected, "I thought she meant to say Alice Bell, which of course was the former owner's name—the woman at the window."

"One thing I should tell you also, there seems to have been a link between the haunting and the presence of children. One of the former owners did have a child, although the neighbors never knew this," Ken Brigham said. "She had a miscarriage. Also, Lowell, Massachusetts, is where these Continental soldiers came from; that was the traditional origin at the time. Maine did not yet exist as a state; the area was still part of Massachusetts. One more thing: both Mr. and Mrs. Bell died without having any funerals performed. She died in a nursing home nearby, he in Florida. But neither had a funeral service."

"Well, they had one now," I remarked and they laughed. It was decided that the Brighams would search the records further regarding some of the other things that Ethel had said in trance, and then get back to me.

Mr. Brigham was as good as his word. On August 21, 1967, he sent me an accounting of what he had further discovered about the house, and the history of the area in which it stands. But it was not as exhaustive as I had hoped even though it confirmed many of the names and facts Ethel had given us in trance. I decided to wait until I myself could follow up on the material, when I had the chance.

Fortunately, as time passed, the Brighams came to visit my ex-wife Catherine and myself in August of the following year at our home in New York, and as a result Ken Brigham went back into the records with renewed vigor. Thus it was that on August 20, 1968, he sent me a lot of confirming material, which is presented here.

Ethel Meyers's mediumship had once again been proved right on target. The names she gave us, Bell, Eben, Murdoch, Blackguard, Willie, Abraham, why there they were in the historical records! Not ghostly fantasies, not guesswork . . . people from out of the past.

August 20, 1968

Dear Hans,

It was good hearing from Cathy and we did enjoy visiting with you. I presume that just about now you're again on one of your trips, but I promised to forward to you some additional information that we've gathered since last summer. Enclosed is a chronology of the history of the house as far as we've been able to trace back. Early this summer (the only time we made it up to Maine) we spent hours in the York, Maine, Registry of Deeds, but the trail is cold. Deeds are so vague that we can't be certain as to whether or not a particular deed refers to our property. We are, however, convinced by style of building, materials, etc., that the back part of our house is much older than thought originally—we suspect it goes back to the mid-1700s.

Although I haven't included reference to it, our reading of the town history (which is extremely garbled and not too accurate) indicates that one of the Willard boys, whose father had an adjoining farm, went off to the Civil War and never returned, although he is not listed as one of the wounded, dead, or missing. If memory serves me right, he was simply listed as W. Willard ("Willie"?). Now the "ghost" said her name was "Isabel"; unfortunately, we can find no records in the town history on the Bell family, although they owned the house from 1851 to 1959 and Eben Bell lived in the town from 1820–1900! This is peculiar in as much as nearly every other family is recounted in the Town History of 1874. Why? Could "Isabel" be a corruption of the Bell name, or perhaps there was an Isabel Bell. Checking backwards in a perpetual calendar it seems that during the mid-1800s, Tuesday, St. Valentine's Day, occurred on February 14, 1865, 1860, and 1854; the first seems most logical since the others do not occur during the Civil War— which ended on [May] 26, 1865!

Some of my other notes are self-explanatory.

Another question of course concerns the term "Blackguard" for our particular road and hill. An archaic term that connotes "rude"—note also that the map of 1850 does not show a family name beside our house . . . this could be because the property was between owners, or it could be that the owners were "rude"—which also could account for the lack of reference in Town History to the Bell family. It's an interesting sidelight.

Now, to more interesting pieces of information for you: 1) we've finally decided to sell the house and it's just like losing a child . . . I'm personally heartbroken, but I'm also a realist and it is ridiculous to try to keep it when we can't get up there often enough to maintain it. We have a couple of prospective buyers now but since we're not under pressure we want to make sure that any new owners would love it like we do and care for it.

2) And, then the strangest . . . Doris was going through

some old photographs of the place and came across a color print from a slide taken by a guest we had there from Dublin, Ireland. And, it truly looks like an image in the long view up the lane to the house. Three persons have noted this now. Then, on another slide it looks as though there were a house in the distance (also looking up the lane) which is only 1H stories in height. We're having the company photographer blow them up to see what we will see. I'll certainly keep you posted on this!

Well, it all adds up to the fact that we did a lot more work and learned a lot more about the place . . . nearly all of which correlates with Ethel's comments. But as a Yankee realist, I'm just going to have to cast sentiment aside and let it go.

Drop us a line when you get a chance.

Sincerely yours,

"Willie left on Tuesday, St. Valentine's Day."

Two points should be made here regarding this story. Ethel Johnson Meyers had many phases or forms of mediumship, but despite her fervent belief that she might also possess the ability to produce so-called extras, or supernormal photographs, she never did during my investigations. What she did produce at times on her own were so-called scotographs, similar to Rorschach effects used in psychiatry; they were the result of briefly exposing sensitive photographic paper to light and then interpreting the resulting shapes.

But genuine psychic photography shows clear cut images, faces, figures that need no special interpretation to be understood, and this, alas, did not occur in this case when I took the photographs with my camera in Mrs. Meyers's presence.

After the Brighams had sold the Maine property, they moved to Hampton, Virginia. Ken and Doris looked forward to many years of enjoying life in this gentler climate.

Unfortunately, exactly two years after our last contact, in August of 1970, Ken slipped and injured an ankle, which in turn led to complications and his untimely and sudden death.

As for the restless ones up in Maine, nothing further was heard, and they are presumed to be where they rightfully belong.

The following research material, supplied by the late Mr. Ken Brigham, is presented here to give the reader a better feel for the territory and times in which this took place.

Brigham's documentation:

1. Roberts, Kenneth, *March to Quebec*, Doubleday, 1938, p. 32. Listed in the King's Service: Thomas Murdock.

2. Carpenter, Allan, *Enchantment of America—Maine*, Children's Press, 1966, p. 27—85 years of Indian warfare, more than 1,000 Maine residents killed, hundreds captured; by year 1675, there were about 6,000 European settlers in what is now Maine.

3. Smith, Bradford, *Roger's Rangers & The French and Indian War*, Random House, 1956, p. 5—Indians began to slaughter them when they marched out of Fort William Henry to surrender—women and children and men (1757); p. 6—Robert Rogers of New York raised company of rangers in 1755, by 1758 had five companies. Ebenezer Webster came from his home in New Hampshire; p. 46—mentioned Colonel Bradstreet; p. 176—Ebenezer, 1761, returned east to Albany as Captain and then to New Hampshire where he married a girl named Mehitable Smith . . . pushed northward with men under Colonel Stevens and settled on 225 acres at northern edge of town of Salisbury. Later fought in revolutionary war.

Oxford County Registry of Deeds

(References: Book 14, p. 18; Bk. 25, p. 295; Bk. 49, p. 254; Bk. 67, p. 264; Bk. 92, p. 158; Bk. 110, p. 149; Bk. 117, p. 268; Bk. 187, p. 197; Bk. 102, p. 135; Bk. 240, p. 477–478; Bk. 260, p. 381)

1805 Abraham (or Abram) Whitney sold to Nathan Jewell

1809 Nathan Jewell sold to William Monroe (part of land and the house) (1/9/09)

1823 Jonathan Stone bankrupt and sold to Peter Gerry (house), Thaddeus Brown and Josiah Shaw (5/19/23)

1836 Peter Gerry sold to Moses M. Mason (6/14/36)

1848 John Gerry sold to Daniel Billings (5/27/48)

1895 Semantha Bell sold to Caroline Bell (3/4/95)

1940 Edna Culhan (daughter of Caroline Bell) sold to Irving and Alice Bell (11/7/40)

1956 Alice Bell transferred to Archie and Ethel Bell (10/12/56)

1959 Archie and Ethel Bell sold to K. E. and D. M. Brigham (1/59)

Bk. 3, p. 484, Feb 7, 1799

Isaac Smith of Waterford for $800 sold to Nathaniel Geary of Harvard, Lot 2 in 6th Range (southerly half). Deed written February 7, 1799, but not recorded until September 24, 1808. (m. Unice Smith) (See notes 1 & 2)

Vol. 3, p. 99, Jan 6, 1800 (Fryeburg)

Nathaniel Geary and Betey Geary, his wife, sold to Peter Geary for $400 westerly end of southern half of Lot 2 in 6th Range. Notarized in York, January 6, 1800. On April 2, 1801 Betey Geary appeared and signed document which was registered on February 11, 1804.

Peter Gerry (or Geary) b. 1776—d. 6/16/1847

m. Mary (b. 1782—d. 3/16/1830)

m. Elizabeth (b. 1787—d. 5/1/1858)

    c. Mary (b. 1834 or 1804—d. 1844)

(see note 3) John C. (b. 1808)

Roland (b. 1810—d. 1842)

m. Maria Farrar (b. 1811—d. 1842)

Abbie (b. 1812—d. 1817)

Elbridge (b. 1815—m. Anna Jenness)

Bk. 92, p. 158, May 27, 1848

John Gerry sold for $100 (?) to Daniel Billings

Daniel Billings (b. 1780 Temple, Massachusetts)

. . . m. Sarah Kimball (b. 1786)

. . . c. Louise (m. William Hamlin)

    Caroline (b. 1810—m. G. F. Wheeler b. 1810)

    George C. (b. 1837—d. 1919)

    . . . m. Rebecca Whitcomb, private F. Co., 9th Reg.—3 years svc.

    Civil War)

    Maria (m. Calvin Houghton)

    James R. (m. Esther Clark)

    John D. (m. Esther Knowlton)

    Miranda

Bk. 102, p. 135, Oct 14, 1851

Daniel Billings sold to William F. Bell of Boston and Timothy Bell for
    $1,400

Bk. 117, p. 268, Dec 24, 1858

William Bell of Waterford paid his father, William F. Bell, $800 for lot
    2 in 6th Range

Bk. 187, p. 197, April 3, 1871

William Bell, "for support of self and wife," transferred to Timothy
C. Bell "homestead farm" and its parts of lots.

Bk. 240, p. 24, 1894
Timothy Bell left property to his wife Semantha Bell

Bk. 240, p. 477–78, Mar 4, 1895
Semantha Hamlin Bell transferred to Caroline Bell of Boston
Caroline Bell (b. 4/4/1848—d. 9/20/1926)
. . . m. T. C. Bell (b. 10/10/1829—d. 7/13/1894)
. . . m. J. B. Bennett

1905
Caroline Bell (d. 1905??) left property to her son Irving Bell, "her sole
    heir."

Bk.442, p. 133, Oct 30, 1940
Edna Bell Culhan (unmarried) of Cambridge, Mass. transferred to
    Irving and Alice Bell
Nov. 7, 1940
Irving Bell transferred to Edna Culhan "premises described in deed from
    Semantha to his mother Caroline Bell and he was her sole heir."

Bk. 560, p. 381, Oct 12, 1956
Archie and Ethel Bell inherited Lot 1 & 2 in the 5th Range and Lots
    1 & 2 in the 6th Range from Alice Bell
Jan 1959
Archie and Ethel Bell sold property to K. E. And D. M. Brigham

Notes
1. According to Bk. 2, pp. 445–46: On December 20, 1802, Nathaniel
    Gerry (wife Betey) for $800 sold to David Whitcomb of Boston,
    Mass., Lot 2 in 6th Range. Deed mentions road running thru land.
    Registered 1807 and notarized and signed by Justice of the Peace

Eber Rice.

2. According to Bk. 9, p. 467–8: On November 13,1810, David Whitcomb for $150 sold to Peter Gerry Lot 2 in the 6th Range, including "Gerry Road." Apparently both these transactions (notes 1 & 2) were concerned with the westerly end of the northern half of Lot 2 in the 6th Range.

3. John C. Gerry (b. 1808): m. Nancy Farrar (b. 1810—d. 1841), Nancy Sawin (b. 1819). He had an apothecary store in Fryeburg.

Interesting Notes

1. Local cemetery has gravestone of Hon. Lewis Brigham, b. 1816, d. 1866 (at Amherst, Mass).

2. Eben Bell, (b. 8/5/1820—d. 6/8/1900)

3. Richard and Samuel Brigham, and David Whitcomb, signed petition for incorporation on December 19, 1795.

4. Historical:

    Waterford was in York County when it applied for incorporation (January 27, 1796).

    Fryeburg (Pequawkett) was settled in 1763, Inc. 1777; in 1768 Fryeburg had population 300 plus.

    November 17, 1796—Isaac Smith petitioned, with others, Massachusetts for incorporation. Document stated there were fifty to sixty families in "said plantation."

History of Waterford, p. 25—"and when the Indians attacked the growing settlements on the Androscoggin in 1781, and carried Lt. Segar* and others into Canadian captivity, Lt. Stephen Farrington led twenty-three men over this trial in hot, although vain pursuit of the savages."

(*Lt. Nathaniel Segar had cleared a few acres in 1774. A few townships, as Waterford and New

Suncook [Lovell and Sweden] had been surveyed and awaited settlers. p. 22)

Waterford, settled 1775, incorporated 1797; population 1790—150; 1800—535

"Spirit of 76" (Commanger/Morris, p. 605)—General Burgoyne surrenders October 1777 . . . General John Stark agreed to work with Seth Warner because Warner was from New Hampshire or the Hampshire Grants (1777).

November 15, 1745—First Massachusetts Regiment, under Sir William Pepperrell—8th company: Capt. Thomas Perkins, Lt. John Burbank, John Gerry (single).

Civil War: "Fifth Regiment commanded by Mark H. Dunnill of Portland." Fifth was engaged in eleven pitched battles and eight skirmishes ere it entered on terrible campaign of the Wilderness which was an incessant battle. It captured 6 rebel flags and more prisoners than it had in its ranks."

5. Local Notes:

A) Androscoggin Trail was the main Indian route from the East Coast to Canada. Below our property, in the area of Lot 3 in the 4th Range, it follows a brook called "Mutiny Brook." The origin of the term used here is vague, but the natives say Indians mutinied there during the French and Indian Wars.

B) When the town was first settled, the pioneers built their homes on our hill rather than the flat land and the only road around Bear Lake was at the foot of Sweden and Blackguard roads.

C) Our road is called by the archaic word "Blackguard" which connotes villain. No one knows why.

D) The second floor of the house was constructed sometime after the first; timbers are hand hewn to the second floor and mill cut above. The house was rebuilt several times apparently; about 1890 or so two brothers and their families intended to live there but one died before taking residence. Also, foundations of an earlier building were uncovered near the back door.

The Haunted Organ at Yale

Yale University in New Haven, Connecticut, is an austere and respectable institution, which does not take such matters as ghostly manifestations very lightly. I must, therefore, keep the identity of my informant a secret, but anyone who wishes to visit Yale and admire its magnificent, historical organ is, of course, at liberty to do so, provided he or she gets clearance from the proper authorities. I would suggest, however, that the matter of ghostly goings-on not be mentioned at such a time. If you happen to experience something out of the ordinary while visiting the organ, well and good, but let it not be given as the reason to the university authorities for your intended visit.

I first heard about this unusual organ in 1969 when a gentleman who was then employed as an assistant organist at Yale had been asked to look after the condition and possible repairs of the huge organ, a very large instrument located in Woolsey Hall. This is the fifth largest organ in the world and has a most interesting history.

Woolsey Hall was built as part of a complex of three buildings for Yale's two-hundredth anniversary in 1901 by the celebrated architects, Carere and Hastings. Shortly after its completion the then university organist, Mr. Harry B. Jepson, succeeded in getting the Newberry family, of the famous department store clan, to contribute a large sum of money for a truly noble organ to be built for the hall.

Even in 1903 it was considered to be an outstanding instrument because of its size and range. By 1915, certain advances in the technology of pipe organs made the 1903 instruments somewhat old-fashioned. Again Jepson contacted the Newberry family about the possibility of updating their gift so that the organ could be rebuilt and the hall enlarged. This new instrument was then dedicated in 1916 or thereabouts.

By 1926 musical tastes had again shifted toward romantic music, and it became necessary to make certain additions to the stops as well as the basic building blocks of the classical ensemble. Once again the Newberry family contributed toward the updating of the instrument. The alterations were undertaken by the Skinner Organ Company of Boston, in conjunction with an English expert by the name of G. Donald Harrison. Skinner and Harrison did not get on well together and much tension was present when they restored and brought the venerable old organ up-to-date.

Professor Harry Jepson was forced to retire in the 1940s, against his wishes, and though he lived down the street only two blocks from Woolsey Hall, he never again set foot into it to play the famous organ that he had caused to be built. He died a bitter and disappointed man sometime in 1952.

The last university organist, Frank Bozyan, retired in the 1970s, with great misgivings. He confided to someone employed by the hall that he felt he was making a mistake; within six months after his retirement he was dead. As time went on, Woolsey Hall, once a temple of beauty for the fine arts, was being used for rock and roll groups and mechanically amplified music. Undoubtedly, those connected with the building of the hall and the organ would have been horrified at the goings-on had they been able to witness them.

The gentleman who brought all of this to my attention, and who shall remain nameless, had occasion to be in the hall and involved with the organ itself frequently. He became aware of a menacing and melancholic sensation in the entire building, particularly in the basement and the organ chambers. While working there at odd hours late at night, he became acutely aware of some sort of unpleasant sensation just lurking around the next corner or even standing behind him! On many occasions he found it necessary to look behind him in order to make sure he was alone. The feeling of a presence became so strong he refused to be there by himself, especially in the evenings. Allegedly, the wife of one of the curators advised him to bring a crucifix whenever he had occasion to go down to the organ chambers. She also claimed to have felt someone standing at the entrance door to the basement, as if to keep strangers out.

I visited Yale and the organ one fine summer evening in the company of my informant, who has since found employment elsewhere. I, too, felt the oppressive air in the organ chambers, the sense of a presence whenever I moved about. Whether we are dealing here with the ghost of the unhappy man who was forced to retire and who never set foot again into his beloved organ chamber, or whether we are dealing with an earlier influence, is hard to say. Not for a minute do I suggest that Yale University is haunted or that there are any evil influences concerning the university itself. But it is just possible that sensitive individuals visiting the magnificent organ at Woolsey Hall might pick up some remnant of an unresolved past.

The Phantom Admiral

I had never heard of Goddard College until I received a letter from Jay Lawrence, a second-semester student at Goddard College in Plainfield, Vermont. Mr. Lawrence was serious about his interest in psychic phenomena and he had some evidence to offer. He did more than ask me to speak at the college on extrasensory perception; he invited me to come and have a look at a ghost he had discovered in Whiteheld, New Hampshire, about two hours' drive from Goddard.

The haunted house in Whitefield belonged to the Jacobsen family who used it as a summer home only. The younger Jacobsen, whose first name was Erlend—they're of Norwegian descent—invited us to come stay at the house, or at least have a look at it. The Goddard College boys offered to pick us up in Boston and drive us up through the scenic White Mountains to Whitefield.

We arrived at dusk, when the country tends to be peaceful and the air is almost still. The house was at the end of a narrow, winding driveway lined by tall trees, hidden away from the road. There was a wooden porch around three sides of the wooden structure, which rose up three stories.

We were welcomed by Erlend Jacobsen, his wife, Martha, and their little boy Erlend Eric, a bright youngster who had met the ghost, too, as we were to find out.

Inside the house with its spacious downstairs dining room and kitchen, decorated in a flamboyant style by the Jacobsens, we found Mr. and Mrs. Nelson, two friends of the owners, and Jeff Broadbent, a young fellow student of Jay Lawrence.

Sybil puttered around the house, indulging her interest in antiques. I mounted my tape recorder to hear the testimony of those who had experienced anything unusual in the house. We went upstairs, where Sybil Leek could not very well hear us, and entered a small bedroom on the second floor, which, I was told, was the main center of ghostly activities, although not the only one.

The house was called "Mis 'n Top" by its original owner and builder. I lost no time in questioning Erlend Jacobsen, a tall young man of thirty on the Goddard College faculty as an instructor, about his experiences in the old house.

"When my parents decided to turn the attic into a club room where I could play with my friends," Erlend Jacobsen began, "they cut windows into the wall and threw out all the possessions of the former owner of the house they had found there. I was about seven at the time.

"Soon after, footsteps and other noises began to be heard in the attic and along the corridors and stairs leading toward it. But it was not until the summer of 1956, when I was a senior in college and had just married, that I experienced the first really important disturbance."

"1955, Erlend," the wife interrupted. Wives have a way of remembering such dates. Mr. Jacobsen blushed and corrected himself.

"1955, you're right," he said. "That summer we slept here for the first time in this room, one flight up, and almost nightly we were either awakened by noises or could not sleep, waiting for them to begin. At first we thought they were animal noises, but they were too much like footsteps and heavy objects being moved across the floor overhead, and down the hall. We were so scared we refused to move in our beds or turn on the lights."

"But you did know of the tradition that the house was haunted, did you not?" I asked.

"Yes, I grew up with it. All I knew is what I had heard from my parents. The original owner and builder of the house, an admiral named

Hawley, and his wife, were both most difficult people. The admiral died in 1933. In 1935, the house was sold by his daughter, who was then living in Washington, to my parents. Anyone who happened to be trespassing on his territory would be chased off it, and I imagine he would not have liked our throwing out his sea chest and other personal possessions."

"Any other experience outside the footsteps?"

"About four years ago," Erlend Jacobsen replied, "my wife and I, and a neighbor, Shepard Vogelgesang, were sitting in the living room downstairs discussing interpretations of the Bible. I needed a dictionary at one point in the discussion and got up to fetch it from upstairs.

"I ran up to the bend here, in front of this room, and there were no lights on at the time. I opened the door to the club room and started to go up the stairs, when suddenly I walked into what I can only describe as a *warm, wet blanket,* something that touched me physically as if it had been hung from wires in the corridor. I was very upset, backed out, and went downstairs. My wife took one look at me and said, 'You're white.' 'I know,' I said. *'I think I just walked into the admiral.'*"

"I suppose he didn't enjoy your bumping into him in this fashion either," I commented. "Anything else?"

"I was alone in the house, in the club room, which is designed like a four-leaf clover—you can see into the section opposite you, but you can't see into the other two. I was lying there, looking out the window at sunset, when I heard someone breathing—rhythmically breathing in, out, in, out."

"What did you do?"

"I held my own breath, because at first I thought I might be doing it. But I was not. The breathing continued right next to me! I became terrified, being then only fifteen years of age, and ran out of the house until my parents returned."

I asked him again about the time *he touched the ghost.*

How did it feel? Did it have the touch of a human body?

"Nothing like it. It was totally dark, but it was definitely warm, and it resisted my passage."

"Has anything happened to you here recently?"

"About two and a half weeks ago, I walked into the house at dusk and I heard very faint crying for about fifteen or twenty seconds. I thought it might be a cat, but there was no cat in the house, and just as suddenly as it had started, the crying stopped. It sounded almost as if it were outside this window, here on the second floor."

"Is there any record of a tragedy attached to this house?"

"None that I know of."

"Who else has seen or heard anything uncanny here?"

"My parents used to have a who was psychic. She had her share of experiences here all right. Her name is Sarah Wheeler and she is about seventy-five now. The admiral had a reputation for disliking people, and she claimed that when she was in bed here, frequently the bedposts would move as if someone were trying to throw her out of bed. The posts would move off the floor and rock the bed violently, held by unseen hands, until she got out of bed, and then they would stop. She was a Catholic and went to the church the next day to fetch some Holy Water. That quieted things down. But the first night of each season she would come without her Holy Water and that was when things were worst for her."

"Poor Sarah," I said.

"She was psychic, and she had an Indian guide," Erlend Jacobsen continued. "I did not put much stock in some of the things she told us, such as there being treasure underneath the house, put there by the old admiral. But eight or nine years ago, I had occasion to recall this. The house has no cellar but rests on stone pillars. We used to throw junk under the house, where wooden steps led down below. I was cleaning up there with a flashlight, when I saw something shiny. It was a cement

95

block with a silver handle sticking out of it. I chipped the cement off, and found a silver bowl, with 'A.H.' engraved on it."

I turned my attention to Mrs. Jacobsen. She had three children, but still gave the impression of being a college sophomore. As a matter of fact, she was taking courses at Goddard, where her husband was an instructor.

It was ten years to the day—our visit was on June 11—that the Jacobsens had come to this house as newlyweds.

"We spent one night here, then went on our honeymoon, and then came back and spent the rest of the summer here," Martha Jacobsen said. "The first night I was very, very frightened—hearing this walking up and down the halls, and we the only ones in the house! There was a general feeling of eeriness and a feeling that there was someone else in the house. There were footsteps in the hall outside our bedroom door. At one point before dawn, the steps went up the stairs and walked around overhead. But Erlend and I were the only ones in the house. We checked."

Imagine one's wedding night interrupted by unseen visitors—this could give a girl a trauma!

"Two weeks later we returned and stayed here alone," Mrs. Jacobsen continued, "and I heard these footsteps several times. Up and down. We've been coming here for the last ten years and I heard it again a couple of weeks ago."

"Must be unnerving," I observed.

"It is. I heard the steps overhead in the club room, and also, while I was downstairs two weeks ago, the door to the kitchen opened itself and closed itself, without anyone being visible. Then the front door did the same—thing opened and shut itself.

"Along with the footsteps I heard things being dragged upstairs, heavy objects, it seemed. But nothing was disarranged afterwards. We checked."

"Any other events of an uncanny nature?" I asked as a matter of record. Nothing would surprise me in *this* house.

"About ten years ago, when we first moved in, I also heard the heavy breathing when only my husband and I were in the house. Then there was a house guest we had, a Mrs. Anne Merriam. She had this room and her husband was sleeping down the hall in one of the single rooms. Suddenly, she saw a figure standing at the foot of her bed."

"What did she do?"

"She called out, 'Carol, is that you?' twice, but got no answer. Then, just as suddenly as it had come, the figure dissolved into thin air.

"She queried her husband about coming into her room, but he told her that he had never left his bed that night. When this happened on another night, she attempted to follow the figure, and found her husband entering through another door!"

"Has anyone else had an encounter with a ghost here?" I asked.

"Well, another house guest went up into the attic and came running down reporting that the door knob had turned in front of his very eyes before he could reach for it to open the door. The dog was with him, and steadfastly refused to cross the threshold. That was Frank Kingston and it all happened before our marriage. Then another house guest arrived very late at night, about five years ago. We had already gone to bed, and he knew he had to sleep in the attic since every other room was already taken. Instead, I found him sleeping in the living room, on the floor, in the morning. He knew nothing about the ghost. 'I'm not going back up there any more,' he vowed, and would not say anything further. I guess he must have run into the admiral."

What a surprise that must have been, I thought, especially if the admiral was all wet.

"Three years ago, my brother came here," Mrs. Jacobsen continued her report. "His name is Robert Gillman. In the morning he complained of having been awake all night. A former skeptic, he knew now that the tales of ghostly footsteps were true, for he, too, had heard them—all night long in fact."

Jeffrey Broadbent was a serious young man who accompanied Jay Lawrence to the house one fine night, to see if what they were saying about the admiral's ghost was true.

They had sleeping bags and stayed up in the attic. It was a chilly November night in 1964, and everything seemed just right for ghosts. Would they be lucky in their quest? They did not have to wait long to find out.

"As soon as we entered the room, we heard strange noises on the roof. They were indistinct and could have been animals, I thought at first. We went off to sleep until Jay woke me up hurriedly around six in the morning. I distinctly heard human footsteps on the roof. They slid down the side to a lower level and then to the ground where they could be heard walking in leaves and into the night. Nothing could be seen from the window and there was nobody up on the roof. We were the only ones in the house that night, so it surely must have been the ghost."

Jay Lawrence added one more thing to this narrative.

"When we first turned out the flashlight up in the attic, I distinctly heard a high-pitched voice—a kind of scream or whine—followed by footsteps. They were of a human foot wearing shoes, but much lighter than the normal weight of a human body would require."

Jerry Weener also had spent time at the haunted house.

"In early March of 1965, Jay and I came over and had dinner at the fireplace downstairs. We decided to sleep downstairs and both of us, almost simultaneously, had a dream that night in which we met the admiral's ghost, but unfortunately on awakening, we did not recall anything specific or what he might have said to us in our dreams. A second time when I slept in the house, nothing happened. The third time I came over with friends, I slept in the attic, and I heard footsteps. We searched the house from top to bottom, but there was no one else who could have accounted for those steps."

Erlend Eric, age eight going on nine, was perhaps the youngest witness to psychic phenomena scientifically recorded, but his testimony should not be dismissed because of his age. He had heard footsteps going up and down and back up the stairs. One night he was sleeping in the room across the hall when he heard someone trying to talk to him.

"What sort of voice was it?" I asked. Children are frequently more psychic than adults.

"It was a man's," the serious youngster replied. "He called my name, but I forgot what else he said. That was three years ago."

Miriam Nelson was a petite young woman, the wife of one of Erlend Jacobsen's friends, who had come to witness our investigation that evening. She seemed nervous and frightened and asked me to take her to another room so I could hear her story in private. We went across the hall into the room where the figure had stood at the head of the bed and I began my questioning.

"My first experience was when Erlend and I brought a Welsh Corgi up here; Erlend's parents were here, too. I was downstairs in the library; the dog was in my lap. Suddenly I felt another presence in the room, and I could not breathe anymore. The dog started to bark and insist that I follow him out of the room. I distinctly felt someone there.

"Then on a cold fall day about four years ago, I was sitting by the stove, trying to get warm, when one of the burners lifted itself up about an inch and fell down again. I looked and it moved again. It could not have moved by itself. I was terrified. I was alone in the house."

I had heard all those who had had an encounter with the ghost and it was time to get back downstairs where the Jacobsens had laid out a fine dinner—just the right thing after a hard day's drive. A little later we all went up the stairs to the top floor, where Sybil stretched out on a couch near the window. We grouped ourselves around her in the haunted attic and waited.

"I had a feeling of a *midde* room upstairs," Sybil said, "but I don't feel anything too strongly yet."

Soon Sybil was in deep trance as we awaited the coming of the admiral—or whoever the ghost would be—with bated breath. The only light in the attic room was a garish fluorescent lamp, which we shut off, and replaced with a smaller conventional lamp. It was quiet, as quiet as only a country house can be. But instead of the ghost speaking to us directly and presumably giving us hell for trespassing, it was Sybil herself, in deep trance "on the other side," reporting what she saw—things and people the ordinary eye could not perceive.

"I'm walking around," Sybil said. "There is a man lying dead in the middle room. Big nose, not too much hair in front, little beard cut short now. There is a plant near him."

"Try to get his name, Sybil," I ordered.

"I'll have to go into the room," she said.

We waited.

"He is not in here all the time," she reported back. "He came here to die."

"Is this his house?"

"Yes, but there is another house also. A long way off. This man had another house. Hawsley . . . Hawsley."

Almost the exact name of the admiral, I thought. Sybil could not have known that name.

"He went from one house to another, in a different country. Something Indian."

"Is he still here and what does he want?"

"To find a place to rest because . . . he does not know in which house it's in!"

"What is he looking for?"

"Little basket. Not from this country. Like a handle . . . it's shiny . . . silver . . . a present. It went to the wrong house. He gave it to the wrong house. He is very particular not to get things confused. It belongs to Mrs. Gerard at the other house. He usually stays in the little room, one flight up. With the fern. By the bed."

"But what about Mrs. Gerard? How can we send the package to her unless we get her address?" I said.

"It's very important. It's in the wrong perspective, he says," Sybil explained.

"What did he have for a profession?" I tried again.

"He says he brought things . . . seeds."

"What are his initials or first name?"

"A. J. H."

Sybil seemed to listen to someone we could not see.

"He's not troublesome," she said. "He goes when I get near to him. Wants to go to the other house."

"Where is the other house?"

"Liang . . . Street . . . Bombay."

"Does he know he is dead?"

"No."

I instructed her to tell him.

"Any family?"

"Two families . . . Bombay."

"Children?"

"Jacob . . . Martin."

It was not clear whether the ghost said Jacob or Jacobsen.

"He is shaking himself," Sybil now reported. "What upset him? He worries about names. A. J. A. name on something he is worried about. The names are wrong on a paper. He said Jacobsen is wrong. It should be Jacob Hawsley son."

Evidently the ghost did not approve the sale of his house by his executors, but wanted it to go to his son.

"Because of two houses, two families, he did not know what to do with the other."

"What does 'A' stand for in his name?"

"Aaron . . . Aaron Jacob."

"Does he have any kind of title or professional standing?"

"A-something . . . A-D-M . . . can't read . . . Administrator A-D-M . . . it's on the paper, but I can't read the paper."

Still, she did get the admiral's rank!

I promised to have the gift delivered to Mrs. Gerard, if we could find her, but he must not stay in this house any further.

"Who waters the plants, he asks," Sybil said.

I assured him the plants would be taken care of.

"But what about the other house, who waters the plants there?" the ghost wanted to know.

"How does he go there?" I asked in return.

"He sails," Sybil replied. "Takes a long time."

Again I promised to find the house in India, if I could.

"What about a date?" I asked. "How long ago did all this happen?"

"About 1867," Sybil replied.

"How old was he then?"

"Fifty-nine."

I implored the admiral not to cause any untidiness in the house by upsetting its inhabitants. The reply via Sybil was stiff.

"As a man with an administrative background, he is always tidy," Sybil reported. "But he is going now."

"He is going now," Sybil repeated, "and he's taking the ferns."

I called Sybil back to her own body, so as not to give some unwanted intruder a chance to stop in before she was back in the driver's seat, so to speak.

None the worse for her travels in limbo, Sybil sat up and smiled at us, wondering why we all stared at her so intently. She remembered absolutely nothing.

Erlend Jacobsen spoke up.

"That basket she mentioned," he said. "When my parents first bought the house, there was hanging over the dining room, on a chain, a stuffed armadillo, which had been shellacked from the outside. It had straw handles and had been turned into a basket. It was around the house until about five years ago, but I have no idea where it is now. For all we know, it may still be around the house somewhere."

"Better find it," I said. "That is, if you want those footsteps to cease!

Just as we were leaving the house, the senior Jacobsens returned. Mr. Eric Jacobsen does not care for ghosts and I was told not to try to get him to talk about the subject. But his wife, Josephine, Erlend's mother, had been pushed down the stairs by the ghost—or so she claims. This is quite possible, judging by the way the admiral was behaving in his post-funeral days and nights.

Our job in Whitefield seemed finished and we continued on to Stowe, Vermont, where we had decided to stay at the famous Trapp Family Lodge. Catherine had become interested in Mrs. Trapp's books, and from *The Sound of Music,* we both thought that the lodge would provide a welcome interlude of peace during a hectic weekend of ghost hunting.

The next morning we rested up from the rigors of our investigation and found the world around us indeed peaceful and promising. The following morning we would go down to Goddard College and address students and teachers on the subject of ghosts, which would leave us with a pleasant afternoon back at Stowe, before flying back to Manhattan. But we had reckoned without the commercial spirit at the lodge. Like most overnight lodgings, they wanted us out of our rooms by eleven o'clock Sunday morning, but finally offered to let us stay until two. I declined.

After my talk at the college, we were taken to one of the girls' dormitories where uncanny happenings had taken place. The college was situated on the old Martin farm, and the manor had been turned into a most elegant girl students' residence, without losing its former Victorian grandeur. Reports of a dead butler still walking the old corridors upstairs had reached my ears. Two students, Madeleine Ehrman and Dorothy Frazier, knew of the ghost. The phenomena were mainly footsteps when no one was about. A teacher who did not believe in ghosts set foot in the manor and later revealed that the name Dawson had constantly impressed itself on her mind. Later research revealed that a butler by that name did in fact live at the manor house long ago.

Sue Zuckerman was a New York girl studying at Goddard.

"One night last semester," she said, "I was up late studying when I heard footsteps approaching my room. After a few seconds I opened my door—there was nobody there. I closed the door and resumed studying. I then heard footsteps walking away from my door. I looked again, but saw nothing.

"During this time for a period of about three weeks, my alarm clock had been shut off every night. I would set it for about seven-thirty, but when I woke up much later than that, the alarm button was always off. I began hiding my clock, locking my door—but it still happened.

"Back in 1962, I was toying with a Ouija board I had bought more in fun than as a serious instrument of communication. I had never gotten anything through it that could not have come from my own mind, but that Friday afternoon in 1962, I worked it in the presence of three other friends, and as soon as we put our hands on it, it literally started to leap around. It went very fast, giving a message one of us took down: 'I am dead . . . of drink. Are you here now in the Manor? One could speak of my presence here.' There was more, but I can't remember it now.

"Afterwards, a strange wind arose and as we walked past a tree outside, it came crashing down."

I don't know about strange "wind," and Ouija boards are doubtful things at times, but the footfalls of the restless butler named Dawson must have been a most unusual extracurricular activity for the co-eds at Goddard College.

The Possession of Mrs. F.

Possession for the sake of evil, or for the sake of continuing indefinitely a physical existence, is probably the most feared form of this phenomenon. But there exists a type of possession which is clearly confined in purpose and frequently also in time. In such cases, the possessor takes hold of an individual on the physical plane in order to finish some uncompleted task he or she was unable to accomplish while alive in the physical sense. Once that task has been accomplished, there is no further need for possession, and the possessor withdraws, continuing an existence in the proper dimension, that is, in the nonphysical world.

Nevertheless, there are aspects of this limited and quasi-intelligent possession that are not acceptable to the one to whom it occurs. In the desire to express a need of sorts or finish something that had been started and not ended, the possessor may overlook the desire of the individual not to be possessed, or to be free of such imposed power. Under such circumstances it is advisable to break the hold of the possessor in spite of any good intentions behind the action.

*   *   *

Virginia F. is an average person of full Irish descent. She describes herself as one of the Black Irish, those who think they are related to the Spanish Armada survivors who took refuge in Ireland in 1588 and later intermingled with the native population. Mrs. F. has five children and lives in a modest home in one of the largest cities in New England. The house was built in February of 1955 and sold to a Mr. and Mrs. J. S.

Evidently the home was far from lucky for the first owner whose wife died of cancer in it after about four years. Then it was rented to a Captain M. for about a year. Apparently the good captain wasn't too happy there either for he left. The next owners were C. and E. B. Within a year of acquiring the house they filed for a divorce. A short time later, their oldest son was run over and killed by a truck. At that point, the house passed into the hands of Mrs. F. and her family. A little over two months after they had moved in, her father had a heart attack in the bathroom and died on the way to the hospital. For nine years Mrs. F. and her family managed to live in the house, but their marriage was not a happy one, and it ended in divorce in 1970. Whether or not the tragic atmosphere of the house has any bearing upon what transpired later is hard to tell, but Mrs. F. thought enough of it to advise me of it, and I'm inclined to think that the depressing atmosphere of a house may very well lead to psychic complications. It could very well be that an earlier dwelling stood on the same spot and that some of the older vibrations are clinging to the new house.

On May 25, 1970, Mrs. F.'s divorce was complete. In the fall of the same year she met another man. Francis and his sister Gloria had visited the house after a club meeting, and from that moment on, Mrs. F. and Francis were inseparable. It was love at first sight. For a few weeks, the two went everywhere together, and then the happiness came to a sudden end. Francis was ill with an incurable disease. He knew he did not have long to live. Instead of a wedding, she helped plan his funeral.

The night before he died, he told her he would never leave her and that nothing or no one could ever separate them. He also told her that he would come for her soon. That night he died. And when he died his electric clock stopped exactly at the moment he passed out of the body. For the last day of his life Francis had been attended day and night by Mrs. F. and her two sons, but nothing could have been done to save him.

When the man knew that his time was short, he started to talk with her about death and what he wanted to have done. She had promised him she would buy the lot in the cemetery next to his; faithful to his request, the day after she had buried him, February 14, 1972, she bought the lot next to his.

That day, strange things started to happen in her home. There was, first of all, a picture, which Francis had bought for her, showing the Minuteman on the Lexington Green. The picture would actually fly off the wall, no matter how many times she refastened it. This happened several times and the picture actually flung itself across the room, making a terrific noise. During the three days between Francis' death and his burial, a little valentine she had given him in the hospital would be moved by unseen hands. Someone took it from a ticket, to which it was fastened with a paper clip, and turned it around so that the side on which was written "Love G." was on top. But no one in the house had done it.

After the funeral, Mrs. F. fell asleep, exhausted from the emotional upset. At four o'clock in the morning she woke up to find that a piece of paper she had put in front of her, had been written upon while she was asleep. The words read, "Remember, I love you, Francis."

Realizing that this was a message somehow using her hands to write even though she might not be aware of it, she tried consciously to receive another message by automatic writing a week later. The first line consisted of scribbled letters that made no sense whatsoever.

But the second line became clearer. It was a love message written in the handwriting of the deceased. There was no mistaking it.

When she confided in her family doctor, he shook his head and prescribed sedatives. In her heartbroken state, Mrs. F. remembered how her fiance had promised her a pearl ring for Christmas but had been too sick then to buy it. The matter of the missing pearl ring had been a private joke between them. Two days after the last automatic message, she was putting some things away in the bedroom of her house. She carefully cleaned the top of her dresser and put everything in its proper place. A short time later her oldest daughter asked her to come up to the bedroom. There, on the dresser, was a pearl! How had it gotten there?

"Do these things truly happen, or am I on the verge of a breakdown?" Mrs. F. asked herself. She remembered how she had written to me some years ago concerning some ESP experiences she had had. Again she got in touch with me, this time for help. "Help me, please, to understand. And if you tell me that I'm losing my mind," she wrote, "then I'll go to the hospital." But I assured her that she was not insane. All she really wanted was to be with her Francis at this point.

Mrs. F. was indeed in a fix. There was nothing wrong with her love relationship, but Francis's promise to take her over to his side of life was another matter. I was convinced that those who were guiding him now would also instruct him accordingly. Gently I explained to Mrs. F. that love cannot fully bridge the gap between the two worlds of existence.

There is a time for them to be joined, but for the present she belonged to the world of the body and must continue to live in it as best she could. When she accepted her true position and also her renewed responsibility towards her children, the hold—which the deceased had had upon her for a while after his passing—lessened. It was as if Francis had understood that his business had indeed been finished. The knowledge of his continued existence in another dimension was all he wanted to convey to his one and only love. That done, he could await her coming in due time in the conviction that they would be together without the shadow of possession between them.

The Ship Chandler's Ghost

It is a well-known fact among ghost hunting experts that structural changes in a house can have dire effects. Take out a wall, and you've got a poltergeist mad as a wet hen. I proved that in the case of the Leighton Buzzard ghost in *Ghosts I've Met*. Take down the building, like the studio building at New York's 51 West Tenth Street, and put up a modern apartment house, and you've got no ghost at all. Just a lot of curious tenants. If the ghost is inside the house before the changes are realized, he may bump into walls and doors that weren't there before—not the way he remembered things at all.

But move a whole house several yards away from the shore where it belongs, and you're asking for trouble. Big trouble. And big trouble is what the historical society in Cohasset, Massachusetts, got when they moved the old Ship's Chandlery in Cohasset. With my good friend Bob Kennedy of WBZ, Boston, I set out for the quaint old town south of Boston on a chilly evening in the fall of 1964.

When we arrived at the wooden structure on a corner of the Post Road—it had a nautical look, its two stories squarely set down as if to withstand any gale—we found several people already assembled. Among them were Mrs. E. Stoddard Marsh, the lively curator of the museum, which was what the Ship's Chandlery became, and her associate, lean, quiet Robert Fraser. The others were friends and neighbors who had heard of the coming of a parapsychologist, and didn't want to miss anything. We entered the building and walked around the downstairs portion of it, admiring its displays of nautical supplies, ranging from fishing tackle and scrimshaw made from walrus teeth to heavy anchors, hoists, and rudders—all the instruments and wares of a ship chandler's business.

Built in the late eighteenth century by Samuel Bates, the building was owned by the Bates family; notably by one John Bates, second of the family to have the place, who had died 78 years before our visit. Something of a local character, John Bates had cut a swath around the area as a dashing gentleman. He could well afford the role, for he owned a fishing fleet of 24 vessels, and business was good in those far-off days when the New England coast was dotted with major ports for fishing and shipping. A handwritten record of his daily catch can be seen next to a mysterious closet full of ladies' clothes. Mr. Bates led a full life.

After the arrival of Dorothy Damon, a reporter from the *Boston Traveler*, we started to question the curator about uncanny happenings in the building.

"The building used to be right on the waterfront, at Cohasset Cove, and it had its own pier," Mrs. Marsh began, "and in 1957 we moved it to its present site."

"Was there any report of uncanny happenings before that date?"

"Nothing I know of, but the building was in a bad state of disrepair.

"After the building was brought to its present site, then," I said, "what was the first unusual thing you heard?"

"Two years ago we were having a lecture here. There were about forty people listening to Francis Hagerty talk about old sailing boats. I was sitting over here to the left—on this ground floor—with Robert Fraser, when all of a sudden we heard heavy footsteps upstairs and things being moved and dragged—so I said to Mr. Fraser, 'Someone is up there; will you please tell him to be quiet?' I thought it was kids."

"Did you know whether there was in fact anyone upstairs at the time?"

"We did not know. Mr. Fraser went upstairs and after a moment he came down looking most peculiar and said, 'There is no one there.'"

"Now, there is no other way to get down from upstairs, only this one stairway. Nobody had come down it. We were interrupted three times on that evening."

I asked Robert Fraser what he had seen upstairs.

"There was enough light from the little office that is upstairs, and I could see pretty well upstairs, and I looked all over, but there was nobody upstairs."

"And the other times?"

"Same thing. Windows all closed, too. Nobody could have come down or gotten out. But I'm sure those were footsteps."

I returned to Mrs. Marsh and questioned her further about anything that might have occurred after that eventful evening of footsteps.

"We were kept so busy fixing up the museum that we paid scant attention to anything like that, but this summer something happened that brought it all back to us."

"What happened?" I asked, and the lady reporter perked up her ears.

"It was on one of the few rainy Sundays we had last July," Mrs. Marsh began. "You see, this place is not open on Sundays. I was bringing over some things from the other two buildings, and had my arms full. I opened the front door, when I heard those heavy footsteps upstairs."

"What did you do—drop everything?"

"I thought it was one of our committee or one of the other curators, so I called out, 'Hello—who's up there?' But I got no answer, and I thought, well, someone sure is pretty stuffy, not answering me back, so I was a little peeved and I called again."

"Did you get a reply?"

"No, but *the steps hesitated* when I called. But then they continued again, and I yelled, 'For Heaven's sake, why don't you answer?'—and I went up the stairs, but just as I got to the top of the stairs, they stopped."

There was a man who had helped them with the work at the museum who had lately stayed away for reasons unknown. Could he have heard the footsteps too and decided that caution was the better part of valor?

"The other day, just recently, four of us went into the room this gentleman occupies when he is here, and the *door closed on us*, by itself. It has never done that before."

I soon established that Fraser did not hear the steps when he was *alone* in the building, but that Mrs. Marsh did. I asked her about anything psychic in her background.

"My family has been interested in psychic matters since I was ten years old," she said in a matter-of-fact tone. "I could have become a medium, but I didn't care to. I saw an apparition of my mother immediately after she passed away. My brother also appeared to me six months after his death, to let me know he was all right, I guess."

"Since last July has there been any other manifestation?"

"I haven't been here much," Mrs. Marsh replied. "I had a lot of work with our costume collection in the main building. So I really don't know."

We decided to go upstairs now, and see if Mr. Bates—or whoever the ghost might be—felt like walking for us. We quietly waited in the semi-darkness upstairs, near the area where the footsteps had been heard, but nothing happened.

"The steps went back and forth," Mrs. Marsh reiterated. "Heavy, masculine steps, the kind a big man would make."

She showed us how it sounded, allowing of course for the fact she was wearing high heels. It sounded hollow enough for ten ghosts.

I pointed at a small office in the middle of the upstairs floor.

"This was John Bates' office," Mrs. Marsh explained, "and here is an Indian doll that falls down from a secure shelf now and then as if someone were throwing it."

I examined the doll. It was one of those early nineteenth-century dolls that Native Americans in New England used to make and sell.

"The people at the lecture also heard the noises," Mrs. Marsh said, "but they just laughed and nobody bothered thinking about it."

I turned to one of the local ladies, a Mrs. Hudley, who had come up with us. Did she feel anything peculiar up here, since she had the reputation of being psychic?

"I feel disturbed. Sort of a strange sensation," she began, haltingly, "as though there was a 'presence' who was in a disturbed frame of mind. It's a man."

Another lady, by the name of McCarthy, also had a strange feeling as we stood around waiting for the ghost to make himself known. Of course, suggestion and atmosphere made me discount most of what those who were around us that night might say, but I still wanted to hear it.

"I felt I had to get to a window and get some air," Mrs. McCarthy said. "The atmosphere seemed disturbed somehow."

I asked them all to be quiet for a moment and addressed myself to the unseen ghost.

"John Bates," I began, "if this is you, may I, as a stranger come to this house in order to help you find peace, ask that you manifest in some form so I know you can hear me?"

Only the sound of a distant car horn answered me.

I repeated my invitation to the ghost to come forward and be counted. Either I addressed myself to the wrong ghost or perhaps John Bates disliked the intrusion of so many people—only silence greeted us.

"Mr. Bates," I said in my most dulcet tones, "please forgive these people for moving your beautiful house inland. They did not do so out of irreverence for your person or work. They did this so that many more people could come and admire your house and come away with a sense of respect and admiration for the great man that you were."

It was so quiet when I spoke, you could have heard a mouse breathe.

Quietly, we tiptoed down the haunted stairs, and out into the cool evening air. Cowboy star Rex Trailer and his wife, who had come with us from Boston, wondered about the future—would the footsteps ever come back? Or was John Bates reconciled with the fact that the sea breezes no longer caressed his ghostly brow as they did when his house was down by the shore?

Then, too, what was the reason he was still around to begin with? Had someone given him his quietus in that little office upstairs? There are rumors of violence in the famous bachelor's life, and the number of women whose affections he had trifled with was legion. Someone might very well have met him one night and ended the highly successful career of the ship chandlery's owner.

A year went by, and I heard nothing further from the curator. Evidently, all was quiet at John Bates' old house. Maybe old John finally joined up with one of the crews that sail the ghost ships on the other side of the curtain of life.

The Somerville Ghost

"**I**'m Mrs. Campano," the letter read in a large, clear handwriting, "and I've been living in this house for four months now." The woman had heard me on station WBZ, Boston, and wanted to report a haunted house.

I called her and found Mrs. Campano a reasonable, well-spoken lady in her middle years. Her elder daughter had recently married and her son was grown, and it made sense for the mother to move to a smaller house. But at the moment she was still at the haunted house on Washington Avenue in Somerville, Massachusetts.

The first impression that something strange went on in her house was when she noticed her dog's unusual behavior. The dog barked constantly and kept running up and down the stairs to the upper floor. When the daughter moved out, she took the dog with her, and Mrs. Campano's house became quiet *except for the ghost.*

There was a light in the downstairs living room of the wooden house, so she found it unnecessary to turn on any additional lights when she wanted to mount the stairs. One night in 1964, when she passed the stairway, she heard someone crying. She entered the bathroom, and when she came out she still heard the sound of someone crying as if hurt. She walked up the stairs, thinking it was one of her children having a nightmare, but when she got to the top of the stairs, the crying stopped.

She checked all the rooms upstairs, and the children were fast asleep. She went back to bed downstairs. Then, above her head, she distinctly heard the shuffling of feet, as if two people were fighting and struggling. She had a puppy, who started to act strangely just as the larger dog had done.

The experience upset Mrs. Campano no end, and she talked it over with her elder daughter, Marsha, now married. The girl was sympathetic, for she, too, had heard the crying and at one time footsteps of someone going up and down the stairs, with the crying continuing for about twenty minutes. It sounded like a woman.

They decided to do something about the noises. A group of young boys, friends of her son's, stayed overnight at the old house. They took the upstairs room where most of the disturbances centered. At first, everything was quiet. The youngest girl and some of her friends went to sleep in another room upstairs. Soon the boys heard tapping and crying, but thought the girls were trying to put over a practical joke. They jumped from their beds and raced across the hall only to find the girls fast asleep in their room.

Mrs. Campano turned to the church for relief, but the local priest refused to come. A friend supplied her with Holy Water but the relief was short lived. A week later, noises started up again.

When Marsha, the elder daughter, had the bedroom to the right upstairs, she often heard the crying and felt as though someone were touching her. But she had kept quiet about these sensations. After she had moved out, the younger daughter, who had the room now, also reported that she felt a presence in her room, and something or someone unseen touching her feet as if to rouse her!

The eighteen-year-old son also had heard the footsteps and crying and had decided to check on the source. When he had reached the hallway, the crying suddenly stopped, but the puppy, which had come with him, kept on growling. Ten minutes later the noises started up again, this time from the cellar.

One more thing Mrs. Campano found strange about the house: on the wall of the room upstairs there was a red spot that looked like blood.

I reached Jim Tuverson, of WBZ's "Contact" program, to arrange for a visit to the haunted house on Washington Avenue, Somerville.

There was a problem, though. Mrs. Campano had decided to move out on May 31, 1965, and our visit would be in June. We took it up with the landlord, Costa & Sons. This is not so easy as it sounds. How do you tell a real estate man one of his properties is haunted? You don't tell him, that's how. You do tell him you've got an interest in old New England houses and could you do a little historical research?

When we arrived at the house I realized immediately how funny the request must have sounded to Mr. Costa. The house was a ramshackle, run-down structure. Since Mrs. Campano had moved, we agreed to see her *after* the investigation and trance session.

It was a warm day for Boston when we met Jim Tuverson and Bob Kennedy of WBZ at Logan Airport. Sybil Leek had flown in directly from San Francisco—using an airplane of course—and joined us for the ride to the haunted house. She knew nothing whatever about the case, not even the location of the house. We left our cars in front of the house where a few curious people had gathered. They rarely saw two radio cars pull up in this unglamorous section of town.

Quickly we went inside the house where a lady from the real estate firm of Costa & Sons was expecting us. The house had been stripped of all its contents except the dirt, which was still around in generous quantities. The aroma was somewhat less than heavenly and it was my fondest wish to get out of there as soon as possible. It was about four in the afternoon and bright, but Sybil never lets such things bother her when we investigate a place.

We hastily borrowed a chair from the house across the street and assembled in the kitchen downstairs. Sybil took to the chair, and I began the session by asking for her impressions of this dismal house.

"As you know, I came in and walked right out again and got a drink next door—that's always a bad sign for me. I don't like this place at all, and

I don't think we're in the right room. The upstairs room is the right place."

"What do you feel about the upstairs?"

"There is a strange smell in one of the rooms upstairs, not just a physical smell, but something beyond that. I always associate this smell with something quite evil and I don't think I'm in for a good time.

"What do you think has taken place in this house?" I asked.

"I think there has been some violence here," Sybil replied without hesitation, "the right hand room upstairs."

"Do you feel any presence in this house?"

"I feel a very bad head right now," Sybil said and touched the back of her own head as if she felt the pain herself. "My head is very bad. There is some lingering evil which pervades not only the inside of the house, but even the outside is not immune."

I then asked Sybil to relax as well as she could under these uncomfortable circumstances, and to allow whatever entity might be hovering about to communicate through her.

Outside the warm air was filed with the distant noises of a bustling city, but inside the drab, dirty house, time seemed to stand still as we tried to wedge open a doorway into another dimension.

"Things are different today," Sybil finally said. "I'm looking in at the house—but nobody can speak through me."

We should have gone upstairs to the room Sybil thought was the center of the haunting, I thought. Still, one never knows. Sometimes just being in a house, any place within the walls, is sufficient to make contact.

I instructed Sybil to remain in trance and to report back anything she could find.

"Right hand side," Sybil said in a quiet, slow voice, different from her habitual speech. "There's someone in the house . . . it's a girl."

"What do you see upstairs?"

"I see the girl on the bed. She's got long, wavy hair, she can't get up, her head is very bad."

"Is she injured?"

"Yes . . . in the back. She's dead. There's a child or a dog, a child . . . this is 1936 . . . I keep going outside the house, you see, because there's someone around . . . I can't find him."

"Can you speak to the woman on the bed?"

"She worries about the child."

I explained about her true status and where the child now was.

"She's getting angry," Sybil reported. "She does not believe you."

I told Sybil to instruct the woman how to call for her child. But the ghost was very confused. We tried to get her to follow Sybil out of the house. I kept explaining what had happened to her.

"She won't leave until she finds the child," Sybil explained and I kept thinking of the scurrying footsteps on those stairs, the crying it all fitted in with a mother trying to find her baby!

"What is her name?" I asked.

There was silence as we waited for more evidence from Sybil's lips.

"Linda Mathews," Sybil said, clearly and distinctly.

"And the child's name?"

"Margaret."

I had never heard these names before in connection with this case, nor had anyone else in the room. Mrs. Campano had not mentioned them to me either.

I instructed Linda to call for her child and then leave the house. But she wouldn't budge.

"She's waiting for someone . . . Robert Shaw was here, she says."

"Did *he* hurt her?"

"She'll kill him, because she hates him enough. He hurt her. He hit her."

"Did he kill her?"

"She doesn't know."

"Did her husband kill her?"

"She doesn't know."

Again Sybil, on my urging, explained her situation to the ghost.

"She's coming a little closer now," Sybil reported. "I think she's Scotch. Country type. She's moving now, off the bed. I'm with her. She's very weak."

I told Sybil to withdraw as soon as the ghost was safely outside the house. Quickly I brought her out of trance.

"Quite an ordeal, somehow," Sybil said, although she did not remember anything that had come through her while in trance. I sent her and my wife on to the radio station with Bob Kennedy, while Jim Tuverson and I drove in his car to Mrs. Campano's new house, a few blocks down Washington Avenue.

The new house was much smaller and the Campanos occupied only a part of it, but it was brighter and much more cheerful than the house we had just left.

A sudden idea struck me. I walked into the Campano living room, and shot a question at Mrs. Campano—"Have you ever heard of Linda Mathews?"

"Yes," Mrs. Campano replied with surprise. "I used to get her mail at the old house all the time, and always sent it back. She used to live in the house. In fact, she died there. But I don't know any more than that."

Here we had immediate corroboration of a name—not a common name like Jones or Smith, but a definite name not easily guessed—and information concerning this name had not been known to anybody in the haunted house while we were there!

Thus Sybil could not have gotten the name from the unconscious minds of any of us in the house, not indeed from me, since I had only learned of the Mathews matter this minute. Jim Tuverson was visibly impressed. Here was proof of the kind that would stand up in any court of law. Sybil had really done a superb job.

I questioned Mrs. Campano about her experiences at the house. Was there anything she had not told me prior to my coming to Somerville?

"It was like a woman crying as if she had been hurt," she reiterated. "Then one night I was the last one to go to bed and everything seemed perfectly normal. In the morning, however, I discovered a series of pictures, which I have in the room between bookends, placed on the floor as if by human hands. Nobody could have done this."

I thought perhaps the unfortunate woman ghost had been trying to get her attention.

"What about your husband?" I asked. "Has he ever heard anything unusual?"

"Yes. One morning we came in around 3 A.M., and we were in the kitchen downstairs cooking, when we both heard someone coming down the stairs. He thought one of the children had smelled the food and was about to join us, but, of course, nobody appeared."

"What about you and your son hearing those footsteps coming up from the cellar?" I asked.

"It sounded like someone in heavy boots coming up the cellar steps," Mrs. Campano explained, "and then we heard the noise of someone handling pots and pans in the kitchen."

"Were they actually moved around?"

"Yes. The next morning we found the kitchen in disorder, but nobody had been in who could have done this. No burglars, either."

I began to wonder if the cellar at the Washington Avenue house did not hold the bodies of two murdered people.

"Did you check the cellar?" I asked.

"The next day," Mrs. Campano replied, "but we found nothing."

Mrs. Campano's father, Peter Cagliano, 73, is a mystic and probably psychic. He came to the house, and for a while things became quiet after that.

Evidently, Mrs. Campano also had inherited some of her family's psychic talents. Her first psychic experience took place when she was 17 years old. She then lived in a house where a murder had been committed and witnessed the noises and physical phenomena accompanying the haunting. Seven years ago, she saw the apparition of a woman known to have died, by the name of Jehasses, but no communication ensued.

"What do you know about a murder committed in the house you just left?" I finally asked her.

"The husband killed his wife and baby, and then himself," she replied, *"with an ax, up in one of the rooms."*

Exactly what Sybil had said in trance!

There was one more witness I wanted to question: Mrs. Campano's married daughter, Marsha Parmesano, who used to sleep in the haunted room upstairs.

"When I was asleep," she said, "I used to feel someone breathing over me, but when I turned around there was nobody there. At the edge of my bed I felt someone sitting there, like gettin' up and sittin' down, but there was no one there. That was the room to the right, upstairs. I felt it a couple of times."

After all, she was occupying Linda Mathews' bed—and adding discomfort to the ghost's unhappy state.

We left the Somerville ghost house with the conviction that the next tenant would have nothing to worry about. No more footsteps, no more crying. That is, unless there is something—or somebody—buried in the cellar that needs to be discovered.

But I doubt it even then. Sybil Leek managed to lead the murdered woman out of her self-imposed prison to join her child. Unless the allegedly guilt-laden husband is still outside the walls of the old house, unable to leave the place of his crimes, everything should be peaceful on Washington Avenue.

The Strange Case of Mrs. C.'s Late but Lively Husband

D eath is not the end, no, definitely not. At least not for Mr. C. who lived the good life in a fair sized-city in Rhode Island. But then he died, or so it would appear on the record. But Mrs. C. came to consult me about the very unusual complaint of her late husband's continuing attentions.

When someone dies unexpectedly, or in the prime of his physical life, and finds that he can no longer express his sexual appetite physically in the world into which he has been suddenly catapulted, he may indeed look around for someone through whom he can express this appetite on the earth plane. It is then merely a matter of searching out opportunities, regardless of personalities involved. It is quite conceivable that a large percentage of the unexplained or inexplicable sexual attacks by otherwise meek, timid, sexually defensive individuals upon members of the opposite sex—or even the same sex—may be due to sudden possession by an entity of this kind. This is even harder to prove objectively than are some of the murder cases involving individuals who do not recall what they have done and are for all practical purposes normal human beings before and after the crime. But I am convinced that the influence of discarnates can indeed be exercised upon susceptible individuals—that is to say, appropriately mediumistic individuals. It also appears from my studies that the most likely recipients of this doubtful honor are those who are sexually weak or inactive. Evidently the unused sexual energies are particularly useful to the discarnate entities for their own gains. There really doesn't seem to be any way in which one can foretell such attacks or prevent them, except, perhaps, by leading a sexually healthy and balanced life. *Those who are fulfilled in their natural drives on the earth plane are least likely to suffer from such invasions.*

On the other hand, there exist cases of sexual possession involving two partners who knew each other before on the earth plane. One partner was cut short by death, either violently or prematurely, and would now seek to continue a pleasurable relationship of the flesh from the new dimension. Deprived of a physical body to express such desires, however, the deceased partner would then find it rather difficult to express the physical desires to the partner remaining on the earth plane. With sex it certainly takes two, and if the remaining partner is not willing, then difficulties will have to be reckoned with. An interesting case came to my attention a few months ago. Mrs. Anna C. lives with her several children in a comparatively new house in the northeastern United States. She bought the house eighteen months after her husband had passed away. Thus there was no connection between the late husband and the new house. Nevertheless, her husband's passing was by no means the end of their relationship.

"My husband died five years ago this past September. Ever since then he has not let me have a peaceful day," she explained in desperation, seeking my help.

Two months after her husband had died, she saw him coming to her in a dream complaining that she had buried him alive. He explained that he wasn't really dead, and that it was all her fault and her family's fault that he died in the first place.

Mr. C. had lived a rather controversial life, drinking regularly and frequently staying away from home. Thus the relationship between himself and his wife was far from ideal. Nevertheless, there was a strong bond between them.

"In other dreams he would tell me that *he was going to have sex relations with me whether I wanted him to or not.* He would try to grab me and I would run all through the house with him chasing after me. I never let him get hold of me. He was like that when he was alive, too. The most important thing in life to him was sex, and he didn't care how or where he got it. Nothing else mattered to him," she complained, describing vividly how the supposedly dead husband had apparently still a great deal of life in him.

"He then started climbing on the bed and walking up and down on it and scaring me half to death. I didn't know what it was or what to do about it," she said, shaking like a leaf.

When Mr. C. could not get his wife to cooperate willingly, he apparently got mad. To express his displeasure, he caused all sorts of havoc around the household. He would tear a pair of stockings every day for a week, knock things over, and even go to the place where his mother-in-law worked as a cook, causing seemingly inexplicable phenomena to occur there as well. He appeared to an aunt in Indiana and told her to mind her own business and stay out of his personal relationship with Mrs. C. (It was the aunt who tried to get rid of him and his influences by performing a spiritualist ritual at the house.) Meanwhile, Mr. C. amused himself by setting alarm clocks to go off at the wrong times or stopping them altogether, moving objects from their accustomed places or making them disappear altogether, only to return them several days later to everyone's surprise. In general, he behaved like a good *poltergeist* should. But it didn't endear him any more to his erstwhile wife.

When Mrs. C. rejected his attentions, he started to try to possess his ten-year-old daughter. He came to her in dreams and told her that her mother wasn't really knowledgeable about anything. He tried everything in his power to drive a wedge between the little girl and her mother. As a result of this, the little girl turned more and more away from her mother, and no matter how Mrs. C. tried to explain things to her, she found the little girl's mind made up under the influence of her late father.

In a fit of destructiveness, the late Mr. C. then started to work on the other children, creating such a state of havoc in the household that Mrs. C. did not know where to turn any longer. Then the psychic aunt from Indiana came to New England to try to help matters. Sure enough, Mr. C. appeared to her and the two had a cozy talk. He explained that he was very unhappy where he was and was having trouble getting along with the people over there. To this, the aunt replied she would be very happy to help him get to a higher plane if that was what he wanted. But that wasn't it, he replied. He just wanted to stay where he was. The aunt left for home. Now the children, one by one, became unmanageable, and Mrs. C. assumed that her late husband was interfering with their proper education and discipline. "I am fighting an unseen force and cannot get through to the children," she explained.

Her late husband did everything to embarrass her. She was working as a clerk at St. Francis' rectory in her town, doing some typing. It happened to be December 24, 1971, Christmas Eve. All of a sudden she heard a thud in her immediate vicinity and looked down to the floor. A heavy dictionary was lying at her feet. The book had been on the shelf only a fraction of a second before. A co-worker wondered what was up. She was hard pressed to explain the presence of the dictionary on the floor since it had been on the shelf in back of them only a moment before. But she knew very well how the dictionary came to land at her feet.

Mr. C. prepared special Christmas surprises for his wife. She went to her parents' house to spend the holiday. During that time her nephew George was late for work since his alarm had not worked properly. On inspection it turned out that someone had stuck a pencil right through the clock. As soon as the pencil was removed, the clock started to work again. On investigation it turned out that no one had been near the clock, and when the family tried to place the pencil into the clock, as they had found it, no one could do it. The excitement made Mrs. C. so ill she went to bed. That was no way to escape Mr. C.'s attentions, however. The day before New Year's Eve, her late husband got to her, walking up and down on the bed itself. Finally she told him to leave her and the children alone, to go where he belonged. She didn't get an answer. But phenomena continued in the house, so she asked her aunt to come back once again. This time the aunt from Indiana brought oil with her and put it on each of the children and Mrs. C. herself. Apparently it worked, or so it seemed to Mrs. C. But her late husband was merely changing his tactics. A few days later she was sure that he was trying to get into one of the children to express himself further since he could no longer get at her. She felt she would be close to a nervous breakdown if someone would not help her get rid of the phenomenon and, above all, break her husband's hold on her. "I am anxious to have him sent on up where he can't bother anyone any more," she explained.

Since I could not go immediately, and the voice on the telephone sounded as if its owner could not hold out a single day more, I asked Ethel Johnson Meyers, my mediumistic friend, to go out and see what she could do. Mrs. C. had to go to Mrs. Meyers' house for a personal sitting first. A week later Ethel came down to Mrs. C.'s house to continue her work. What Mrs. Meyers discovered was somewhat of a surprise to Mrs. C. and to myself. It was Ethel's contention that the late husband, while still in the flesh, had himself been the victim of possession and had done the many unpleasant things (of which he was justly accused) during his lifetime, not of his own volition but under the direction of another entity. That the possessor was himself possessed seemed like a novel idea to me, one neither Mrs. Meyers nor I could prove. Far more important was the fact that Mrs. Meyers' prayers and commands to the unseen entity seemed to have worked, for he walks up and down Mrs. C.'s bed no more, and all is quiet. I believe the hold Mr. C. had upon his wife after his death was so strong because of an unconscious desire on her part to continue their relationship. Even though she abhorred him—and the idea of being sexually possessed by a man who had lost his physical body in the usual way—something within her, perhaps deeply buried within her, may have wanted the continuous sexual attention he had bestowed upon her while still in the body.

The Terror on the Farm

North Woodstock, Connecticut, is New England at its best and quietest: rolling farmland seldom interrupted by the incursions of factories and modern city life.

The village itself seems to have weathered the passage of time rather well and with a minimum of change. Except for the inevitable store signs and other expressions of contemporary American bad taste, the village is as quiet today as it must have been, say, two hundred years ago, when America was young.

On Brickyard Road, going toward the outer edges of the village and standing somewhat apart from the inhabited areas, is an old farmhouse. At the time this incident takes place, it had obviously seen better days; it was totally dilapidated and practically beyond repair. Still, it was a house of some size and quite obviously different from the ordinary small farmhouses of the surrounding countryside.

For the past fifty years, the sixteen-room house, had been the property of the Duprey family. The house itself was built in pre-revolutionary times by the Lyons family, who used it as a tavern. The place was a busy spot on the Boston-Hartford road, and a tavern here did well indeed in the days when railroads had not yet come into existence.

After the Lyons Tavern changed hands, it belonged successfully to the Potters, Redheads, Ides, and then the Dupreys. But it finally became a private dwelling, the center of the surrounding farm, and no longer a public house.

Very little is known about its early history beyond what I've told here; at least that is what Mrs. Florence Viner discovered when she considered buying the house. She did learn, however, that Mrs. Emery Duprey, a previous owner, had suffered great tragedy in the house. One morning she had taken a group of neighbor children to school. The school was in a one-room house, less than a mile distant. Her fourteen-year-old daughter Laura was left behind at the house because she had not been feeling well that day. When Mrs. Duprey returned home a short time later, she found the girl gone. Despite every effort made, the girl was never seen again nor was any trace found of her disappearance.

Mr. and Mrs. Charles Viner decided to buy the house in 1951 despite its deplorable condition. They wanted a large country house and did not mind putting it in good condition; in fact, they rather looked forward to the challenging task.

It was on Good Friday of that year that they moved in. Although they started the restoration immediately, they stayed at the house and made do, like the pioneers they felt they had now become.

The farm itself was still a working farm, and they retained a number of farm workers from the surrounding area to work it for them. The only people staying at the house at all times were the Viners, their daughter Sandra, and the help.

Two months after their arrival, one evening Mrs. Viner and her daughter, then eleven years old, were alone in the house, sitting in the kitchen downstairs, reading.

"Who is upstairs?" the girl suddenly inquired.

Mrs. Viner had heard furtive footsteps also, but had decided to ignore them. Surely, the old house was settling or the weather was causing all sorts of strange noises.

But the footsteps became clearer. This was no house settling. This was someone walking around upstairs. For several minutes, they sat in the kitchen, listening as the steps walked all over the upper floor. Then Mrs. Viner rose resolutely, went to her bedroom on the same floor and returned with a .22 revolver she had in the drawer of her night table just in case prowlers showed up. The moment she re-entered the kitchen, she clearly heard two heavy thumps upstairs. It sounded as if a couple of heavy objects had fallen suddenly and hit the floor. Abruptly, the walking ceased as if the thumps were the end of a scene being re-enacted upstairs.

Too frightened to go up and look into what she *knew* to be an empty room, Mrs. Viner went to bed. When her husband returned a little later, however, they investigated upstairs together. There was nothing out of place nor indeed any sign that anyone had been up there.

But a few days later, the same phenomenon recurred. First, there were the footsteps of someone walking up and down upstairs, as if in great agitation. Then two heavy thumps and the sound of a falling object and abrupt silence. The whole thing was so exactly the same each time it almost became part of the house routine, and the Viners heard it so many times they no longer became panicky because of it.

When the house regained its former splendor, they began to have overnight guests. But whenever anyone stayed at the house, inevitably, the next morning they would complain about the constant walking about in the corridor upstairs. Mrs. Ida Benoit, Mrs. Viner's mother, came downstairs the morning after her first night in the house and assured her daughter, "I'll never sleep in *this* house again. Why, it's haunted. Someone kept walking through my bedroom."

Her daughter could only shrug and smile wanly. She knew very well what her mother meant. Naturally, the number of unhappy guests grew, but she never discussed the phenomena with anyone beforehand. After all, it was just possible that *nothing* would happen. But in ten years of occupancy, there wasn't a single instance where a person using a bedroom upstairs was not disturbed.

A year after they had moved in, Mrs. Viner decided to begin to renovate a large upstairs bedroom. It was one of those often used as a guest room. This was on a very warm day in September, and despite the great heat, Mrs. Viner liked her work and felt in good spirits. She was painting the window sash and singing to herself with nothing particular on her mind. She was quite alone upstairs at the time and for the moment the ghostly phenomena of the past were far from her thoughts.

Suddenly, she felt the room grow ice cold. The chill became so intense she began to shudder and pulled her arms around herself as if she were in mid-winter on an icy road. She stopped singing abruptly and at the same time she felt the strong presence of another person in the room with her.

"Someone's resenting very much what I'm doing," she heard herself think.

Such a strong wave of hatred came over her she could not continue. Terrified, she nevertheless knew she had to turn around and see who was in the room with her. It seemed to take her an eternity to muster sufficient strength to move a single muscle.

Suddenly, she felt a cold hand at her shoulder. Someone was standing behind her and evidently trying to get her attention. She literally froze with fear. When she finally moved to see who it was the hand just melted away.

With a final effort, she jerked herself around and stared back into the room. There was no one there. She ran to the door, screaming, "I don't know who you are or what you are, but you won't drive me out of this house."

Still screaming, she ran down the stairs and onto the porch. There she caught her breath and quieted down. When her daughter came home from school, she felt relieved. The evil in that room had been overpowering, and she avoided going up there as much as possible after that experience.

"I'll never forget that hand, as long as I live," she explained to her husband.

In the years that followed, they came to terms with the unseen forces in the house. Perhaps her determined effort not to be driven out of her home had somehow gotten through to the specter. At any rate, the Viners were staying and making the house as livable as they could. Mrs. Viner gave birth to two more children, both sons, and as Sandra grew up, the phenomena seemed to subside. In 1958, a second daughter was born, and Sandra left for college. But three weeks later the trouble started anew.

One night in September, she was sitting in the downstairs living room watching television with James Latham, their farm worker. The two boys and the baby had been in bed for hours. Suddenly, there was a terrific explosion in the general direction of the baby's room. She ran into the room and found it ice cold—cold as an icebox. From the baby's room another door leads out into the hall, which was usually closed for obvious reasons. But now it stood wide open, evidently thrust open with considerable force. The lock was badly bent from the impact and the radiator, which the door had hit in opening, was still reverberating from it. The baby was not harmed in any way, but Mrs. Viner wondered if perhaps the oil burner had blown up.

She went down into the basement to check but found everything normal. As she returned to the baby's room she suddenly had the distinct impression that the phenomenon was somehow connected with the presence of a *young girl.*

She tried to reason this away since no young girl was present in the household, nor was there any indication that this tied in in any way with the tragic disappearance of Mrs. Duprey's girl, of which she, of course, knew about. Try as she might, she could not shake this feeling that a young girl was the focal point of the disturbances at the house.

One night her sister had joined her in the living room downstairs. Suddenly there was a loud crash overhead in what they knew was an empty bedroom. Mrs. Viner left her worried sister downstairs and went up alone. A table in the bedroom had been knocked over. No natural force short of a heavy earthquake could have caused this. The windows were closed, and there was no other way in which the table could topple over by itself. She was so sure that this could not have been caused by anything but human intruders, she called the state police.

The police came and searched the house from top to bottom but found no trace of any intruder.

Mrs. Viner then began to wonder about the goings-on. If these unseen forces had the power to overturn heavy tables, surely they might also harm people. The thought frightened her. She had until then considered living with a ghost or ghosts rather on the chic side; now it took on distinctly threatening overtones. She discussed it with her husband but they had put so much work and money into the house that the thought of leaving again just did not appeal to them.

It was inevitable that she should be alone in the house, except for the children, at various times. Her husband was away on business, and the farm help were out where they belonged. Often Mrs. Viner found herself walking through the rooms hoping against rational reasoning that she would come face to face with the intruder. Then she could address her or him—she was not sure how many there were—and say, "Look, this is my house now, we've bought it and rebuilt it, and we don't intend to leave it. Go away and don't hang around; it's no use." She often rehearsed her little speech for just such a confrontation. But the ghost never appeared when she was ready.

Meanwhile the footsteps followed by the heavy thumps kept recurring regularly, often as many as four times in a single week. It was usually around the same time of the evening, which led her to believe that it represented some sort of tragedy that was being re-enacted upstairs by the ghostly visitors. Or was she merely tuning in on a past tragedy and what she and the others were hearing was in fact only an echo of the distant past? She could not believe this, especially as she still remembered vividly the ice cold hand that grabbed her shoulder in the bedroom upstairs on that hot September day. And a memory would not cause a heavy door to swing open by itself with such violence that it burst the lock.

No, these were not memory impressions they were hearing. These were actual entities with minds of their own, somehow trapped between two states of being and condemned by their own violence to live forever in the place where their tragedy had first occurred. What a horrible fate, Mrs. Viner thought, and for a moment she felt great compassion for the unfortunate ones.

But then her own involvement reminded her that it was, after all, her house and her life that was being disrupted. She had a better right to be here than they had, even if they had been here before.

Defiantly, she continued to polish and refine the appointments in the house until it looked almost as if it had never been a dilapidated, almost hopelessly derelict, house. She decided to repaper one of the bedrooms upstairs, so that her guests would sleep in somewhat more cheerful surroundings. The paper in this particular room was faded and very old and deserved to be replaced. As she removed the dirty wallpaper, the boards underneath became visible again. They were wide and smooth and obviously part of the original boards of the house.

After she had pulled down all the paper from the wall facing away from the window, she glanced up at it. The wall, exposed to light after goodness knows how many years, was spattered with some sort of paint.

"This won't do at all," she decided, and went downstairs to fetch some rags and water. Returning to the room, she started to remove what she took for some very old paint. When she put water on the stains, the spots turned a bright red!

Try as she might, she could not remove the red stains. Finally she applied some bleach, but it only turned the spots a dark brown. It finally dawned on her that this wasn't paint but blood. On closer investigation, her suspicion was confirmed. She had stumbled upon a blood-spattered wall—but what had taken place up here that had caused this horrible reminder?

Somehow she felt that she had gotten a lead in her quest for the solution to the phenomena plaguing the house. Surely, someone had been killed up there, but who and why?

She went into the village and started to talk to the local people. At first, she did not get much help. New Englanders are notoriously shy about family matters. But eventually Mrs. Viner managed to get some information from some of the older, local people who had known about the house on Brickyard Road for a long time.

When the house was still a public tavern, that is somewhere around the turn of the nineteenth century or the very end of the eighteenth, there had been two men at the tavern who stayed overnight as guests. Their names are shrouded in mystery, and perhaps they were very unimportant as history goes.

But there was also a young girl at the tavern, the kind innkeepers used to hire as servant girls in those days. If the girl wanted to be just that, well and good; if she wanted to get involved with some of the men that passed through on their way to the cities, that was her own business. Tavern keepers in those days were not moral keepers and the hotel detective had not yet been conceived by a Puritan age. So the servant girls often went in and out of the guests' rooms, and nobody cared much.

It appears that one such young girl was particularly attractive to two men at the same time. There were arguments and jealousy. Finally the two men retired to a room upstairs and a fight to the finish followed. As it was upstairs, most likely it was in the girl's own room, with one suitor discovering the other obtaining favors he had sought in vain, perhaps. At any rate, as the horrified girl looked on, the two men killed each other with their rapiers, and their blood, intermingled in death, spattered upon the wall of the room.

As she walked back from the village with this newly gained knowledge, Mrs. Viner understood clearly for the first time, why her house was indeed haunted. The restless footsteps in the room upstairs were the hurried steps of the unhappy suitor. The scuffling noises that followed and the sudden heavy thumps would be the fight and the two falling bodies—perhaps locked in death. The total silence that always ensued after the two heavy falls clearly indicated to her that the stillness of death following the struggle was being re-enacted along with the tragedy itself.

And how right she had been about a girl being the central force in all this!

But why the hostility towards her? Why the icy hand on the shoulder? Did the girl resent her, another woman, in this house? Was she still hoping her suitor would come for her, and did she perhaps take Mrs. Viner for competition? A demented mind, especially when it has been out of the body for a hundred and fifty years, can conjure up some strange ideas.

But her fighting energies were somehow spent, and when an opportunity arose to sell the house, Mrs. Viner agreed readily to do so. The house then passed into the hands of Samuel Beno after the Viners had lived in it from 1951 to 1961. For five years, Mr. Beno owned the house but never lived in it. It remained unoccupied, standing quietly on the road.

Only once was there a flurry of excitement about it in recent years. In 1966 someone made off with $5,000 worth of plumbing and copper piping. The owner naturally entrusted the matter to the state police, hoping the thieves would eventually return for more. The authorities even placed tape recorders in the house in case the thieves did return.

Since then not much has been heard about the house and one can only presume that the tragic story of the servant girl and her two suitors has had its final run. But one can't be entirely sure until the next tenant moves into the old Lyons Tavern. After all, blood does not come off easily, either from walls or from men's memories.

New York

A Revolutionary Corollary:
Patrick Henry, Nathan Hale, et al.

Nathan Hale, as every schoolboy knows, was the American spy hanged by the British. He was captured at Huntington Beach and taken to Brooklyn for trial. How he was captured is a matter of some concern to the people of Huntington, Long Island. The town was originally settled by colonists from Connecticut who were unhappy with the situation in that colony. There were five principal families who accounted for the early settlement of Huntington, and to this day their descendants are the most prominent families in the area. They were the Sammes, the Downings, the Busches, the Pauldings, and the Cooks. During the Revolutionary War, feelings were about equally divided among the town people: some were Revolutionaries and some remained Tories. The consensus of historians is that members of these five prominent families, all of whom were Tories, were responsible for the betrayal of Nathan Hale to the British.

All this was brought to my attention by Mrs. Geraldine P. of Huntington. Mrs. P. grew up in what she considers the oldest house in Huntington, although the Huntington Historical Society claims that theirs is even older. Be that as it may, it was there when the Revolutionary War started. Local legend has it that an act of violence took place on the corner of the street, which was then a crossroads in the middle of a rural area. The house in which Mrs. P. grew up, stands on that street. Mrs. P. suspects that the capture—or, at any rate, the betrayal—of the Revolutionary agent took place on that crossroads. When she tried to investigate the history of her house, she found little cooperation on the part of the local historical society. It was a conspiracy of silence, according to her, as if some people wanted to cover up a certain situation from the past.

The house had had a "strange depressing effect on all its past residents," according to Mrs. P. Her own father, who studied astrology and white magic for many years, has related an incident that occurred several years ago in the house. He awoke in the middle of the night in the master bedroom because he felt unusually cold. He became aware of "something" rushing about the room in wild, frantic circles. Because of his outlook and training, he spoke up, saying, "Can I help you?" But the rushing about became even more frantic. He then asked what was wrong and what could be done. But no communication was possible. When he saw that he could not communicate with the entity, Mrs. P.'s father finally said, "If I can't help you, then go away." There was a snapping sound, and the room suddenly became quiet and warm again, and he went back to sleep. There have been no other recorded incidents at the house in question. But Mrs. P. wonders if some guilty entity wants to manifest, not necessarily Nathan Hale, but perhaps someone connected with his betrayal.

At the corner of 43rd Street and Vanderbilt Avenue, Manhattan, one of the busiest and noisiest spots in all of New York City, there is a small commemorative plaque explaining that Nathan Hale, the Revolutionary spy, was executed on that spot by the British. I doubt that too many New Yorkers are aware of this, or can accurately pinpoint the location of the tragedy. It is even less likely that a foreigner would know about it. When I suggested to my good friend Sybil Leek that she accompany me to a psychically important spot for an experiment, she readily agreed. Despite the noises and the heavy traffic, the spot being across from Grand Central Station, Sybil bravely stood with me on the street corner and tried to get some sort of psychic impression.

"I get the impression of food and drink," Sybil said. I pointed out that there were restaurants all over the area, but Sybil shook her head. "No, I was thinking more of a place for food and drink, and I don't mean in the present. It is more like an inn, a transit place, and it has some connection with the river. A meeting place, perhaps, some sort of inn. Of course, it is very difficult in this noise and with all these new buildings here."

"If we took down these buildings, what would we see?"

"I think we would see a field and water. I have a strong feeling that there is a connection with water and with the inn. There are people coming and going—I sense a woman, but I don't think she's important. I am not sure . . . unless it would mean foreign. I hear a foreign language. Something like *Verchenen.** I can't quite get it. It is not German."

"Is there anything you feel about this spot?"

"This spot, yes. I think I want to go back two hundred years at least, it is not very clear, 1769 or 1796. That is the period. The connection with the water puzzles me."

"Do you feel an event of significance here at any time?"

"Yes. It is not strong enough to come through to me completely, but sufficiently *drastic* to make me feel a little nervous."

"In what way is it drastic?"

"Hurtful, violent. There are several people involved in this violence. Something connected with water, papers connected with water, that is part of the trouble."

Sybil then suggested that we go to the right to see if the impressions might be stronger at some distance. We went around the corner and I stopped. Was the impression any stronger?

"No, the impression is the same. Papers, violence. For a name, I have the impression of the letters P.T. Peter. It would be helpful to come here in the middle of the night, I think. I wish I could understand the connection with water, here in the middle of the city."

"Did someone die here?"

Sybil closed her eyes and thought it over for a moment. "Yes, but the death of this person was important at that time and indeed necessary. But there is more to it than just the death of the person. The disturbance involves lots of other things, lots of other people. In fact, two distinct races were involved, because I sense a lack of understanding. I think that this was a political thing, and the papers were important."

"Can you get anything further on the nature of this violence you feel here?"

"Just a disturbed feeling, an upheaval, a general disturbance. I am sorry I can't get much else. Perhaps if we came here at night, when things are quieter."

I suggested we get some tea in one of the nearby restaurants. Over tea, we discussed our little experiment and Sybil suddenly remembered an experience she had had when visiting the Hotel Biltmore before. (The plaque in question is mounted on the wall of the hotel.) "I receive many invitations to go to this particular area of New York," Sybil explained, "and when I go I always get the feeling of repulsion to the extent where I may be on my way down and get into a telephone booth and call the people involved and say, 'No, I'll meet you somewhere else.' I don't like this particular area we just left; I find it very depressing. *I feel trapped.*"

I am indebted to R. M. Sandwich of Richmond, Virginia, for an intriguing account of an ESP experience he has connected to Patrick Henry. Mr. Sandwich stated that he has had only one ESP experience and that it took place in one of the early estate-homes of Patrick Henry. He admitted that the experience altered his previously dim view of ESP. The present owner of the estate has said that Mr. Sandwich has not been the only one to experience strange things in that house.

The estate-home where the incident took place is called Pine Flash and is presently owned by E. E. Verdon, a personal friend of Mr. Sandwich. It is located in Hanover County, about fifteen miles outside of Richmond. The house was given to Patrick Henry by his father-in-law. After Henry had lived in it for a number of years, it burned to the ground and was not rebuilt until fifteen years later. During that time Henry resided in the old cottage, which is directly behind the house, and stayed there until the main house had been rebuilt. This cottage is frequently referred to in the area as the honeymoon cottage of young Patrick Henry. The new house was rebuilt exactly as it had been before the fire. As for the cottage, which is still in excellent condition, it is thought to be the oldest wood frame dwelling in Virginia. It may have been there even before Patrick Henry lived in it.

On the Fourth of July, 1968, the Sandwiches had been invited to try their luck at fishing in a pond on Mr. Verdon's land. Since they would be arriving quite early in the morning, they were told that the oars to the rowboat, which they were to use at the pond, would be found inside the old cottage. They arrived at Pine Flash sometime around 6 A.M. Mrs. Sandwich started unpacking their fishing gear and food supplies, while Mr. Sandwich decided to inspect the cottage. Although he had been to the place several times before, he had never actually been inside the cottage itself.

Here then is Mr. Sandwich's report.

"I opened the door, walked in, and shut the door tight behind me. Barely a second had passed after I shut the door when a strange feeling sprang over me. It was the kind of feeling you would experience if you were to walk into an extremely cold, damp room. I remember how still everything was, and then I distinctly heard footsteps overhead in the attic. I called out, thinking perhaps there was someone upstairs. No one answered, nothing. At that time I was standing directly in front of an old fireplace.

I admit I was scared half to death. The footsteps were louder now and seemed to be coming down the thin staircase toward me. As they passed me, I felt a cold, crisp, odd feeling. I started looking around for something, anything that could have caused all this. It was during this time that I noticed the closed door open very, very slowly. The door stopped when it was half opened, almost beckoning me to take my leave, which I did at great speed! As went through that open door, I felt the same cold mass of air I had experienced before. Standing outside, I watched the door slam itself, almost in my face! My wife was still unpacking the car and claims she neither saw nor heard anything."

Revolutionary figures have a way of hanging on to places they like in life. Candy Bosselmann of Indiana has had a long history of psychic experiences. She is a budding trance medium and not at all ashamed of her talents. In 1964 she happened to be visiting Ashland, the home of Henry Clay, in Lexington, Kentucky. She had never been to Ashland, so she decided to take a look at it. She and other visitors were shown through the house by an older man, a professional guide, and Candy became somewhat restless listening to his historical ramblings. As the group entered the library and the guide explained the beautiful ash paneling taken from surrounding trees (for which the home is named), she became even more restless. She knew very well that it was the kind of feeling that forewarned her of some sort of psychic event. As she was looking over toward a fireplace, framed by two candelabra, she suddenly saw a very tall, white-haired man in a long black frock coat standing next to it. One elbow rested on the mantel, and his head was in his hand, as if he were pondering something very important.

Miss Bosselmann was not at all emotionally involved with the house. In fact, the guided tour bored her, and she would have preferred to be outside in the stables, since she has a great interest in horses. Her imagination did not conjure up what she saw: she knew in an instant that she was looking at the spirit imprint of Henry Clay.

In 1969 she visited Ashland again, and this time she went into the library deliberately. With her was a friend who wasn't at all psychic. Again, the same restless feeling came over her. But when she was about to go into trance, she decided to get out of the room in a hurry.

Rock Ford, the home of General Edward Hand, is located four miles south of Lancaster, Pennsylvania, and commands a fine view of the Conestoga River. The house is not a restoration but a well-preserved eighteenth-century mansion, with its original floors, railings, shutters, doors, cupboards, panelings, and window glass. Even the original wall painting can be seen. It is a four story brick mansion in the Georgian style, with the rooms grouped around a center hall in the design popular during the latter part of the eighteenth century. The rooms are furnished with antiquities of the period, thanks to the discovery of an inventory of General Hand's estate which permitted the local historical society to supply authentic articles of daily usage wherever the originals had disappeared from the house.

Perhaps General Edward Hand is not as well known as a hero of the American Revolution as others are, but to the people of the Pennsylvania Dutch country he is an important figure, even though he was of Irish origin rather than German. Trained as a medical doctor at Trinity College, Dublin, he came to America in 1767 with the Eighteenth Royal Irish Regiment of Foote. However, he resigned British service in 1774 and came to Lancaster to practice medicine and surgery. With the fierce love of liberty so many of the Irish possess, Dr. Hand joined the Revolutionaries in July of 1775, becoming a lieutenant colonel in the Pennsylvania Rifle Battalion. He served in the army until 1800, when he was discharged as a major general. Dr. Hand was present at the Battle of Trenton, the Battle of Long Island, the Battle of White Plains, the Battle of Princeton, the campaign against the Iroquois, and the surrender of Cornwallis at Yorktown. He also served on the tribunal which convicted Major John André, the British spy, and later became the army's adjutant general. He was highly regarded by George Washington, who visited him in his home toward the end of the war. When peace came, Hand became a member of the Continental Congress and served in the Assembly of Pennsylvania as representative of his area. He moved into Rock Ford when it was completed in 1793 and died there in September 1802.

Today, hostesses from a local historical society serve as guides for the tourists who come to Rock Ford in increasing numbers. Visitors are taken about the lower floor and basement and are told of General Hand's agricultural experiments, his medical studies, and his association with George Washington. But unless you ask specifically, you are not likely to hear about what happened to the house after General Hand died. To begin with, the General's son committed suicide in the house. Before long the family died out, and eventually the house became a museum since no one wanted to live in it for very long. At one time, immigrants were contacted at the docks and offered free housing if they would live in the mansion. None stayed. There was something about the house that was not as it should be, something that made people fear it and leave it just as quickly as they could.

Mrs. Ruth S. lives in upstate New York. In 1967 a friend showed her a brochure concerning Rock Ford, and the house intrigued her. Since she was traveling in that direction, she decided to pay Rock Ford a visit. With her family, she drove up to the house and parked her car in the rear. At that moment she had an eerie feeling that something wasn't right. Mind you, Mrs. S. had not been to the house before, had no knowledge about it nor any indication that anything unusual had occurred in it. The group of visitors was quite small. In addition to herself and her family, there were two young college boys and one other couple. Even though it was a sunny day, Mrs. S. felt icy cold.

"I felt a presence before we entered the house and before we heard the story from the guide," she explained. "If I were a hostess there, I wouldn't stay there alone for two consecutive minutes." Mrs. S. had been to many old houses and restorations before but had never felt as she did at Rock Ford.

It is not surprising that George Washington should be the subject of a number of psychic accounts. Probably the best known (and most frequently misinterpreted) story concerns General Washington's vision which came to him during the encampment at Valley Forge, when the fortunes of war had gone heavily in favor of the British, and the American army, tattered and badly fed, was just about falling to pieces. If there ever was a need for divine guidance, it was at Valley Forge. Washington was in the habit of meditating in the woods at times and saying his prayers when he was quite alone. On one of those occasions he returned to his quarters more worried than usual. As he busied himself with his papers, he had the feeling of a presence in the room. Looking up, he saw opposite him a singularly beautiful woman. Since he had given orders not to be disturbed, he couldn't understand how she had gotten into the room. Although he questioned her several times, the visitor would not reply. As he looked at the apparition, for that is what it was, the General became more and more entranced with her, unable to make any move. For a while he thought he was dying, for he imagined that the apparition of such unworldly creatures as he was seeing at that moment must accompany the moment of transition.

Finally, he heard a voice, saying, "Son of the Republic, look and learn." At the same time, the visitor extended her arm toward the east, and Washington saw what to him appeared like white vapor at some distance. As the vapor dissipated, he saw the various countries of the world and the oceans that separated them. He then noticed a dark, shadowy angel standing between Europe and America, taking water out of the ocean and sprinkling it over America with one hand and over

Europe with the other. When he did this, a cloud rose from the countries thus sprinkled, and the cloud then moved westward until it enveloped America. Sharp flashes of lightning became visible at intervals in the cloud. At the same time, Washington thought he heard the anguished cries of the American people underneath the cloud. Next, the strange visitor showed him a vision of what America would look like in the future, and he saw villages and towns springing up from one coast to the other until the entire land was covered by them.

"Son of the Republic, the end of the century cometh, look and learn," the visitor said. Again Washington was shown a dark cloud approaching America, and he saw the American people fighting one another. A bright angel then appeared wearing a crown on which was written the word Union. This angel bore the American Flag, which he placed between the divided nation, saying, "Remember, you are brethren." At that instant, the inhabitants threw away their weapons and became friends again.

Once more the mysterious voice spoke. "Son of the Republic, look and learn." Now the dark angel put a trumpet to his mouth and sounded three distinct blasts. Then he took water from the ocean and sprinkled it on Europe, Asia, and Africa. As he did so, Washington saw black clouds rise from the countries he had sprinkled. Through the black clouds, Washington could see red light and hordes of armed men, marching by land and sailing by sea to America, and he saw these armies devastate the entire country, burn the villages, towns, and cities, and as he listened to the thundering of the cannon, Washington heard the mysterious voice saying again, "Son of the Republic, look and learn."

Once more the dark angel put the trumpet to his mouth and sounded a long and fearful blast. As he did so, a light as of a thousand suns shone down from above him and pierced the dark cloud which had enveloped America. At the same time the angel wearing the word

Union on his head descended from the heavens, followed by legions of white spirits. Together with the inhabitants of America, Washington saw them renew the battle and heard the mysterious voice telling him, once again, "Son of the Republic, look and learn."

For the last time, the dark angel dipped water from the ocean and sprinkled it on America; the dark cloud rolled back and left the inhabitants of America victorious. But the vision continued. Once again Washington saw villages, towns, and cities spring up, and he heard the bright angel exclaim, "While the stars remain and the heavens send down dew upon the earth, so long shall the Union last." With that, the scene faded, and Washington beheld once again the mysterious visitor before him. As if she had guessed his question, the apparition then said:

"Son of the Republic, what you have seen is thus interpreted: Three great perils will come upon the Republic. The most fearful is the third, during which the whole world united shall not prevail against her. Let every child of the Republic learn to live for his God, his land, and his Union." With that, the vision disappeared, and Washington was left pondering over his experience.

One can interpret this story in many ways, of course. If it really occurred, and there are a number of accounts of it in existence which lead me to believe that there is a basis of fact to this, then we are dealing with a case of prophecy on the part of General Washington. It is a moot question whether the third peril has already come upon us, in the shape of World War II, or whether it is yet to befall us. The light that is stronger than many suns may have ominous meaning in this age of nuclear warfare.

Washington himself is said to have appeared to Senator Calhoun of South Carolina at the beginning of the War between the States. At that time, the question of secession had not been fully decided, and Calhoun, one of the most powerful politicians in the government, was not sure whether he could support the withdrawal of his state from the

Union. The question lay heavily on his mind when he went to bed one hot night in Charleston, South Carolina. During the night, he thought he awoke to see the apparition of General George Washington standing by his bedside. The General wore his presidential attire and seemed surrounded by a bright outline, as if some powerful source of light shone behind him. On the senator's desk lay the declaration of secession, which he had not yet signed. With Calhoun's and South Carolina's support, the Confederacy would be well on its way, having closed ranks. Earnestly, the spirit of George Washington pleaded with Senator Calhoun not to sign the declaration. He warned him against the impending perils coming to America as a divided nation; he asked him to reconsider his decision and to work for the preservation of the Union. But Calhoun insisted that the South had to go its own way. When the spirit of Washington saw that nothing could sway Senator Calhoun, he warned him that the very act of his signature would be a black spot on the Constitution of the United States. With that, the vision is said to have vanished.

One can easily explain the experience as a dream, coming as it did at a time when Senator Calhoun was particularly upset over the implications of his actions. On the other hand, there is this to consider: Shortly after Calhoun had signed the document taking South Carolina into the Confederacy, a dark spot appeared on his hand, a spot that would not vanish and for which medical authorities had no adequate explanation.

Mrs. Margaret Smith of Orlando, Florida, has had a long history of psychic experiences. She has personally seen the ghostly monks of Beaulieu, England; she has seen the actual lantern of Joe Baldwin, the famous headless ghost of Wilmington, North Carolina; and she takes her "supernatural" experiences in her stride the way other people feel about their musical talents or hobbies. When she was only a young girl, her grandmother took her to visit the von Steuben house in Hackensack, New Jersey. (General F. W. A. von Steuben was a German supporter of the American Revolution who aided General Washington with volunteers who had come over from Europe because of repressions, hoping to find greater freedom in the New World.) The house was old and dusty, the floorboards were creaking, and there was an eerie atmosphere about it. The house had been turned into an historical museum, and there were hostesses to take visitors through.

While her grandmother was chatting with the guide downstairs, the young girl walked up the stairs by herself. In one of the upstairs parlors she saw a man sitting in a chair in the corner. She assumed he was another guide. When she turned around to ask him a question about the room, he was gone. Since she hadn't heard him leave, that seemed rather odd to her, especially as the floorboards would creak with every step. But being young she didn't pay too much attention to this peculiarity. A moment later, however, he reappeared. As soon as she saw him, she asked the question she had on her mind. This time he did not disappear but answered her in a slow, painstaking voice that seemed to come from far away. When he had satisfied her curiosity about the room, he asked her some questions about herself, and finally asked the one which stuck in her mind for many years afterward—"What is General Washington doing now about the British?"

Margaret was taken aback at this question. She was young, but she knew very well that Washington had been dead for many years. Tactfully, she told him this and added that Harry Truman was now president and that the year was 1951. At this information, the man looked stunned and sat down again in the chair. As Margaret watched him in fascinated horror, he faded away.

Morgan Hall

Alice is a twenty-two-year-old blond, way above average in looks and intelligence. She lives in Manhattan, has a decent, law-abiding seaman for a father and an Irish heritage going back, way back, but mixed in with some French and various other strains that have blended well in Alice's face, which is one of continual curiosity and alertness. Alice's work is routine, as are most of her friends. She takes this in her stride now, for she has another world waiting for her where nothing is ever ordinary.

When she was born, her parents moved into an old house in Brooklyn that had the reputation of being queer. Alice was only a few months old when they left again, but during those months she would not go into her mother's bedroom without a fierce struggle, without breaking into tears immediately—a behavior so markedly different from her otherwise "good" behavior as a baby that it could not help but be noticed by her parents. While her father had no interest in such matters, her mother soon connected the child's strange behavior with the other strange things in the house: the doors that would open by themselves, the footsteps, the strange drafts, especially in the bedroom little Alice hated so much.

When Alice was about twelve years old, and the family had moved from the old neighborhood into another house, she found herself thinking of her grandmother all of a sudden one day. Her grandparents lived a distance away upstate and there had been no recent contact with them.

"Grandmother is dead," Alice said to her mother, matter-of-factly. Her mother stared at her in disbelief. Hours later the telephone rang. Grandmother, who had been in excellent health, had suddenly passed away.

Her mother gave the girl a queer look but she had known of such gifts and realized her daughter, an only child, was something special. Within six months, the telephone rang twice more. Each time, Alice looked up and said:

"Grandfather's dead."

"Uncle's dead."

And they were.

While her father shook his head over all this "foolishness," her mother did not scoff at her daughter's powers. Especially after Alice had received a dream warning from her dead grandmother, advising her of an impending car accident. She was shown the exact location where it would happen, and told that if her mother were to sit in front, she would be badly hurt but if Alice were to change places with her, Alice would not be as badly hurt.

After the dream, without telling her mother her reasons, she insisted on changing places with her on the trip. Sure enough, the car was hit by another automobile. Had her mother been where Alice sat, she might not have reacted quickly enough and been badly hurt. But Alice was prepared and ducked—and received only a whiplash.

Afterward, she discussed all this with her mother. Her mother did not scoff, but asked her what grandmother, who had given them the warning, had looked like in the vision.

"She had on a house dress and bedroom slippers," Alice replied. Her mother nodded. Although the grandmother had lost both legs due to diabetes, she had been buried with her favorite bedroom slippers in the coffin. Alice had never seen nor known this.

When she was seventeen years of age, Alice had a strong urge to become a nun. She felt the world outside had little to offer her and began to consider entering a convent. Perhaps this inclination was planted in her mind when she was a camp counselor for a Catholic school on Long Island. She liked the serenity of the place and the apparently quiet, contemplative life of the sisters.

On her very first visit to the convent, however, she felt uneasy. Morgan Hall is a magnificently appointed mansion in Glen Cove, Long Island, that had only been converted to religious purposes some years ago. Prior to that it was the Morgan estate with all that the name of that wealthy family implies. Nothing about it was either ugly or frightening in the least, and yet Alice felt immediately terrified when entering its high-ceilinged corridors.

As a prospective postulant, it was necessary for her to visit the place several times prior to being accepted, and on each occasion her uneasiness mounted.

But she ascribed these feelings to her lack of familiarity with the new place. One night, her uncle and grandfather appeared to her in a dream and told her not to worry, that everything would be all right with her. She took this as an encouragement to pursue her religious plans and shortly after formally entered the convent.

She moved in just a few days before her eighteenth birthday, looking forward to a life totally different from that of her friends and schoolmates. The room she was assigned to adjoined one of the cloisters, but at first she was alone in it as her future roommate was to arrive a week late. Thus she spent her very first days at Morgan Hall alone in the room. The very first night, after she had retired, she heard someone walking up and down outside the door. She thought this strange at that hour of the night, knowing full well that convents like their people to retire early. Finally her curiosity overcame her natural shyness of being in a new place, and she peaked out of her door into the corridor. The footsteps were still audible. But there was no one walking about outside.

Quickly, she closed the door and went to bed.

The next morning, she discussed the matter with six other postulants in rooms nearby. They, too, had heard the footsteps that night. In fact, they had heard them on many other nights as well when there was positively no one walking about outside.

As she got used to convent routine, Alice realized how impossible it would be for one of them—or even one of the novices, who had been there a little longer than they— to walk around the place at the hour of the night when she heard the steps. Rigid convent rules included a bell, which rang at 10 P.M. Everybody had to be in their rooms and in bed at that time, except for dire emergencies. One just didn't walk about the corridors at midnight or later for the sheer fun of it at Morgan Hall, if she did not wish to be expelled. All lights go out at ten also and nothing moves.

At first, Alice thought the novices were playing tricks on the new arrivals by walking around downstairs to create the footsteps, perhaps to frighten the postulants in the way college freshmen are often hazed by their elder colleagues. But she soon realized that this was not so, that the novices were no more allowed out after ten than they were.

Her psychic past did not allow Alice to let matters rest there and her curiosity forced her to make further inquiries as best she could under the circumstances. After all, you don't run to the Mother Superior and ask, Who walks the corridors at night, Ma'am?

It was then she learned that the house had been J. P. Morgan's mansion originally and later had been used by the Russian Embassy for their staff people. She recalled the battles the Russians had fought with the Glen Cove township over taxes and how they finally vacated the premises in less than perfect condition. As a sort of anticlimax, the Catholic nuns had moved in and turned the Hall into a convent and school.

A conversation with the convent librarian wasn't particularly fruitful, either. Yes, Mr. Morgan built the house in 1910. No, he didn't die here, he died in Spain. Why did she want to know?

Alice wondered about Mr. Morgan's daughter.

Alice Morgan had lived in this house and died here of typhoid fever in the early years of her life.

But try as she might, she never got the librarian to tell her anything helpful. Naturally, Alice did not wish to bring up the real reason for her curiosity. But it seemed as if the librarian sensed something about it, for she curtly turned her head sideways when speaking of the Morgans as if she did not wish to answer.

Frustrated in her inquiry, Alice left and went back to her chores. One night in October of 1965, Alice was walking in the hall of the postulancy, that part of the building reserved for the new girls who were serving their apprenticeship prior to being admitted to the convent and to taking their final vows.

It was a cool night, and Alice had walked fairly briskly to the extreme end of the hall and then stopped for a moment to rest. As she turned around and faced toward the opposite end of the hall, whence she had just come, she noticed a girl standing there who had not been there before. She wore a long, black dress similar to the dresses the postulants wore and Alice took her to be her girl friend.

She noticed the figure enter the room at the end of the hall. This room was not a bedroom but used by the postulants for study purposes.

"It's Vera," Alice thought, and decided to join her and see what she was up to in that room.

Quickly, she walked towards the room and entered it.

The lights were off and Alice thought this peculiar. Was her friend perhaps playing games with her? The room at this hour was quite dark.

So she turned on the lights, and looked around. There was no one in the room now, and there was no way anyone could have left the room without her noticing it, Alice reasoned. She examined the windows and found them tightly closed. Not that she expected her friend to exit the room by that way, but she wanted to be sure the person—whoever she might have been—could not have left that way. This was on the third floor and anyone trying to leave by the windows would have had to jump, or have a ladder outside.

Suddenly it hit Alice that she had not heard anything at all. All the time she had seen the figure walk into the room, there had been no footsteps, no noise of a door opening, nothing at all. Morgan Hall's doors open with a considerable amount of squeaking and none of that was audible when she had seen the figure before.

Alice quickly left and hurried to her own room to figure this out quietly.

On recollection, she visualized the figure again and it occurred to her at once that there was something very odd about the girl. For one thing, the long gown the postulants wear moves when they walk. But the figure she had seen was stiff and seemed to glide along the floor rather than actually walk on it. The corridor was properly lit and she had seen the figure quite clearly. What she had not seen were her ankles and socks, something she would have observed had it been one of her friends.

Although the door was not closed, the room was actually a corner room that could be entered in only one way, from the front door. Alice was sure she had not seen the figure emerge from it again. There was no place to hide in the room, had this been her girl friend playing a joke on her. Alice had quickly examined the closet, desk, and beds—and no one was hiding anywhere in that room.

Eventually, she gathered up enough courage to seek out her friend Vera and discuss the matter with her. She found that there was a "joke" going around the convent that Alice Morgan's ghost was roaming the corridors, but that the whole matter was to be treated strictly as a gag. Yet she also discovered that there was one part of the Hall that was off limits to anyone *alone*. In what the girls called the catacombs, at ground level, was the laundry room. The third section, way back, was never to be entered by any of them at night, and in the daytime only if in pairs. Yet, the area was well lit. Alice could not get any information for the reasons for this strange and forbidding order. In a convent, speaking to anyone but one's own group is extremely difficult without "proper permission" and this was not a fitting subject to discuss.

The novices, whom she approached next, suddenly became serious and told her to forget it: there were things going on in the building that could not be explained. She was not to pay attention, and pray hard instead.

Alice wondered about this attitude, and perhaps it was then that her first doubts concerning her ecclesiastical future began to enter her mind.

Shortly after, it was still October 1965, she lay awake in bed at night, thinking of her future at the convent. The clock had just chimed eleven and she was still wide awake. Night after night, she had heard the walking in the hall. After weeks of these manifestations, her nerves began to get edgy and she could not sleep as easily as she used to when she still lived in Brooklyn. Sure enough, there they were again, those incessant footsteps. They seemed to her the steps of a medium-heavy person, more like a woman's than a man's, and they seemed to be bent on some definite business, scurrying along the hall as if in a hurry.

Suddenly the night was pierced by a shriek: it seemed directly outside her door, but below. Since she was on the top floor, the person would have to be on the second floor.

There was no mistaking it, this was the outcry of a woman in great pain, in the agony of being hurt by someone!

This time she was almost too scared to look, but she did open the door only to find the corridor abandoned and quiet now.

She ran in to speak to the other postulants, regulations or no regulations. She found them huddled in their beds in abject fear. All eight of them had heard the bloodcurdling scream!

By now Alice was convinced that something strange had taken place here and that a restless personality was stalking the corridors. A short time later, she and Vera were in their room, getting ready to retire.

It was a cold night, but no wind was about. The windows were the French window type that locked with a heavy iron rod from top to bottom. No one could open the window from the outside, the only way it could be opened would be from the inside, by pushing the rod up.

"We don't have to lock the window tonight, do we?" Vera said. "It isn't windy."

But they decided to do it anyway as they did every night. They put their shoes on the window sill, something they were in the habit of doing frequently so that the small draft coming in below the windows would "air them out."

After the window was locked, they retired.

It was well into the night, when the girls awoke to a loud noise. The French window had broken open by itself and the shoes had been tossed inside the room as if by a strong storm!

They checked and found the air outside totally still. Whatever had burst their window open had not been the wind. But what was it?

The room was ice cold now. They shuddered and went back to bed.

There is only a small ledge, for pigeons to sit on outside the window, so no one could have opened the window from that vantage point. One could hardly expect pigeons to burst a window open, either.

The girls then realized that the novices who had been complaining about the windows in their room being constantly open had not been fibbing. Alice and Vera always kept their windows closed, yet some unseen force had apparently opened them from inside on a number of occasions. Now they had seen for themselves how it happened.

Alice realized that the window had been broken open as if by force from *inside,* not outside.

"Someone's trying to get out, not in," she said, and her roommate could only shudder.

There were other peculiar things she soon noticed. Strange cold drafts upstairs and in the attic. Crosses nailed to the wall next to the entrance to the upstairs rooms. Only to those rooms, and to no others, and not inside the rooms, as one might expect in a convent, but just outside as if they had been placed there to keep something, or someone evil out!

In the main dining room, a door, when closed, could not be distinguished from the surrounding wall. A trick window near the head of the table was actually a mirror which allowed the man at the head of the table to see who was coming towards him from all sides.

Banker Morgan lived in considerable fear of his life, whether imagined or real, but certainly the house was built to his specifications. In fact, trick mirrors were so placed in various parts of the main house so that no one could approach from downstairs and surprise anyone upstairs, yet no one could see the one watching through them.

Shortly after Alice had moved into the convent, she began to have strange dreams in which a blond young girl named Alice played a prominent role.

In the dream, the girl's blond hair changed to curls, and she heard a voice say, "This is Alice Morgan, I want to introduce you to her."

But when she woke up Alice thought this was only due to her having discussed the matter with the novices. Alice Morgan was not the disturbed person there, her psychic sense told her.

To her, all ghostly activities centered around that attic. There were two steps that always squeaked peculiarly when someone stepped on them. Many times she would hear them squeak and look to see who was walking on them, only to find herself staring into nothingness. This was in the daytime. On other occasions, when she was at work cleaning garbage cans downstairs—postulants do a lot of ordinary kitchen work—she would feel herself observed closely by a pair of eyes staring down at her from the attic. Yet, no one was up there then.

The torture of the nightly footsteps together with her doubts about her own calling prompted her finally to seek release from the convent and return to the outside world, after three months as a postulant. After she had made this difficult decision, she felt almost as if all the burdens had lifted from the room that had been the center of the psychic manifestations.

She decided to make some final inquiries prior to leaving and since her superiors would not tell her, she looked the place over by herself, talked to those who were willing to talk and otherwise used her powers of observation. Surely, if the haunted area was upstairs, and she knew by now that it was, it could not be Alice Morgan who was the restless one.

But then who was?

The rooms on the third floor had originally been servant quarters as is customary in the mansions of the pre–World War I period. They were built to house the usually large staffs of the owners. In the case of the Morgans, that staff was even larger than most wealthy families.

Was "the restless one" one of the maids who had jumped out the window in a final burst for freedom, freedom from some horrible fate?

Then her thoughts turned to the Communist Russian occupancy of the building. Had they perhaps tortured someone up there in her room? The thought was melodramatically tempting, but she dismissed it immediately. The figure she had seen in the hall was dressed in the long dress of an earlier period. She belonged to the time when the Morgan Hall was a mansion.

No, she reasoned, it must have been a young girl who died there while the Morgans had the place and perhaps her death was hushed up and she wanted it known. Was it suicide, and did she feel in a kind of personal hell because of it, especially now that the place was a convent?

Somehow Alice felt that she had stumbled upon the right answers. That night, the last night she was to spend at the convent prior to going home, she slept soundly.

For the first time in three months, there were no footsteps outside her door.

For a while she waited, once the ten o'clock bell had sounded, but nothing happened. Whoever it was had stopped walking.

Return to Clinton Court

When I investigated Clinton Court, New York, in 1960, and wrote about it in *Ghost Hunter*, I never dreamed I'd have to come back and talk to a ghost again. But sometimes the dead won't stay still. Our first visit had been somewhat impaired by a nervous real estate firm who wanted us out of the house as quickly as possible. Ethel Johnson Meyers went into trance in the lower portion of what was once the stables and carriage house of Governor Clinton. Now located in the heart of Hell's Kitchen, it was then a rural neighborhood in which the Clinton Mansion, now gone, was surrounded by fields and woodlands close to the North River.

Ethel Meyers' trance was fully described in the chapter called "The Clinton Court Ghosts" in *Ghost Hunter*. When we left the downstairs apartment where Ethel and I had spent a quiet hour, I was pretty sure there would be no further need for our services. The apartment was then in a state of disrepair, there was no tenant as yet, and all we had to sit on were a bench and a completely worn-out chair someone had left behind.

I thought no more of charming Clinton Court so neatly tucked away behind an iron gate and probably unknown to most New Yorkers, until 1964, when a Miss Alyce Montreuil wrote to me of her experiences in the house at 422H West Forty-sixth Street, New York.

As a friend of the tenants who had taken one of the two apartments making up the former carriage house, she had had her brush with the uncanny. I reported this in detail in *Ghosts I've Met;* how the upstairs door near the porch atop the stairs would not stay closed, how the door seemingly unlocked itself, and how her dogs would freeze when approaching the staircase leading to the upper apartment.

Again I thought I had done my duty to restless Clinton Court by reporting these later developments during the tenancy of Danny Brown and Frank Benner, between 1959 and 1963. Meanwhile, the tower apartment had also acquired new tenants, Mr. and Mrs. Dan Neary, who had lived there since 1963.

Somehow Clinton Court would not leave me alone. A young student of the occult named Bob Nelson wrote to me of doors opening by themselves. But he had read my book, and I was afraid it might have inspired him to look for these things. Then in February of 1965, Mrs. Leo Herbert contacted me after seeing Sybil Leek and myself "de-ghosting" (or trying to "de-ghost") June Havoc's house, situated behind theirs, on Miss Havoc's television program.

Her husband, a direct descendant of Victor Herbert, was property master for all David Merrick shows, and Mrs. Herbert was a dancer. They had lived in the two top floors composing the upper apartment since 1964. There were some odd things going on in the place, and would Sybil Leek and I please come and have a talk with whoever it was who was causing them?

No sooner said than done. On March 28, about a dozen people assembled in the upstairs living room of the Herberts. They included the downstairs neighbors, the Nearys; some people living in the front, or un-haunted section of Clinton Court; Bob Nelson, Carl Gewritz, the Herbert children, and Mr. and Mrs. Biff Liff; Gail Benedict, public relations director, Bill Hazlett, and Peter Hahn of North American Newspaper Alliance; Catherine and I; and, of course, Sybil Leek, resplendent in purple dress, stockings, and cape.

Promptly at nine, we dimmed the lights and grouped ourselves around the room roughly in a circle, with Sybil stretching out on a chair in the upper center.

After the usual few moments of hypnosis, I had Sybil safely entranced, and I waited for the ghost to make himself or herself known. I knew there were several layers of consciousness in the place, and I could not be sure about the ones who would break through the barrier and use Sybil's vocal cords to communicate with us.

Her lips moved silently for a few moments while I strained not to miss the first words. Gradually the sounds became intelligible and I moved closer.

"What is your name?" I asked.

"Walker."

I asked the ghost to speak up.

"George . . . Walker," the voice said, plainly now.

"Is this your house?"

"No. George . . . I have blood in my mouth . . . hurt."

"Who hurt you?"

"Don't know . . . dying . . . I'm dying . . . too late . . ."

"Do you live here?"

"No . . . Brice."

"What street?"

"No street. Brice. South."

"What year is this?"

"Ninety-two."

"What can we do to help you?"

"I want to live . . . doctor."

"Which doctor do you want us to call?"

"Warren. East . . . Easton."

It sounded like East Hampton to me, but I wasn't sure. The voice had difficulty maintaining an even tone.

"How did you get to this house?" I inquired.

"Went to the river . . . everybody . . . friends, soldiers . . . Alfred . . . came to rest . . ."

"Why did you come to this house?"

"I like it . . . remembered . . . coming here to see George . . . two Georgies."

"What is this other George's name?"

"Clinton. George Clinton . . . I die . . ."

"Are you a soldier?"

"Yeah . . . Colonel . . . George . . . Walker."

"What regiment?"

"Two-four."

"Who is the commanding general?"

"Wilson."

"First name?"

"Amos . . . nobody bothers . . ."

"Yes, I do. I will help you. Who attacked you?"

"I don't know."

I asked what he wanted in this house.

"I want to stay . . . no house, field! Can't get to the house."

"Where were you born?" I changed the subject before the ghost could get too upset to give us information.

"Brice . . . Carolina . . ."

"When did you come up here?"

The voice hesitated.

"Eight-three . . . no, ninety-three . . . eighty-eight."

"How did you get hurt?"

"Blood in my chest . . . knife . . ." He added that it was a man, a soldier, but he did not recognize him.

Suddenly, the jaws of the medium started to quiver and the voice began to give out.

"Can't talk . . ." I calmed him, and his tone became once more steadier.

"What other regiments were here?" I resumed.

"Queens . . . Nine . . . "

"Were you in any campaign?"

"Brice . . ."

"What town is Brice near?"

"Pike's Hill."

"What colony?"

"Carolina . . . North Carolina."

"Any other town it is near to?"

"Pike's Hill, Three Hills . . ."

I asked him whether he knew anyone else here, but the ghost replied he couldn't see things in the "field," only smoke.

"The house is too far. I can't get there," he repeated.

"What is your wife's name?"

"Martha . . . Brice."

"Children?"

"Three."

"Your father's name?"

"Stephen . . . Brice . . . Burnt Oak."

"Is that the name of a house?"

"Yes . . ."

"Is he alive or dead?"

"Dead."

"When did he die?"

"Fifty-nine."

"Where is he buried?"

"Burnt Oak."

"Cemetery?"

"In the garden."

"What denomination was he?"

"Catholic."

"Were you Catholic?"

"Yes . . . French Catholic."

"Were you baptized?"

"St. Teresa."

"Where is this?"

"Pike Hill."

"What year were you born?"

"Thirty-four."

"Any brothers who were officers?"

"Clifford . . . Colonel . . . fourteenth regiment, stationed Pike Hill."

"Cavalry or infantry?"

"Infantry."

"Any other brothers who were officers?"

"Aaron . . . Captain . . ."

"Where stationed?"

"Don't know."

I felt it was time to release this unhappy one. Gently, I suggested his pain was no more, and asked him to join his loved ones.

A moment later he slipped away. I then asked that Sybil Leek, still deeply entranced, answer my questions, without awakening. This is actually switching from deep trance to clairvoyant trance in the middle of the séance, but Sybil has extraordinary powers of the mind and is a disciplined medium. Sybil's own voice responded to me now. She sounded somewhat sleepy and wasn't her usual crisp self, but nevertheless she was clearly audible.

I asked her to look around and report what she saw. Sybil's etheric body was now "on the other side" for the time being, and she was able to see the same things a permanent resident of that other world would be seeing.

She described a house with three windows, with a "sort of office" inside.

"There are people here who should not be here . . . girls!" she said.

"What happens here?" I asked.

"Something to do with the staircase . . . something happened . . . trying to see . . . I don't like it . . . someone hanging . . . don't like it . . . a man . . ."

"What does he look like?"

"Six . . . young men . . . gray clothes . . . someone hung *him* . . . I don't want to look . . ."

"Is there anyone else on the staircase?" I inquired.

"Yes," Sybil said in halting tones. "That girl."

"How old is she?"

"Twenty-five, twenty-six."

"What is she doing on the staircase?"

"She has seen *him*. Doesn't care. She wants someone to take him away, but then she forgets about it. She was wrong about the man . . . liking him . . . I see her living in this house and she is very happy, until she gets frightened by the man. She doesn't like the staircase. Someone takes the staircase and *puts it somewhere else* . . . I don't want to stay here . . . bad house."

"What about the staircase?" I pressed Sybil.

"She moved the staircase and then got to go back to the old staircase and then they caught up with her."

"Who caught up with her?"

"The man's friends. The man who was hung. She was very ill. He had her move the staircase. They knew it was there. And so she kept going back. And then she died . . . *somebody pushed her*. And she hurt her back, she couldn't walk, bad house."

"The girl—because she's frightened. She throws things onto the ground. She runs up the stairs—the other stairs trying to get away—she doesn't like music—reminds her of sad song—the music starts things off here."

"How long ago did she die?"

"Eighteen-four-o—about . . . "

"Is she causing all the disturbances in this house?" I asked.

"No . . . a man, and she, and others . . . lot of people pass through . . . to the river."

"Anyone else on the staircase?"

"No."

"Look at the door. Is anybody at the door?"

"Animal . . . dog . . . scratching . . . nobody there to let it in . . . she's inside."

"Is this her house?"

"Sort of. Lives here . . . Goes to the door because of the scratching noise."

"Is it her dog?"

"Dog lives in the house . . . strange, she wants to go, and she can't."

"Why?"

"Because she would have no money. She is wanting to open the door, let the dog in."

"Is the woman on the other side?"

Sybil's voice was somewhat puzzled.

"*I'm* on the other side."

Of course she was . . . temporarily.

"Is she the same girl you saw on the stairs?"

"Yes."

"Is there anyone else here?"

"No."

"Do you see any children here?"

"Four children. Not here now. Not very strong."

"Look at the staircase once more. Was there any kind of tragedy on the staircase?"

"I see someone who falls. Older man. The girl . . . is used to the staircase now. She keeps *staying* on this staircase."

172

"You mean like the man who was hanged?"

"Yes. It is very confusing. She is on the staircase waiting for something else, I think. Someone and something else to happen. Someone to come, she is very confused."

I felt Sybil had been "under" long enough and decided to bring her out of her trance. This was accomplished quickly. When Sybil awoke, she remembered very little, as usual.

The group was animated now as everyone sought to sum up reactions and feelings. Our bearded host, Leo Herbert, who was next to Sybil with the entrance door at his back, was the first to speak.

"It is very strange, but just before Hans put Sybil under, I felt that there was a draft. I got up, and shut the door, but I could still feel this coldness, right here, on me. It just never left, and feels pretty much like that this moment, though not with the intensity it had when you were hypnotizing Sybil. I had the feeling if I moved out of this spot, Sybil would talk louder."

Sybil's entranced voice was not loud on this occasion, and some of the group farther back in the room had difficulty hearing her.

"Did you have any psychic experiences in this house prior to our session tonight?" I asked Leo Herbert.

"I have heard noises from upstairs, where I sleep, and I came down here to investigate and found no one here," Herbert said, "but I had the feeling of a *presence* here. As if somebody had just been here. This was only two and a half weeks ago. The first time when I awakened, I thought that I heard footsteps down here, and I waited a long time and heard nothing, and after fifteen minutes, I went back to bed. An hour later I was awakened again, went directly down, checked the windows and door and found them all locked. Yet I felt someone had been present here."

I then turned to Mrs. Herbert, who was sitting on the comfortable couch next to Catherine.

"What about you—have you had any uncanny experiences here?"

"About a year ago, I was alone in the apartment," the slender brunette answered, "when I was sure someone was throwing pebbles against the skylight of the roof above our bedrooms. I also heard footsteps on the roof."

"Did you look to see who it was?"

"No, I was terrified."

"Did you find any pebbles on the roof?"

"No, nothing. I went up the next morning, but there was nothing on the roof. No pebbles."

I thanked Mrs. Herbert and approached the Nearys, who live below the Herberts. Mrs. Neary was quite willing to talk to me, although she had originally been a skeptic about ghosts.

"The sounds in the house are so much more varied than ever before," she volunteered. "I have heard a bell ringing, yet there is no bell. On at least six occasions lately, I have felt someone brush past me, yet nobody could be seen. I have had a sense of shadow. There are all sorts of strange noises. Primarily in the area of the wall between the living room and kitchen. Sometimes there is ticking in the wall."

I asked for quiet, and read aloud Miss Montreuil's letter to me, relating the experiences she had had at the house while a guest of previous tenants. I stressed that Sybil Leek did not know where we would be going that evening. She had no advance information, because we never discuss cases beforehand. I had directed the driver to take us to 420 West Forty-sixth Street, carefully avoiding the use of "Clinton Court." On arrival, I had hustled her upstairs, so that she had no chance to study the house or familiarize herself with it.

And yet much of what came through Sybil Leek's entranced lips matched the earlier testimony of Ethel Johnson Meyers. Much was new, too, and could be checked without much difficulty. I felt Ethel had "sensed" a girl on the staircase, and so had Sybil.

That the stairs had been moved was unknown to both Ethel and Sybil at the time, yet both said they had been. Sybil spoke of a man hanged on the stairs, which might very well refer to Old Moor, the sailor hanged for mutiny on the Battery, but buried here in Potter's Field. Clinton Court was built above the old Potter's Field.

The girl, waiting for someone and for something to happen, was felt by both mediums. And the story of the pebbles and footsteps on the roof meshes with Mrs. Meyer's tale of a girl pushed off the roof to her death.

The officer named Walker was a new character in the everexpanding ghostly cast of Clinton Court. Could he be traced?

Sometimes it is even difficult to trace a living officer, and tracing a dead one isn't easy. I did not expect to be completely successful, but I had hoped that at least one or two names could be traced or proved correct.

Sybil, in trance speaking with the voice and mind of Col. George Walker, had referred to a commanding officer by the name of Amos Wilson. He also said his doctor was one Dr. Warren, and that he had come to New York in 1788. We don't know, at least from the psychic end, whether he was still on active duty in 1792, when presumably his death occurred. He might have been retired and his visit to New York might not have been connected with his military career at all.

It was therefore with considerable interest that I found in Heitman's *Historical Register of Officers of the Continental Army* that a George Walker had been a Second Lieutenant, serving in that capacity to 1783, and that one Amos Wilson, First Lieutenant, had served at least in 1776; also, one John Warren, Surgeon, is recorded for the period from 1777 to 1783. These officers served with Northern regiments, while Walker claimed North Carolina as his home. However, it was not unusual for officers, or men, for that matter, to serve in regiments based in other regions of the country than their own colony. Many

Southerners did indeed come north during the revolutionary and post-revolutionary period to serve with established "Yankee" regiments.

In trance, Walker claimed to have had a brother named Aaron Walker, with the rank of Captain. I found a Lt. Aaron Walker, attached to a Connecticut regiment in 1776. George Walker—the one I found listed—served in New Jersey, incidentally, which could have brought him into nearby New York.

I did not locate Walker's other brothers, nor did I come across his father or wife, but we must keep in mind that the records of the period are not complete. Certainly the claimed friendship with George Clinton fits in chronologically. The ghost also spoke several times of a place called Brice, North Carolina, and described it as being near Pike's Hill. There is a Pikes*ville*, North Carolina.

As for Brice, North Carolina—or perhaps Bryce, as the spelling was never given—this took a bit more searching. Finally, the reference librarian of the North Carolina State Library in Raleigh, Mrs. Helen Harrison, was able to supply me with some information.

The *Colonial Records,* which is a list of incorporated towns, early maps, postal guides, etc., revealed nothing about such a place. The State Department of Archives and History also checked their files without success. But in *Colonial Records,* vol. IV, page 16, there is *mention* of a sawmill being erected at Brice's Creek, Newbern, in 1735, and of Samuel Pike receiving a land grant at Newbern in 1748.

"Brice started to acquire land grants as early as 1707," Mrs. Harrison pointed out, "and it is known that Brice built a fort on his plantation and that patents were granted for land on Brice's Creek as late as 1758. It seems possible that this settlement may be the Brice to which you refer."

What about Pike's Hill and Three Hills, which the ghost said were close to each other and to Brice?

"In 1755," Mrs. Harrison stated, "there was a movement to build the capital at Tower Hill, Craven County, N.C. It interested me to find that *all three* of these places are located in Craven County, though Tower Hill may have no connection with Three Hills."

On re-hearing the tapes, I find I cannot be absolutely sure whether the ghost said Tower Hill or Three Hills. It could have been either.

So there you have it. How could Sybil Leek (or I, for that matter) know these minute details that are so obscure even a local historian had difficulty tracing them?

Not a ghost of a chance, I think.

The Ghost of Gay Street

Frank Paris and T. E. Lewis were puppeteers. Children came to admire the little theater the two puppeteers had set up in the high-ceilinged basement of their old house in Greenwich Village, that old section of New York going back to the 1700s. The house at number 12 Gay Street was a typical old townhouse, smallish, the kind New Yorkers built around 1800 when "the village" meant *far uptown.*

In 1924, a second section was added to the house, covering the garden that used to grace the back of the house. This architectural graft created a kind of duplex, one apartment on top of another, with small rooms at the sides in the rear.

The ownership of the house in the early days is hazy. At one time a sculptor owned number 12, possibly before the 1930s. Evidently he was fond of bootleg liquor, for he built a trap door in the ground floor of the newer section of the house, probably over his hidden liquor cabinet. Before that, Mayor Jimmy Walker owned the house, and used it *well,* although not *wisely.* One of his many loves is said to have been the tenant there. By a strange set of circumstances, the records of the house vanished like a ghost from the files of the Hall of Records around that time.

Later, real-estate broker Mary Ellen Strunsky lived in the house. In 1956, she sold it to the puppeteer team of Paris and Lewis, who had been there ever since, living in the upstairs apartment and using the lower portion as a workroom and studio for their little theater.

None of this, incidentally, was known to me until after the visit I paid the house in the company of my medium for the evening, Betty Ritter.

It all started when a reporter from the *New York World-Telegram*, Cindy Hughes, came to interview me, and casually dropped a hint that she knew of a haunted house. Faster than you can say *Journal-American*, I had her promise to lead me to this house. On a particularly warm night in May of 1963, I followed Miss Hughes down to Gay Street. Betty Ritter knew nothing at all about the case; she didn't even know the address where we were going.

We were greeted warmly by Frank Paris, who led us up the stairs into the upper apartment. The sight of the elaborately furnished, huge living room was surprising. Oriental figurines, heavy drapes, paintings, statuary, and antiques filed the room.

In two comfortable chairs we found awaiting us two friends of the owners: an intense looking man in his thirties, Richard X., who, I later discovered, was an editor by profession, and Alice May Hall, a charming lady of undetermined age.

I managed to get Betty out of earshot, so I could question these people without her getting impressions from our conversation.

"What is this about the house being haunted?" I asked Frank Paris.

He nodded gravely.

"I was working downstairs with some lacquer. It was late, around 3 A.M. Suddenly, I began to smell a strong odor of violets. My black spaniel here also smelled it, for he started to sniff rather strangely. And yet, Ted, my partner, in the same room with me, did not get the strange scent at all. But there is more. People waltz up and down the stairs at night, time and again."

"What do you mean, *waltz*?"

"I mean they go up and down, up and down, as if they had business here," Frank explained, and I thought, perhaps they had, perhaps they had.

"A weekend visitor also had a most peculiar experience here," Frank Paris continued. "He knew nothing about our haunted reputation, of course. We were away on a short trip, and when we got back, he greeted us with—'Say, who are all these people going up and down the stairs?' He had thought that the house next door was somehow connected to ours, and that what he heard were people from next door. But of course, there is no connection whatever."

"And did you ever investigate these mysterious footsteps?" I asked.

"Many times," Frank and Ted nodded simultaneously, "but there was never anyone there—anyone of flesh-and-blood, that is."

I thanked them, and wondered aloud if they weren't psychic, since they had experienced what can only be called psychic phenomena.

Frank Paris hesitated, then admitted that he thought both of them were to some extent.

"We had a little dog which we had to have put away one day. We loved the dog very much, but it was one of those things that had to be done. For over a year after the dog's death, both of us felt him poking us in the leg—a habit he had in life. This happened on many occasions to both of us."

I walked over to where Miss Hall, the gray-haired little lady, sat.

"Oh, there is a ghost here all right," she volunteered. "It was in February of 1963, and I happened to be in the house, since the boys and I are good friends. I was sitting here in this very spot, relaxing and casually looking toward the entrance door through which you just came—the one that leads to the hallway and the stairs. There was a man there, wearing evening clothes, and an Inverness Cape—I saw him quite plainly. He had dark hair. It was dusk, and there was still some light outside."

"What did you do?"

"I turned my head to tell Frank Paris about the stranger, and that instant he was gone like a puff of smoke."

Paris broke in.

"I questioned her about this, since I didn't really believe it. But a

180

week later, at dawn this time, I saw the ghost myself, exactly as Alice had described him—wearing evening clothes, a cape, hat, and his face somewhat obscured by the shadows of the hallway. Both Alice and I are sure he was a youngish man, and had sparkling eyes. What's more, our dog also saw the intruder. He went up to the ghost, friendly-like, as if to greet him."

Those were the facts of the case. A ghost in evening clothes, an old house where heaven knows what might have happened at one time or another, and a handful of psychic people.

I returned to Betty Ritter, and asked her to gather psychic impressions while walking about the house.

"A crime was committed here," the medium said, and described a terrible argument upstairs between an Asian man and a woman. She described a gambling den, opium smokers, and a language she could not understand. The man's name was Ming, she said. Ming is a very common Chinese word meaning, I believe, Sun.

Betty also told Frank Paris that someone close to him by the name of John had passed on and that he had something wrong with his right eye, which Paris acknowledged was correct. She told Ted Lewis that a Bernard L. was around him, not knowing, of course, that Lewis' father was named Bernham Lewis. She told Richard X. that he worked with books, and it was not until after the séance that I learned he was an editor by profession. I don't know about the Chinese man and the opium den, but they are possibilities in an area so far removed from the bright lights of the city as the Village once was.

We went downstairs and, in the almost total darkness, formed a circle. Betty fell into trance, her neck suddenly falling back as if she were being possessed by a woman whose neck had been hurt.

"Emil," she mumbled, and added the woman had been decapitated, and her bones were still about. She then came out of trance and we walked back up the stairs to the oldest part of the house. Still "seeing" clairvoyantly, Betty Ritter again mumbled "Emil," and said she saw documents with government seals on them. She also felt someone named Mary Ellen had lived here and earlier some "wellknown government official named Wilkins or Wilkinson."

Betty, of course, knew nothing about real-estate broker Mary Ellen Strunsky or Jimmy Walker, the former New York Mayor, who had been in this house for so long.

It now remained for us to find those bones Betty had talked about. We returned to the downstairs portion of the house, but Betty refused to go farther. Her impression of tragedy was so strong she urged us to desist.

Thus it was that the Ghost of Gay Street, whoever he may be, would have to wait just a little longer until the bones could be properly sorted out. It wasn't half bad, considering that Frank Paris and Ted Lewis put on a pretty nice puppet show every so often, down there in the murky basement theater at number 12 Gay Street.

The Ghosts of Barbery Lane

"I know a house in Rye, New York, with a ghost," painter Mary Melikian said to me, and there was pleasure in her voice at being the harbinger of good news. Mary knew how eager I was to find a haunted house, preferably one that was still haunted.

"A ghost," Mary repeated and added, tantalizingly, "a ghost that *likes to slam doors.*"

I pumped Mary for details. One of her friends was the celebrated portrait painter Molly Guion, known in Rye as Mrs. John Smythe. Molly and her husband, an architect, lived in a sprawling mid-nineteenth-century house atop a bluff overlooking the old New Haven Railroad bed, surrounded by houses built in later years. The Smythes' house was the first one on the tract, the original Manor House, built there around 1860 by one Jared B. Peck.

I arranged with Mrs. Smythe to visit the house the following week, in August of 1963. My wife Catherine and I were met at the train by Mrs. Smythe, whose husband also came along to welcome us. The drive to the house (originally called "The Cedars" but now only known as a number on Barbery Lane) took less than five minutes, yet you might well have entered another world—so serene and rural was the atmosphere that greeted us that moonlit evening, when the station wagon pulled up to the gleaming-white 100-year old house the Smythes had called home since the summer of 1957.

Rising to four floors, the structure reminded me of the stylized paintings of Victorian houses associated with another world. A wide porch went around it at the ground level, and shady trees protected it from view and intrusion.

The huge living room was tastefully furnished with fine antiques and all over the house we encountered the marvelously alive portraits painted by Molly Guion, which blended naturally into the decor of the house. This was a stately mansion, only an hour from New York but as quiet and removed from the city of subways as if it stood in the Deep South or Down East. We seated ourselves comfortably. Then I came right to the point.

"This ghost," I began. "What exactly does it do and when did you first notice anything unusual in the house?"

This is my standard opener. Molly Guion was more than happy to tell us everything. Her husband left for a while to tend to some chores.

"We arrived in this house on a hot summer day in 1957—in July," she recalled. "About a week later—I remember it was a particularly hot night—we heard a door slam. Both my husband and I heard it."

"Well?"

"But there was absolutely nobody in the house at the time except us," Molly said, significantly. "We heard it many times after that. Maybe six or seven separate instances. Once around ten o'clock at night I heard the front door open and close again with a characteristic squeak. Mother was living with us then and I was not feeling well, so that a nurse was staying with me. I called out 'Mother,' thinking she had come home a bit early, but there was no reply. Since then I've heard the front door open many times, but there is never anyone there."

"Is it the front door then?"

"No, not always. Sometimes it is the front door and sometimes it is this door on the second floor. Come, I'll show you."

Molly led us up the winding stairs to a second floor containing many small rooms, all exquisitely furnished with the solid furniture of the Victorian period. There was a tiny room on one side of the corridor

184

leading to the rear of the house, and across from it, the door that was heard to slam. It was a heavy wooden door, leading to a narrow winding staircase which in turn led up another flight of stairs to the third floor. Here Molly Guion had built herself a magnificent studio, taking up most of the floor space.

"One day in January of 1962," she volunteered, "I was downstairs in the kitchen talking to an exterminator, when I heard a door slam hard—it seemed to me. Yet, there was no one in the house at the time, only we two downstairs."

"Outside of yourself and your husband, has anyone else heard these uncanny noises?"

Molly nodded quickly.

"There was this man that worked for me. He said, 'Mrs. Smythe, every time I'm alone in the house, I hear a door slam!'"

"Anyone else?"

"A Scottish cleaning woman, name of Roberta Gillan. She lives in Harrison, New York. She once came to me and said, 'Did you just slam a door?' Of course, I hadn't."

We were now seated in a small room off the second-floor corridor. The light was moody and the air dank. There was a quietness around the house so heavy I almost wished I could hear a door slam. Molly had more to reveal.

"Once, a little girl named Andree, age eleven, came to visit us and within seconds exclaimed 'Mamma, there is a ghost in this house!'"

Our hostess admitted to being somewhat psychic, with some times comical results. Years ago, when a boyfriend had failed to keep their date, she saw him clearly in a dream-vision with a certain blonde girl. He later explained his absence in a casual way, but she nailed him with a description of his blonde—and he confessed the truth.

Two years after she moved into the house, Molly developed a case of asthma, the kind very old people sometimes suffer from. Strangely, it bothered her only in certain rooms and not at all in others. It started like a kind of allergy, and gradually worsened until it became a fully grown asthmatic condition. Although two rooms were side by side, sleeping in one would aggravate the condition, but sleeping in the other made her completely free of it!

"Did you hear any other noises—I mean, outside of the door slamming?" I asked.

"Yes. Not so long ago we had a dinner party here, and among the guests was a John Gardner, a vice president of the Bankers Trust Company.

Suddenly she had heard someone rap at the window of the big room downstairs. They tried to ignore the noise, but Gardner heard it too.

"Is someone rapping at your window?" he inquired.

He was assured it was nothing. Later he took Molly aside and remonstrated with her. "I distinctly heard the raps," he said. Molly just smiled.

Finally the Smythes called on the American Society for Psychic Research to find an explanation for all these goings-on. But the Society was in no hurry to do anything about the case. They suggested Molly write them a letter, which she did, but they still took no action.

I thoroughly inspected the premises—walked up the narrow staircase into Molly Guion's studio where some of the best portrait oils hung. Her paintings of famous Britons had just toured as an exhibition and the house was full of those she owned (the greater part of her work was commissioned and scattered in collections, museums, and private homes).

There was a tiny bedroom next to the landing in back of the studio, evidently a servant's room, since the entire floor had originally been servants' quarters. The house had sixteen rooms in all.

By now Mr. Smythe had joined us and I explained my mission. Had he ever noticed anything unusual about the house?

"Oh yes," he volunteered, speaking slowly and deliberately. "There are all sorts of noises in this house and they're not ordinary noises—I mean, the kind you can *explain*."

"For instance?"

"I was sleeping up here one night in the little bedroom here," he said, pointing to the servant's room in back of the landing, "when I heard footsteps. They were the steps of an older person."

But there was no one about, he asserted.

Jared Peck, who built the house in 1860, died in 1895, and the house passed into the hands of his estate to be rented to various tenants. In 1910, Stuyvesant Wainwright bought the property. In the following year, his ex-wife, now Mrs. Catlin, bought it from him and lived in it until her death in the 1920s.

The former Mrs. Wainwright turned out to be a colorful person. Born wealthy, she had a very short temper and the servants never stayed long in her house.

"She certainly liked to slam doors," Mr. Smythe observed. "I mean she was the kind of person who would do that sort of thing."

"One day she became very ill and everybody thought she would die," Molly related. "There she was stretched out on this very couch and the doctor felt free to talk about her condition. 'She won't last much longer,' he said, and shrugged. Mrs. Wainwright sat up with a angry jolt and barked, 'I intend to!' And she did, for many more years of hot-tempered shenanigans."

In her later years Mrs. Wainwright moved to the former servants' quarters on the second floor—whether out of economy or for reasons of privacy no one knows for sure. The *slamming door* was right in the heart of her rooms and no doubt she traveled up those narrow stairs to the floor above many times.

The plumber, painter, and carpenter who worked for Mrs.

187

Wainwright were still living in Rye and they all remembered her as a willful and headstrong woman who liked to have her own way. Her granddaughter, Mrs. Condit, recalled her vividly. The Smythes were pretty sure that Mrs. Wainwright slept up there on the second floor— they found a screen marked "My bedroom window" that fit no other window in any of the rooms.

The Smythes acquired the handsome house from the next owner, one Arthur Flemming, who used Mrs. Wainwright's old room. But he didn't experience anything unusual, or at any rate said nothing about it.

There was a big theft once in the house and Mrs. Wainwright may have been worried about it. Strongly attached to worldly possessions, she kept valuables in various trunks on the third floor, and ran up to look at them from time to time to make sure everything was still there.

Could the slamming of the door be a re-enactment of these frequent nervous expeditions up the stairs? Could the opening and closing of the entrance door be a fearful examination of the door to see if the lock was secure, or if there was anyone strange lurking about outside?

The very day after our visit to this haunted house, a young painter friend of Molly's named Helen Charleton, of Bronxville, New York, was alone in the studio that Molly let her use occasionally to do some painting of her own. She was quite alone in the big house when she clearly heard the front door open. Calling out, she received no answer. Thinking that the gardener might have a key, and that she might be in danger, she took hold of what heavy objects she could put her hands on and waited anxiously for the steps that were sure to resound any moment. No steps came. An hour later, the doorbell rang and she finally dashed down to the entrance door. *The door was tightly shut*, and no one was about. Yet she *had* heard the characteristic noise of the opening of the old-fashioned door!

The mailman's truck was just pulling away, so she assumed it was he who had rung the bell. Just then Molly returned.

"I've heard the door slam many times," Helen Charleton said to me, "and it always sounds so far away. I think it's on the first floor, but I can't be sure."

Was Mrs. Wainwright still walking the Victorian corridors of "The Cedars," guarding her treasures upstairs?

When Catherine and I returned from Europe in the fall of 1964, Molly Guion had news for us. All was far from quiet in Rye. In the upstairs room where Molly's invalid mother was bedridden, a knob had flown off a table while Mrs. Guion stood next to it. In the presence of a nurse, the bathroom lights had gone on and off by themselves. More sinister, a heavy ashtray had taken off on its own to sail clear across the room. A door had opened by itself, and footsteps had been heard again.

A new nurse had come, and the number of witnesses who had heard or seen uncanny goings-on was now eight.

I decided it was time for a séance, and on January 6, 1965, medium Ethel Meyers, Mary Melikian, Catherine and I took a New Haven train for Rye, where John Smythe picked us up in his station wagon.

While Ethel Meyers waited in the large sitting room downstairs, I checked on the house and got the latest word on the hauntings. Molly Guion took me to the kitchen to show me the spot where one of the most frightening incidents had taken place.

"Last Christmas, my mother, my husband, and I were here in the kitchen having lunch, and right near us on a small table next to the wall was a great big bread knife. Suddenly, to our amazement, *the knife took off into the air*, performed an arc in the air and landed about a yard away from the table. This was about noon, in good light."

"Was that the only time something like this happened?"

"The other day the same thing happened. We were down in the kitchen again at nighttime. My husband and I heard a terrific crash upstairs. It was in the area of the servants' quarters on the second floor, which is in the area where that door keeps slamming. I went up to investigate and found a heavy ashtray lying on the floor about a yard away from the table in my husband's den."

"And there was no one upstairs—flesh-and-blood, that is?"

"No. The object could not have just slipped off the table. It landed some distance away."

"Amazing," I conceded. "Was there more?"

"Last week I was standing in the upstairs sitting room with one of the nurses, when a piece of a chair that was lying in the center of a table took off and landed in the middle of the floor."

"Before your eyes?"

"Before our eyes."

"What would you say is the most frequent phenomenon here?" I asked.

"The opening of the front door downstairs. We and others have heard this characteristic noise any number of times, and there is never anyone there."

I turned to Mrs. Witty, the nurse currently on duty with Molly Guion's mother.

"How long have you been in this house?"

"Since October, 1964."

"Have you noticed anything unusual in these four months?"

"Well, Mrs. Smythe and I were in the patient's bedroom upstairs, when we heard the front door downstairs open. I remarked to Mrs. Smythe that she had a visitor, and went down to the front door, and looked. *The heavy chain was swinging loose, and the front door was slightly ajar!*"

"Did you see any visitor?"

"No. I opened the door, looked all around, but there was no one there. "

"Anything else?"

"A couple of weeks later, the same thing happened. I was alone in the house with the patient, and the door was locked securely. An hour after I had myself locked it, I heard the door shut tightly, but the chain was again swinging by itself."

I next turned to Mr. Smythe to check up on his own experiences since we had last talked. Mr. Smythe was a naval architect and very cautious in his appraisal of the uncanny. He was still hearing the "measured steps" in the attic room where he sometimes slept, even when he was all alone in the house.

I returned to Ethel Meyers, the medium, who had seated herself in a large chair in the front sitting room downstairs.

"Anything happening?" I asked, for I noticed a peculiar expression on Ethel's face, as if she were observing something or someone.

"I picture a woman clairvoyantly," Ethel said. "She looks at me with a great deal of defiance."

"Why are you pointing across the room at that sofa?" I asked my wife.

"I saw a light from the corner of my eye and I thought it was a car, but no car has passed by," Catherine said.

If a car *had* passed by, no reflection could have been seen at that spot, since no window faced in that direction.

While Ethel prepared for the trance sitting, I went outside the room to talk to Georgia Anne Warren, a young dancer who had modeled for some of Molly Guion's paintings. Her full-length nude study graced the studio upstairs, and there amid the Churchill portraits and faces of the famous or near-famous, it was like a shining beacon of beauty. But Miss Warren wasn't only posing for a painter, we discovered—she was also modeling for a ghost.

"I heard a thumping noise, as if someone were going upstairs. I was in the kitchen. The steps sounded as if they were coming from the dining room. There was no one coming in. The only people in the house at the time were Molly Guion and myself. No doubt about it."

I thanked the redheaded model and followed Ethel Meyers up the stairs, to which she seemed propelled by a sudden impulse. There, on the winding Victorian steps, Ethel made her first contact with the ghost.

"Make the body very cold. Don't put it in the ground when it's warm. Let it get very cold!" she mumbled, as if not quite herself.

"Let her speak through you," I suggested.

"She is," Ethel replied, and continued in a somewhat strange voice. "Ring around the rosies, a pocketful of posies . . ."

I turned toward the stairwell and asked the ghost to communicate with us, tell her tale, and find help through us. There was no further answer.

I led Mrs. Meyers back to her chair, and asked Molly Guion to dim the lights a little so we could all relax. Meanwhile, other witnesses had arrived. They included New York Times reporter N. Berkowitz, Benton & Bowles vice-president Gordon Webber, publicist Bill Ryan, and book critic John K. Hutchins. We formed a long oval around Ethel Meyers and waited for the ghost to make her appearance.

We did not have to wait long. With a sudden shriek, Ethel, deep in trance, leapt to her feet, and in the awkward posture of an old crone, walked toward the front door. Nothing I could do would hold her back. I followed her quickly, as the medium, now possessed by the ghost, made her way through the long room to the door.

As if a strong wind had swept into the sitting room, the rest of the guests were thrown back by the sheer drive of Ethel's advance. She flung herself against the heavy wooden door and started to alternately gnaw at it and pound against it in an unmistakable desire to open it and go through. Then she seized the brass chain—the one Mrs. Witty had twice seen swinging by itself—and pulled it with astonishing force. I had all I could do to keep the medium from falling as she threw her body against the door.

In one hand I held a microphone, which I pressed close to her lips to catch as much of the dialogue as possible. I kept the other hand ready to prevent Ethel's fall to the floor.

"Rotten," the entranced medium now mumbled, still clutching the chain.

I tried to coax her back to the chair, but the ghost evidently would have none of it.

"It stinks . . . Where is it?"

"Is this your house?" I asked.

Heavy breathing.

"Yes. Get out!"

"I've come to help you. What is your name?"

"Get out!" the microphone picked up.

"What is it that you want?" I asked.

"My body."

"You've passed on, don't you understand?"

"No . . . I want my body. Where is it?"

I explained again that this was no longer her house, but she kept calling for the return of "her body" in such anger and despair that I began to wonder if it had not been buried on the premises.

"They took it, my body. I saw them, I saw them!"

"You must let go of this house. It is no longer yours," I said.

"No, my house, my house. They took it. My body. I have nothing. Get it. I feel I have one."

I explained that we had lent her a body to speak through for the moment.

"Who are you?" *It* sounded quieter.

"A friend," I replied, "come to help you."

Instead of replying, the entranced medium grabbed the door again.

"Why do you want to open the door?" I asked. It took a moment for the answer to come through trembling lips.

"Go out," she finally said. "I don't know you. Let me go, let me go."

I continued to question the ghost.

"Who are you? Did you live in this house?"

"My house. They took it out. My body is out there!"

I explained about the passage of time.

"You were not well. You've died."

"No, no . . . I wasn't cold."

"You are free to go from this door. Your loved ones, your family, await you outside."

"They hate me."

"No, they have made up with you. Why should they hate you?"

"They took me out the door."

Then, suddenly the medium's expression changed. Had someone come to fetch her?

"Oh, Baba, darling . . . Oh, he loved me."

There was hysterical crying now.

"He's gone . . . My beloved . . . "

"What is his name?"

" *Wain* . . . Where is he . . . Let me go!"

The crying was now almost uncontrollable, so I sent the ghost on her way. At the same time I asked that Albert, Ethel's control on the etheric side of the veil, take over her physical body for the moment to speak to us.

It took a moment or two until Albert was in command. The medium's body visibly straightened out and all traces of a bent old crone vanished. Albert's crisp voice was heard.

"She's a former tenant here, who has not been too well beloved. She also seems to have been carried out before complete death. This has brought her back to try and rectify it and make contact with the physical body. But here is always unhappiness. I believe there was no love toward her as she was older."

"Can you get a name?" I asked.

"If she refuses, I cannot."

"How long ago was this?"

"During the Nineties. Between 1890 and 1900."

"Is this a woman?"

"Yes. "

"Anything peculiar about her appearance?"

"Large eyes, and almost a harelip."

"Why is she concerned about her body?"

"There was no great funeral for her. She was put in a box and a few words were said over her grave. That is part of her problem, that she was thus rejected and neglected."

"Why does she run up to the attic?"

"This was her house, and it was denied to her later in life."

"By whom?"

"By those living here. Relatives to her."

"Her heirs?"

"Those who took it over when she could no longer function. She was still alive."

"Anything else we should know?"

"There is a great deal of hate for anyone in this house. Her last days were full of hate. Should she return, if she is spoken to kindly, she will leave. We will help her."

"Why is she so full of hate?"

"Her grief, her oppressions. She never left her tongue quiet when she was disrupted in her desire to go from her quarters to the rest of the house."

"What was her character?"

"As a young person she was indeed a lady. Later in life, a strong personality, going slightly toward dual personality. She was an autocrat. At the very end, not beloved."

"And her relationship with the servants?"

"Not too friendly. Tyrannical."

"What troubled her about her servants?"

"They knew too much."

"Of what?"

"Her downfall. Her pride was hurt."

"Before that, how was she?"

"A suspicious woman. She could not help but take things from others which she believed were hers by right."

"What did she think her servants were doing?"

"They pried on her secret life. She trusted no one toward the end of life."

"Before she was prevented, as you say, from freely going about the house—did she have any belongings in the attic?"

"Yes, hidden. She trusted no one."

I then suggested that the "instrument" be brought back to herself. A very surprised Ethel Meyers awakened to find herself leaning against the entrance door.

"What's the matter with my lip?" she asked when she was able to speak. After a moment, Ethel Meyers was her old self, and the excursion into Mrs. Wainwright's world had come to an end.

The following morning Molly Smythe called me on the phone. "Remember about Albert's remarks that Mrs. Wainwright was restrained within her own rooms?"

Of course I remembered.

"Well," Molly continued, "we've just made a thorough investigation of all the doors upstairs in the servants' quarters where she spent her last years. They all show evidence of locks having been on them, later removed. *Someone was locked up there for sure.*"

Ironically, death had not released Mrs. Wainwright from confinement. To her, freedom still lay beyond the heavy wooden door with its brass chain.

Now that her spirit self had been taken in hand, perhaps she would find her way out of the maze of her delusions to rejoin her first husband, for whom she had called.

The next time Molly Smythe hears the front door opening, it'll be just her husband coming home from the office. *Or so I thought.*

But the last week of April, 1965, Molly called me again. Footsteps had been heard *upstairs* this time, and the sound of a door somewhere being opened and closed, and of course, on inspection, there was no one *visible* about.

Before I could make arrangements to come out to Rye once again, something else happened. Mr. Smythe was in the bathtub, when a large tube of toothpaste, safely resting well back on a shelf, flew off the shelf by its own volition. No vibration or other *natural* cause could account for it. Also, a hypodermic needle belonging to one of the nurses attending Molly's invalid mother had somehow disappeared.

I promised to bring Sybil Leek to the house. The British medium knew nothing whatever of the earlier history of the case, and I was curious to see if she would make contact with the same or different conditions, as sometimes happens when two mediums are used in the same house. It's like tuning in on different radio wavelengths.

It was a cool, wet day in May when we seated ourselves in a circle upstairs in the "haunted room." Present in addition to the hosts, Sybil Leek, and myself, were Mrs. Betty Salter (Molly's sister); David Ellingson, a reporter from the Port Chester, N.Y., *Item;* Mr. and Mrs. Robert Bendick, neighbors and friends of the Smythes; and Mary Melikian. Mr. Bendick was a television producer specializing in news programs.

Sybil went into hypnotic trance. It took several minutes before anything audible could be recorded.

"Who are you?" I asked.

A feeble voice answered:

"Marion . . . Marion Gernt . . . "

Before going into trance, Sybil had volunteered the information that the name "Grant," or something like it, had been on her mind ever since she set foot into the house.

"What year is this?" I asked.

"1706."

"Who built the house?"

"My father. . . Walden."

She then complained that people in the house were disturbing *her*, and that therefore she was *pulling it down*.

"My face is swollen," she added. "I'm sick . . . Blood."

Suddenly, something went wrong with my reliable tape recorder. In all my previous investigations it had worked perfectly. Now it wouldn't, and some parts of the conversation were not recorded. The wheels would turn and then stop, and then start again, as if someone were sticking their fingers into them at will!

I tried my camera, and to my amazement, I couldn't take any pictures. All of a sudden, the mechanism wouldn't function properly, and the shutter could not be un-cocked. I did not get any photographs. Bob Bendick, after the séance, took a good look at the camera. In a moment it was working fine again. After the séance, too, we tried to make the tape recorder work. It started and then stopped completely.

"The batteries have run out," I explained, confident that there was nothing more than that to it. So we put the machine on house current. Nothing happened. It wasn't the batteries. It was something else.

After we left the "haunted room" and went downstairs, I put the tape recorder into my traveling case. About ten minutes later, I heard a ghostly voice coming from my case. *My* voice. The tape recorder that I had left in a secure turn-off position had started up by itself . . . or . . . so it seemed.

But one can't be sure in haunted houses. *Item* reporter David

Ellingson and Mary Melikian were standing next to me when it happened. John Smythe was wondering if someone had turned on the radio or TV. So much for the instruments that didn't work—temporarily.

But, let us get back to Sybil and the ghost speaking through her. She claimed to have been burned all over in a fire. John Smythe confirmed later that there were traces of a fire in the house that have never been satisfactorily explained.

The ghost seemed confused about it. She was burned, on this spot, in what was then a little house. The place was called Rocher. Her named was spelled M-a-r-i-o-n G-e-r-n-t. She was born at Rodey, eight miles distant. She was not sure about her age. At first she said 29, then it was 57. The house was built by one Dion, of Rocher.

I then tried to explain, as I always do, that the house belonged to someone else and that she must not stay.

"Go away," the ghost mumbled, not at all pleased with the idea of moving. But I insisted. I told her of her husband who wanted her to join him "over there."

"I hate him!" she volunteered, then added—"I start moving things . . . I break things up . . . I want my chair."

"You must not stay here," I pleaded. "You're not wanted here."

"He said that," she replied in a sullen voice. "Alfred did. My husband."

"You must join him and your children."

"I'll stay."

I repeated the incantation for her to leave.

"I can't go. I'm burned. I can't move," she countered.

I explained that these were only memories.

Finally she relented, and said—"I'll need a lot of rags . . . to cover myself."

Gently now, she started to fade.

"I need my chair," she pleaded, and I told her she could have it.

Then she was gone.

Sybil came back now. Still in trance, she responded quickly to my questions about what she saw and felt on the other side of the veil. This is a technique I find particularly effective when used prior to bringing the medium out of trance or from under hypnosis.

"An old lady," Sybil said. "She is quite small. I think she is Dutch. Shriveled. She is very difficult. Can't move. Very unpleasant. Throws things because she can't walk. This is her house. She lived here about three hundred years ago. She wants everything *as it was*. She has marks on her face. She was in a fire."

"Did she die in it?" I asked.

"No. She died near here. Doesn't communicate well."

"There is a box with two hearts, two shields," Sybil said. "It means something to this woman."

"Were there any others around?" I asked.

"Lots, like shadows," Sybil explained, "but this little woman was the one causing the commotion."

"She likes to throw things," Sybil added, and I couldn't help thinking that she had never been briefed on all the objects the ghost had been throwing.

"She doesn't know where any doors are, so she just goes on. The door worries her a lot, because she doesn't know where it is. The front and rear have been changed around."

Sybil, of course, knew nothing of the noises centering around the main door, nor the fact that the rear of the house was once the front.

I told Sybil to send her away, and in a quiet voice, Sybil did so.

The seance was over, at least for the time being.

A little later, we went up to the top floor, where both Molly and Sybil suddenly sensed a strong odor of perfume. I joined them, and I smelled it, too. It was as if *someone were following us about the house!*

But it was time to return to New York. Our hosts offered to drive us to the city.

"Too bad," I said in parting, "that nobody has seen an apparition here. Only sounds seem to have been noticed."

Betty Salter, Mrs. Smythe's perky sister, shook her head.

"Not true," she said. "I was here not so long ago when I saw a black figure downstairs in the dining room. I thought it was Molly, but on checking found that I was quite alone downstairs . . . That is, except for her."

Mrs. Wainwright, of course, was of Dutch ancestry, and the description of the character, appearance, and general impression of the ghost Sybil gave did rather fit Mrs. Wainwright.

Was the 1706 lady an ancestor or just someone who happened to be on the spot when only a small farm house occupied the site?

The Smythes really didn't care whether they have two ghosts or one ghost. They preferred to have none.

The Girl Ghost on Riverside Drive

One day in January of 1965, a gentleman named H. D. Settel called me on the phone to report a ghost in his Victorian apartment on Riverside Drive in New York City. Since I also live on the Drive, it seemed the neighborly thing to do to go have a look. Mr. Settel, who was in his late twenties or early thirties, had lived in the fourth floor walk-up apartment of what was once a small townhouse for some time. He got married and his wife joined him there in October of 1964.

Since moving in, his normally cheerful wife had gone into fits of despondency for which there seemed to be no rational explanation. Spending a lot of time at home, she felt a great anxiety at times, as if something momentous were about to happen. Gradually, the sensation changed to one of dissociation, a desire to leave her physical body. Fighting this tendency, she reported the strange sensations to her husband, who was sympathetic, and suggested she stop fighting the "take-over." When she followed his advice, she found herself crying for no apparent reason.

This was followed by most unusual behavior on her part. In the middle of the night, she sat up in bed and started to talk in a most irritated fashion. Unfortunately, neither of the Settels remembered the substance of her outbreak.

About mid-January, Mrs. Settel was on the threshold of sleep when she heard a curious tapping sound on the dresser. Quickly she turned on the light and the tapping stopped, but she had the fleeting impression that there was someone else in the apartment, and the strange, floating sensation came back.

Her husband also had an unusual experience. He awoke one night toward five in the morning, and asked his wife whether she had screamed. She assured him that she hadn't. Trying to get hold of himself, Settel explained that he had just heard a young girl scream. He had seen a girl dressed in a maid's uniform standing in the doorway of the two-room apartment, looking into the bedroom, and holding a large white dog on a leash. *Her look was one of pure evil.*

Somehow he had the impression that her name was Eudrice, and he felt himself compelled to write down the words "Eudrice was a girl of young looks." Neither phrasing nor handwriting was his own. The Settels had never heard of anyone named Eudrice, so they called the public library and were told that it was a Colombian form of the Greek name Eurydice.

I asked whether either of them had had psychic experiences before coming to the house on Riverside Drive.

On their honeymoon, Mr. Settel saw a very old lady during the night, and described the vision in great detail to his wife the next morning. From the details of appearance, dress, brooch, room, and chair in which he saw her sitting, Mrs. Settel realized that her husband had seen her long-dead grandmother, with whom she had lived as a child. Her husband had never seen a picture of her. Mr. Settel was in the textile business, and Mrs. Settel used to be a radio and television broadcaster.

I offered to visit the house, and did so the last week of February, 1965. The apartment on the fourth floor was done in modern style, and the Settels had made the most of the small area. There was a curious closet that suggested there had once been a door near the entrance to the bedroom. In the old days, the servants' quarters usually were located on the top floors, and this apartment undoubtedly was once just that.

I questioned Mr. Settel about the ghostly maid. Was there any light in the room at the time?

"Well, the sun was just coming up, and I could distinguish her out-line quite clearly. She was a girl in her middle twenties, I'd say," he replied. "She was completely solid and real, not transparent or waver-ing. She had very long black hair, extremely white skin. I was terrified, stared at her for about thirty seconds, just lying there. Next thing, she was gone. We turned on the light, but, of course, there was nobody but us two in the apartment."

"What else have you observed here?" I asked.

"There was, and is, an oppressive heaviness in the atmosphere of this place, and a constant feeling of a presence other than our own," Mr. Settel replied. "Usually at night, between 9 and 3 A.M."

I turned again to Mrs. Settel.

"I almost committed suicide here once, something I would not normally think of," she confided. "Sometimes I seem to be almost pos-sessed—I have the feeling if I allowed myself to leave my physical body, I would not be able to return."

The house had been built in 1897, and bought in 1910 from the builder by a Mrs. Gillen from Detroit. Before the house was built, the area had just been woods. From the time Mrs. Gillen bought the house, around 1910, Wall Streeters and such notables as Thomas Dewey had lived in the house. It had been a townhouse, subdivided by Mrs. Gillen into plush apartments.

There were five floors. The Settels had the fourth floor. A man named Alleyn had come to the house in 1925. From Panama, and mar-ried to a West Indian woman, he died in the house in 1956—he dropped dead, it seems, on the second floor.

For twenty years, the Settel apartment had been owned by a retired Army colonel named Villaflora and his wife. He was from Panama and she was Polish.

The Settels were able to get a lot of information about the building from one of the older tenants, a Mrs. Morgan. The superintendent's wife had committed suicide in the apartment downstairs.

The information thus obtained left a gap between 1897 when the house was built, and 1910 when it was sold to Mrs. Gillen. Thirteen years of mystery. Many interesting tenants coming and going!

I encouraged the Settels to use a Ouija board to see if their combined psychic acumen would obtain anything evidential.

"Did you get anything worthwhile?" I asked. Ouija boards often aren't reliable. It all depends on what checks out, of course.

"Yes indeed," Mr. Settel replied. "We got so much we stopped—in a hurry. The communicator identified herself as Eudrice Fish. She claimed to have come from Germany, and to have died in 1957 by suicide. Much of it was garbled."

I took some photographs of the apartment, but none of them showed anything unusual. I had decided there was nothing more I could do in this case, when I received an urgent call from Mrs. Settel.

"Three nights after your visit, Mr. Holzer," she said, "I was lying in bed. It was about 4 A.M., and I was not asleep, having just turned out the lights. Suddenly, the bedsheet was pulled down from around my neck to below my chest. I did not move or attempt to awaken my husband, who was asleep beside me. A few minutes later, the corner of the pillow beneath my head moved *as though it were being tugged,* and I began to sense a presence. The air seemed heavy and expectant, and briefly I felt myself floating again. To my surprise, nothing further occurred, and I fell asleep in about five minutes after that.

"The night before—it was a Thursday; you were here on Tuesday—I went into the bathroom to find the water running in the sink. Neither of us had left it on. We are quite neat about such things. The bathroom also houses our cat, who seems to behave strangely at times lately. Last Christmas we went out and left the bathroom door open for her to go to her sandbox. On our return it was firmly closed—something the cat could not have done!"

I promised to come again, and this time bring Sybil Leek with me to see if contact with the ghost could be made.

Before I came, Mrs. Settel had a strange dream. She saw a male figure, and received the impression that she was very fond of this unknown man. She believed in him, but he was really quite evil. He seemed to be trying to talk her into something, and sway her. She was wondering if the ghost was trying to tell her something about her own life.

When I brought Sybil Leek to the apartment, a change took place in Sybil's face almost as soon as she set foot inside the door. The Victorian staircase and appointments outside had pleased my antique-loving friend, but when she had settled herself into the easy chair in the larger of the two rooms, she said immediately:

"It's not very pleasant here. I feel a person here who died very badly. It's a man. Something affecting his back. There is a younger person with him. They are dark, curly head, the man has a beard. European, Polish. About 1900. Something was lost here."

We adjourned to the bedroom, and Sybil went into trance. Soon she would be deeply "under."

A heavy male voice announced his presence.

"Oscar."

"Do you live here?" I asked.

"Yes."

"Your second name."

"Tratt. Oscar Tratt."

"Where are you from?"

"Efla. Near Cracow."

"What is your profession?"

"Make shoes. Out of wood. Wood shoes."

"Who lives here with you?"

"Mella. Woman. My *Gnaedige Frau*. My wife."

"Whom do you pay rent to?"

"Flynn. Sammy Flynn."

"What year is this?"

"1902."

"How old are you now?"

"Sixty-three."

"Are you well?"

"No. I'm waiting for Ernst to come back."

"Who is Ernst?"

"Mella's boy."

"Your son?"

"Who knows?"

"Why do you want him to come back?"

"Burn him."

"Why?"

"Took too much money from me." The ghost's voice rose in anger. "She let him take it!"

It wasn't clear whether he worked for Mella or whether she was his wife or both.

I continued the questioning.

"Did you get hurt here?"

"Yes, I broke my back. Ernst . . . his door by the steps, on this floor." Now the ghost broke into tears.

"I'm lost . . . find Ernst."

"Is there anyone else here? A woman perhaps?"

You could imagine the ghost shrugging, if ghosts can shrug.

"Common girl. They come and go. Looking for Ernst. Bad. Takes anybody's money . . . my back . . . bad boy."

"What is his family name?"

"Tratt . . . my son."

Schratt or Tratt—I couldn't be quite sure.

The son was about 35 and single, the ghost claimed. He belonged to the Jewish faith, and was somehow connected with a synagogue on Ninety-sixth Street. He also went to school on Ninety-sixth Street.

The ghostly voice began to falter and Oscar complained that he could not remember some things, and that his back hurt him.

"Did you go to the hospital?" I asked.

"No. Stayed here till they come for me."

"Why are you troubled?"

"Lost a lot of money here. Want to make some more shoes."

I began to send him away, gently, but firmly. After he had slipped out of Sybil's body, the medium's own personality reappeared, called back by me.

I asked Sybil, still entranced, to look around and report to me what she observed.

"There are lots of people at the top of the stairs . . . two men and two women. A man is falling down the stairs . . . and a little girl is crying."

"How old is the little girl?"

"Very pretty, like a little foreign girl. She's a servant. Perhaps 20 years old. She has a gray dress with a high neck. She's very unhappy because of what happened. She was upstairs, then she came down and hid in the cupboard . . . here. She was frightened of the young man that he might hurt her."

"Did she know him well?"

"Very well. He liked her."

"Was there anything between her and the young man?"

"Yes. She liked him, but she liked the old people, too. She used to listen to them quarrel."

"What were her duties in this house?"

"She had to look after a lot of gentlemen who lived in this house, but not really after these two here."

"What was her name?"

"Irene . . . Eurine . . . Erundite . . . Eireene." Sybil's voice expressed uncertainty.

"Why is she here?"

"No place to go."

"How did she die?"

"Very sick in her throat . . . died here. She never told anyone about the old man. My throat's bad . . ." Sybil was taking on the "passing symptoms" of the spectral maid.

"How long ago did she die?"

"1912."

Suddenly another person was speaking to us. A very agitated voice calling for "Mella!" Evidently, the servant girl had taken over. The throat seemed to hurt her still. Eventually she calmed down.

"What is your name?" I asked.

"Erundite." It could have been Erundice, or something like that.

"Where were you born?"

"Here . . . 27 London Place . . . down by the river."

I asked her to repeat her name. It now sounded like "Irene Dyke."

Her mother's name, she said, was Martha, and her father's Mostin Dyke. Or it could have been Austin Dyke. The voice was faint.

She did not know where her father came from. Only that it was far away where there were ships.

"What was your work here?"

"Servant. Laundry maid."

"Were there any pets in the house?"

"There was always something to fall over. Parrot. Ten cats."

"Any dogs in the house?"

"Oh, there was this big old monster . . . he was gray."

"Did you take him out?"

"He followed me."

"What sort of clothes did you wear when you served here?"

"Gray dress, and black apron . . . there is no water in the house, you know. Got to get some across the road. Dog fell into the river."

"What year is this?"

"1907-1908."

"Did you have an affair with Ernst?"

"I'm not going to say."

"Did you see him hurt his father?"

"Yes."

"What did you do after that?"

"I came in with Mella and I waited in the cupboard. I cried. Somebody came, that's why I stayed in the cupboard."

"Was Oscar gone then?"

"Think so. Never saw him again."

Everybody, it would seem, accused Ernst. He came back, and she saw him, but then her throat started to bother her.

"Why are you still here?"

"Mella said wait here in the cupboard."

She thought it was 1913. I coaxed her to leave the closet, and to forget about her bad throat.

"1913 I had my worst bad throat. It was very cold by the river. I went back to the cupboard."

"You're free now," I said. "You may leave this cupboard . . . this house . . . and join your loved ones."

Gradually, the tense body of the medium slackened as the servant girl left.

Soon, Sybil Leek was back to her old self.

"I feel fine," she said, and looked around. She remembered nothing of Oscar or the servant girl.

And there it is. How do you trace the name of a servant girl, even so unusual a name as Eurydice, or Irene Dyke, or whatever it was, in a rooming house in 1913? You can't. Telephones were still rare then, and the directories were far from complete.

Needless to say, Sybil knew nothing whatever about "Eurydice" or that a servant girl had been seen here by Mr. Settel. I had kept all that to myself.

Apparently, Oscar has made his peace with Ernst, and the pale young servant girl is forever out of the cupboard. The spot where Mr. Settel had seen her apparition was indeed where an old cupboard had been made into a walk-in closet. As for the big dog, why, there may be a place for him, too, on the other side. At any rate, the Settels have heard, seen, and felt nothing since Sybil's visit.

The Specter in the Hallway

Port Washington is a busy little town on Long Island, about forty-five minutes from New York City. A lot of people who live there commute daily to their jobs downtown or midtown, and the flavor of the town is perhaps less rustic than other places further out on Long Island. Still, there are a few back roads and quiet lanes that are as quiet and removed from the pace of Main Street as any small town might boast. Such a street is Carlton, and a house in about the middle of the block not far from the waterfront fits the description of a country home to a tee. It is a two-story wooden structure about fifty years old, well-preserved and obviously redecorated from time to time. The house sits back from the street on a plot of land, and all in all, one could easily overlook it if one were not directly searching for it. There is nothing spectacular about this house on Carlton, and to this day the neighbors think of it only as a nice, old house usually owned by nice, respectable people whose lives are no different from theirs and whose problems are never of the kind that make headlines.

But the house behind the nice, old trees has not always been so pleasant looking. When Mr. and Mrs. F. first saw it, it was nothing more than a dilapidated shell of its former splendor, yet it was imbued with a certain nobility that translated itself, in their minds, into the hope of being capable of restoration, provided someone lavished enough care and money on the place. Mr. F. was not wealthy, but he had a going business and could afford a good-sized house.

Mrs. F.'s own father had been involved in the building of the house on Carlton though she did not realize it at the time she first saw it. He had been in the building trade in this town, and Mrs. F. had grown up here. It seemed the natural thing to her to settle in a town she was familiar with, now that their two girls were of school age, and she had to think of the future. The house was for sale and as they walked through it they realized that it had been neglected for some time. The real estate man was properly vague about previous owners, and would say only that it had been built by respectable people fifty-three years ago, and they could have it very reasonably. Real estate agents are not historians, they are not even concerned with the present, but only the future: tomorrow's sale and commission. If the F.'s did not want to buy the old house, sooner or later someone else would, or perhaps the house could be torn down and another one built here. The land was almost more valuable than the house itself. Suburbia was stretching further and further and Port Washington was a most convenient location.

But the F.'s did buy the house in 1961 and even though the place was a shambles, they managed to move in right away and live in it while they were restoring and redecorating it. There were twelve rooms in all, on two floors. A broad staircase with two landings led up to the second story. The second landing led directly into a hallway. To the left was the master bedroom, to the right a second bedroom they turned over to their two girls, aged thirteen and eight. The first few days were busy ones indeed, as the family tried to settle down in unfamiliar surroundings. Mr. F. worked in the city, and the girls were in school mornings, so Mrs. F. was alone in the house a good part of the day. The master bedroom in particular was an eyesore, dark and forbidding as it was, and wholly depressing to her.

She decided to start work immediately on the bedroom, and had it painted white. That caused some problems in the mornings when one wanted to sleep late, for they had morning sun, and the white walls made the room even brighter. But this occasional inconvenience was

213

more than offset by the general cheerfulness the change in color gave the room. Mrs. F. felt optimistic about the house and was sure it would make a splendid home for them.

One day soon after their arrival, she was hanging curtains in the bedroom. Suddenly she felt a hostile glare in back of her and turned to see who had entered the room. There was no one to be seen. And yet, she was sure another person was next to her in the room, a person whose hatred she could literally feel!

Immediately, Mrs. F. put down the curtains and left the house. For a few hours, she went shopping in town. As it became time to return home, she dismissed the whole incident as imagination. She had no interest in the occult even though over the years she had shown a marked degree of ESP powers. Whenever someone close to her, or even a mere acquaintance, was involved in a tragedy, she knew it beforehand. Often she would anticipate what someone was about to say to her, but she had learned to play down this peculiar talent lest people in the community might think her an oddball. If anything, she hated being "different," or causing her husband dismay for leanings that did not sit well with his employers or the people they socialized with.

Shortly after this incident, she was in bed asleep when she awoke to the incessant ringing of the telephone. The telephone was downstairs, so she got up and started on her way down the stairs to answer it. Who would call them at that hour? Theirs was an unlisted number.

She was fully awake as she reached the stairs. The phone was still demanding her attention. As she put one foot onto the top step, she felt herself pushed by unseen hands and fell down to the first landing. As soon as she fell, the telephone stopped ringing. As a consequence of this "accident," she was crippled for several months. Her husband ascribed the fall to her drowsiness, but she knew better. She had felt a hard push in the back: she had not slipped on the stairs. They patiently went over the entire list of those who had their unlisted phone number. None of them had called.

From this moment on, her optimistic outlook about the house changed. She longed for the time she could be outside the house, have the choice of running away from it when she felt like it. But her legs were still bruised and the time passed slowly.

Then one evening, while her husband was away, she sat quietly in the living room downstairs, reading a book. For some unexplainable reason, she suddenly felt that someone was watching her. She lifted her eyes from the book, turned, and glanced up at the stairway. There, at the very spot where she had fallen, stood a man. His face was in the shadows, but he was tall and wearing dark clothes. She stared at the figure with amazement for several moments. When she was fully aware of it, the apparition vanished, as if it had only wanted to let her know of its presence.

Too horrified to move from the chair, Mrs. F. just sat there until her husband returned. She knew the man on the stairs wanted her to come up to him, and she could not bring herself to do it. Neither could she tell her husband what had happened.

Much later, when she confided in him, she found out that he did not think her mad, and his compassion only increased their deep affection for each other.

The larger incidents were accompanied by a continuing plethora of odd sounds, creaking noises on the stairs or in the master bedroom. Most of the latter noises she had heard downstairs in the living room, which is located directly underneath the master bedroom. Old houses make odd noises, she rationalized to herself, and probably the house was just settling. But to make sure, she decided to call in some termite specialists. They came and removed paneling from some of the basement walls in that part of the house and gave the place a thorough examination. As she watched, they inspected the beams and the foundation of the house. They found nothing. The house was neither settling nor shifting, the experts explained, thus removing the pat explanation Mrs. F. had given to herself for the odd noises. She wished she had never called in the termite experts, for now that she knew there were no natural causes for the disturbances, what was she to do?

So far neither her husband nor her children had noticed anything odd, or if they had, they had not said anything to her. Mrs. F. dreaded the thought of discussing such matters with her children. One night she busied herself in the living room after dinner. Her husband was out and the two girls were presumably in their own room upstairs. Suddenly there was a loud thumping and knocking overhead in the master bedroom.

"The girls are out of their beds," she thought, and called up to them to go back to bed immediately. There was no reply. When she went upstairs to check, she found both girls fast asleep in their room. She went back to continue her chores in the living room. Immediately, the noises started up again overhead. Despite her fears that he was up there waiting for her, Mrs. F. went up again. There are seven doors opening onto that hallway and yet she knew immediately which door he was lurking behind: her bedroom's. She turned around and grabbed the banister of the stairs firmly. This time he wasn't going to push her down again. Slowly, she descended the stairs. She knew in her heart the specter would not follow her down. His domain was the upstairs part of the house. She soon realized that the uncanny house guest had his limitations as far as movements were concerned and it gave her unsuspected strength: she knew he could not follow her outside, or even into the living room; there she was safe from him. Often, when she was outside in the yard, she could *feel* him peering out at her, watching, always watching with slow-burning eyes. When she went out to market and closed the door behind her, a wave of hatred hit her from inside the empty house. He resented being left alone. Had the ghostly presence developed an attachment toward her?

Psychic feelings had been a subject studiously avoided by Mrs. F. in her conversations, but when she mentioned her problem accidentally to her mother, she was surprised to find not a questioning gaze but an understanding acknowledgment.

"I too have always felt there is someone in the house," her mother admitted, "but I think it's friendly."

Mrs. F. shook her head. She knew better. Her mother then suggested that a portrait of Jesus be placed in the entrance foyer to ward off "evil influences." Mrs. F. was not religious, but under the circumstances, she was willing to try *anything*. So a portrait of Christ was duly placed in the foyer at the landing. It apparently made a difference, for the presence of the man in black faded away from the spot from that day. However, he was as strongly present as ever in the bedroom.

One night, the F.'s intimate relationship was literally interrupted by the ghostly presence, and it took them years to get over the shock. They could never be sure that they were truly "alone," and even if they moved to another room, Mrs. F. feared the jealous specter would follow them there.

During the day, she continuously felt a call to go up to the bedroom, but she never went when she was alone in the house. That was "his" domain and she had hers in the downstairs area of the house.

One evening, while her husband was taking a shower, she felt encouraged enough to venture alone into the bedroom. A thought ran through her mind, "Why, he isn't here after all!" Scarcely had she finished thinking this, when she clearly heard a voice shout into her ear: "I am here!" And as if to underscore his presence, a necktie rose off its clasp and placed itself on her shoulder!

Mrs. F. tried to behave as if that happened every day of her life. As if speaking to herself she said, aloud, "Oh, stupid tie, falling like that!" But she knew she was not fooling him, that he knew he had terribly frightened her with this performance. That was the straw that broke the camel's back.

The same evening, she and her husband had a quiet discussion about the house. They both loved it and they had spent considerable money and much time in fixing it up. It was most inconvenient to move after four years. But what were they to do? Share it forever with a ghost?

She found that her husband had felt odd in the house for a long time also, and had thought of selling it. While he failed to see how a ghost could possibly harm them—having had plenty of chances to do so and not having done so, apart from the "accident" on the stairs he did not wish to subject his family to any form of terror.

They placed an ad in *The New York Times* and listed their telephone for the first time. At least, Mrs. F. thought, if the phone rang now, it would be someone calling about the house, not a ghost trying to rouse her from deep sleep.

But houses do not always sell overnight, especially old ones. They wanted to sell, but they didn't want to lose money. Still, having made the decision to move eventually made things easier for Mrs. F. She was even able to muster some curiosity about their unbidden guest and made inquiries among neighbors, especially some old-timers who knew the area well. Nobody, however, could shed any light on the situation. Of course, Mrs. F. did not come right out and speak of her experiences in the house, but she did ask if any unusual events had ever occurred in it or what the history of the house had been. Still, the result was not encouraging and they realized they would leave the house without ever knowing who it was that had caused them to do so!

Then Mrs. F. discovered that she was, after all, a natural medium. She would simply sit back in her chair and rest and gradually her senses would become clouded and another person would speak to her directly. It felt as if that person was very close to her and she could take the message the way a telegraph operator takes down a telegram, word for word, and the more relaxed she was and the less fear she showed, the more clear the words were to her.

She fought this at first, but when she realized that it meant only more discomfort, she relaxed. Then, too, she knew the specter would not harm her—their relationship had somehow changed since the time he had pushed her down those stairs. She felt no fear of him only compassion, and sensed he needed help badly and that she was willing to extend it to him.

While they were waiting for a buyer for the house, she would often lapse into semiconsciousness and commune with her tormentor, who had now become a kind of friend. Gradually she pieced together his story and began to understand his reasons for doing what he was doing to get her attention. As she listened to the ghost, his anger gave way to an eagerness to be heard and understood.

A young man of about seventeen and of small build, he had light hair, high cheekbones, and deep-set eyes. At that tender age he was lost at sea as a member of the Canadian Navy. A French Canadian, he desperately wanted her to deliver a message to someone, but she was unable to clearly get either the message or the name of the individual. Perhaps the very emotionalism of such an attempt caused its failure. But she did get the name of his ship, something that sounded to her like Tacoma. Whenever Mrs. F. awoke from her trance state, that word stood strongly in her mind. Finally she wrote to the United States Navy Department. Unfortunately, there had been four ships by that name! But her intuition told her to contact the Canadian Navy also. The boy had been lost during World War II, while on duty, and while she did not have his name, perhaps the name of the ship could be traced. No, the Canadians did not have a Tacoma, but they did have a mine sweeper named Transcona, and instantly she felt that was the right ship. It had been in war service from 1942 to 1945.

As her inquiries went on, she felt the atmosphere in the house change. It was no longer heavy with frustration, but the presence was still there. Twice during that month he was seen by the children. The thirteen-year-old girl wanted to know who was "the big boy walking back and forth in the hallway all night" and Mrs. F. told her she had dreamed it all, for there was no one in the hall that night.

Either unable or unwilling to question this explanation, the girl thought no further about it. The younger girl, however, reported another incident a few days later. She knew nothing of her older sister's experience. As she was bathing, a young man had opened the door and then turned and walked into her sister's room! Mrs. F. was hard put to explain that away, but eventually she managed to calm the little girl.

But despite Mrs. F.'s willingness to let him communicate with her in trance, the young man was unable to give either his name or that of the person whom he tried to reach. His own emotions were still pitched high from the sudden death he had suffered and he did not know how to cope with the situation.

In October of that year, after a wait of half a year, they sold the house. The new owner was a police officer in retirement with little sympathy for ghosts. Both he and his wife are devout Catholics and any suggestion at investigating the disturbances to free the unfortunate soul was simply not answered. The F.'s had moved out but stayed in town, so they could not help hearing some of the local gossip concerning the house.

If the police officer was bothered by the ghostly sailor, he certainly did not speak of it to anyone. But word of mouth was that the new owners were disappointed with their new home: it wasn't as happy a place to them as they had anticipated when they bought it. Lots of little things were going wrong seemingly for no apparent reasons. For example, no matter how often the bedroom door was opened, it would "close itself."

Mrs. F. smiled wryly, for she remembered that the ghostly sailor always liked that door open. She, too, had closed it to have privacy, only to find it opened by unseen hands. Finally, she understood that it wasn't curiosity or evil thoughts on his part, but simple loneliness, the desire not to be shut out from the world, and she left it open, the way he wanted it.

How long would it take the lieutenant to understand the lad? She mused and wondered if perhaps he could leave the house of his own free will, now that he had told her at least part of his story. Shortly after, the F.'s moved to Florida. They wondered if the power for the manifestations had come from their young daughters, who were at the time of "poltergeist" age. If so, the police lieutenant will have the same problem: he has six children of his own.

The Vindication of Aaron Burr

Very few historical figures have suffered as much from their enemies or have been as misunderstood and persistently misrepre-
sented as the onetime Vice-President of the United States, Aaron
Burr, whose contributions to American independence are frequently
forgotten while his later troubles are made to represent the man.

Burr was a lawyer, a politician who had served in the Revolutionary
forces and who later established himself in New York as a candidate of
the Democratic-Republican party in the elections of 1796 and 1800.
He didn't get elected in 1796, but in 1800 he received exactly as many
electoral votes as Thomas Jefferson. When the House of
Representatives broke the tie in Jefferson's favor, Burr became Vice-
President.

Burr soon realized that Jefferson was his mortal enemy. He found
himself isolated from all benefits, such as political patronage, normally
accruing to one in his position, and he was left with no political future
at the end of his term. Samuel Engle Burr, a descendant of Theodosia
Barstow Burr, Aaron's first wife, and the definitive authority on Aaron
Burr himself, calls him "the American Phoenix," and truly he was a man
who frequently rose from the ashes of a smashed career.

Far from being bitter over the apparent end of his career, Burr
resumed his career by becoming an independent candidate for governor
of New York. He was defeated, however, by a smear campaign in which
both his opponents, the Federalists, and the regular Democratic-
Republican party took part.

"Some of the falsehoods and innuendoes contained in this campaign literature," writes Professor Burr in his namesake's biography, "have been repeated as facts down through the years. They have been largely responsible for much of the unwarranted abuse that has heaped upon him since that time."

Aside from Jefferson, his greatest enemies were the members of the Hamilton-Schuyler family, for in 1791 Burr had replaced Alexander Hamilton's father-in-law, General Philip Schuyler, as the senator from New York. Hamilton himself had been Burr's rival from the days of the Revolutionary War, but the political slurs and statements that had helped to defeat Burr in 1804, and that had been attributed to Hamilton, finally led to the famed duel.

In accepting Burr's challenge, Hamilton shared the illegality of the practice. He had dueled with others before, such as Commodore Nicholson, a New York politician, in 1795. His own son, Philip Hamilton, had died in a duel with New York lawyer George Eacker in 1801. Thus neither party came to Weehawken, New Jersey that chilly July morning in 1804 exactly innocent of the rules of the game.

Many versions have been published as to what happened, but to this day the truth is not clear. Both men fired, and Burr's bullet found its mark. Whether or not the wound was fatal is difficult to assess today. The long voyage back by boat, and the primitive status of medicine in 1804 may have been contributing factors to Hamilton's death.

That Alexander Hamilton's spirit was not exactly at rest I proved a few years ago when I investigated the house in New York City where he had spent his last hours after the duel. The house belonged to his physician, but it has been torn down to make room for a modern apartment house. Several tenants have seen the fleeting figure of the late Alexander Hamilton appear in the house and hurry out of sight, as if trying to get someplace fast. I wonder if he was trying to set the record straight, a record that saw his opponent Burr charged with *murder* by the State of New Jersey.

Burr could not overcome the popular condemnation of the duel; Hamilton had suddenly become a martyr, and he, the villain. He decided to leave New York for a while and went to eastern Florida, where he became acquainted with the Spanish colonial system, a subject that interested him very much in his later years. Finally he returned to Washington and resumed his duties as the Vice-President of the United States.

In 1805 he became interested in the possibilities of the newly acquired Louisiana Territory, and tried to interest Jefferson in developing the region around the Ouachita River to establish there still another new state.

Jefferson turned him down, and finally Burr organized his own expedition. Everywhere he went in the West he was cordially received. War with Spain was in the air, and Burr felt the United States should prepare for it and, at the right time, expand its frontiers westward.

Since the government had shown him the cold shoulder, Burr decided to recruit a group of adventurous colonists to join him in establishing a new state in Louisiana Territory and await the outbreak of the war he felt was sure to come soon. He purchased four hundred thousand acres of land in the area close to the Spanish-American frontier and planned on establishing there his dream state, to be called Burrsylvania.

In the course of his plans, Burr had worked with one General James Wilkinson, then civil governor of Louisiana Territory and a man he had known since the Revolutionary War. Unfortunately Burr did not know that Wilkinson was actually a double agent, working for both Washington and the Spanish government.

In order to bolster his position with the Jefferson government, Wilkinson suggested to the President that Burr's activities could be considered treasonable. The immediate step taken by Wilkinson was to alter one of Burr's coded letters to him in such a way that Burr's statements could be used against him. He sent the document along with an alarming report of his own to Jefferson in July of 1806.

Meanwhile, unaware of the conspiracy against his expedition, Burr's colonists arrived in the area around Natchez, when a presidential proclamation issued by Jefferson accused him of treason. Despite an acquittal by the territorial government of Mississippi, Washington sent orders to seize him.

Burr, having no intention of becoming an insurrectionist, disbanded the remnants of his colonists and returned east. On the way he was arrested and taken to Richmond for trial. The treason trial itself was larded with paid false witnesses, and even Wilkinson admitted having forged the letter that had served as the basis for the government's case. The verdict was "not guilty," but the public, inflamed against him by the all-powerful Jefferson political machine, kept condemning Aaron Burr.

Under the circumstances, Burr decided to go to Europe. He spent the four years from 1808 to 1812 traveling abroad, eventually returning to New York, where he reopened his law practice with excellent results.

The disappearance at sea the following year of his only daughter Theodosia, to whom he had been extremely close, shattered him; his political ambitions vanished, and he devoted the rest of his life to an increasingly successful legal practice. In 1833 he married for the second time—his first wife, Theodosia's mother, also called Theodosia, having died in 1794. The bride was the widow of a French wine merchant named Stephen Jumel, who had left Betsy Jumel a rich woman indeed. It was a stormy marriage, and ultimately Mrs. Burr sued for divorce. This was granted on the 14th of September 1836, the very day Aaron Burr died. Betsy never considered herself anything but the *widow* of the onetime Vice-President, and she continued to sign all documents as Eliza B. Burr.

Burr had spent his last years in an apartment at Port Richmond, Staten Island, overlooking New York Harbor. His body was laid to rest at Princeton, the president of which for many years had been Burr's late father, the Reverend Aaron Burr.

I had not been familiar with any of this until after the exciting events of June 1967, when I was able to make contact with the person of Aaron Burr through psychic channels.

My first encounter with the name Aaron Burr came in December of 1961. I was then actively investigating various haunted houses in and around New York City as part of a study grant by the Parapsychology Foundation. My reports later grew into a popular book called *Ghost Hunter*.

One day a publicist named Richard Mardus called my attention to a nightclub on West Third Street doing business as the Cafe Bizarre. Mr. Mardus was and is an expert on Greenwich Village history and lore, an he pointed out to me that the club was actually built into remodeled stables that had once formed part of Richmond Hill, Aaron Burr's estate in New York City. At the time of Burr's occupancy this was farmland and pretty far uptown, as New York City went.

But Mardus did not call to give me historical news only: Psychic occurrences had indeed been observed at the Burr stables, and he asked me to took into the matter. I went down to have a look at the edifice. It is located on a busy side street in the nightclub belt of New York, where after dark the curious and the tourists gather to spend an evening of informal fun. In the daytime, the street looks ugly and ordinary, but after dark it seems to sparkle with an excitement of its own.

The Cafe Bizarre stood out by its garish decor and posters outside the entrance, but the old building housing it, three stories high, was a typical early nineteenth-century stone building, well preserved and showing no sign of replacement of the original materials.

Inside, the place had been decorated by a nightmarish array of paraphernalia to suggest the bizarre, ranging from store dummy arms to devil's masks, and colorful lights played on this melee of odd objects suspended from the high ceiling. In the rear of the long room was a stage, to the left of which a staircase led up to the loft; another staircase was in back of the stage, since a hayloft had occupied the rear portion of the building. Sawdust covered the floor, and perhaps three dozen assorted tables filled the room.

It was late afternoon and the atmosphere of the place was cold and empty, but the feeling was nevertheless that of the unusual—uncanny, somehow. I was met by a pretty, dark-haired young woman, who turned out to be the owner's wife, Mrs. Renée Allmen. She welcomed me to the Cafe Bizarre and explained that her husband, Rick, was not exactly a believer in such things as the psychic, but that she herself had indeed had unusual experiences here. On my request, she gave me a written statement testifying about her experiences.

In the early morning of July 27, 1961, at 2:20 A.M., she and her husband were locking up for the night. They walked out to their car when Mrs. Allmen remembered that she had forgotten a package inside. Rushing back to the cafe, she unlocked the doors again and entered the deserted building. She turned on the lights and walked toward the kitchen, which is about a third of the way toward the rear of the place. The cafe was quite empty, and yet she had an eerie sensation of not being alone. She hurriedly picked up her package and walked toward the front door again. Glancing backward into the dark recesses of the cafe, she then saw the apparition of a man, staring at her with piercing black eyes. He wore a ruffled shirt of the kind nobody wears in our time, not even in colorful Greenwich Village. He seemed to smile at her, and she called out to him, "Who is it?"

But the figure never moved or reacted.

"What are you doing here?" Renée demanded, all the while looking at the apparition.

There was no answer, and suddenly Renée's courage left her. Running back to the front door, she summoned her husband from the car, and together they retuned to the cafe. Again unlocking the door, which Renée had shut behind her when she fled from the specter, they discovered the place to be quite empty. In the usual husbandly fashion, Mr. Allmen tried to pass it off as a case of nerves or tired eyes, but his wife would not buy it. She knew what she had seen, and it haunted her for many years to come.

Actually, she was not the first one to see the gentleman in the white ruffled shirt with the piercing black eyes. One of their waiters also had seen the ghost and promptly quit. The Village was lively enough without psychic phenomena, and how much does a ghost tip?

I looked over the stage and the area to the left near the old stairs to see whether any reflecting surface might be blamed for the ghostly apparition. There was nothing of the sort, nothing to reflect light. Besides, the lights had been off in the rear section, and those in the front were far too low to be seen anywhere but in the immediate vicinity of the door.

Under the circumstances I decided to arrange for a visit with psychic Ethel Johnson Meyers to probe further into this case. This expedition took place on January 8, 1962, and several observers from the press were also present.

The first thing Mrs. Meyers said, while in trance, was that she saw three people in the place, psychically speaking. In particular she was impressed with an older man with penetrating dark eyes, who was the owner. The year, she felt, was 1804. In addition, she described a previous owner named Samuel Bottomslee, and spoke of some of the family troubles this man had allegedly had in his lifetime. She also mentioned that the house once stood back from the road, when the road passed farther away than it does today. This I found to be correct.

"I'm an Englishman and I have my rights here," the spirit speaking through Mrs. Meyers thundered, as we sat spellbound. Later I found out that the property had belonged to an Englishman before it passed into Burr's hands.

The drama that developed as the medium spoke haltingly did not concern Aaron Burr, but the earlier settlers. Family squabbles involving Samuel's son Alan, and a girl named Catherine, and a description of the building as a stable, where harness was kept, poured from Ethel's lips. From its looks, she could nor have known consciously that this was once a stable.

The period covered extended from 1775 to 1804, when another personality seemed to take over, identifying himself as one John Bottomsley. There was some talk about a deed, and I gathered that all was not as it should have been. It seemed that the place had been sold, but that the descendants of Samuel Bottomslee didn't acknowledge this too readily.

Through all this the initials A.B. were given as prominently connected with the spot.

I checked out the facts afterward; Aaron Burr's Richmond Hill estate had included these stables since 1797. Before that the area belonged to various British colonials.

When I wrote the account of this séance in my book *Ghost Hunter*, I thought I had done with it. And I had, except for an occasional glance at the place whenever I passed it, wondering whether the man with the dark, piercing eyes was really Aaron Burr.

Burr's name came to my attention again in 1964 when I investigated the strange psychic phenomena at the Morris-Jumel Mansion in Washington Heights, where Burr had lived during the final years of his life as the second husband of Mme. Betsy Jumel. But the spectral manifestations at the Revolutionary house turned out to be the restless shades of Mme. Jumel herself and that of her late first husband, accusing his wife of having murdered him.

One day in January of 1967 I received a note from a young lady named Alice McDermott. It concerned some strange experiences of hers at the Cafe Bizarre—the kind one doesn't expect at even so oddly decorated a place. Miss McDermott requested an interview, and on February 4 of the same year I talked to her in the presence of a friend.

She had been "down to the Village" for several years as part of her social life—she was now twenty—and visited the Bizarre for the first time in 1964. She had felt strange, but could not quite pinpoint her apprehension.

"I had a feeling there was *something* there, but I let it pass, thinking it must be my imagination. But there was something on the balcony over the stage that seemed to stare down at me—I mean something besides the dummy suspended from the ceiling as part of the decor."

At the time, when Alice was sixteen, she had not yet heard of me or my books, but she had had some ESP experiences involving premonitions and flashes of a psychic nature.

Alice, an only child, works as a secretary in Manhattan. Her father is a barge officer and her mother an accountant. She is a very pretty blonde with a sharp mind and a will of her own. Persuaded to try to become a nun, she spent three months in a Long Island convent, only to discover that the religious life was not for her. She then returned to New York and took a job as a secretary in a large business firm.

After she left the convent she continued her studies also, especially French. She studied with a teacher in Washington Square, and often passed the Cafe Bizarre on her way. Whenever she did, the old feeling of something uncanny inside came back. She did not enter the place, but walked on hurriedly.

But on one occasion she stopped, and something within her made her say, "Whoever you are in there, you must be lonely!" She did not enter the place despite a strong feeling that "someone wanted to say hello to her" inside. But that same night, she had a vivid dream. A man was standing on the stage, and she could see him clearly. He was of medium height, and wore beige pants and black riding boots. His white shirt with a kind of Peter Pan collar fascinated her because it did not look like the shirts men wear today. It had puffy sleeves. The man also had a goatee, that is, a short beard, and a mustache.

"He didn't took dressed in today's fashion, then?"

"Definitely not, unless he was a new rock'n'roll star."

But the most remarkable features of this man were his dark, piercing eyes, she explained. He just stood there with his hands on his hips, looking at Alice. She became frightened when the man kept looking at her, and walked outside.

That was the end of this dream experience, but the night before she spoke to me, he reappeared in a dream. This time she was speaking with him in French, and also to an old lady who was with him. The lady wore glasses, had a pointed nose, and had a shawl wrapped around her—"Oh, and a plain gold band on her finger."

The lady also wore a Dutch type white cap, Alice reported. I was fascinated, for she had described Betsy Jumel in her old age—yet how could she connect the ghostly owner of Jumel Mansion with her Cafe Bizarre experience? She could not have known the connection, and yet it fit perfectly. Both Burr and Betsy Jumel spoke French fluently, and often made use of that language.

"Would you be able to identify her if I showed you a picture?" I asked.

"If it were she," Alice replied, hesitatingly.

I took out a photograph of a painting hanging at Jumet Mansion, which shows Mme. Jumel in old age.

I did not identify her by name, merely explaining it was a painting of a group of people I wanted her to took at.

"This is the lady," Alice said firmly, "but she is younger looking in the picture than when I saw her."

What was the conversation all about? I wanted to know.

Apparently the spirit of Mme. Jumel was pleading with her on behalf of Burr, who was standing by and watching the scene, to get in touch with *me!* I asked Alice, who wants to be a commercial artist, to draw a picture of what she saw. Later, I compared the portrait with known pictures of Aaron Burr. The eyes, eyebrows, and forehead did indeed resemble the Burr portraits. But the goatee was not known.

After my initial meeting with Alice McDermott, she wrote to me again. The dreams in which Burr appeared to her were getting more and more lively, and she wanted to go on record with the information thus received. According to her, Aaron poured his heart out to the young girl, incredible though this seemed on the face of it.

The gist of it was a request to go to "the white house in the country" and find certain papers in a metal box. "This will prove my innocence. I am not guilty of treason. There is written proof. Written October 18, 1802 or 1803." The message was specific enough, but the papers of course were long since gone.

The white house in the country would be the Jumel Mansion.

I thanked Alice and decided to hold another investigation at the site of the Cafe Bizarre, since the restless spirit of the late Vice-President of the United States had evidently decided to be heard once more.

At the same time I was approached by Mel Bailey of Metromedia Television to produce a documentary about New York haunted houses, and I decided to combine these efforts and investigate the Burr stables in the full glare of television cameras.

On June 12, 1967 I brought Sybil Leek down to the Bizarre, having flown her in from California two days before. Mrs. Leek had no way of knowing what was expected of her, or where she would be taken. Nevertheless, as early as June 1, when I saw her in Hollywood, she had remarked to me spontaneously that she "knew" the place I would take her to on our next expedition—then only a possibility and she described it in detail. On June 9, after her arrival in New York, she telephoned and again gave me her impressions.

"I sense music and laughter and drumbeat," she began, and what better is there to describe the atmosphere at the Cafe Bizarre these nights? "It is a three-story place, not a house but selling something; two doors opening, go to the right-hand side of the room and something is raised up from the floor, where the drumbeat is."

Entirely correct; the two doors lead into the elongated room, with the raised stage at the end.

"Three people . . . one has a shaped beard, aquiline nose, he is on the raised part of the floor; very dark around the eyes, an elegant man, lean, and there are two other people near him, one of whom has a name starting with a Th...."

In retrospect one must marvel at the accuracy of the description, for surely Sybil Leek had no knowledge of either the place, its connection with Burr, nor the description given by the other witnesses of the man they had seen there.

This was a brief description of her first impressions given to me on the telephone. The following day I received a written account of her nocturnal impressions from Mrs. Leek. This was still two days before she set foot onto the premises!

In her statement, Mrs. Leek mentioned that she could not go off to sleep late that night, and fell into a state of semiconsciousness, with a small light burning near her bed. Gradually she became aware of the smell of fire, or rather the peculiar smell when a gun has just been fired. At the same time she felt an acute pain, as if she had been wounded in the left side of the back.

Trying to shake off the impression, Mrs. Leek started to do some work at her typewriter, but the presence persisted. It seemed to her as if a voice was trying to reach her, a voice speaking a foreign language and calling out a name, Theo.

I questioned Mrs. Leek about the foreign language she heard spoken clairvoyantly.

"I had a feeling it was French," she said.

Finally she had drifted into deeper sleep. But by Saturday afternoon the feeling of urgency returned. This time she felt as if someone wanted her to go down to the river, not the area where I live (uptown), but "a long way the other way," which is precisely where the Burr stables were situated.

Finally the big moment had arrived. It was June 12, and the television crews had been at work all morning in and around the Cafe Bizarre to set up cameras and sound equipment so that the investigation could be recorded without either hitch or interruption. We had two cameras taking turns, to eliminate the need for reloading. The central area beneath the "haunted stage" was to be our setting, and the place was reasonably well lit, certainly brighter than it normally is when the customers are there at night.

Everything had been meticulously prepared. My wife Catherine was to drive our white Citroën down to the Bizarre with Sybil at her side. Promptly at 3:00 P.M. the car arrived, Sybil Leek jumped out and was greeted at the outer door by me, while our director, Art Forrest, gave the signal for the cameras to start. "Welcome to the Cafe Bizarre," I intoned and led my psychic friend into the semidark inside. Only the central section was brightly lit.

I asked her to walk about the place and gather impressions at will.

"I'm going to those drums over there," Sybil said firmly, and walked toward the rear stage as if she knew the way.

"Yes—this is the part. I feel cold. Even though I have not been here physically, *I know this place.*"

"What do we have to do here, do you think?" I asked.

"I think we have to relieve somebody, somebody who's waited a long time."

"Where is this feeling strongest?"

"In the rear, where this extra part seems to be put on."

Sybil could not know this, but an addition to the building was made years after the original had been constructed, and it was precisely in that part that we were now standing.

She explained that there was more than one person involved, but one in particular was dominant; that this was something from the past, going back into another century. I then asked her to take a chair, and Mrs. Renée Allmen and my wife Catherine joined us around a small table.

This was going to be a séance, and Sybil was in deep trance within a matter of perhaps five minutes, since she and I were well in tune with one another, and it required merely a signal on my part to allow her to "slip out."

At first there was a tossing of the head, the way a person moves when sleep is fitful.

Gradually, the face changed its expression to that of a man, a stern face, perhaps even a suspicious face. The hissing sound emanating from her tightly closed lips gradually changed into something almost audible, but I still could not make it out.

Patiently, as the cameras ground away precious color film, I asked "whoever it might be" to speak louder and to communicate through the instrument of Mrs. Leek.

"Theo!" the voice said now. It wasn't at all like Sybil's own voice.

"Theo . . . I'm lost . . . where am I?" I explained that this was the body of another person and that we were in a house in New York City.

"Where's Theo?" the voice demanded with greater urgency. "Who are you?"

I explained my role as a friend, hoping to establish contact through the psychic services of Mrs. Leek, then in turn asked who the communicator was. Since he had called out for Theo, he was not Theo, as I had first thought.

"Bertram Delmar. I want Theo," came the reply.

"Why do you want Theo?"

"Lost."

Despite extensive search I was not able to prove that Bertram Delmar ever existed or that this was one of the cover names used by Aaron Burr; but it is possible that he did, for Burr was given to the use of code names during his political career and in sensitive correspondence.

What was far more important was the immediate call for Theo, and the statement that she was "lost." Theodosia Burr was Burr's only daughter and truly the apple of his eye. When she was lost at sea on her way to join him, in 1813, he became a broken man. Nothing in the up-and-down life of the American Phoenix was as hard a blow of fate than the loss of his beloved Theo.

The form "Theo," incidentally, rather than the full name Theodosia, is attested to by the private correspondence between Theodosia and her husband, Joseph Alston, governor of South Carolina. In a rare moment of foreboding, she had hinted that she might soon die. This letter was written six months before her disappearance in a storm at sea and was signed, "Your wife, your fond wife, Theo."

After the séance, I asked Dr. Samuel Engle Burr whether there was any chance that the name Theo might apply to some other woman.

Dr. Burr pointed out that the Christian name Theodosia occurred in modern times only in the Burr family. It was derived from Theodosius Bartow, father of Aaron Burr's first wife and mother of the girl lost at sea. The mother had been Theodosia the elder, after her father, and the Burrs had given their only daughter the same unusual name.

After her mother's passing in 1794, the daughter became her father's official hostess and truly "the woman in the house." More than that, she was his confidante and shared his thoughts a great deal more than many other daughters might have. Even after her marriage to Alston and subsequent move to Carolina, they kept in touch, and her family was really all the family he had. Thus their relationship was a truly close one, and it is not surprising that the first thought, after his "return from the dead," so to speak, would be to cry out for his Theo!

I wasn't satisfied with his identification as "Bertram Delmar," and insisted on his real name. But the communicator brushed my request aside and instead spoke of another matter.

"Where's the gun?"

"What gun?"

I recalled Sybil's remark about the smell of a gun having just been fired. I had to know more.

"What are you doing here?"

"Hiding."

"What are you hiding from?"

"You."

Was he mistaking me for someone else?

"I'm a friend," I tried to explain, but the voice interrupted me harshly.

"You're a soldier."

In retrospect one cannot help feeling that the emotionally disturbed personality was reliving the agony of being hunted down by U.S. soldiers prior to his arrest, confusing it, perhaps, in his mind with still another unpleasant episode when he was being hunted, namely, after he had shot Hamilton!

I decided to pry farther into his personal life in order to establish identity more firmly.

"Who is Theo? What is she to you?"

"I have to find her, take her away . . . it is dangerous, the French are looking for me."

"Why would the French be looking for you?" I asked in genuine astonishment. Neither I nor Mrs. Leek had any notion of this French connection at that time.

"Soldiers watch...."

Through later research I learned that Burr had indeed been in France for several years, from 1808 to 1812. At first, his desire to have the Spanish American colonies freed met with approval by the then still revolutionary Bonaparte government. But when Napoleon's brother Joseph Napoleon was installed as King of Spain, and thus also ruler of the overseas territories, the matter became a political horse of another color; now Burr was advocating the overthrow of a French-owned government, and that could no longer be permitted.

Under the circumstances, Burr saw no point in staying in France, and made arrangements to go back to New York. But he soon discovered that the French government wouldn't let him go so easily. "All sorts of technical difficulties were put in his way," writes Dr. Samuel Engle Burr, "both the French and the American officials were in agreement to the effect that the best place for the former Vice-President was within the Empire of France." Eventually, a friendly nobleman very close to Napoleon himself managed to gee Burr out. But it is clear that Burr was under surveillance all that time and probably well aware of it!

I continued my questioning of the entity speaking through an entranced Sybil Leek, the entity who had glibly claimed to be a certain Bertram Delmar, but who knew so many things only Aaron Burr would have known.

What year was this, I asked.

"Eighteen ten."

In 1810, Burr had just reached France. The date fit in well with the narrative of soldiers watching him.

"Why are you frightened?" I asked.

"The soldiers, the soldiers...."

"Have you done anything wrong?"

"Who are you?"

"I'm a friend, sent to help you!"

"Traitor! You ... you betrayed me...."

"Tell me what you are doing, what are you trying to establish here?"

"Traitor!"

Later, as I delved into Burr's history in detail, I thought that this exchange between an angry spirit and a cool interrogator might refer to Burr's anger at General James Wilkinson, who had indeed posed as a friend and then betrayed Burr. Not the "friend" ostensibly helping Burr set up his western colony, but the traitor who later caused soldiers to be sent to arrest him. It certainly fit the situation. One must understand that in the confused mental state a newly contacted spirit personality often finds himself, events in his life take on a jumbled and fragmentary quality, often flashing on the inner mental screen like so many disconnected images from the emotional reel of his life. It is then the job of the psychic researcher to sort it all out.

I asked the communicator to "tell me all about himself" in the hope of finding some other wedge to get him to admit he was Aaron Burr.

"I escaped . . . from the French."

"Where are the French?"

"Here."

This particular "scene" was apparently being re-enacted in his mind, during the period he lived in France.

"Did you escape from any particular French person?" asked.

"Jacques ... de la Beau...."

The spelling is mine. It might have been different, but it *sounded* like "de la Beau."

"Who is Jacques de la Beau?"

Clenched teeth, hissing voice—"I'm . . . not . . . telling you. Even . . . if you . . . kill me."

I explained I had come to free him, and what could I do for him?

"Take Theo away . . . leave me . . . I shall die. . . ."

Again I questioned him about his identity. Now he switched his account and insisted he was French, born at a place called Dasney near Bordeaux. Even while this information was coming from the medium's lips, I felt sure it was a way to throw me off his real identity. This is not unusual in some cases. When I investigated the ghost of General Samuel Edward McGowan some years ago, it took several weeks of trance sessions until he abandoned an assumed name and admitted an identity that could later be proven. Even the discarnates have their pride and emotional "hangups," as we say today.

The name Jacques de la Beau puzzled me. After the séance, I looked into the matter and discovered that a certain Jacques Prevost (pronounced pre-voh) had been the first husband of Aaron Burr's first wife, Theodosia. Burr, in fact, raised their two sons as his own, and there was a close link between them and Burr in later years. But despite his French name, Prevost was in the British service.

When Burr lived in New York, he had opened his home to the daughter of a French admiral, from whom she had become separated as a consequence of the French Revolution. This girl, Natalie, became the close companion of Burr's daughter Theodosia, and the two girls considered themselves sisters. Natalie's father was Admiral de Lage de Volade. This name, too, has sounds similar to the "de la Beau" I thought I had understood. It might have been "de la voh" or anything in between the two sounds. Could the confused mind of the communicator have drawn from both Prevost and de Lage de Volade? Both names were of importance in Burr's life.

"Tell me about your wife," I demanded now.

"No. I don't like her."

I insisted, and he, equally stubborn, refused.

"Is she with you?" I finally said.

"Got rid of her," he said, almost with joy in the voice.

"Why ?"

No good to me . . . deceived me . . . married. . . ."

There was real disdain and anger in the voice now.

Clearly, the communicator was speaking of the second Mrs. Burr. The first wife had passed away a long time before the major events in his life occurred. It is perfectly true that Burr "got rid of her" (through two separations and one divorce action), and that she "deceived him," or rather tricked him into marrying her: He thought she was wealthier than she actually was, and their main difficulties were about money. In those days people did not always marry for love, and it was considered less immoral to have married someone for money than to deceive someone into marrying by the prospects of large holdings when they were in fact small. Perhaps today we think differently and even more romantically about such matters; in the 1830s, a woman's financial standing was as negotiable as a bank account.

The more I probed, the more excited the communicator became; the more I insisted on identification, the more cries of "Theo! Theo!" came from the lips of Sybil Leek.

When I had first broached the subject of Theo's relationship to him, he had quickly said she was his sister. I brought this up again, and in sobbing tones he admitted this was not true. But he was not yet ready to give me the full story.

"Let me go," he sobbed.

"Not until you can go in peace," I insisted. "Tell me about yourself. You are proud of yourself, are you not?"

"Yes," the voice came amid heavy sobbing, "the disgrace ... the disgrace...."

"I will tell the world what you want me to say. I'm here as your spokesman. Use this chance to tell the world your side of the facts!"

There was a moment of hesitation, then the voice, gentler, started up again.

"I . . . loved . . . Theo. . . . I have to . . . find her. . . ."

The most important thought, evidently, was the loss of his girl. Even his political ambitions took a back seat to his paternal love.

"Is this place we're n part of your property?"

Forlornly, the voice said,

"I had . . . a lot . . . from the river . . . to here."

Later I checked this statement with Mrs. Leroy Campbell, curator of the Morris-Jumel Mansion, and a professional historian who knew the period well.

"Yes, this is true," Mrs. Campbell confirmed, "Burr's property extended from the river and Varick Street eastward."

"But the lot from the river to here does not belong to a Bertram Delmar," I said to the communicator. "Why do you wish to fool me with names that do not exist?"

I launched this as a trial balloon. It took off.

"She calls *me* Bertram," the communicator admitted now. "I'm not ashamed of my name."

I nodded. "I'm here to help you right old wrongs, but you must help me do this. I can't do it alone."

"I didn't kill . . . got rid of her. . . ." he added, apparently willing to talk.

"You mean, your wife?"

"Had to."

"Did you kill *anyone*?" I continued the line of discussion.

"Killed . . . to protect . . . not wrong!"

"How did you kill?"

242

"A rifle. . . ."

Was he perhaps referring to his service in the Revolutionary War? He certainly did some shooting then.

But I decided to return to the "Bertram Delmar" business once more. Constant pressure might yield results.

"Truthfully, will you tell us who you are?"

Deliberately, almost as if he were reading an official communique, the voice replied, "I am Bertram Delmar and I shall not say *that name*. . . ."

"You must say 'that name' if you wish to see Theo again." I had put it on the line. Either cooperate with me, or I won't help you. Sometimes this is the only way you can get a recalcitrant spirit to "come across"— when this cooperation is essential both to his welfare and liberation and to the kind of objective proof required in science.

There was a moment of ominous quiet. Then, almost inaudibly, the communicator spoke.

"An awful name . . . *Arnot*."

After the investigation I played the sound tapes back to make sure of what I had heard so faintly. It was quite clear. "The communicator" had said "*Arnot*."

My first reaction was, perhaps she is trying to say Aaron Burr and pronounce Aaron with a broad ah. But on checking this out with both Mrs. Campbell and Dr. Burr I found that such a pronunciation was quite impossible. The night after the séance I telephoned Dr. Burr at his Washington home and read the salient points of the transcript to him.

When I came to the puzzling name given by the communicator I asked whether Arnot meant anything inasmuch as I could not find it in the published biographies of Burr. There was a moment of silence on the other end of the line before Dr. Burr spoke.

"Quite so," he began. "It is not really generally known, but Burr did use a French cover name while returning from France to the United States, in order to avoid publicity. That name was *Arnot*."

But back to the Cafe Bizarre and our investigation.

Having not yet realized the importance of the word Arnot, I continued to insist on proper identification.

"You must cleanse yourself of ancient guilt," I prodded.

"It is awful . . . awful. . . ."

"Is Theo related to you?"

"She's mine."

"Are you related to her?"

"Lovely . . . little one . . . *daughter*."

Finally, the true relationship had come to light.

"If Theo is your daughter, then you are not 'Bertram.'"

"You tricked me . . . go away . . . or else I'll kill you!" The voice sounded full of anger again.

"If you're not ashamed of your name, then I want to hear it from your lips."

Again, hesitatingly, the voice said,

"*Arnot*."

"Many years have gone by. Do you know what year we're in now?"

"Ten. . . ."

"It is not 1810. A hundred fifty years have gone by."

"You're mad."

"You're using the body of a psychic to speak to us...."

The communicator had no use for such outrageous claims.

"I'm not going to listen. . . ."

But I made him listen. I told him to touch the hair, face, ears of the "body" he was using as a channel and to see if it didn't feel strange indeed.

Step by step, the figure of Sybil, very tensed and angry a moment before, relaxed. When the hand found its way to the chin, there was a moment of startled expression:

"No beard...."

I later found that not a single one of the contemporary portraits of Aaron Burr shows him with a chin beard. Nevertheless, Alice McDermott had seen and drawn him with a goatee, and now Sybil Leek, under the control of the alleged Burr, also felt for the beard that was not there any longer.

Was there ever a beard?

"Yes," Dr. Burr confirmed, "there was, although this, too, is almost unknown except of course to specialists like myself. On his return from France, in 1812, Burr sported a goatee in the French manner."

By now I had finally gotten through to the person speaking through Sybil Leek, that the year was 1967 and not 1810.

His resistance to me crumbled.

"You're a strange person," he said, "I'm tired."

"Why do you hide behind a fictitious name?"

"People . . . ask . . . too many . . . questions."

"Will you help me clear your name, not Bertram, but your real name?"

"I was betrayed."

"Who is the President of the United States in 1810?" I asked and regretted it immediately. Obviously this could not be an evidential answer. But the communicator wouldn't mention the hated name of the rival.

"And who is Vice-President?" I asked.

"Politics . . . are bad . . . they kill you . . . I would not betray anyone. . . I was wronged . . . politics . . . are bad. . . ."

How true!

"Did you ever kill anyone?" I demanded.

"Not wrong . . . to kill to . . . preserve. . . . I'm alone."

He hesitated to continue.

"What did you preserve? Why did you have to kill another person?"

"*Another* . . . critical . . . I'm not talking!"

"You must talk. It is necessary for posterity."

"I tried . . . to be . . . *the best*. . . . I'm not a traitor . . . soldiers . . . beat the drum . . . then you die . . . politics!!"

As I later listened to this statement again and again, understood the significance of it, coming, as it did, from a person who had not yet admitted he was Aaron Burr and through a medium who didn't even know where she was at the time.

He killed to *preserve his honor*—the accusations made against him in the campaign of 1804 for the governorship of New York were such that they could not be left unchallenged. Another was indeed *critical* of him, Alexander Hamilton being that person, and the criticisms such that Burr could not let them pass.

He "tried to be the best" also—tried to be President of the United States, got the required number of electoral votes in 1800, but deferred to Jefferson, who also had the same number.

No, he was not a traitor, despite continued inference in some history books that he was. The treason trial of 1807 not only exonerated the former Vice President of any wrongdoing, but heaped scorn and condemnation on those who had tried him. The soldiers beating the drum prior to an execution could have become reality if Burr's enemies had won; the treason incident under which he was seized by soldiers on his return from the West included the death penalty if found guilty. That was the intent of his political enemies, to have this ambitious man removed forever from the political scene.

"Will you tell the world that you are not guilty?" I asked.

"I told them . . . trial . . . I am not a traitor, a murderer. . . ."

I felt it important for him to free himself of such thoughts if he were to be released from his earthbound status.

"I . . . want to die . . ." the voice said, breathing heavily.

"Come, I will help you find Theo," I said, as promised.

But there was still the matter of the name. I felt it would help "clear the atmosphere" if I could get him to admit he was Burr.

I had already gotten a great deal of material, and the séance would be over in a matter of moments. I decided to gamble on the last minute or two and try to shock this entity into either admitting he was Burr or reacting to the name in some telling fashion.

I had failed in having him speak those words even though he had given us many incidents from the life of Aaron Burr. There was only one more way and I took it. "Tell the truth," I said, "are you Aaron Burr?"

It was as if I had stuck a red hot poker into his face. The medium reeled back, almost upsetting the chair in which she sat. With a roar like a wounded lion, the voice came back at me,

"Go away . . . GO AWAY!! . . . or I'll kill you!"

"You will not kill me," I replied calmly. "You will tell me the truth."

"I will kill you to preserve my honor!!"

"I'm here to preserve your honor. I'm your friend."

The voice was like cutting ice.

"You said that once before."

"You are Aaron Burr, and this is part of your place."

"I'M BERTRAM!"

I did not wish to continue the shouting match.

"Very well," I said, "for the world, then, let it be Bertram, if you're not ready to face it that you're Burr."

"I'm Bertram . . ." the entity whispered now.

"Then go from this place and join your Theo. Be Bertram for her."

"Bertram . . . you won't tell?" The voice was pleading.

"Very well." He would soon slip across the veil, I felt, and there were a couple of points I wanted to clear up before. I explained that he would soon be together with his daughter, leaving here after all this time, and I told him again how much time had elapsed since his death.

"I tarried . . . I tarried . . ." he said, pensively.

"What sort of a place did you have?" I asked.

"It was a big place . . . with a big desk . . . famous house. . . ." But he could not recall its name.

Afterward, I checked the statement with Mrs. Campbell, the curator at the Morris-Jumel Mansion. "That desk in the big house," she explained, "is right here in our Burr room. I was originally in his law office." But the restless one was no longer interested in talking to me.

"I'm talking to Theo . . ." he said, quietly now, "in the garden. . . . I'm going for a walk with Theo . . . go away."

Within a moment, the personality who had spoken through Sybil Leek for the past hour was gone. Instead, Mrs. Leek returned to her own self, remembering absolutely nothing that had come through her entranced lips.

"Lights are bright," was the first thing she said, and she quickly closed her eyes again.

But a moment later, she awoke fully and complained only that she felt a bit tired.

I wasn't at all surprised that she did.

Almost immediately after I had returned home, I started my corroboration. After discussing the most important points with Dr. Samuel Engle Burr over the telephone, I arranged to have a full transcript of the séance sent to him for his comments.

So many things matched the Burr personality that there could hardly be any doubt that it vas Burr we had contacted. "I'm not a traitor and a murderer," the ghostly communicator had shouted. "Traitor and murderer" were the epithets thrown at Burr in his own lifetime by his enemies, according to Professor Burr, as quoted by Larry Chamblin in the *Allentown Call-Chronicle.*

Although he is not a direct descendant of Aaron Burr, the Washington educator is related to Theodosia Barstow Burr, the Vice-President's first wife. A much-decorated officer in both world wars, Professor Burr is a recognized educator and the definitive authority on his famous namesake. In consulting him, I was getting the best possible information.

Aaron Burr's interest in Mexico, Professor Burr explained, was that of a liberator from Spanish rule, but there never was any conspiracy against the United States government. "That charge stemmed from a minor incident on an island in Ohio. A laborer among his colonists pointed a rifle at a government man who had come to investigate the expedition."

Suddenly, the words about the rifle and the concern the communicator had shown about it became clear to me: It had led to more serious trouble for Burr.

Even President Wilson concurred with those who felt Aaron Burr had been given a "raw deal" by historical tradition. Many years ago he stood at Burr's grave in Princeton and remarked, "How misunderstood . . . how maligned!"

It is now 132 years since Burr's burial, and the falsehoods concerning Aaron Burr are still about the land, despite the two excellent books by Dr. Samuel Engle Burr and the discreet but valiant efforts of the Aaron Burr Association which the Washington professor heads.

In piecing together the many evidential bits and pieces of the trance session, it was clear to me that Aaron Burr had at last said his piece. Why had he not pronounced a name he had been justly proud of in his lifetime? He had not hesitated to call repeatedly for Theo, identify her as his daughter, speak of his troubles in France and of his political career—why this insistence to remain the fictitious Bertram Delmar in the face of so much proof that he was indeed Aaron Burr?

All the later years of his life, Burr had encountered hostility, and he had learned to be careful whom he chose as friends, whom he could trust. Gradually, this bitterness became so strong that in his declining years he felt himself to be a lonely, abandoned old man, his only daughter gone forever, and no one to help him carry the heavy burden of his life. Passing across into the nonphysical side of life in such a state of mind, and retaining it by that strange quirk of fate that makes some men into ghostly images of their former selves, he would not abandon that one remaining line of defense against his fellow men: his anonymity.

Why should he confide in me, a total stranger, whom he had never met before, a man, moreover, who spoke to him under highly unusual conditions, conditions he himself neither understood nor accepted? It seemed almost natural for Burr's surviving personality to be cautious in admitting his identity.

But his ardent desire to find Theo was stronger than his caution; we therefore were able to converse more or less freely about this part of his life. And so long as he needed not say he was Burr, he felt it safe to speak of his career also, especially when my questions drove him to anger, and thus lessened his critical judgment as to what he could say and what he should withhold from me.

Ghosts are people, too, and they are subject to the same emotional limitations and rules that govern us all.

Mrs. Leek had no way of obtaining the private, specific knowledge and information that had come from her entranced lips in this investigation; I myself had almost none of it until after the séance had ended, and thus could not have furnished her any of the material from my own unconscious mind. And the others present during the séance—my wife, Mrs. Allmen, and the television people knew even less about all this.

Neither Dr. Burr nor Mrs. Campbell were present at the Cafe Bizarre, and their minds, if they contained any of the Burr information, could not have been tapped by the medium either, if such were indeed possible.

Coincidence cannot be held to account for such rare pieces of information as Burr's cover name Arnot, the date, the goatee, and the very specific character of the one speaking through Mrs. Leek, and his concern for the clearing of his name from the charges of treason and murder.

That we had indeed contacted the restless and unfree spirit of Aaron Burr at what used to be his stables is now the only physical building still extant that was truly his own, I do not doubt in the least.

The defense rests, and hopefully, so does a happier Aaron Burr, now forever reunited with his beloved daughter Theodosia.

When the Dead Stay On

Nothing is so exasperating as a dead person in a living household. I mean a ghost has a way of disturbing things far beyond the powers held by the wraith while still among the quick. Very few people realize that a ghost is not someone out to pester you for the sake of being an annoyance, or to attract attention for the sake of being difficult. Far from it. We know by now that ghosts are unhappy beings caught between two states and unable to adjust to either one.

Most people "pass over" without difficulty and are rarely heard from again, except when a spiritualist insists on raising them, or when an emergency occurs among the family that makes intervention by the departed a desired, or even necessary, matter.

They do their bit, and then go again, looking back at their handiwork with justified pride. *The dead are always among us*, make no mistake about that. They obey their own set of laws that forbids them to approach us or let us know their presence except when conditions require it. But they can do other things to let us feel them near, and these little things can mean a great deal when they are recognized as sure signs of a loved one's nearness.

Tragedies create ghosts through shock conditions, and nothing can send them out of the place where they found a sad end except the realization of their own emotional entanglement. This can be accomplished by allowing them to communicate through trance. But there are also cases in which the tragedy is not sudden, but gradual, and the unnatural attachment to physical life creates the ghost syndrome. The person who refuses to accept peacefully the transition called death, and holds on to material surroundings, becomes a ghost when these feelings of resistance and attachment become psychotic.

Such persons will then regard the houses they lived and died in as still theirs, and will look on later owners or tenants as merely unwanted intruders who must be forced out of the place by any means available. The natural way to accomplish this is to show themselves to the living as often as possible, to assert their continued ownership. If that won't do it, move objects, throw things, make noises—let them know whose house this is!

The reports of such happenings are many. Every week brings new cases from reliable and verified witnesses, and the pattern begins to emerge pretty clearly.

A lady from Ridgewood, New York, wrote to me about a certain house on Division Avenue in Brooklyn, where she had lived as a child. A young grandmother, Mrs. Petre had a good education and an equally good memory. She remembered the name of her landlord while she was still a youngster, and even the names of all her teachers at Public School 19. The house her family had rented consisted of a basement, parlor floor, and a top floor where the bedrooms were located.

On a certain warm October day, she found herself in the basement, while her mother was upstairs. She knew there was no one else in the house. When she glanced at the glass door shutting off the stairs, with the glass pane acting almost like a mirror, she saw to her amazement a man peeking around the doorway. Moments before she had heard heavy footsteps coming down the stairs, and wondered if someone had gotten into the house while she and her mother had been out shopping. She screamed and ran out of the house, but did not tell her family about the stranger.

Sometime after, she sat facing the same stairs in the company of her brother and sister-in-law, when she heard the footsteps again and the stranger appeared. Only this time she got a good look at him and was able to describe his thin, very pale face, his black hair, and the black suit and fedora hat he wore.

Nobody believed the girl, of course, and even the landlady accused her of imagining all this. But after a year, her father became alarmed at his daughter's nervousness and decided to move. Finally, the landlady asked for details of the apparition, and listened as the girl described the ghost she had seen.

"My God," the landlady, a Mrs. Grimshaw, finally said. "I knew that man—he hanged himself on the top floor!"

* * *

Sometimes the dead will only stay on until things have been straightened out to their taste. Anna Arrington was a lady with the gift of mediumship who lived in New York State. In 1944, her mother-in-law, a woman of some wealth, passed on in Wilmington, North Carolina, and was buried there. There was some question about her will. Three days after her death, Mrs. Arrington was awakened from heavy sleep at 3 A.M. by a hand touching hers.

Her first thought was that one of her two children wanted something. On awakening, however, she saw her mother-in-law in a flowing white gown standing at the foot of her bed. While her husband continued to snore, the ghost put a finger to Mrs. Arrington's lips and asked her not to awaken her son, but to remember that the missing will was in the dining room of her house on top of the dish closet under a sugar bowl. Mrs. Arrington was roundly laughed at by her husband the next morning, but several days later his sister returned from Wilmington (the Arringtons lived in New York City at the time) and confirmed that the will had indeed been found where the ghost had indicated.

* * *

Back in the 1960s, I was approached by a gentleman named Paul Herring, who was born in Germany, and who lived in a small apartment on Manhattan's Eastside as well as in a country house in Westchester County, New York. He was in the restaurant business and not given to dreaming or speculation. He struck me as a simple, solid citizen. His aged mother, also German-born, lived with him, and a large German shepherd dog completed the household.

Mr. Herring was not married, and his mother was a widow. What caused them to reach me was the peculiar way in which steps were heard around the Westchester house when nobody was walking. On three separate occasions, Mrs. Herring saw an apparition in her living room.

"It was sort of blackish," she said, "but I recognized it instantly. It was my late husband."

The "black outline" of a man also appeared near light fixtures, and there were noises in the house that had no natural origins.

"The doors are forever opening and closing by themselves," the son added. "We're going crazy trying to keep up with that spook."

Their bedspreads were being pulled off at night. They were touched on the face by an unseen hand, especially after dark.

The September before, Mrs. Herring was approaching the swinging doors of the living room, when the door moved out by itself and met her! A table in the kitchen moved by its own volition in plain daylight.

Her other son, Max, who lived in Norfolk, Virginia, always left the house in a hurry because "he can't breathe" in it. Her dog, Noxy, was forever disturbed when they were out in the Westchester house.

"How long has this been going on, Mrs. Herring?" I asked.

"About four years at least," the spunky lady replied, "but my husband died ten years ago."

It then developed that he had divorced her and married another woman, and there were no surviving children from that union. Still, the "other woman" had kept all of Mr. Herring Sr.'s money—no valid will was ever found. Was the ghost protesting this injustice to his companion of so many years? Was he regretting his hasty step divorcing her and marrying another?

The Herrings weren't the only ones to hear the footsteps. A prospective tenant who came to rent the country house fled after hearing someone walk *through a closed door.*

*   *   *

Mrs. E. F. Newbold seems to have been followed by ghosts since childhood as if she were carrying a lamp aloft to let the denizens of the nether world know she had the sixth sense.

"I'm haunted," she said. "I've been followed by a 'what's it' since I was quite young. It simply pulls the back of my skirt. No more than that, but when you're alone in the middle of a room, this can be awfully disconcerting."

I thought of Grandma Thurston's ghost, and how she had pulled my elbow a couple of years before while I was investigating an empty room in a pre-Colonial house in Connecticut, and I couldn't agree more. Mrs. Newbold's family had psychic experiences also. Her little girl had felt a hand on her shoulder. It ran in the family.

"My husband's aunt died in Florida, while I was in New Jersey. We had been very close, and I said good-bye to her body here at the funeral at 10 A.M. At 9 P.M. I went into my kitchen and though I could not see her, I *knew* she was sitting at the table, staring at my back, and pleading with me."

"What about this skirt pulling?"

"It has followed me through a house, an apartment, a succession of rented rooms, two new houses, and two old houses. I've had a feeling of not being alone, and of sadness. I've also felt a hand on my shoulder, and heard pacing footsteps, always overhead.

"The next house we lived in was about 35 years old, had had only one owner, still alive, and no one had died there. It looked like a haunted house, but it was only from neglect. We modernized it, and *then* it started! Pulling at my skirt went on fairly often. One night when I was alone, that is, my husband was out of town and our three children were sound asleep—I checked them just before and just after—I was watching TV in the living room, when I heard the outside cellar door open. I looked out the window to see if someone was breaking in, since I had locked the door shortly before. While I was watching, I heard it close firmly. The door didn't move, however. This door had a distinctive sound so I couldn't have mistaken it.

"I went back to my seat and picked up my scissors, wishing for a gun. I was sure I heard a prowler. Now I heard slow footsteps come up from the cellar, through the laundry room, kitchen, into the living room, right past me, and up the stairs to the second floor. They stopped at the top of the stairs, and I never heard it again. Nor do I want to. Those steps went past me, no more than five feet away, and the room was empty. Unfortunately, I have no corroboration, but I was wide awake and perfectly sober!"

So much for the lady from Harrington Park, New Jersey.

*   *   *

Miss Margaret C. and her family lived in what surely was a haunted house, so that I won't give her full name. But here is her report.

"In December of 1955, just two days before Christmas, I traveled to Pennsylvania to spend the holidays with my sister and her husband. They lived on the second floor (the apartment I am now renting) of a spacious mid-Victorian-style home built around a hundred years ago.

"Due to the death of my sister's mother-in-law, who had resided on the first floor of the house, the occasion was not an entirely joyous one, but we came for the sake of my brother-in-law.

"Having come all the way from Schenectady, New York, we retired between ten-thirty and eleven o'clock. The room I slept in was closest to the passage leading to the downstairs, and the two were separated only by a door.

"Once in bed, I found it rather difficult to sleep. As I lay there, I heard a piano playing. It sounded like a very old piano and it played church music. I thought it quite strange that my brother-in-law's father would be listening to his radio at that hour, but felt more annoyed than curious.

"The next morning, as we were having coffee, I mentioned this to my sister. She assured me that her father-in-law would *not* be listening to the radio at that hour and I assured *her* that I *had* heard piano music. It was then she mentioned the old piano her husband's mother had owned for many years and which sat in the downstairs front room.

"We decided to go and have a look at it. The dust that had settled on the keyboard was quite thick, and as definite as they could possibly be were the imprints of someone's fingers. Not normal fingers, but apparently quite thin and bony fingers. My sister's mother-in-law had been terribly thin and she loved to play her piano, especially church music. There was positively no one else in the house who even knew how to play the piano, except my mother, who lived with my sister and her husband."

*　　*　　*

Another New Jersey lady named Louise B., whose full name and address I have in my files, told me of an experience she will never forget.

"I cannot explain why I am sending this on to you, merely that I feel compelled to do so, and after many years of following my compulsions, as I call them, must do so.

"My mother had a bachelor cousin who died and was buried around

Valentine's Day, 1932. He had lived with two maiden aunts in Ridgewood, New Jersey, for most of his lifetime. He was a well-known architect in this area. He designed local monuments, one of which is standing in the Park in Ridgewood today. He was short of stature, with piercing eyes and a bushy gray full beard, and he smoked too many cigars. I was not quite 14 years old when he passed away.

"My parents decided to spare me the burial detail, and they left me at home on the way to the cemetery with instructions to stay at home until they returned. They planned on attending the burial, going back to the house with my great-aunts and then coming home before dinner, which in our house was 6 P.M.

"I have no recollection of what I did with my time in the afternoon, but remember that just before dusk I had gone indoors and at the time I was in our dining room, probably setting the table for dinner, as this was one of my chores.

"We had three rooms downstairs: the living room faced north and ran the full length of the house, while the kitchen and dining room faced southeast and southwest respectively, and a T-shaped partition divided the rooms. There was a large archway separating the dining and living rooms.

"I don't recall when I became aware of a 'presence.' I didn't see anything with my eyes, rather I felt what I 'saw,' or somehow sensed it and my sense 'saw.' This is not a good explanation, but about the closest I can come to what I felt.

"This presence was not in any one spot in the room, but something that was gradually surrounding me, like the air that I was breathing, and it was frightening and menacing and very evil and stronger, and somehow the word *denser* seemed to apply and I knew that it was 'Uncle' Oscar. I could feel him coming at me from every direction (like music that gets louder and louder), and my senses 'saw' him as he had been dressed in the casket, with a red ribbon draped across his chest, only he was alive and I was aware of some terrible determination on his part and suddenly I knew that somehow he was trying to 'get inside me' and I began to back away. I don't recall speaking, nor his speaking to me. I just knew what his intention was and who he was. I last remember screaming helplessly and uselessly at him to go away. I do not know how long this lasted. I only know that suddenly he was gone, and my parents came into the room. I was hysterical, they tell me, and it took some doing to quiet me."

Many years later Mrs. B. discovered that "Uncle" Oscar had died a raving maniac to the last.

*   *   *

Grace Rivers was a secretary by profession, a lady of good background, and not given to hallucinations or emotional outbursts. I had spoken with her several times and always found her most reluctant to discuss what to her seemed incredible.

It seemed that on weekends, Miss Rivers and another secretary, by the name of Juliet, were the house guests of their employer, John Bergner, in Westbrook, Connecticut. Miss Rivers was also a good friend of this furniture manufacturer, a man in his middle fifties. She had joined the Bergner firm in 1948, six years after John Bergner had become the owner of a country house built in 1865.

Bergner liked to spend his weekends among his favorite employees, and sometimes asked some of the office boys as well as his two secretaries to come up to Connecticut with him. All was most idyllic until the early 1950s, when John Bergner met an advertising man by the name of Philip Mervin. This business relationship soon broadened into a social friendship, and before long Mr. Mervin was a steady and often self-invited house guest in Westbrook.

At first, this did not disturb anyone very much, but when Mervin noticed the deep and growing friendship between Bergner and his right-hand girl, something akin to jealousy prompted him to interfere with this relationship at every turn. What made this triangle even more difficult for Mervin to bear was the apparent innocence with which Bergner treated Mervin's approaches. Naturally, a feeling of dislike grew into hatred between Miss Rivers and the intruder, but before it came to any open argument, the advertising man suddenly died of a heart attack at age 51.

But that did not seem to be the end of it by a long shot.

Soon after his demise, the Connecticut weekends were again interrupted, this time by strange noises no natural cause could account for. Most of the uncanny experiences were witnessed by both girls as well as by some of the office boys, who seemed frightened by it all. With the detachment of a good executive secretary, Miss Rivers lists the phenomena:

Objects moving in space.

Stones hurried at us inside and outside the house.

Clanging of tools in the garage at night (when nobody was there).

Washing machine starting up at 1 A.M., *by itself.*

Heavy footsteps, banging of doors, in the middle of the night.

Television sets turning themselves on and off at will.

A spoon constantly leaping out of a cutlery tray.

The feeling of a cold wind being swept over one.

And there was more, much more.

When a priest was brought to the house to exorcise the ghost, things only got worse. Evidently the deceased had little regard for holy men.

Juliet, the other secretary, brought her husband along. One night in 1962, when Juliet's husband slept in what was once the advertising man's favorite guest room, he heard clearly a series of knocks, as if someone were hitting the top of the bureau. Needless to say, her husband had been alone in the room, and he did not do the knocking.

It became so bad that Grace Rivers no longer looked forward to those weekend invitations at her employer's country home. She feared them. It was then that she remembered, with terrifying suddenness, a remark the late Mr. Mervin had made to her fellow workers.

"If anything ever happens to me and I die, I'm going to walk after those two girls the rest of their lives!" he had said.

Miss Rivers realized that he was keeping his word.

Her only hope was that the ghost of Mr. Mervin would someday be distracted by an earlier specter that was sharing the house with him. On several occasions, an old woman in black had been seen emerging from a side door of the house. A local man, sitting in front of the house during the weekdays when it was unoccupied—Bergner came up only on weekends—was wondering aloud to Miss Rivers about the "old lady who claimed she occupied the back part of the house." He had encountered her on many occasions, always seeing her disappear into the house by that same, seldom-used, side door. One of the office boys invited by Tom Bergner also saw her around 1:30 A.M. on a Sunday morning, when he stood outside the house, unable to go to sleep. When she saw him she said hello, and mentioned something about money, then disappeared into a field.

Grace Rivers looked into the background of the house and discovered that it had previously belonged to a very aged man who lived there with his mother. When she died, he found money buried in the house, but he claimed his mother had hidden more money that he had never been able to locate. Evidently the ghost of his mother felt the same way about it, and was still searching. For that's how it is with ghosts sometimes—they become forgetful about material things.

Mid-Atlantic

How the Little Girl Ghost Was Sent Out to Play

Ed Harvey ran a pretty good talk show called "Talk of Philadelphia" on WCAU radio. It was the sort of program people listened to in their homes and cars. They listened in large numbers. I know, for the telephone calls came in fast and furious in the show's final half hour, when calls from the public were answered on the air.

One day in April, 1965, Ed and his charming wife, Marion, went to a cocktail party at a friend's house. There he got to talking to Jack Buffington, who was a regional director of a world-wide relief organization and a pretty down-to-earth fellow, as Ed soon found out. Somehow the talk turned to ghosts, and Buffington had a few things to say on that subject since he lived in a haunted house. At that point, Ed Harvey asked permission for Sybil Leek and myself to come down and have a go at the house.

We arrived at Buffington's house on Lansdowne Avenue, in Lansdowne, a Philadelphia suburb, around 10 o'clock. It was a little hard to find in the dark, and when we got there it did not look ghostly at all, just a nice old Victorian house, big and sprawling. Jack Buffington welcomed us at the door.

As I always do on such occasions, I asked Sybil to wait in another room where she could not hear any of the conversation, while I talked to those who had had experiences in the house.

After Sybil had graciously left, we seated ourselves and took inventory. What I saw was a tastefully furnished Victorian house with several wooden staircases and banisters, and lots of fine small antiques. Our host was joined by his dark-haired Italian-born wife, and two friends from his office. My wife Catherine immediately made friends with Mrs. Buffington, and then we started to find out what this was all about.

The Buffingtons, who had a four-year-old daughter named Allegra, had come to the house just nine months before. A lot had happened to them in those nine months.

"We came home from a trip to Scranton," Jack Buffington began, "and when we got back and I inserted the key in the front door, the hall light went on by itself. It has two switches, one on the upstairs level, so I raced upstairs to see who was in the house, but there was no one there. Periodically this happens, and I thought it was faulty wiring at first, but it has been checked and there is nothing wrong with it. The cellar light and the light in the third floor bathroom also go on and off by themselves. I've seen it, and so have my wife and our little girl."

"Anything else happening here?" I asked casually.

"There are many things that go bump in the night here. The first noise that happened recurrently was the sound of an old treadle sewing machine, which is heard on the average of once every month. This happens in a small room on the second floor, which we now use as a dressing room, but which may well have been a sewing room at one time."

I walked up the narrow stairs and looked at the little room. It had all the marks of a Victorian sewing room where tired servants or a worried mother worked at the clothes for her child.

"It's always around three in the morning, and it awakens us," Mr. Buffington continued, "and then there are footsteps and often they sound like children's footsteps."

"Children's footsteps?"

"Yes, and it is rather startling," Mr. Buffington added, "since we do have a small child in the house and inevitably go and check that it isn't she who is doing it. It never is."

"Is it downstairs?"

"All over the place. There are two stories, or three flights, including the basement. And there are a front and back stairway. There is never any pattern about these things. There may be a lot of happenings at the same time, then there is nothing for weeks, and then it starts again."

"Outside of the child's footsteps, did you ever have any indication of a grown-up presence?" I asked.

"Well, I saw the figure of a woman in the doorway of the dining room, walking down this hall, and through these curtains here, and I heard footsteps in conjunction with it. I thought it was my wife, and I called to her. I was hanging a picture in the dining room at the time. No answer. I was getting annoyed and called her several times over, but there was no response. Finally she answered from the second floor—she had not been downstairs at all."

"What happened to the other woman in the meantime?"

"I walked in here—the hall—and there was no one here."

"How was she dressed?"

"She had on a long skirt, looking like a turn-of-the-century skirt, and she did have her hair on top of her head, and she was tall and slender. "

Mrs. Buffington is not very tall, but she does wear dark clothes.

"It was a perfectly solid figure I saw—nothing nebulous or transparent," our host added. "The spring lock at the entrance door was locked securely. "

"Did anyone else see an apparition here?"

"My brother met a woman on the stairway—that is, the stairway leading to the third floor. He was spending the night with us, around Thanksgiving time. There was a party that evening and he mistook her for a guest who had somehow remained behind after all the other guests had gone home. She passed him going *up* while he was coming *down*, and she walked into his room, which he thought odd, so he went back to ask if he could help her, but there wasn't anybody there!"

Jack Buffington gave a rather nervous laugh.

I took a good look at the upstairs. Nobody could have gotten out of the house quickly. The stairs were narrow and difficult to negotiate, and the back stairs, in the servants' half of the house, were even more difficult. Anyone descending them rapidly was likely to slip and fall. The two brothers hadn't talked much about all this, I was told, since that time.

"Our little girl must be seeing her, too, for she frequently says she is going up to play with her lady friend," Jack Buffington said.

I started to wander around the house to get the feeling of it. The house was built in 1876 to the specifications of George Penn, a well-known local builder. Although it was now a duplex, it was originally a townhouse for just one family.

The upper stories contained several small, high-ceilinged rooms, and there was about them the forbidding atmosphere of a mid-Victorian house in a small town. The Buffingtons had furnished their house with taste, and the Italian background of the lady of the house was evident in the works of art and antiques strewn about the house.

As I soon discovered, tragedy had befallen the house on Lansdowne Avenue at least twice as far as it was known. The original builder had a sister who suffered from mental illness and was hospitalized many times. She also spent many years in this house. Then a family named Hopkins came to live in it, and it was at that time that the house was divided into two parts. Incidentally, no manifestations had been reported from the other half of the house. About six years before—the exact time was none too clear, and it may be further back—a family named Johnson rented the half now occupied by the Buffingtons. They had a retarded child, a girl, *who was kept locked up in a room on the third floor.* She died in her early teens, they say, in a hospital not far away. Then the house stood empty, looking out onto quiet Lansdowne Avenue with an air of tragedy and secret passion.

Three years went by before the Buffingtons, returning from Italy, took over the house.

"Have there been any unusual manifestations on the third floor?" I asked Mr. Buffington.

"Just one. Something carries on in the trunk up on the third floor. The trunk is empty and there is no reason for those frightful noises. We have both heard it. It is above where the child sleeps."

Mr. Buffington added that a book he read at night in bed often disappeared and showed up in the most peculiar spots around the house— spots that their little four year old couldn't possibly reach. On one occasion, he found it in a bathroom; at least once it traveled from his room upstairs to the top bookshelf downstairs, all by itself.

"My impression of this ghost," Mr. Buffington said, "is that it means no harm. Rather, it has the mischievousness of a child."

I now turned my attention to petite Mrs. Buffington, who had been waiting to tell me of her own most unusual experiences in the house.

"On one occasion I was on the second floor with the child," she began. "It was about eleven in the morning, and I was taking some clothes out of a cabinet. The back staircase is very close to this particular cabinet. Suddenly, I very distinctly heard a voice calling 'Mamma,' a voice of a person standing close to the cabinet, and it as a girl's voice, a child's voice and quite distinct—in fact, my daughter, Allegra, also heard it, for she turned to me and asked 'Mammi, who is it?'"

"What did you do?"

"I pretended to be nonchalant about it, looked all over, went up the stairs, opened cabinets—but, of course, there was no one there. "

"And your daughter?"

"When we did not find anyone, she said, 'Oh, it must be our lady upstairs.'"

"Any other experiences you can recall?"

"Yes, tonight, in fact," Mrs. Buffington replied. "I was in the kitchen feeding the child, and I was putting something into the garbage container, when I heard a child's voice saying 'It's lower down'—just that, nothing more."

"Amazing," I conceded.

"It was a young girl's voice," Mrs. Buffington added. "I looked at Allegra, but it was obvious to me that the voice had come from the opposite direction. At any rate, Allegra was busy eating. I've been very nervous the past few days and about a week ago, when my husband was away in Washington, I spent the night alone, and having had some strong coffee, could not find sleep right away. I had moved the child in with me, so I did not have to stay by myself. I switched the light off, and the door to the landing of the second floor staircase was open. Just on that spot I suddenly heard those crashing noises as if somebody were rolling down. I was terrified. As soon as I switched the light back on, it stopped. There was nothing on the stairs. I sat on the bed for a moment, then decided it was my nerves, and turned the light off again. Immediately, the same noise returned, even louder. There was no mistaking the origin of the noises this time. They came from the stairs in front of the room. I switched the light on again and they stopped, and I left the lights burning the rest of the night. I finally fell asleep from sheer exhaustion."

"One more thing," Jack Buffington broke in. "On the back staircase, there is an area about four feet long which is a terribly frigid area sporadically. My little girl wouldn't walk up that staircase if she could possibly help it. Both my wife and I felt the cold spot."

"Is this in the area of the room where the little child was kept?" I asked.

"It is one floor below it, but it is the area, yes," Mrs. Buffington admitted.

I had heard enough by now to call in Sybil Leek, who had been outside waiting patiently for the call to lend her considerable psychic talents to the case.

After she had seated herself in one of the comfortable leather chairs, and we had grouped ourselves around her in the usual fashion, I quickly placed her into trance. Within a few minutes, her lips started to quiver gently, and then a voice broke through.

"Can't play," a plaintive child's voice said.

"Why not?" I asked immediately, bringing the microphone close to Sybil's entranced lips to catch every word.

"No one to play with. I want to play."

"Who do you want to play with?"

"Anyone. I don't like being alone."

"What is your name?"

"Elizabeth."

"What is your family name?"

"Streiber."

"How old are you?"

"Nine."

"What is your father's name?"

"Joseph Streiber."

Now Sybil had no knowledge that a child's ghost had been heard in the house. Nor had she overheard our conversation about it. Yet, the very first to manifest when trance had set in was a little girl! I continued to question her. "Your mother's name?"

"Mammi."

"What is her first name?"

The child thought for a moment, as if searching, then repeated: "Mammi."

With sudden impact, I thought of the ghostly voice calling for "Mamma" heard on the steps by Mrs. Buffington and her little daughter.

"Do you go to school?"

The answer was almost angry.

"No! I play."

"Where do you live in this house?"

"Funny house . . . I get lost . . . too big."

"Where is your room?"

"On the stairs."

"Who else lives in the house?"

"Mammi."

"Anyone else?"

"No one."

"Where were you born?"

"Here."

"What is your birthday?"

"Eight . . . Eighteen . . . Twenty-One."

"What month?"

"March."

Did she mean that she was born in 1821? The house was built in 1876 and before that time, only a field existed on the site. Or was she trying to say: March 8th, 1921? Dates always confuse a ghost, I have found.

"Are you feeling well?"

A plaintive "no" was the answer. What was wrong with her, I wanted to know.

"I slip on the stairs," the ghost said. "I slipped down the stairs. I like to do that."

"Did you get hurt?"

"Yes. "

"What happened then?"

"So I sit on the stairs," the little girl ghost said, "and sometimes I run down one staircase. Not the other. Then I have fun."

"Is there anyone else with you?"

"Mammi."

Again I thought of the apparition in the Victorian dress Jack Buffington had seen in the hall.

"Do you see her now?" I asked.

An emphatic "no" was the answer.

"When have you seen her last?"

She thought that one over for a moment.

"Two days."

"Is she living?"

"Yes . . . she goes away, and then I'm lost."

"Does she come back?"

"Yes."

"What about your father?"

"Don't like my father. Not very nice time with my father. He shouts."

"What floor is your room on?"

"At the top."

I recalled that the retarded little girl had been kept in a locked room on the top floor.

"Do you ever go downstairs?"

"Of course I go downstairs. I play on the stairs. And I'm going to sit on the stairs all the time until somebody plays with me!"

"Isn't there any other little girl or boy around?" I asked.

"I don't get at him . . . they take him away and hide him."

"Who does?"

"People here."

"Do you see people?"

"Yes."

"Do people see *you*?"

"They think they do . . . they're not very nice, really."

"Do you talk to them?" She seemed to nod. "What do you tell them?"

"I want to play."

"Do you call out for anyone?" I asked.

"Mammi."

"Is there anyone else in this house you can see? Any children?"

"Yes, but they won't play."

"What sort of children are there in this house?"

"They won't play."

How do you explain to a child that she is a ghost?

"Would you like to meet some other children like yourself who do want to play?" I asked. She liked that very much. I told her to imagine such children at play and to think of nothing else. But she wanted to play in this house.

"I live here."

I persisted in telling her that there were children outside, in a beautiful meadow, just waiting for her to join them.

"My father tells me not to."

"But he is not here."

"Sometimes I see him."

"Come outside now."

"I don't go outside in the daytime."

"What do you do in the daytime then?"

"I get up early and play on the stairs."

She was afraid to go outside, she said, but preferred to wait for "them" in the house, so she would not miss them. I explained things to her ever so gently. She listened. Eventually, she was willing to go, wondering only—"When do I come back?"

"You won't want to come back, Elizabeth," I replied, and asked if she understood these things now.

She thought for a moment, then said:

"Funny man . . ."

"You see, something happened to you, and you are not quite the same as before," I tried to explain. "People in this house are not like you and that's why you can't play with them. But outside in the meadow there are many like you. Children to play with all your life!"

And then I sent her away.

There was a strange, rapping noise on the staircase now, as if someone were saying good-bye in a hurry. Abruptly, the noise ceased and I recalled Sybil, still entranced, to her own body.

I asked her to describe what she saw on her side of the veil.

"The child is difficult," she said. "Doesn't want to leave the house. She's frightened of her father. She's about ten. Died here, fell. "

I instructed the medium to help the child out of the house and across the border. This she did.

"There is also a woman here," Sybil said. "I think she followed the child. She is tied to this house because the child would not go."

"What does she look like?"

"Medium fair, full face, not thin—she wears a green dress in one piece, dark dress—she comes and goes—she worries about the child—I think *she left the child*."

Guilt, I thought, so often the cause of a haunting!

"When she came back, something had happened," Sybil continued. "The child had been injured and now she keeps coming back to find the child. But the child only wants to play and sit on the stairs. "

"Can you contact the woman for us?" I asked.

"The woman is not a good person," Sybil replied slowly. "She is sorry. She listens now."

"Tell her we've sent the child away."

"She knows."

"Tell her she need no longer haunt this house; her guilt feelings are a matter of the past."

275

"She wants to follow the child. She wants to go now."

"She should think of the child with love, and she will join her."

"She doesn't love the child."

"She will have to desire to see her family again, then, to cross over. Instruct her."

In a quiet voice, Sybil suggested to the ghost that she must go from the house and never return here.

"She won't upset the house, now that the child is gone," Sybil assured us. "The search for the child was the cause of it all."

"Was the child ill?" I asked.

"The child was difficult and lonely, and she fell."

Again I heard rapping noises for a moment.

"Was there anything wrong with this child?"

"I'm not so sure. I think she was a little *fou*. She was florid, you know, nobody to look after her, looking for things all the time and frightened to go out."

"Did she die in this house or was she taken somewhere?"

"She died here."

Sometimes the ghost reattaches himself to the last refuge he had on the earth plane, even though the body may expire elsewhere, and instantly returns to that place, never to leave it again, until freed by someone like myself.

"The woman is gone now," Sybil mumbled. "The child went a long way, and the woman is gone now, too."

I thanked Sybil and led her back to consciousness, step by step, until she woke up in the present, fully relaxed as if after a good night's rest, and, of course, not remembering a thing that had come through her entranced lips the past hour.

Mr. Buffington got up, since the spell of the foregoing had been broken, and motioned me to follow him to the next room.

"There is something I just remembered," he said. "My daughter,

Allegra, took a fall on the staircase on the spot where those chills have been felt. She wore one of her mother's high heels and the likelihood of a spill was plausible—still, it was on *that* very spot."

The next morning, I called a number of people who knew Lansdowne history and past residents well enough to be called experts. I spoke to the librarian at the Chester County Historical Society and the librarian at Media, and to a long-time resident Mrs. Susan Worell, but none of them knew of a Joseph Streiber with a little girl named Elizabeth. The records back into the twenties or even earlier are pretty scanty in this area and research was almost hopeless. Quite conceivably, the Streibers were among the tenants who had the house in a transitory way during the years of which Jack Buffington had no records—but then again, there are certain parallels between fact and trance results that cannot be dismissed lightly.

Jack Buffington thought the description of the woman he saw and that given by the medium do not fully correspond, but then he did not see the specter long enough to be really sure.

The retarded child Sybil Leek brought through had an amazing similarity to the actual retarded girl of about ten who had lived in the house and died in a nearby hospital, and the word "Mamma" that Mrs. Buffington had heard so clearly was also close to what the ghost girl said she kept calling her mother.

There was some mystery about the dates—and even the longtime residents of the area I interviewed could not help me pin down the facts. Was there a man by that name with a little girl?

Records were not well kept in this respect and people in America could come and go far more easily than in European countries, for instance, where there was an official duty to report one's moves to either the police or some other government office.

A day or two after our visit, Jack Buffington reported that the noises were worse than ever! It was as if our contact with the wraiths had unleashed their fury; having been told the truth about their status, they would naturally have a feeling of frustration and resentment, or at least the woman would. This resentment often occurs after an investigation in which trance contact is made. But eventually things quiet down and I had the feeling that the woman's guilt feelings would also cease. That the little girl ghost had been sent out to play, I have no doubt. Perhaps that aftermath was the mother's fury at having her no longer in her sight. But then I never said that ghosts are the easiest people to live with.

Goings-On in Maryland

Norma Martin's family has been psychic all the way back, usually on the female side. There was a great-grandmother who ran a boarding house for the brakemen and motormen who worked on the trolley line to Owings Mills, Maryland. One foggy night a motorman was killed in an accident. Her great-grandmother had forgotten all about the unfortunate fellow when she got off a trolley a year later to walk home. Who would join her but the dead motorman. Since she had befriended him in life she assumed he wanted to protect her on a foggy and rainy night. Every anniversary since she has seen the dead fellow walking with her.

Norma is a young girl living near Baltimore. She likes to spend her summer holidays at her aunt's house in Harford County. Although Norma is aware of her family's background in the occult, she is herself not exactly a believer. At least she wasn't until her cousin complained to her about seeing a ghost. Now Norma had been in her aunt's house before and had not experienced anything, so she questioned her cousin further. Since the other girl was an excellent student and a very logical person, Norma felt that her testimony might be of value. Apparently the cousin had gotten into the habit of staying up very late at night to do her homework. That was in the summer of 1966. In the still of the night she would look up and see a white form go past her toward the bedroom door. Startled, she would turn around but the figure was gone. Not much later she was asleep in the living room when she felt herself awakened by the sound of someone breathing very hard near her. She opened her eyes slightly, and to her bewilderment a strange little man with white hair and a long beard stood next to her bed. A moment later the apparition had vanished. When Norma came back to her aunt's house she wondered about the experience her cousin had reported to her. She was still doubtful and wondered if the whole thing might have been a dream. Shortly after her arrival she woke up in the middle of the night because she had the feeling of a human presence in the room. She looked up and there was the figure of a little man. The sound of his breathing came to her consciousness at the same time. A moment later he had disappeared. It occurred to Norma then that certain spots in her aunt's house had been unusually chilly all along even though it might be very hot outside. Finally convinced that there was something uncanny in her aunt's house, Norma made some inquiries. The little man had been a long-time servant and he had died here, although on the grounds, not in the house directly. Perhaps he had no other place to go than to return to his master's house, still trying to serve.

When I was lecturing on extrasensory perception in Baltimore in October of 1968 a pleasant-looking woman came up to me and asked to speak to me quietly. "We have an earthbound restless spirit in our home," she explained and looked around as if she had said something no one else should hear. I assured her that there were thousands of people with similar problems and not to be ashamed of being overheard, especially not in an audience that had come to hear me speak on that very same subject. After the lecture I questioned her further. The Schaefers had moved into their home in Baltimore in November of 1967. They knew that the home was very old but had no idea as to its background or prior tenants. The man who had sold them the house was of very little help except to say there had been many tenants before them. Much later Mrs. Schaefer discovered that no tenant had ever stayed there more than three months and that the list of those who had moved in and out of the house was very long indeed. The owner of the house lived out of town and would not come down to be present at the sale. The Schaefers had never met him, and that too seemed unusual. But at the time they moved in they were excited and happy with their new old home and did not worry about such matters as prior problems, or, heaven forbid, ghosts. As a matter of fact, between November of 1967 and the early spring of 1968 there was nothing in the atmosphere of the house suggesting anything out of the ordinary. One Sunday evening the Schaefers had the visit of a young artist and his wife. In the course of the evening the conversation turned to psychic phenomena and the increased interest the subject seemed to find these days among college people. More as a lark than for serious reasons the young man suggested the use of a Ouija board. He added that he had a feeling there were spirits present in the atmosphere and that they should contact them and find out who they were and why they were present. The Schaefers went along more for amusement's sake than because they felt there was anything haunted about their house. A board was found and immediately the four of them put their hands on it. To their amazement the board came alive instantly. Messages came from it spelled at a rapid pace far more speedily than they could have spelled them even if these messages had originated in their own minds, consciously or unconsciously. What the Ouija kept telling them was that a spirit communicator named David wished to speak to Sara. He identified himself as the son of Elmer and, in a pointed move toward Mrs. Schaefer, kept repeating over and over that he wanted to be her friend. At this point the young artist rose quickly from the board and pointed to one end of the room. His face was pale and sweat pearls appeared on his forehead. Staring toward that end of the room, he said he saw someone standing there and would have no more truck with the Ouija board. Suddenly what had started as light entertainment became heavy with forbidding silence. The Schaefers put the board away with great haste and tried to dismiss the incident with light banter.

Mrs. Schaefer did not really feel that way, for she was aware of the existence of things beyond the pale of the material and had had some interest in research of this kind. She too felt strange at that moment, but thanks to their conversation the young man regained his composure and a moment later was back to his old self. However, so strong had the impact been on him that he refused to discuss the incident then or at any time thereafter. All he would explain to the Schaefers was that something of this kind had happened to him once before and he did not wish to have it happen again. Neither one of the Schaefers had seen anything in the corner of the room to which the young artist had pointed.

After their guests had left the Schaefers went up the stairs to bed. As she went up Mrs. Schaefer had a strange feeling of a human presence. Before she realized what she was saying she heard herself speak aloud, "You are welcome." There was no fear in her at that time nor ever since, but she had within her the certainty that their home had a spirit resident and that the spirit had made himself known to them through the Ouija board that evening. From that moment on they became increasingly aware of a presence. Their two-year-old grandson would play on the stairs and point at something they couldn't see, describing "the man" standing there. They would hear footsteps crossing the living room, ascending the stairs, and were quite sure that someone was coming up. On one occasion Mr. Schaefer was so sure that a flesh-and-blood person had invaded their home that he came downstairs with a revolver. The phenomena increased in frequency both in the daytime and at night. Knockings would come from all parts of the house—knocking for which there was no natural explanation. Finally Mrs. Schaefer wondered about the original communicator. Since her given name is Sara she thought that he had tried to contact her, but she knew no David who would fit into a close relationship with her. She decided to search the title of their old home and with some effort found the original land grant which was dated 1836. To her amazement she discovered it had been given to a certain David Patterson. David Patterson had four children, three sons and a daughter. The daughter was named Sara. After her discovery things quieted down. Then they would pick up again. On such occasions she would ask the spirit to please leave and not disturb the house. This would always work for a few days but eventually the noises returned. Mrs. Schaefer then realized that David Patterson was still concerned with his old house and liked to continue living in it.

The Gridiron Club in Baltimore is an up-to-date establishment belying its unusual past. If you look closely you will realize that the house itself is very old and its colonial origins though fixed up are nevertheless still in evidence. There is even a swimming pool now where the old slave quarters used to be. And thereby hangs a ghostly tale. The house goes back about two hundred years and was originally known as the Hillen House. If it weren't for a psychically oriented young lady by the name of Linda Merlo I would never have heard of the Gridiron Club or the Hillen House. Fortunately, for posterity, Miss Merlo lives about a mile away and knows all about it. In the colonial period a Mrs. Hillen owned much of the land around it. In her later years she fell sick and had a nurse in attendance twenty-four hours a day. One day the nurse went out into the hallway for a moment. When she returned her patient was gone. The nurse realized that the slaves might have abducted her patient in order to blackmail her into concessions of freedom, but how could she had disappeared from the room? If there was a secret passage leading down into the slave quarters it was never found. She could not have been kidnapped through the window since the room was on the third floor of the house. The door was impossible too, since the nurse had not left the hallway long enough for people to pass through it, and there was no other door to the room. Whichever way the owner of the house was spirited down into the slave quarters, it appears, according to the tradition which may very well be true, that the slaves tried to make her come to terms with them. In the excitement of the moment the sick woman died.

In the course of time the house changed hands often. Eventually it became the property of a family who owned it before it became the Gridiron Club. They were the first ones to realize that something very unusual was going on in their home. The noise of people talking downstairs when no one was about was only one of the phenomena they had to get used to. One of the sons, Ralph, liked to work on motorcycles and cars and frequently went downstairs to wash up. He would walk smack into a party going full blast although he could not understand a single word the voices were saying. As soon as he entered, the noise stopped abruptly. When he left the basement and shut the door behind him he heard the noise resume immediately in what he knew was an empty basement. He would put his working tools carefully away and lock them up. The next day he would find them scattered all over the floor, with some of them missing and never found again. Yet he was sure that no burglar had come into the house. Because of the goings-on Ralph took to securely locking all doors and windows. Nevertheless, whenever he did so he would find them wide open the next morning. On one occasion the owner of the house was in the basement locking the windows one by one. As he locked the first window and went on to the second to continue his task he saw the first window open itself again. He locked it again and went on but the phenomenon repeated itself. At that point he said, "All right, Mrs. Hillen, I give up," and up he went.

Two of the owner's sons, Ralph and Billy, were sitting in the kitchen when they saw a window open by itself right in front of their very eyes. They jumped to their feet when they heard someone approaching wearing chains dragging behind him. Many slaves were chained at the ankles to prevent them from running away. But it wasn't just the noises that kept reminding the owners of the history of their house. Ralph's fiancée, Barbara, once saw a woman's face in the window and on turning around realized there was no one there who could have caused a reflection. Not much later the figure of a person holding a candle was seen walking down the hall. The owners had the house checked out for any defects, whether structural or electrical, to account for the many strange noises. That, however, was before the apparition. They realized then that the restless spirit of Mrs. Hillen was still about and that those who had tormented her hadn't found rest either. It is difficult to say whether the patrons of the Gridiron Club are much bothered by these goings-on. If they saw the ghost of Mrs. Hillen or of some of the slaves passing by, they might think that the club was putting on a floor show for them. There is no telling what the ghostly slaves think of the swimming pool that now occupies the area where they had to live in those far-off days.

Joseph P. Rosinski is a professional radio announcer in Baltimore, Maryland. He is in his early forties and has had some interest in the occult but not to the point of pursuing it deeply or in great detail. As an avocation Mr. Rosinski has been interested in working with the blind. It was on an autumn night in 1965 that he happened to be reading aloud a textbook to his friend Ed Maff at the Maryland School for the Blind in Overlea, which is a suburb of Baltimore. About eight o'clock in the evening the supervisor of the institution came into the classroom where Rosinski and the blind man were sitting, apparently in great agitation. A blind student by the name of Mike Moran was faced with an emergency and had telephoned for help. Apparently the young man had lost his talking book needle. It had rolled somewhere on the rug in his room and he just couldn't find it. Would Mr. Rosinski be kind enough to help out? The radio announcer gladly volunteered to go to Mike Moran's place and read him the text.

That place turned out to be the cupola of an old gingerbread house built in the 1870s located at the corner of the thirteen-hundred block of North Calvert Street in Baltimore. The house seemed unusually quiet on the outside, somewhat neglected, but still showing its once proud exterior, built in a period when houses were far more solid than they are today. There was a proprietor by the name of O'Malley, a white-haired Irishman who spoke with a thick brogue. Somewhat gruffly he pointed toward the stairs to indicate that the blind man lived up there. Rosinski started to walk up. Leaving the dimly lit vestibule he suddenly found himself wondering who he really was. He didn't quite feel like himself at that point. Suddenly he found himself transported back into the gaslit area. Walking up the stairs, he arrived at the top floor and rang the bell to Mike Moran's room. Passing through heavy mahogany doors, he saw that the entire cupola was occupied with one large room. There was an old bedstead with a menacingly high headboard which was about a foot shy of hitting the ceiling. Nearby were a candle stand, an antique marble washstand and other authentic period pieces all done in dark mahogany. Somehow the room seemed frightening to Rosinski. He realized that the room and the furniture had been untouched for years. The room was filled with cigar smoke and an undefinable aroma of the past. However, Rosinski didn't wish to let the strange atmosphere of the room prevent him from doing the job he had come to do. He immediately proceeded to read to the young man the text and then prepared to go home, but the hour was late and it was decided he should spend the night and return in the morning. The bed was large enough to accommodate both of them, so they turned in for the night. Even though Rosinski was very tired from his efforts, he couldn't sleep. As he lay there on the old bed he suddenly felt a female softness under him. In surprise he sat up, thereby awakening Mike Moran also. Rosinski could not see anything but he felt sure there was someone else with them in bed. Mike was blind, yet he immediately "saw" the figure of a young woman on the bed. He was glad Rosinski had come to stay with him, for he was frightened. Rosinski looked toward the head of the bed and what he saw was not very reassuring. There on the bed was the form of a young woman surrounded by an aura of green and blue-gray mist. Somehow he felt that the girl had suffered in the room, and he also had the impression that a baby was connected with the woman in some dramatic way. But the most disturbing feeling of all was *the fact that he no longer felt that he was himself.* He knew for sure now that he was a nineteenth-century doctor visiting a patient in this cupola room. He felt he had to help the poor woman and suffered her agonies with her. Even the way he walked about the room was not his usual gait. It seemed to him that he walked straighter and with a firmer, lighter step than was his usual custom. There was nothing he could do to change this transformation, yet at the same time he was able to observe it clinically and to wonder about it.

After a sleepless night Rosinski returned to his own home. He implored me to go to the house on Calvert Street and do something about the ghostly woman on the bed. I tried to as soon as I was able. I found the house on Calvert Street near Mount Royal without trouble. It is situated just opposite the old Mount Royal Hotel. But I looked in vain for O'Malley. In fact, the house gave every impression of being abandoned or pretty nearly so. The vestibule was dirty and dark. No one opened the door for me and I began to feel I had come too late. Time was of the essence and I did not want to hang around and see whether a living soul might eventually turn up and let me in. Regretfully I started to walk down the stairs that led from the vestibule to the street outside. Once more I turned and looked back. I had the distinct impression that I was not alone. I could not see anything, but somewhere in the murky dark of the vestibule I felt two outstretched arms. I went back and said in a soft voice, "You are over now and must find peace. Ask for your loved ones to come and get you and take you away from this house where you have found so much unhappiness. There is no need to stay. Everyone you once knew, everyone you once loved, has gone on. You too must go on." I turned and went back to the street. When I looked back once more, the arms were no longer reaching out to me.

The Bayberry Perfume Ghost

If there is anything more staid than a North Philadelphia banker I wouldn't know it. But even bankers are human and sometimes psychic. In William Davy's case there had been little or no occasion to consider such a matter except for one long forgotten incident when he was eight years of age. At that time he lived with his parents in Manchester, England. On one particular morning, little William insisted that he saw a white shadow in the shape of a man passing in front of the clock. The clock, it so happened, was just striking the hour of 8:30 A.M. His mother, reminded by the sound of the clock, hurriedly sent the boy off to school, telling him to stop his foolishness about white shadows.

By the time the boy returned home, word had reached the house that his favorite grandfather, who lived halfway across England in Devon, had passed away. The time of his death was 8:30 A.M. Eventually, Mr. Davy moved to Philadelphia where he is an officer in a local bank, much respected in the community and not the least bit interested in psychic matters. His aged father, William Sr., came to live with him and his family in the home they bought in 1955. The house is a splendid example of Victorian architecture, built on three levels on a plot surrounded by tall trees in what is now part of North Philadelphia, but what was at the time the house was built a separate community, and originally just farmland.

The ground floor has a large kitchen to one side, a large living room, with fireplace, separated from a dining room by a sliding double door. Upstairs are bedrooms on two floors, with the third floor the onetime servant quarters, as was customary in Victorian houses. The Davy family did some remodeling downstairs, but essentially the house is as it was when it was first built, sometime in the late 1880's, according to a local lawyer named Huston, who is an expert on such things. At any rate, in 1890 it already stood on the spot where it is today.

William Sr. was a true English gentleman given to historical research, and a lover of ghost stories, with which he liked to regale his family on many occasions. But what started as a purely literary exercise soon turned into grim reality. Shortly after his arrival, William Sr. complained of hearing unusual noises in the house. He had a room on the third floor and was constantly hearing strange noises and floor boards creaking as if someone were walking on them.

His son laughed at this and ascribed it to his father's vivid imagination, especially after his many fictional ghost stories had set the mood for that sort of thing. But the older Davy insisted to his last day that he was being troubled by an unseen entity. After he passed away in February of 1963, Mr. and Mrs. Davy thought no more of the matter. The house was a peaceful home to them and they enjoyed life.

Several months later, Mr. Davy was sitting by himself in the living room, reading. He was tired, and the time was 10 P.M. He decided to call it a day, and got up to go to bed. As he walked toward the hallway between the living room and the staircase, he literally stepped into a cloud of very pungent perfume which he instantly identified as a very strong bayberry smell. For a moment he stood in utter amazement, then slowly continued into the hall and up the stairs. The perfume still surrounded him, as if someone invisible, wearing this heavy perfume, were walking alongside him!

Upon reaching the first landing he went into the bedroom. At that point, the perfume suddenly left him, just as suddenly as it had come.

"Mary," he asked his wife, "did you by any chance spill some perfume?" She shook her head emphatically. She did not even own any such scent, and there had been no one else in the house that day or evening.

Puzzled but not particularly upset, Mr. Davy let the matter drop and he would have forgotten it entirely had not another event taken him by surprise.

Several months later he was again sitting in the living room, the time being around 10 P.M. He put down his book, and went toward the hallway. Again, he walked into a heavy cloud of the same perfume! Again it followed him up the stairs. As he climbed he felt something— or someone—brush against his right leg. It made a swishing sound but he could not see anything that could have caused it. When he got to the landing, he stopped and asked Mary to come out to him.

His wife had suffered a fractured skull when she was young and as a consequence had lost about seventy percent of her sense of smell.

When Mary joined him at the landing, he asked her if she smelled anything peculiar. "Oh my word," she said, immediately, "what a heavy perfume!" They were standing there looking at each other in a puzzled state. "What on earth is it?" Mary finally asked. He could only shrug his shoulders.

At that precise moment, they clearly heard footsteps going up the stairs from where they were standing, to the third floor!

Since neither of them saw any person causing the footsteps, they were completely unnerved, and refused to investigate. They did not follow the footsteps up to the third floor. They knew only too well that there wasn't any living soul up there at the moment.

One evening Mary was reading in bed, on the second floor, when she found herself surrounded by the same bayberry perfume. It stayed for several seconds, then died away. Since she was quite alone in the house and had been all evening, this was not very reassuring. But the Davys are not the kind of people that panic easily, if at all, so she shrugged it off as something she simply could not explain. On another occasion, Mr. Davy saw a patch of dull, white light move through the living room. From the size of the small cloud it resembled in height either a large child or a small person, more likely a woman than a man. This was at 3 A.M. when he had come downstairs because he could not sleep that night.

In April of 1966 the Davys had gone to Williamsburg, Virginia for a visit. On their return, Mr. Davy decided to take the luggage directly upstairs to their bedroom. That instant he ran smack into the cloud of bayberry perfume. It was if some unseen presence wanted to welcome them back!

One of Mary's favorite rings, which she had left in her room, disappeared only to be discovered later in the garden. How it got there was as much of a mystery then as it is now, but no one of flesh and blood moved that ring. Naturally, the Davys did not discuss their unseen visitor with anyone. When you're a Philadelphia banker you don't talk about ghosts.

In September of the same year, they had a visit from their niece and her husband, Mr. and Mrs. Clarence Nowak. Mr. Nowak is a U.S. government employee, by profession a chemical engineer. Their own house was being readied and while they were waiting to move in, they spent two weeks with their uncle and aunt. The niece was staying on the second floor, while Mr. Nowak had been assigned the room on the third floor that had been the center of the ghostly activities in the past. After they had retired, Mr. Nowak started to read a book. When he got tired of this, he put the book down, put the lights out and got ready to doze off.

At that precise moment, he clearly heard footsteps coming up and he was so sure it was Mary coming up to say goodnight that he sat up and waited. But nobody came into his room and the footsteps continued!

Since he is a man of practical outlook, this puzzled him and he got out of bed and looked around. The corridor was quite empty, yet the footsteps continued right in front of him. Moreover, they seemed to enter the room itself and the sound of steps filled the atmosphere of the room as if someone were indeed walking in it. Unable to resolve the problem, he went to sleep.

The next night, the same thing happened. For two weeks, Mr. Nowak went to sleep with the footsteps resounding promptly at 10 P.M. But he had decided to ignore the whole thing and went to sleep, steps or no steps.

"It seemed, when I was in bed," he explained to his aunt, somewhat sheepishly, "the footsteps were coming up the stairs, and when I was lying there it seemed as if they were actually in the room, but I could not distinguish the actual location. When I first heard them I thought they were Mary's, so I guess they must have been the footsteps of a woman."

Mr. Nowak is not given to any interest in psychic phenomena, but on several occasions his wife, also named Mary, as is her aunt, did have a rapport bordering on telepathic communication with him. These were minor things, true, but they were far beyond the possibilities of mere chance. Thus it is very likely that the chemist's natural tendency towards extrasensory perception played a role in his ability to hear the steps, as it certainly did in the case of the banker, Mr. Davy, whose own childhood had shown at least one marked incident of this sort.

But if the ghostly presence favored anyone with her manifestations, it would seem that she preferred men. Mary Nowak slept soundly through the two weeks, with nary a disturbance or incident.

Clifford Richardson, another nephew of the Davys, came from Oklahoma to visit the Nowaks one time, and in the course of the visit he decided to stay a night at the Davys. Mr. Richardson is the owner of an insurance agency and not the least bit interested in the occult. On his return to the Nowaks the following day, he seemed unusually pensive and withdrawn. Finally, over coffee, he opened up.

"Look, Mary," he said, "your husband Bucky has stayed over at Uncle Ned's house for a while. Did he sleep well?"

"What do you mean?" Mary asked, pretending not to know.

"Did he ever hear any sounds?"

Mary knew what he meant and admitted that her husband had indeed "heard sounds."

"Thank God," the insurance man sighed. "I thought I was going out of my mind when I heard those footsteps."

He, too, had slept in the third floor bedroom.

What was the terrible secret the little bedroom held for all these years?

The room itself is now plainly but adequately furnished as a guest room. It is small and narrow and undoubtedly was originally a maid's room. There is a small window leading to the tree-studded street below. It must have been a somewhat remote room originally where a person might not be heard, should he cry for help for any reason.

The Davys began to look into the background of their house. The surrounding area had been known as Wright's Farm, and a certain Mrs. Wright had built houses on the property towards the late 1880's. The house was owned by four sets of occupants prior to their buying it and despite attempts to contact some of those who were still alive, they failed to do so. They did not discuss their "problem" with anyone, not even Mary's aged mother who was now staying with them. No sense frightening the frail old lady. Then again the Davys weren't really frightened, just curious. Mary, in addition to being a housewife, was also a student of group dynamics and education at nearby Temple University, and the phenomena interested her mildly from a researcher's point of view. As for William Davy, it was all more of a lark than something to be taken seriously, and certainly not the sort of thing one worries about.

When their inquiries about the history of the house failed to turn up startling or sensational details, they accepted the presence as something left over from the Victorian age and the mystique of it all added an extra dimension, as it were, to their fine old home.

Then one day, in carefully looking over the little room on the third floor, Mr. Davy made an interesting discovery. At waist height, the door to the room showed heavy dents, as if someone had tried to batter it down! No doubt about it, the damage showed clear evidence of attempted forcing of the door.

Had someone violated a servant up there against her wishes? Was the door to the bedroom battered down by one of the people in the house, the son, perhaps, who in that age was sacrosanct from ordinary prosecution for such a "minor" misdeed as having an affair with the maid?

The strong smell of bayberry seemed to indicate a member of the servant class, for even then, as now, an overabundance of strong perfume is not a sign of good breeding.

There have been no incidents lately but this does not mean the ghost is gone. For a Victorian servant girl to be able to roam the *downstairs* at will is indeed a pleasure not easily abandoned—not even for the promised freedom of The Other Side!

The Ghost-Servant Problem
at Ringwood Manor

Ringwood, in the south of England, has an American counterpart in New Jersey. I had never heard of Ringwood Manor in New Jersey until Mrs. Edward Tholl, a resident of nearby Saddle River, brought it to my attention. An avid history buff and a talented geographer and map maker, Mrs. Tholl had been to the Manor House and on several occasions felt "a presence." The mountain people who still inhabited the Ramapo Mountains of the region wouldn't go near the Manor House at night.

"Robert Erskine, geographer to Washington's army, is buried on the grounds," Mrs. Tholl told me.

The Manor House land was purchased by the Ogden family of Newark in 1740, and an iron-smelting furnace was built on it two years later. The area abounds in mine deposits and was at one time a center of iron mining and smelting. In 1762, when a second furnace was built, a small house was also built. This house still stands and now forms part of the haphazard arrangement that constitutes the Manor House today. One Peter Hasenclever bought the house and iron works in 1764. He ran the enterprise with such ostentation that he was known as "The Baron." But Hasenclever did not produce enough iron to suit his backers, and was soon replaced by Robert Erskine. When the War of Independence broke out, the iron works were forced to close. Erskine himself died "of exposure" in 1780.

By 1807, the iron business was going full blast again, this time under the aegis of Martin Ryerson, who tore down the ramshackle old house and rebuilt it completely. After the iron business failed in the 1830s, the property passed into the hands of famed Peter Cooper in 1853. His son-in-law Abram S. Hewitt, one-time Mayor of New York, lived in the Manor House.

Mrs. Hewitt, Cooper's daughter, turned the drab house into an impressive mansion of 51 rooms, very much as it appears today. Various older buildings already on the grounds were uprooted and added to the house, giving it a checkered character without a real center. The Hewitt family continued to live at Ringwood until Erskine Hewitt deeded the estate to the State of New Jersey in 1936, and the mansion became a museum through which visitors were shown daily for a small fee.

During troubled times, tragedies may well have occurred in and around the house. There was a holdup in 1778, and in the graveyard nearby, many French soldiers were buried who died there during an epidemic. There is also on record an incident, in later years, when cook was threatened by a butler with a knife, and there were disasters that took many lives in the nearby iron mines.

One of the Hewitt girls, Sally, had been particularly given to mischief. If anyone were to haunt the place, she'd be a prime candidate for the job. I thanked Claire Tholl for her help, and called on Ethel Johnson Meyers to accompany me to New Jersey. Of course, I didn't give her any details. We arranged to get to the house around dusk, after all the tourists had gone.

My wife Catherine and I, with Ethel Meyers as passenger, drove out to the house on a humid afternoon in May, 1965. Jim Byrne joined us at the house with *Saturday Review* writer Haskell Frankel in tow.

We were about an hour late, but it was still light, and the peaceful setting of the park with the Manor House in its center reminded one indeed of similar houses gracing the English countryside.

We stood around battling New Jersey mosquitoes for a while, then I asked Catherine to take Ethel away from the house for a moment, so I could talk to Mrs. Tholl and others who had witnessed ghostly goings-on in the house.

"I've had a feeling in certain parts of the house that I was not alone," Mrs. Tholl said, "but other than that I cannot honestly say I have had uncanny experiences here."

Alexander Waldron had been the superintendent of Ringwood Manor for many years, until a year before, in fact. He consented to join us for the occasion. A jovial, gray-haired man, he seemed rather deliberate in his report, giving me only what to him were actual facts.

"I was superintendent here for eighteen years," Mr. Waldron began. "I was sitting at my desk one day, in the late afternoon, like today, and the door to the next room was closed. My office is on the ground floor. I heard two people come walking toward me at a fast pace. That did not seem unusual, for we do have workmen here frequently. When the steps reached my door, nothing happened. Without thinking too much, I opened the door for them. But there was no one there. I called out, but there was no answer. Shortly after, two workmen did come in from outside, and together we searched the whole building, but found no one who could have made the sound."

"Could anyone have walked away without being seen by you?"

"Impossible. There was good light."

"Did anything else happen after that?"

"Over the years we've had a few things we could not explain. For instance, doors we had shut at night, we found open the next morning. Some years ago, when I had my boys living here with me, they decided to build a so-called monster down in the basement. One boy was of high-school age, the other in grammar school—sixteen and thirteen. One of them came in by himself one night, when he heard footsteps overhead, on the ground floor. He thought it was his brother who had come over from the house.

"He thought his brother was just trying to scare him, so he continued to work downstairs. But the footsteps continued and finally he got fed up with it and came upstairs. All was dark, and nobody was around. He ran back to the house, where he found his brother, who had never been to the Manor at all."

Bradley Waldron probably never worked on his "monster" again after that.

There are stories among the local hill folk of Robert Erskine's ghost walking with a lantern, or sitting on his grave half a mile down the road from the Manor House, or racing up the staircase in the house itself.

Wayne Daniels, who had accompanied Mrs. Tholl to the House, spoke up now. Mr. Daniels had lived in the region all his life, and was a professional restorer of early American structures.

"I have felt strange in one corner of the old dining room, and in two rooms upstairs," he volunteered. "I feel hostility in those areas, somehow."

It was time to begin our search in the house itself.

I asked Ethel Meyers to join us, and we entered the Manor House, making our way slowly along the now-deserted corridors and passages of the ground floor, following Ethel as she began to get her psychic bearings.

Suddenly, Ethel remarked that she felt a man outside the windows, but could not pin down her impression.

"Someone died under a curse around here," she mumbled, then added as if it were an afterthought, "Jackson White . . . what does that mean?"

I had never heard the name before, but Claire Tholl explained that "Jackson White" was a peculiar local name for people of mixed blood, who live in the Ramapo hills. Ethel added that someone had been in slavery at one time.

Ethel was taken aback by the explanation of "Jackson White." She had taken it for granted that it was an individual name. Jackson Whites, I gathered, are partly Native American and partly black, but not white.

We now entered a large bedroom elegantly furnished in the manner of the early nineteenth century, with a large bed against one wall and a table against the other. Ethel looked around the room uncertainly, as if looking for something she did not yet see.

"Someone with a bad conscience died in this room," she said. "A man and a woman lived here, who were miles apart somehow."

It was Mrs. Erskine's bedroom we were in. We went through a small door into another room that lay directly behind the rather large bedroom; it must have been a servant's room at one time. Nevertheless, it was elegant, with a marble fireplace and a heavy oak table, around which a number of chairs had been placed. We sat down but before I had time to adjust my tape recorder and camera, Ethel Meyers fell into deep trance. From her lips came the well-modulated voice of Albert, her control. He explained that several layers of consciousness covered the room, that there were blacks brought here by one Jackson, who came in the eighteenth century. One of them seemed present in the room, he felt.

"One met death at the entrance . . . a woman named Lucy Bell, she says. She was a servant here."

Suddenly, Albert was gone. In his stead, there was a shrill, desperate female voice, crying out to all who would listen.

"No . . . I didn't . . . before my God I didn't . . . I show you where . . . I didn't touch it . . . never. . ."

She seemed to be speaking to an unseen tormentor now, for Ethel, possessed by the ghost, pulled back from the table and cried:

"No . . . don't . . . don't!" Was she being beaten or tortured?

"He didn't either!" the ghost added.

I tried to calm her.

"I didn't touch . . . I didn't touch . . ." she kept repeating.

I asked for her name.

"Lucy," she said in a tormented, high-pitched voice completely different from Ethel Meyers' normal tones.

"I believe you," I said, and told the ghost who we were and why we had come. The uncontrollable crying subsided for the moment.

"He's innocent too," she finally said. "I can't walk," she added. Ethel pointed to her side. Had she been hurt?

"I didn't take it," she reiterated. "It's right there."

What didn't she take? I coaxed her gently to tell me all about it. "I've come as a *friend*," I said, and the word finally hit home. She got very excited and wanted to know where I was since she could not see me.

"A friend, Jeremiah, do you hear?" she intoned.

"Who is Jeremiah?"

"He didn't do it either," she replied. Jeremiah, I gathered, lived here, too, but she did not know any family name—just Jeremiah. Then Ethel Meyers grabbed my hand, mumbling "friend," and almost crushed my fingers. I managed to pull it away. Ethel ordinarily has a very feminine, soft grip—a great contrast to the desperately fierce gasp of the ghost possessing the medium!

"Don't go!"

I promised to stay if she would talk.

"I have never stolen," she said. "It's dark . . . I can't see now . . . where do I go to see always?"

"I will show you the way," I promised.

"Marie . . . Marie . . . where are you?" she intoned pleadingly.

"What is Jeremiah doing?"

"He is begging for his honor."

"Where is he now?"

"Here with me."

"Who is the person you worked for?" I asked.

"Old lady. . . I don't want her . . ."

"If she did you wrong, should we punish her? What is her name?"

"I never wished evil on anyone . . . I would forgive her . . . if she forgives me. She is here . . . I saw her, and she hates me . . ."

The voice became shrill and emotional again. I started to send her away, and in a few moments, she slipped out. Suddenly, there was an entirely different person occupying Ethel's body. Proudly sitting up, she seemed to eye us, with closed eyes, of course, as if we were riffraff invading her precincts.

"What is your name?" I demanded.

"I am in no court of justice," was the stiff reply in a proper upper-middle-class accent. "I cannot speak to you. I have no desire. It is futile for you to give me any advice."

"What about this servant girl?" I asked.

"You may take yourself away," the lady replied, haughtily. "Depart!"

"What did the girl take?" I asked, ignoring her outburst of cold fury.

"I am not divulging anything to you."

"Is she innocent then?"

This gave her some thought, and the next words were a little more communicative.

"How come you are in my house?" she demanded.

"Is it your house?"

"I will call the servants and have you taken out by the scruff of your neck," she threatened.

"Will the servants know who you are?" I countered.

"I am lady in my own."

"What is your name?"

"I refuse to reveal myself or talk to you!"

I explained about the passage of time. It made no impression.

"I will call her . . . Old Jeremiah is under his own disgrace. You are friend to him?"

I explained about Ethel Meyers and how she, the ghost, was able to communicate with us.

She hit the table hard with Ethel's fist.

"The man is mad," the ghost said. "Take him away!"

I didn't intend to be taken away by ghostly men-in-white. I continued to plead with "the lady" to come to her senses and listen. She kept calling for her servants, but evidently nobody answered her calls.

"Jeremiah, if you want to preserve yourself in my estimation and not stand by this girl, take this . . ."

Somehow the medium's eyes opened for a moment, and the ghost could "see." Then they closed again. It came as a shock, for "the lady" sullenly stopped her angry denunciation and instead "looked" at me in panic.

"What is this? Doctor . . . where is he . . . Laura! Laura! I am ill. Very ill. I can't see. I can't see. I hear something talking to me, but I can't see it. Laura, call a doctor. I'm going to die!"

"As a matter of fact," I said calmly, "you have died already. "

"It was my mother's." The ghost sobbed hysterically. "Don't let her keep it. Don't let it go to the scum! I must have it. Don't let me die like this. Oh, oh . . ."

I called on Albert, the control, to take the unhappy ghost away and lead her to the other side of the veil, if possible. The sobbing slowly subsided as the ghost's essence drifted away out of our reach in that chilly Georgian room at Ringwood.

It wasn't Albert's crisp, precise voice that answered me. Another stranger, obviously male, now made his coughing entry and spoke in a lower-class accent.

"What's the matter?"

"Who is this?" I asked.

The voice sounded strangely muffled, as if coming from far away.

"Jeremiah . . . What's the matter with everybody?" The voice had distinct black overtones.

"I'm so sleepy," the voice said.

"Who owns this house?"

"Ho, ho, I do," the ghost said. "I have a funny dream, what's the matter with everybody?" Then the voice cleared up a little, as he became more aware of the strange surroundings into which he had entered.

"Are you one of these white trashes?" he demanded.

"What is the old lady's name?" I asked.

"She's a Bob," he replied, enigmatically, and added, "real bumby, with many knots in it, many knots in the brain."

"Who else is here?"

"I don't like you. I don't know you and I don't like who I don't know," the servant's ghost said.

"You're white trash," he continued. "I seed you!" The stress was on *white*.

"How long have you been living here?"

"My father. . . Luke."

Again, I explained about death and consequences, but the reception was even less friendly than I had received from "the lady."

Jeremiah wanted no truck with death.

"What will the old squaw say? What will she say?" he wondered.

"She needs me."

"Not really," I replied. "After all, she's dead, too." He could hardly believe the news. Evidently, the formidable "squaw" was immune to such events as death in his mind.

"What do you have against my mother?" he demanded now. Things were getting confusing. Was the "old lady" his mother?

"Lucy white trash too," he commented.

"Was she your wife?"

"Call it that."

"Can you see her?"

"She's here."

"Then you know you have died and must go from this house?" I asked.

"'dominable treek, man, 'dominable treek," he said, furiously.

"This house is no longer yours."

"It never was," he shot back. "The squaw is here. We're not dead, great white spirit—laugh at you."

"What do you want in this house?"

"Squaw very good," he said. "I tell you, my mother, squaw very good. Lucy Bell, white trash, but good. Like Great White Spirit. Work my fingers down to the bone. I am told! I am thief, too. Just yesterday. Look at my back! Look at my squaw! Red Fox, look at her. Look at my back, look at it!"

He seemed to have spent his anger. The voice became softer now.

"I am so sleepy," he said. "So sleepy. . . my Lucy will never walk again . . . angel spirit . . . my people suffer . . . her skin should be like mine . . . help me, help my Lucy . . . "

I promised to help and to send him to his father, Luke, who was awaiting him.

"I should have listened to my father," the ghost mumbled.

Then he recognized his father, evidently come to guide him out of the house, and wondered what he was doing here.

I explained what I thought was the reason for his father's presence. There was some crying, and then they all went away.

"Albert," I said. "Please take over the instrument."

In a moment, the control's cool voice was heard, and Ethel was brought out of trance rather quickly.

"My hip," she complained. "I don't think I can move."

"Passing conditions" or symptoms the ghost brings are sometimes present for a few moments after a medium comes out of trance. It is nothing to be alarmed about.

I closed Ethel's eyes again, and sent her back into trance, then brought her out again, and this time all was "clear." However, she still recalled a scream in a passage between the two rooms.

I wondered about the Indian nature of the ghost. Were there any Indians in this area?

"Certainly," Mr. Waldron replied. "They are of mixed blood, often African American blood, and are called Jackson Whites. Many of them worked here as servants."

The footsteps the superintendent had heard on the floor below were of two persons, and they could very well have come from this area, since the room we were in was almost directly above his offices.

There was, of course, no record of any servants named Jeremiah or Lucy. Servants' names rarely get recorded unless they do something that is most unusual.

I asked Mrs. Tholl about ladies who might have fitted the description of the haughty lady who had spoken to us through Ethel Meyers in trance.

"I associate this with the Hewitt occupancy of the house," she explained, "because of the reference to a passage connecting two parts of the house, something that could not apply to an early structure on the spot. Amelia Hewitt, whose bedroom we had come through, was described in literature of the period as 'all placidity and kindliness.' Sarah Hewitt, however, was quite a cut-up in her day, and fitted the character of 'the lady' more accurately."

But we cannot be sure of the identity of the ghost-lady. She elected to keep her name a secret and we can only bow to her decision and let it remain so.

What lends the accounts an air of reality and evidence is, of course, the amazing fact that Ethel Meyers spoke of "Jackson Whites" in this house, an appellation completely new to her and me.

I am also sure that the medium had no knowledge of Indians living in the area. Then, too, her selecting a room above the spot where the ghostly steps had been heard was interesting, for the house was sprawling and had many rooms and passages.

The Octagon Revisited

B ack in 1965 I published a comprehensive account of the hauntings and strange goings-on at one of Washington's most famous houses. Frequently referred to as "the second White House" because it served in that capacity to President Madison during the War of 1812, the Octagon still stands as a superb monument to American architecture of the early nineteenth century. Most people hear more about the Pentagon than about the Octagon when referring to Washington these days, but the fact is that the Octagon, or eight-sided house, is still a major tourist attraction, although not for the same reasons that brought me there originally. As a matter of fact, The American Institute of Architects, who own the building, were and are quite reluctant to discuss their unseen tenants. It took a great deal of persuasion and persistence to get various officials to admit that there was something amiss in the old building.

After my first account appeared in *Ghosts I've Met*, I received a number of calls from people in Washington who had also been to the Octagon and experienced anything ranging from chills to uncanny feelings. I also found that the executives of The American Institute of Architects were no longer quite so unfriendly towards the idea of a parapsychologist investigating their famous old headquarters. They had read my account and found in it nothing but truthful statements relating to the history and psychic happenings in the house, and there really was nothing they could complain about. Thus, over the years I remained on good terms with the management of The American

Institute of Architects. I had several occasions to test the relationship because once in a while there seemed to be a chance to make a documentary film in Washington, including, of course, the Octagon. It didn't come to pass because of the difficulties involved not with The American Institute of Architects but the more worldly difficulties of raising the needed capital for such a serious-minded film. It may yet come to pass.

Originally I became aware of the potential hauntings at the Octagon because of a *Life* magazine article in 1962. In a survey of allegedly haunted houses, *Life* claimed that some visitors to the Octagon had seen a shadow on the spot where a daughter of Colonel Tayloe, who had built the house, had fallen to her death. As far as I could ascertain at the time, there was a tradition in Washington that Colonel John Tayloe, who had been the original owner of the Octagon, had also been the grieving father of a daughter who had done the wrong thing marriage-wise. After she had run away from home, she had later returned with her new husband asking forgiveness from her stern father and getting short shrift. In desperation, so the tradition goes, she then flung herself from the third-floor landing of the winding staircase, landing on a spot near the base of the stairs. She died instantly. That spot, by the way, is one of those considered to be the most haunted parts of the Octagon.

A somewhat different version is given by Jacqueline Lawrence in a recent survey of Washington hauntings published by the Washington *Post* in October of 1969. According to Miss Lawrence, Colonel Tayloe had more than one daughter. Another daughter, the eldest one, had fallen in love with a certain Englishman. After a quarrel with her father, who did not like the suitor, the girl raced up the stairs and when she reached the second landing, went over the banister and fell two flights to her death. This, then, would have been not a suicide but an accident.

As for the other daughter, the one who had brought home the wrong suitor according to tradition, Miss Lawrence reports that she did not marry the man after all. Her father thought of this young Washington attorney as a man merely after his daughter's money and refused to accept him. This was especially necessary as he himself had already chosen a wealthy suitor for his younger daughter. Again an argument ensued, during which he pushed the girl away from him. She fell over that same ill-fated banister, breaking her neck in the fall. This also according to Miss Lawrence was an accident and not suicide or murder.

In addition to these two unfortunate girls, she also reports that a slave died on that same staircase. Pursued by a British naval officer, she threw herself off the landing rather than marry him. According to Miss Lawrence, the young man immediately leaped after her and joined her in death.

It is a moot question how easily anyone could fall over the banister, and I doubt that anyone would like to try it as an experiment. But I wondered whether perhaps the story of the two girls had not in the course of time become confused into one tradition. All three deaths would have had to take place prior to 1814. In that year Washington was taken by the British, and after the burning of the White House President Madison and his family moved temporarily into the Octagon. They stayed there for one full year, during which the Octagon was indeed the official White House.

Only after President Madison and his family had left the Octagon did accounts of strange happenings there become known. People in Washington started to whisper that the house was haunted. Allegedly, bells could be heard when there was no one there to ring them. The shade of a girl in white had been observed slipping up the stairway. The usual screams and groans associated with phantoms were also reported by those in the know. According to Miss Lawrence, seven years after the Civil War five men decided to stay in the house after dark to prove to themselves that there was nothing to the stories about the haunting. They too were disturbed by footsteps, the sound of a sword rattling, and finally, human shrieks. Their names, unfortunately, are not recorded, but they did not stay the night.

After some correspondence with J. W. Rankin, Director of the Institute, my wife, Catherine, and I finally started out for Washington on May 17, 1963. The beautiful Georgian mansion greeted us almost as if it had expected us. At the time we did not come with a medium. This was our first visit and I wanted to gain first impressions and interview those who actually had come in contact with the uncanny, be it visual or auditory. First I asked Mr. Rankin to supply me with a brief but concise rundown on the history of the house itself. It is perhaps best to quote here my 1965 report in *Ghosts I've Met*.

Mr. Rankin received us with interest and showed us abound the house which was at that time fortunately empty of tourists and other visitors. It was he who supplied some of the background information on the Octagon, from which I quote:

The White House and the Octagon are relations, in a way. Both date from the beginning of government in the national capital; the White House was started first but the Octagon was first completed. Both have served as the official residence of the President.

It was early in 1797 that Colonel John Tayloe of Mount Airy, Virginia, felt the need for a town house. Mount Airy was a magnificent plantation of some three thousand acres, on which the Colonel, among many activities, bred and raced horses, but the call of the city was beginning to be felt, even in that early day; Philadelphia was the Colonel's choice, but his friend General Washington painted a glowing picture of what the new national capital might become and persuaded him to build the Octagon in surroundings that were then far removed from urbanity.

Dr. William Thornton, winner of the competition for the Capitol, was Colonel Tayloe's natural selection of architect.

On April 19, 1797, Colonel Tayloe purchased for $1000 from Gustavus W. Scott—one of the original purchasers from the Government on November 21, 1796—Lot 8 in Square 170 in the new plot of Washington. Although, as the sketch of 1813 shows, the site was apparently out in a lonely countryside, the city streets had been definitely plotted, and the corner of New York Avenue and Eighteenth Street was then where it is today.

Obviously, from a glance at the plot plan, Colonel Tayloe's house derived its unique shape from the angle formed at the junction of these two streets. In spite of the name by which the mansion has always been known, Dr. Thornton could have had no intention of making the plan octagonal; the house planned itself from the street frontages.

Work on the building started in 1798 and progressed under the occasional inspection of General Washington, who did not live to see its completion in 1800. The mansion immediately took its place as a center of official and nonofficial social activities. Through its hospitable front door passed Madison, Jefferson, Monroe, Adams, Jackson, Decatur, Porter, Webster, Clay, Lafayette, Von Steuben, Calhoun, Randolph, Van Rensselaer, and their ladies.

Social activities were forgotten, however, when the War of 1812 threatened and finally engulfed the new nation's capital. On August 24, 1814, the British left the White House a fire-gutted ruin. Mrs. Tayloe's foresight in establishing the French Minister—with his country's flag—as a house guest may have saved the Octagon from a like fate.

Colonel Tayloe is said to have dispatched a courier from Mount Airy, offering President Madison the use of the mansion, and the Madisons moved in on September 8, 1814.

For more than a year Dolly Madison reigned as hostess of the Octagon. In the tower room just over the entrance President Madison established his study, and here signed the Treaty of Ghent on February 17, 1815, establishing a peace with Great Britain which endures to this day.

After the death of Mrs. John Tayloe in 1855, the Octagon no longer served as the family's town house. That part of Washington lost for a time its residential character and the grand old mansion began to deteriorate.

In 1865 it was used as a school for girls. From 1866 to 1879 the Government rented it for the use of the Hydrographic Office. As an office and later as a studio dwelling, the Octagon served until about 1885, when it was entrusted by the Tayloe heirs to a caretaker.

Glenn Brown, a longtime secretary of The American Institute of Architects, suggested in 1889 that the house would make an appropriate headquarters for the Institute.

When the architects started to rehabilitate the building, it was occupied by ten black families. The fine old drawing room was found to be piled four feet deep with rubbish. The whole interior was covered with grime, the fireplaces closed up, windows broken, but the structure, built a century before, had been denied no effort or expense to make it worthy of the Tayloes, and it still stood staunch and sound against time and neglect.

Miraculously the slender balusters of the famous stairway continued to serve, undoubtedly helped by the fact that every fifth baluster is of iron, firmly jointed to the handrail and car-

riage. Even the Coade Stone mantels in drawing room and dining room, with their deeply undercut sculpture, show not a chip
nor scar. They had been brought from London in 1799 and
bear that date with the maker's name.

On January 1, 1899, the Institute took formal possession of
the rehabilitated mansion, its stable, smokehouse and garden.

So much for the house itself. I was given free rein to interview the staff, and proceeded to do so. Some of them are white,
some black; all displayed a high degree of intelligence and dig-
nity of the kind one often finds among the staff in old Southern
mansions.

I carefully tabulated the testimony given me by the
employees individually, and checked the records of each of
them for reliability and possible dark spots. There were none.

In view of the fact that nobody was exactly eager to be put
down as having heard or seen ghosts, far from seeking publicity or public attention, I can only regard these accounts as
respectable experiences of well-balanced individuals.

The building itself was then in the care of Alric H. Clay.
The museum part of the Octagon, as different from the large
complex of offices of The American Institute of Architects, was
under the supervision of Mrs. Belma May, assisted by a staff of
porters and maids, since on occasion formal dinners or parties
took place in the oldest part of the Octagon.

Mrs. May was not given to hallucinations or ghost stories,
and in a matter-of-fact voice reported to me what she had
experienced in the building. Most of her accounts were of very
recent date.

Mrs. May saw the big chandelier swing of its own volition
while all windows in the foyer were tightly shut; she mentioned

the strange occurrence to a fellow worker. She also heard strange noises, not accounted for, and mostly on Saturdays. On one occasion, Mrs. May, accompanied by porters Allen and Bradley, found tracks of human feet in the otherwise undisturbed dust on the top floor, which had long been closed to the public. The tracks looked to her as "if someone were standing on toes, tiptoeing across the floor." It was from there that the daughter of Colonel Tayloe had jumped.

Mrs. May often smelled cooking in the building when there was no party. She also felt "chills" on the first floor landing.

Caretaker Mathew reported that when he walks up the stairs, he often feels as if someone were walking behind him, especially on the second floor. This is still happening to him now.

Ethel Wilson, who helps with parties, reports "chills" in the cloakroom.

Porter Allen was setting up for a meeting on the ground floor in the spring of 1962 when he heard noises "like someone dragging heavy furniture across the floor upstairs." In March 1963 he and his colleague saw the steps "move as if someone was walking on them, but there was no one there." This happened at 9:30 A.M.

Porter Bradley has heard groaning, but the sound is hard to pin down as to direction. Several times he has also heard footsteps.

Alric H. Clay, in charge of buildings, was driving by with his wife and two children one evening in the spring of 1962, when he noticed that the lights in the building were on. Leaving his family in the car, he entered the closed building by the back door and found everything locked as it should be.

However, in addition to the lights being on, he also noticed that the carpet edge was flipped up at the spot where the girl had fallen to her death in the 1800s.

Clay, not believing in ghosts, went upstairs; there was nobody around, so he turned the lights off, put the carpet back as it should be, and went downstairs into the basement where the light controls are.

At that moment, on the main floor above (which he had just left) he clearly heard someone walk from the drawing room to the door and back. Since he had just checked all doors and knew them to be bolted firmly, he was so upset he almost electrocuted himself at the switches. The steps were heavy and definitely those of a man.

In February of 1963 there was a late party in the building. After everybody had left, Clay went home secure in the knowledge that he alone possessed the key to the back door. The layout of the Octagon is such that nobody can hide from an inspection, so a guest playing a prank by staying on is out of the question.

At 3:00 A.M. the police called Clay to advise him that all lights at the Octagon were blazing and that the building was wide open. Mr. Woverton, the controller, checked and together with the police went through the building, turning off all lights once more. Everything was locked up again, in the presence of police officers.

At 7:00 A.M., however, they returned to the Octagon once more, only to find the door unlocked, the lights again burning. Yet, Clay was the only one with the key!

Only one prior account of any unusual goings-on at the Octagon had come to my attention before my visit in 1963. The July 1959 issue of The American Institute of Architects' Journal contains a brief account of the long service record of a certain employee named James Cypress. Although Mr. Cypress himself had never seen any ghosts, he did report that there was an unusual occurrence at one time when his wife was ill and in need of a doctor. The doctor had reported that he had seen a man dressed in the clothes of about 150 years ago coming down the spiral staircase. The doctor looked at the stranger somewhat puzzled. At that instant the apparition dissolved into thin air, leaving the medical man even more bewildered. A short time before publication of *Ghosts I've Met*, Joy Miller of the Associated Press wrote to me about the Octagon ghosts, adding a few more details to the story.

Legend has it that on certain days, particularly the anniversary of the traffic affair, no one may cross the hall at the foot of the stairway where the body landed without unconsciously going around an unseen object lying there.

The story of the bells that ring without due cause also is embroidered in this account.

Once, so a story goes, a skeptic leaped up and caught hold of the wires as they started to ring. He was lifted off the floor but the ringing kept on. To keep superstitious servants, the house was entirely rewired, and this apparently did the trick.

Of course, accounts of this kind are usually anonymous, as a parapsychologist I do not accept reports no matter how sincere or authentic they sound unless I can speak personally to the one to whom the event has occurred.

When I started to assemble material for this book, I wondered what had happened at the Octagon since 1963. From time to time I keep reading accounts of the hauntings that used to be, but nothing startling or particularly new had been added. It became clear to me that most of these newspaper articles were in fact based on earlier pieces and that the writers spent their time in the research libraries rather than in the Octagon. In April of 1969 I contacted The American Institute of Architects again, requesting permission to revisit the Octagon, quietly and discreetly but with a medium. The new executive director, William H. Scheick, replied courteously in the negative: "The Octagon is now undergoing a complete renovation and will be closed to visitors until this work is completed. We hope the Octagon will be ready for visitors in early 1970. I am sorry that you and your guest will not be able to see the building when you are in Washington."

But Mr. Scheick had not reckoned with the persistence and flexibility of an erstwhile ghost hunter. I telephoned him and after we had become somewhat better acquainted, he turned me over to a research staff member who requested that I let him remain anonymous. For the purpose of this account, then, I will refer to him simply as a research assistant. He was kind enough to accompany us on a tour of the Octagon, when we managed to come to Washington, despite the fact that the house was in repair or, rather, disrepair.

The date was May 6, 1969; the day was hot and humid, as so many days in May are in Washington. With me was my good friend Ethel Johnson Meyers, whom I had brought to Washington for the purpose of investigating several houses, and Mrs. Nicole Jackson, a friend who had kindly offered to drive us around. I can't swear that Mrs. Meyers had not read the account of my earlier investigation of the Octagon. We never discussed it particularly, and I doubt very much that she had any great interest in matters of this kind, since she lives in New York City and rarely goes to Washington. But the possibility exists that she had read the chapter, brief as it is, in my earlier book. As we will see in the following pages, it really didn't matter whether she had or had not. To her, primary impressions were always the thing, and I know of no instance where she referred back to anything she had done before or read before.

When we arrived at the Octagon, we first met with the research assistant. He received us courteously and first showed us the museum he had installed in the library. We then proceeded through the garden to the Octagon building itself, which is connected with the library building by a short path. Entering the building from the rear rather than the imposing front entrance as I had in 1963, we became immediately aware of the extensive work that was going on inside the old building. Needless to say, I regretted it, but also realized the necessity of safeguarding the old structure. Hammering of undetermined origin and workmen scurrying back and forth were not particularly conducive to any psychic work, but we had no choice. From noon to one o'clock was the agreed-upon time for us, and I hoped that we could at least learn something during this brief period. I urged Ethel to find her own bearings the way she always does, and the three of us followed her, hoping to catch what might come from her lips clairvoyantly or perhaps even in trance.

Immediately inside the building, Ethel touched me, and I tried to edge closer to catch what came from her. She was quite herself and the impressions were nothing more than clairvoyant descriptions of what raced through her mind. We were standing in the room to the left of the staircase when I caught the name "Alice."

"What about Alice?" asked. "Who is she?"

"I don't know. It just hit me."

"I won't tell you any more than that you should try to find your way around this general area we are in now, and upstairs as far as you feel like."

"Oh yes, my goodness, there's so many, they won't stay still long enough. There's one that has *quite a jaw*—I don't see the top of the face yet; just a *long jaw.*"

"Man or woman?"

"Man."

"Is this an imprint from the past or is this a *person?*"

"From the past."

"Go over to this banister here, and touch the banister and see whether this helps you establish contact."

"I see a *horse face.*"

"Is this part of his character or a physical impairment?" "Physical impairment."

"What is his connection with this house?"

"I just see him here, as if he's going to walk out that door. Might have a high hat on, also. I keep hearing, 'Alice. Alice.' As if somebody's calling."

"Are there several layers in this house, then?"

"I would say there are several layers."

"Is there anything about this area we're standing in that is in any way interesting to you?" We were now in front of the fatal banister.

"Well, this is much more vivid. This is fear."

She seemed visibly agitated now, gripping the banister with both hands. Gently, I pried her loose and led her up a few steps, then down again, carefully watching her every move lest she join the hapless Tayloe girls. She stopped abruptly at the foot of the stairs and began to describe a man she sensed near the staircase—a phantom man, that is. Connected with this male ghost, however, was another person, Ethel indicated.

"Someone has been carried down these steps after an illness, and out of here. That's not the man, however. It seems to be a woman."

"What sort of illness?"

"I don't know. I just see the people carrying her down— like on a stretcher, a body, a sick person."

"Was this person alive at the time when she was carried down?"

"Alive, but very far gone."

"From where did she come?"

"I think from down here." Ethel pointed toward the spot beneath the banister. "There is also a Will, but during this time I don't think Will is alive, when this happens. I also find the long-faced man walking around. *I can see through him.*"

"Is he connected with the person on the stretcher?"

"I would say so, because he follows it." Then she added, "Someone comes here who is still alive from that. Moved around."

"A presence, you mean?" She nodded. "This man with the horse face—what sort of clothes did he wear?"

"A formal suit with a long coat. Turn of the century or the twenties?"

"The *nineteen*-twenties?"

"Somewhere in here, yes."

"And the person on the stretcher—do you see her?"

"No, she's covered up. It is the woman I still see in here."

"Why don't you go up those stairs, to about the first landing."

"I am afraid of that, *for some reason or other.*"

"Why do you suppose that is?"

"I don't like it."

"Did something happen in that area?"

"I don't know. I'm just getting a feeling as if I don't want to go. But I'll go anyway."

"See whether you get any more impressions in doing that!"

"I'm getting a cerebral heaviness, in the back of the head."

"Was somebody hurt there?"

"I would say. Or—stricken."

"What is the connection? Take one or two steps only, and see whether you feel anything further in doing this. You're now walking up the stairs to the first landing."

"Oh, my head. Whew!"

"You feel—?"

"Numb."

"We're not going further than the first landing. If it is too difficult, don't do it."

"No. I'll take it for what it is." Suddenly, she turned. "Don't push me!"

"Somebody's trying to push you?"

"Yes."

I didn't feel like testing the matter. "All right, come back here. Let us stand back of the first landing."

"I get a George, too. And Wood, and something else. I'm holding onto my head, that hurts, very badly."

"Do you know who is this connected with, the injury to the head?"

"It sounds like Jacques."

"Is he connected with this house in any official capacity?"

"Well, this is a definite ghost. He's laughing at me. I don't like it!"

"Can you get any name for this person?"

"Again I get Jacques."

"Did anything tragic ever happen here?"

"I would say so. I get two individuals here—the long-faced man, and a shorter-faced man who is much younger."

"Are they of the same period?"

"No."

"Where does the woman on the stretcher fit in?"

"In between, or earlier."

"What is this tragic event? What happened here?"

"I can hardly get anything. It feels like my brains are gone."

"Where do you think it happened? In what part of the building?"

"Here, of course, *here.*"

"Did somebody die here? Did somebody get hurt?"

"According to my head, I don't know how anybody got through this. It is like blown off. I can't feel it at all. I have to put my hand up to find it."

"Are the presences still here?"

Instead of replying, Ethel put up her hands, as if warding off an unseen attack. "Oh, no!"

"Why did you just move like this? Did you feel anyone present?"

"Yes—as if somebody was trying to get hold of me, and I don't want that. I don't know how long I can take the head business, right here . . ."

"All right, we'll go down. Tell them, whoever might be present, that if they have to say something, they should say it. Whatever information they have to pass on, we are willing to listen. Whatever problem they might have."

Ethel seemed to struggle again, as if she were being possessed.

"There's something foreign here, and I can't make out what is being said."

"A foreign language?"

"Yes."

"What language is it?"

"I'm not sure; it's hard to hear. It sounds more Latin than anything else."

"A Latin language? Is there anything about this house that makes it different from any other house?"

"There's a lot of foreign influence around it."

"Was it used in any way other than as a dwelling?"

"There were séances in this place."

"Who do you think held them?"

"Mary."

"Who is this Mary?"

"She parted her hair in the middle. Heavy girl. I've got to put my hand up, always to my head, *it hurts so.*"

"Do you get the names of the people involved in this horrible accident, or whatever it is that you describe, this painful thing?"

"That has to be Mary who's taken down the steps. I think it's this one."

"The tragedy you talk about, the pain . . ."

"It seems like it should be *here,* but it could have been somewhere else. I don't understand. There are two layers here."

"There may be many layers."

"There are so many people around here, it's so hard to keep them separate."

"Do you get the impression of people coming and going? Is there anything special about the house in any way?"

"I would say there is. *The highest people in the land have lived here.* I'm positively torn by the many things. Someone married here with the name of Alice. *That* has nothing to do with the head."

"Alice is another layer?"

"That's right."

"Mary has the injury to her head. Is the marriage of Alice later or earlier?"

"Much later." Then she added. "This house is terribly psychic, as it were—it is as if I have been able to find the easiest possible connections with a lot of people through what has been done here, psychically. There's a psychic circle around this place. From the past."

"Do you feel that these manifestations are still continuing?"

"I would say there are, yes. I don't know what all this rebuilding is doing to it, particularly when the painting starts. Has Lincoln had anything to do with this house? I feel that I see him here."

"What would be his connection with the house?"

"Nothing at all, but *he's been here.*"

"Why would he be here?"

"I see an imprint of him."

"As a visitor?"

"I would say, yes. Some other high people have been here, too."

"As high as he?"

"That's right."

"Before him or after him?"

"After."

"What about before? Has anybody been as high as he here?"

"I would say so." Ethel, somewhat sheepishly, continued. "The man with the long face, he looks like Wilson!"

At that I raised my eyebrows. The mention of President Lincoln, and now Wilson, was perhaps a little too much name-dropping. On the other hand, it immediately occurred to me that both of these dignitaries must have been present at the Octagon at one time or other in their careers. Even though the Octagon was not used as a second White House after the disastrous War of 1812, it had frequently been used as a major reception hall for official or semiofficial functions. We do not have any record as to President Lincoln's presence or, for that matter, Wilson's, but it is highly likely that both of these men visited and spent time at the Octagon. If these occasions included some festivities, an emotional imprint might very well have remained behind in the atmosphere and Ethel would, of course, pick that up. Thus her mention of Lincoln and Wilson wasn't quite as outlandish as I had at first thought.

For several minutes now I had noticed a somewhat disdainful smile on the research assistant's face. I decided to discontinue questioning Ethel, especially as it was close to one o'clock now and I knew that the assistant wanted to go to lunch.

I wondered whether any of the foregoing material made any sense to him. Frankly, I didn't have much hope that it did, since he had been honest enough to communicate his lack of faith in the kind of work I was doing. But he had been kind enough to come along, so the very least I could do was use his services such as they might turn out to be.

The name Alice meant nothing to him, but then he was tuned in on the history of the Octagon rather than Washington history in general. Later, at the Wilson House I realized that Ethel was in some peculiar way catapulting her psychic readings. It appeared that Alice meant a good deal in the history of President Wilson.

What about Lincoln? The assistant shook his head.

"The family left the house about eighteen fifty-four, and I guess Lincoln was a Congressman then. He could have been here, but . . ."

"You're not sure?"

"I mean, he's not on the list that we have of people who have been here. I have no knowledge of it."

Colonel Tayloe died in 1854, and the house was owned by the family until after 1900 when the Institute bought it. But it was not occupied by the Tayloe family after the Colonel's death. I wondered why.

As to the names of the Tayloes' daughters, the research assistant wasn't very helpful either. He did have the names of some of the daughters, but he couldn't put his hands on them right now. He did not remember Mary. But, on reflection, there might have been.

I turned to Ethel. It was clear to me that the noise of the returning workmen, who had just finished their lunch hour, and the general tone of the conversation did not help to relax her. I thanked the assistant for his presence, and we left the building. But before we had walked more than a few steps, Ethel stopped suddenly and turned to me and said, "Somebody was murdered here, or badly wounded at least." She felt it was the woman on the stretcher. She was not completely sure that death had been due to murder, but it was certainly of a violent kind. I pointed at a portrait on the wall; the picture was that of Colonel Tayloe. Did

Ethel recognize the man in the picture, I asked, without of course indicating who he was. Perhaps she knew anyway. She nodded immediately.

"That's the man. I saw him."

He was one of the men she had seen walking about with a peculiar tall hat. She was quite sure. The face somehow had stuck in her mind. Ethel then pointed at another portrait. It was a photograph of Mrs. Wilson. She too had been at the Octagon. Ethel felt her presence.

"Would this be nineteen fifty-eight?" she asked somewhat unsure. The date seemed possible.

In evaluating Ethel's performance, I kept in mind that she had rarely if ever been wrong in pinpointing presences in haunted houses. Under the circumstances, of course, there was no possibility of Ethel going into full trance. Her contact with the entities was at the very best on the surface. Nevertheless, if three lady ghosts mentioned by Jacqueline Lawrence in her article had been present, then Ethel would surely have felt, seen, or otherwise indicated them. I am quite sure that Ethel never saw the article in the Washington *Post*. I am also equally sure that had she seen it, it would have made no difference to her, for she is a dedicated and honest medium. In the building itself she found her way to the psychic "hot spot" without my help, or in any way relying on my guidance. Had she been there before it would have macle no difference, since the renovation had completely altered the impression and layout of the downstairs. I myself was hard put to find my way around, even though I had been to the Octagon on two previous occasions.

Thus, Ethel Johnson Meyers tended to confirm the original contention published by me in 1965. One girl ghost and one male ghost, daughter and father, would be the logical inhabitants of the Octagon at this time. Whether or not the entities themselves are aware of their plight is a moot question.

It appears to be equally difficult to ascertain the true nature of the girl's problem. Had she merely brought home a suitor whom her father did not like, or had she actually gotten married? Strange as it seems, the records are not clear in this case. What appears to be certain, at least to me, is her death by falling from the upper story. Ethel Johnson Meyers would not have picked up the "passing condition" had she not genuinely felt it. Furthermore, these impressions were felt by the medium on the very spot where traditionally the girl landed. Thus, Ethel was able to confirm the continuous presence of an unfortunate young woman in what used to be her father's house. Since the two Presidents whom the medium felt in some way attached to the house are hardly of the ghostly kind, it remains for Colonel Tayloe himself to be the man whose footsteps have been identified by a number of witnesses.

The American Institute of Architects no longer considers the Octagon the kind of museum it was before the renovation. It prefers that it be known primarily as their headquarters. Also, it is doubtful that the frequent parties and social functions that used to take place inside its walls will be as frequent as in the past, if indeed the Institute will permit them altogether.

If you are a visitor to the nations capital and are bent on unusual sights, by all means include the Octagon in your itinerary. Surely once the renovation is completed there can be no reason—I almost said no earthly reason—for a visitor to be denied the privilege of visiting the American Institute of Architects. And as you walk about the Octagon itself and look up at the staircase perhaps wondering whether you will be as fortunate, or unfortunate as the case may be, as to see one of the two phantoms, remember that they are only dimly aware of you if at all. You can't command a ghost to appear. If you manage to wangle an invitation to spend the night, perhaps something uncanny might happen— but then again, it might not. What you can be sure of, however, is that

I haven't "de-ghosted" the Octagon by any means even though a medium, Ethel Johnson Meyers, was briefly almost on speaking terms with its two prominent ghosts.

It remains to be seen, or heard, whether further psychic phenomena take place at the Octagon in the future.

South

Charlottesville and the Revolution

W hen people think of the American Revolution, they think primarily of Boston and the Tea Party, Paul Revere and his uncle, and Philadelphia and its Liberty Bell. Very few people realize that Charlottesville, Virginia, was the focal point of the emerging United States for a while—that it was at the little, conveniently situated town in northern Virginia that much of the early planning of the Revolution took place. That was so because some of the leaders of American independence, such as Thomas Jefferson and James Monroe, made their homes in and around Charlottesville. Foreign tourists who are eager to see Washington, D.C., and cannot get enough of its majestic government buildings should take an extra hour to fly down to Charlottesville to see where it all began.

I hadn't been to Charlottesville since 1964, when Horace Burr, professor of speech and director of drama at Madison College in Harrisonburg, Virginia, and Virginia Cloud, the noted librarian and historian, had invited me. At that time, however, my main interest was in ferreting out some of the local ghosts and discussing them in a book I was then writing. Professor Burr was instrumental in prearranging my visit in early February 1973, knowing what I was hoping for, and clearing permission for me and a mediumistic friend to visit some private homes of the area. Virginia Cloud was on hand too, and it felt like old times revisited when my friend Ingrid Beckman and I emerged from the jet plane at the little Charlottesville airport. We were going to stay for two days, which had been tightly planned by

Professor Burr and Miss Cloud. Even a television interview with a crew from nearby Richmond, Virginia, had been penciled into the schedule, and I gave it while standing on the historical staircase of the Burr house, Carrsgrove.

Immediately upon arriving, we checked in at the Monticello Hotel in downtown Charlottesville. In retrospect, it seems odd that such a patently third-rate provincial hotel should bear the illustrious name of Monticello. The rooms weren't at all what we had ordered, the service and food were below standard, and it occurred to me how Jefferson would have felt had he been forced to put up some of his friends at this hostelry. Fortunately, it didn't exist during Jefferson's lifetime.

It turned out that February 9 was also Professor Burr's birthday, and he had accepted an invitation for the evening from the president of the University. Nevertheless, he spent the after-noon with us. Promptly at two o'clock, he picked us up at the hotel and, together with Miss Cloud, who had arranged our visit, drove us to Foxhill Farm, now the home of Mrs. Isabelle Palmer, a prominent society leader in Charlottesville. The house is somewhat on the outskirts of the town itself, on a knoll set back from the street. Although of pre-Revolutionary origin, it has been nicely fixed up and contains the latest comforts. Its dozen or so rooms are distributed on two floors, with a large kitchen downstairs and an imposing dining room to the right of the entrance. Upstairs, there are mainly bedrooms. Behind the house is the loveliest of gardens, enclosed by a brick wall behind which extend the rolling hills of Virginia's horse country, as far as the eye can reach.

Mrs. Palmer received us with much cordiality, and, as she had been briefed beforehand not to divulge anything about the house while Ingrid and I were inspecting it, only formalities and generalities were exchanged between us at first. As in my custom, I let my mediumistic associate go about the house as her intuition commanded her. Immediately on entering the large room to the right of the entrance, Ingrid stopped. She found herself now in the left-hand corner of what was obviously a dining room.

"What's the matter?" I asked, realizing that she was picking up some imprint from the past.

"I have a generally heavy feeling here. I can't describe it as yet, but the area is loaded with impressions," Ingrid replied, still trying to get her psychic bearings.

Ever since I had started to work with Ingrid, my own ESP ability has also sharpened, and on occasion I was able to sense things along with her. Thus I heard myself say, "Walk around and see whether you feel anything. I get the feeling of a meeting of some importance having taken place here." I had no idea why I said it, but both Ingrid and I agreed that a meeting of some importance had taken place in that very room, that someone had been arguing and had gotten up to leave in order to warn someone about a matter of importance.

"I feel there is a series of meetings here, not just one," Ingrid added, and then we walked over to the kitchen area. Since Ingrid felt nothing particularly strong in that area, we proceeded upstairs.

As soon as Ingrid walked into the bedroom to the left of the stairs, she stopped. "Guests on government business stayed here," she said, touching the bed to receive stronger psychometric impressions. "I 'get' a woman here; she is the wife of someone who has gone away, and I think she is very anxious for him. I get the feeling that she is worried for the man to get through the lines, and she is sitting up in an all-night vigil."

While Ingrid was speaking, I received the impression of the name Margaret, followed by the initial L. I have no idea why, but the imprint was quite strong.

"I have the feeling a lot of people went up and down the front stairway in the middle of the night," Ingrid said, "and that this is in a sense like a refuge."

I turned to Mrs. Palmer and Horace Burr, asking them to comment on the psychic impressions received by Ingrid and myself.

"Well," Professor Burr began, "this house, Foxhill Farm, stood halfway between Brown's Cove and the new village of Charlottesville at the time of the Revolutionary War. Our civilization came in through this part, through the valley, along the river. So this was actually a very important location; people who lived here were well-to-do, and it was a huge plantation. The owner was a certain John Rodes, and his son David was made sheriff of the county in 1775. During Colonial days, the post of sheriff was a very important government position, and Rodes had his own son filling that office.

"Since this house was a place halfway between the Revolutionary lines and the British, I felt it would be interesting to see what your psychic friend would get from the vibrations in the house," Burr added.

"What about the important meetings both Ingrid and I felt in the dining room downstairs?" I asked.

Professor Burr nodded emphatically. "Yes, if there were meetings they would undoubtedly have been held here."

At this point, Mrs. Palmer explained that the corner of the dining room where Ingrid had felt such strong vibrations had always puzzled her. It was on that spot that she had felt chills and had a sense of presence. Not being a medium, however, she could do very little with it. Nevertheless, she felt that whatever psychic activities might be present in her house would center around that corner of the dining room. I then questioned her about the room upstairs where Ingrid had had such a vivid impression. It turned out that the room was exactly above the library and not far from the area where the meetings had been held in the dining room. The house itself consisted originally of two separate houses that were joined together in the middle. The area where Ingrid had felt the strongest impressions had been built in 1765; the other, where she had felt nothing special, had been built in 1807.

I then directed a question to Burr. "Was there any particular meeting where people were sitting down at a long table, wearing a kind of severe dark brown coat, with lots of buttons running down the middle? Somebody at the end of the meeting would be getting up with a rather serious face, saying, 'I'll let him know,' and then take some papers and leave the assembly. This would have been very late at night or early in the morning, and someone would have to ride quite a distance to notify someone of a decison taken here for some area to join up with some other forces." As I finished speaking, I wondered where I had gotten all that information; it seemed to me that it was simply coming out of me, as if I had been *impressed* with it by some external source. I could tell by the took on Ingrid's face that she felt pretty much the same but that I had somehow expressed it first.

Burr thought this over for a moment. "It sounds very reasonable, since it was the time when they were recruiting and the sheriff would have had his hands in it, of course."

Again I followed a hunch. "Has anyone ever left here who was connected with this house and whose life was in jeopardy if he were caught?"

"Well, okay," Burr replied, "then let us go into the bloodstain on the floor, which you can see plainly even now." Sure enough, in the door jamb between the library and the next room there was a bloodstain deeply soaked into the wood.

Isabelle Palmer took up the explanation from this point on. "This has some connection with a Revolutionary person," she explained. "That is why when you mentioned refuge it hit home with me. Tradition has it that a wounded man came here during the Revolution and sought refuge. But we don't know who he was or whether he died here."

We walked back into the sumptuous library and sat down, surrounded by eighteenth-century oil paintings of great historical value. I asked about the men dressed in the reddish brown long coats which I had been impressed with a little while earlier. Could it have any meaning in terms of historical fact?

"Well," Burr replied, "that was the most typical homespun yarn that you could have in the 1770s in Piedmont, which is where we are. The material was produced on a loom and dyed with tobacco dyes, so the colors were dark brown."

Since the old pre-Revolutionary houses were once the centers of large plantations, they are not clustered in or around the town of Charlottesville but stand in lonely majesty in the countryside, even though much of the land has long since been sold off. Such was the case with Castalia, an imposing three-story manor house with red brick at the bottom, a veranda going around most of the house, and a portico dressing up the rest. The tall red brick chimneys, which supplied the fireplaces with outlets in the days before central heating, look like imposing flagpoles peering out into the Virginia hills. Castalia is surrounded by tall, old trees and is reached by a driveway from a dirt road which in turn branches off the main highway. Even in its reduced size, Castalia is the center of an estate which takes a full fifteen minutes to drive through.

As we were halfway between the town of Charlottesville and the estate, Virginia Cloud, who had been chatting incessantly, as is her custom, happened to say something about a ghost. Now, don't get me wrong. Virginia Cloud has a lot to say, and nothing she ever tells you is without interest. She probably knows more about motion pictures and stars than any living soul, and nearly everything there is to know about Charlottesville and the American Revolution.

"About that ghost," I said, and turned around. I was seated next to Horace Burr, and Ingrid and Virginia were in the rear seats.

"Well," Virginia said, "this very road we are riding on is the road where my friend Mrs. Emily Money Kelly had a remarkable experience with a ghost."

"Tell me more," I coaxed her, as if that were necessary.

"Emily lived nearby because her father was Colonel Money, an Englishman who worked for John Armstrong Chandler, a very famous gentleman of the area. One night Emily and her sister were on this long road which, as you know, connects Castle Hill with Castalia."

I knew that fact very well. In 1964 I had visited Castle Hill, where there is a haunted bedroom, allegedly visited at times by a lady ghost who appears only to people she doesn't like so she can tell them to leave "her" bedroom. At the time of my visit to Castle Hill, I had questioned the owner, Colonel Clark Lawrence, about any psychic occurrences. Politely, he informed me that he had none to report.

"Emily and her sister were turning into the driveway of their house, when they saw a rider very clearly—so clearly, in fact, that upon arriving at the door they asked one of their servants, 'Who was right in front of us when we came here?' The man seemed surprised. 'Why, Miss Emily, I've been out here all evening and I didn't see anybody.' Other people living in the area have also reported seeing a lonely rider ahead of them, heading up the road from Castle Hill to Castalia. Nobody knows who he is, or where he goes."

I thanked Virginia for her contribution to the local ghost lore, and just then the sleek blue car turned into the driveway leading up to Castalia. There we were welcomed by the owners, the Boocock family. We were exactly eighteen miles from Charlottesville and in the very heart of the Virginia horse country. The several ladies and gentlemen assembled to greet us in the large parlor downstairs were all members of the family, eager to contribute their experiences to the investigation. As I had requested that nothing be said about the house or the occurrences therein, only polite chitchat was exchanged at first. Ingrid took a look at the downstairs part of the house, and explained how pleasing it was to her artistic taste. But within a matter of minutes, she was on her way upstairs and I followed her, tape recorder and camera in hand. Behind me came Horace Burr and Virginia Cloud, followed at a respectful distance by the lady of the house.

The house was living proof that the Southern gentry still knows how to furnish homes. Elegantly decorated in the proper style, without so much as a single intrusion of modernism or so-called improvements, the interior of Castalia was a joy to the eye. Four-posters, heavy drapes, thick carpets, early nineteenth-century furniture, beautifully carved staircases and, above all, rooms upon rooms, space upon space, and all of it deep in the country, far away from pressures and the onrushing traffic.

As soon as we reached the second-floor landing, Ingrid made an immediate dash for a corner room, later identified as the chintz room. It had windows on both outside walls, giving a person an excellent view of the drive and thus of anyone coming up to the house. There was a period bed, or rather a double bed, in the center, and heavy drapes at the tall windows, reaching almost to the floor in the French manner. Opposite the bed stood a dresser with a large mirror. Horace and I kept back, close to the entrance door, while Ingrid walked slowly around the room.

"There is an impression here of an older woman; I get the feeling of an all-night vigil," she said finally. "I think she is worried about someone at a distance." I queried her about the person this woman worried over. "It is a man," Ingrid replied. "He's away on a war campaign. I think he is either a general or some other high-ranking officer; a leader and a patriot."

"Try to see what he looks like," I instructed her, "what his name is, what his connection is with this house, anything you can get on him."

Ingrid closed her eyes, breathed deeply for a moment, then reopened them again and said, "He is at a great distance right now, a hundred miles or more. She is worried that he may never return."

"Is he in any kind of action at the moment?"

"Yes. There is a decision, a turning point in the war, and she is worried that he may not come back from it. I get 1760 or '70. Her name is Margaret."

"What happened to this man? Does he come back?"

Ingrid's face took on a sad expression, almost as if she were feeling what "Margaret" must have felt at the time. "I don't think he comes back."

"What happens to her?"

"She stays here in great sadness."

"Is she still attached to this house, or do you merely feel her imprint?"

"Oh, I think she comes here. I think this is the room where she did most of her worrying. She comes back in the hopes that *he* will return."

"Did he die in battle?"

"Yes."

"How did she hear of it?"

"A carrier came with the news."

"How is it connected with this house?"

"He owned it; he was in the family."

"When the news came to her, was she in this room?"

"Yes, she was ill."

"As you speak, do you sense her close to you? Is she in some way telling you this? What was she dressed like?"

"I think she wore a nightgown," Ingrid replied, closing her eyes again to better describe what her psychic senses told her. "She wears perfume, her hair is pulled back, it is of dark brown color. She's a woman of perhaps forty-five. She likes to wear flowered clothes, gauzy material, and beads around her neck."

"What keeps her in this house?"

"He never returned and she is *still waiting*."

"Is she aware of his death?"

"She's confused."

"Does she realize that her own death has occurred?"

"I don't think so."

Next, we entered the so-called lavender room, also on the second floor of the house. It was situated opposite the chintz room, on the right of the stairwell, but also facing toward the road so that one could observe it from the window. The lavender room was considerably smaller than the chintz room we had just left. I decided to leave Ingrid and Virginia alone in it for a few moments, to see whether they could gather up some impressions from the past. Meanwhile, I went outside to change film and tape.

When I returned, both ladies seemed agitated and said they had news for me. "I think a woman was brought in here. She was very ill and stayed here until her death," Ingrid said firmly. "I think it is the same woman I felt in the chintz room except that she actually stayed in this one. I think she received the shock when she was in the other room, and then her condition became hopeless and she was moved in here. I don't know whether it was because of drink, but she never recovered emotionally. She was in here for several years, and eventually she died here. In this room I feel only sadness and the long-drawn-out period of her suffering. I think she wants to tell her story, she is so lonely and sad."

I instructed Ingrid to try and contact the entity, in trance if possible. Obediently, Ingrid sat back in a deep, comfortable chair in the corner, closed her eyes and waited. Although full trance did not occur, she seemed very much under the influence of an outside entity.

David," Ingrid said, her voice barely audible. "David or Davis," she added, "I think that is the man. She is very confused and still waiting for him." I instructed Ingrid to inform the lady that the man had passed on and that she herself was no longer in the flesh. Did the spirit understand her condition? "She understands what I am saying," Ingrid replied, "but I don't think she pays attention."

I decided to follow a different route of questioning. "Ask her to eveal more about herself."

"I think she was a very delicate lady, with lots of perfumes and fineries and beads; she catered to herself. She was a socially prominent woman."

"Was there anything among her habits that was particularly out-standing, such as a hobby or interest of some sort?"

"I think she liked to read a lot. Poetry. Especially Emerson, I think. But she didn't do any more reading after her loss; she was too confused. She thinks she is still here. *She is afraid to leave.*"

As is my custom under such circumstances, I explained to the entity that she could join her loved one merely by calling out to him and displaying a sincere desire to join him. Did the spirit lady under-stand what I was saying to her? "She listens," Ingrid explained. "She is showing herself to me with a shawl now, a white shawl bordered with fringes. Maybe she does needlework. She is always watching out the windows. *But the news does not come.* She grows old in this room."

"Does she understand why the man she is waiting for is not eturning?"

"No. She is very stubborn."

But eventually, Ingrid and I persuaded her that there was no point in waiting any longer, and with our blessings we sent her away to the

343

man who had also been waiting for her on *his* side of the road.

We continued our inspection of the large house, walking down half a flight of stairs and up another half on the other side of the house, which apparently had been built at a different time. The house presented a fascinating pattern of staircases and corridors, not laid out in a perfectly straight pattern but allowing for unexpected corners, turns, and hidden nooks. The master bedroom was located at the other end of the house, its windows looking down onto the land and toward the main road in the distance. It was a bright, large, and well-appointed room, beautifully decorated and well kept. Again, I let Ingrid step into it first by herself to pick up whatever she could in the way of psychic impressions.

"I don't feel anything here," Ingrid announced with a determined tone of voice. I had learned to respect her judgment, for whenever she felt nothing in the atmosphere of a room, there usually was nothing to be felt. On the other hand, whenever I had taken her to allegedly haunted rooms, she had picked up the scent without fail. I thanked her, and we descended to the ground floor, where the members of the family awaited us with great curiosity. Briefly, I filled them in on what Ingrid had discovered and in turn asked them to brief us on the house and make comments about Ingrid's discoveries.

Horace Burr was the first to speak. "The grandson of the famous Dr. Thomas Walker of Castle Hill, about whom you have written in *Ghosts I've Met*," he said, "had a grandson named Lewis. The house, as it stands now, was built around 1850, but there was an older house here before that time." Burr got up and showed me the dividing line where the old part ended and the newer portion began. About two-thirds of the living room was in the older section, while the frontal third actually occupied the newer part of the house. "So the first part, that is, the first room we were in, wasn't standing when the phenomena occurred," Burr explained. "Yet the apparition of a woman which has been observed by many of the people around here always occurred in the chintz room, the room where Ingrid correctly identified her. This was Mrs. Sally Lewis, the wife of Robert Lewis."

"Who saw her?" I asked.

"Mrs. Lila Boocock, the present Mrs. Boocock's sister-in-law. It happened prior to her marriage when she, her mother, and her intended were visiting here from New York. In the middle of the night she was awakened by a little woman with dark brown hair, pulled back, wearing a shawl and a striped taffeta dress. The woman was in her bedroom busying herself with a briefcase which Lila had brought with her and which contained some real estate papers. *The ghostly lady tried to go through it as if she were checking things out.* As Lila sat in bed, amazed at what she saw, she heard a sound reminding her of crisp onions being cut while the woman was going through her papers. Finally the woman walked straight over to the bed, with a faint smile on her face, and leaned over as if she wanted to say something. The next moment she was gone."

Mrs. Lila Boocock lives in Florida now. The experience occurred in 1926.

I turned to my hostess, Mrs. Elizabeth Boocock. "Have you yourself had an experience along these lines?"

"Yes," she replied. "Before we actually lived here, we used to come down to visit, and we would take the bedroom in the left part. That was in 1929. One morning I woke up around five o'clock because I heard footsteps with a regular rhythm to them. It sounded like, one-two-three-stop. At first I thought that my husband was ill. He hadn't been very well and was in the bed next to me, so I turned on the lights. But he was sound asleep. After that, I heard the same footsteps again and again, always at five o'clock in the morning. Finally I asked my mother-in-law what it all meant, and she replied, 'Oh, that's Mrs. Lewis.' But I never heard it again after we moved into the house."

I turned to the attractive lady to her right, Gwendolyn Goss, Mrs. Boocock's daughter, asking for any first-hand experiences.

"When I was at school in 1943, I brought a roommate home for Thanksgiving weekend," she began. "My friend, Marie de France, and I stayed in the chintz room, and it was a very cold, windy night, so we had a fire going in the fireplace. We put our clothes over a chair near the fireplace and went to bed. Sometime after midnight I heard some noise, as if someone were moving around the room, and I assumed Marie had gotten up. At the same time, Marie thought I had gotten up, so we both got out of bed and turned on the lights. Imagine our surprise when we found all our clothes on the floor *and the chair turned toward the fireplace with an open book on it!* Neither of us had put the book there. All that time the wind was blowing hard and the room was icy cold."

"Someone must have sat in that chair, reading a favorite book by the fireplace," I interjected. Horace Burr gave me a significant took.

"When we first moved down here, we lived in this house for a while before we moved out to the cottage, which you can see out the window," Gwendolyn continued. "When mother mentioned again and again to me that she had heard footsteps of an unseen person over-head, I finally said, 'Why, that's ridiculous.' But one night I heard the footsteps myself and immediately went upstairs to look. They sounded like four very definite footsteps going in one direction, then turning around and coming back. Immediately I went upstairs to look above the room I was in, and there was nothing."

"What sort of footsteps were they?" I asked.

"It sounded almost as if someone were pacing up and down," Gwendolyn replied.

"But that wasn't all," she continued. "During the 1930s my grand-parents had gone to Europe for a while, and the house was locked up. Not only was it closed from the outside but each individual room in the house itself was also locked. When they sent word by cablegram that they were coming home and asked the maid and the farm manager to open the house for them, these people came in. When they got to the lavender room and unlocked the door, they found the bedspread off the bed and on the floor, the bureau scarf off it, and all the silver in a mess. It looked as if someone had gone through it in a fit of temper, yet there had been no one in the house. No one could have gotten in. A mouse couldn't have gotten in.

"On one occasion, Mrs. Boocock and her mother were sleeping in the room next to the chintz room, when she heard a crash in the middle of the night which sounded to her as if someone had jerked off the dresser scarf and everything had gone to the floor. When the two women checked, they found everything in order. This happened two or three times in a row, both in the chintz room and in the lavender room."

"It would seem that somebody was looking for something, wouldn't it?" I said. "But I wonder who the ghost was waiting for?" "I think I can answer that," Horace Burr said. "Mrs. Lewis's son had been hunting nearby when he shot himself accidentally, or so they say. That was in 1855. Naturally she was upset, pacing up and down, waiting for someone who never came. Ingrid mentioned someone who was part of the family, and she mentioned her reading Emerson. That would fit. George Lewis is buried here in the grounds."

A tall heavy-set man who had been listening to the conversations in patience and silence spoke up now. He turned out to be Gwendolyn's husband, Edward Goss. Since he was an expert in engineering matters, he wanted us to know that important structural changes had taken place in the house. Both the lavender room and the chintz room had been changed, in 1904 and then again in 1909. He understood that the late Mrs. Sally Lewis was "unhappy" about the changes in her house. He explained that during the Revolutionary period there was a double cabin about two minutes away from the main house, and that this cabin was built in 1747 by a man named Jack, not far from the Castalia spring, which had been named after the legendary spring on Mount Parnassus.

"About two years after Lila Boocock had seen the apparition of Mrs. Lewis in her bedroom," Goss said, "she happened to be introduced to a granddaughter of the late Mrs. Lewis. After describing the apparition in detail, she asked the granddaughter whether she recognized it. 'That is my grandmother,' the granddaughter said firmly. 'She was little and had straight, pulled-back hair. She wore a shawl and a striped taffeta dress.'"

"Did you yourself ever have an experience in the house?"

"Yes, I did. In 1947 the then owner of the house, Mrs. Marmie Boocock, was away in Florida, and the house was quite empty except for myself. One night I noticed a light shining from a distance, and when I went up to investigate, I realized the light was coming from the chintz room. Sure enough, the lights had been turned on in that room. Since I had been the only one in the house and hadn't turned them on, there was no natural explanation for it."

I suddenly recalled that Ingrid had "gotten" the name Margaret when we had first entered the chintz room. Certainly Marmie and Margaret are close enough.

When we had first entered the house, I had asked Virginia Cloud to observe what she could, psychically speaking, and to make notes of her impressions. She too had a very strong impression in the chintz room of a woman named Louise, which of course, could have been Lewis. She "saw" her as a woman with white hair and blue eyes, wearing a kind of filmy nightgown, possibly with a cap on her head, and felt that she had lived quite a long time ago. Virginia senses that the woman had some anxiety about another person *whom she also felt present in the room.* The other person Virginia thought was a very vital individual, and she "got" the name Henry or Alexander. Local tradition has had it that a restless spirit from another century lived on in the patrician rooms of Castalia. Is it a Revolutionary wraith, or indeed Mrs. Lewis, waiting for her beloved son to return from the hunt?

As we were about to leave, I noticed a book on the table in the library downstairs. It was *A Pride of Lions,* by Lately Thomas. The book deals with the life of a local celebrity, John Armstrong Chandler. When Ingrid saw it, she let out a little cry. The book seemed to have been placed there, as if to greet her. You see, it was Ingrid who had designed the jacket for it.

The Farm is a most unlikely name for one of Charlottesville's oldest buildings. Actually, it is a handsome two-story brick house, with a prominent fireplace on one end. The downstairs is now divided into two rooms—a front room very much the way it was in colonial days, and a back room now used by the owner, the postmaster of Charlottesville, as a kind of storage room. Upstairs are two bedrooms. The house stands in a tree studded lot right in the very center of Charlottesville. A little to the left of the house, the postmaster pointed out the spot where the old Kings Highway used to go through. It was here also that Ingrid felt the vibration of many men passing by.

On the outside of The Farm, a simple plaque reminds visitors that this is one of the most historical spots in the area. Carefully avoiding any opportunity for my mediumistic friend to see that plaque, Horace Burr, Virginia Cloud, Ingrid, and I arrived at The Farm at three o'clock in the afternoon and immediately proceeded to the main room downstairs, where Ingrid stood transfixed in front of the colonial fireplace. To her, the little house looked like any other pre-colonial stone building; there was nothing to indicate that it had been of any significance in the past. As Ingrid stared at the fireplace, another strange thing happened. Almost simultaneously and frequently complementing one another, she and I got impressions from the past, rapidly, as it were; we both said whatever came to our minds. "I'm getting something about sickness in this room," Ingrid said, while I heard myself say, "I get the feeling of people with long rifles, shooting from the upper story. They are wearing gray jackets and light colored pants, and the rifles are very long. This is in the direction away from the fireplace." Both of us said that men were making plans in the house at one time, and that it had to do with the defense of the building.

"I have the feeling that wounded people are being brought in right down here," Ingrid said. "I get the name Langdon or Langley and the name Nat." She walked around the room and then returned to her position near the fireplace. "I think the people with the light-colored breeches and the brown waistcoats and the long rifles are watching the road nearby for someone to come up that road. This is like a blockhouse, and there is some great anxiety about someone on his way up here. This is a last-ditch defense; there are perhaps five or six men, and they are militia men. I get the feeling of them lying on their stomachs upstairs with those huge rifles pointing with their long barrels and bayonets on top of them. The bullets are homemade, and it is the middle of the night. And then I get the feeling of a skirmish."

"It is like a flank," I said, feeling my way through an indefinite something in the air. "Someone is coming from the *wrong direction* to defend it. They should be coming this way, but they're coming the other way. They are coming up rather than down, and this is a terrible catastrophe for the defenders. I think if they get through, then it is all over."

I asked Virginia Cloud whether she had felt anything in the place. "I had a feeling of sickness here, as if it might be a hospital. I see Redcoats, Tories."

I turned to Horace Burr, asking him to comment on our observations. He seemed plainly delighted. "Well, I thought the most amazing thing that you said was this kind of replay of a group of armed forces, a flank, because there was a very interesting little maneuver that happened down the road, an attempt to cut off the main body of the armed forces coming here. The attempt went awry, though. The American troops were entrenched along the road here, expecting the British to come *this* way. Unfortunately, they came the *other* way, so the British did take Charlottesville for one night. This is a very little known fact of history, and I'm sure you wouldn't have been aware of it. What you said was so interesting because it was one of those little events that are enormously important but did not become generally known because the stratagem didn't work."

"What about the defense outpost here and the men with their rifles upstairs? Do they make any sense?"

"Yes, indeed. From upstairs you could see where this flank should have been down the road, and so they probably were up there looking out for the oncoming troops."

"What about their dress?"

"Of course, they were all colonial, not professional soldiers."

"What about the name Nat?"

"This house was owned at the time by Nicholas Merriweather Lewis. He was a colonel and George Washington's aide. Nat was a colonial nickname for Nicholas."

"What about sick people in here?"

"This was an important center, and the owner's wife, Mary Walker Lewis, was well known for her interest in the public and public affairs. Her father owned Castle Hill. She and her husband were first cousins, both descended from the original Nicholas Merriweather, who had come here from Wales via Jamestown."

Why had Ingrid been so fascinated by the fireplace and the area immediately before it? Although she couldn't pinpoint it in so many words, she insisted that something terribly important had taken place in that very room. To be sure, no ghost had stayed behind in The Farm. But an indelible imprint of an important link with the past was indeed still alive in the atmosphere of the little house.

It was on June 14, 1781, that Colonel Banastre Tarleton, the British commander, had been seen by John Jouett, who then took his famous ride to warn Jefferson and the legislature of the approaching British. About that, anon. When Tarleton finally got to Charlottesville late the same day, proceeding along the old Kings Highway and destroying several wagonloads of Continental supplies on the way, he thwarted the carefully laid plans of the defenders of Charlottesville, two hundred men to whom the defense of the village had been entrusted. They had been planning an ambush in the gorge below Monticello. Captain John Marson, in command of the detachment, was disappointed, but there was nothing to be done. As Tarleton entered Charlottesville, he saw The Farm, with Mrs. Lewis standing at the door, far more curious than frightened. "I think maybe I'll stay here," Tarleton is quoted as saying, and decided to make The Farm his headquarters for the night. Mrs. Lewis had heard all sorts of stories about the handsome Tarleton. The Colonel was twenty-seven and very courteous. "Madam, you dwelt in a little paradise," she quoted him in her diary.

Tarleton spent the night in front of the fireplace which had so attracted Ingrid, leaving the rest of the house to Mrs. Lewis, whose husband was away with the Continental Army. He spent the night wrapped in his greatcoat, in a chair which once stood in front of the fireplace but which was taken to Carrsgrove, the home of Horace Burr, several years ago.

It had been an unforgettable day, as Horace Burr put it, and the only night Tarleton spent in the area. Evidently the imprint of the expected but never realized ambush and the feelings of the men lying in wait for their feared foe had been left so strongly in the atmosphere of the house that Ingrid and, to some extent, I were able to tune in on it and reconstruct it.

What can one possibly say about Carrsgrove that the owners, Horace and Helen Burr, direct descendants of Aaron Burr, have not said at one time or another, either in person or in print? Carrsgrove is their home, and they live in it happily and with great style. But it is more than just a home; it is a landmark of great importance, meticulously maintained by Burr and gradually turned into a personal museum. Where else can you find a Gainsborough, a Hogarth portrate of the young King George III, and dozens upon dozens of fine paintings and art works of the seventeenth and eighteenth centuries? Where else can you find a complete blend of antiquities and today's way of life, a little garden with a terra cotta statuette, and, above all, so many important pieces of furniture directly associated with the American Revolution? Not only is Professor Burr the foremost art authority in Albemarle County, as the area is now called, but he can tell you within a fraction of a second who was married to whom two hundred years ago, who their children were, and who they married in turn; his genealogical knowledge is absolutely fascinating, if not frightening. However, all those whose births Horace Burr knows so intimately are the right kind of people, from the Virginia horse country's point of view—the old families. The Randolphs, the Carrs, the Merriweathers, the Lewises, and last but certainly not least, the Burrs.

When I visited the house for the first time in 1964, I was already overwhelmed by its historical atmosphere. People have lived continuously on the spot where Carrsgrove now stands, but the stone house was erected in 1748 by a certain David Reese. This was fourteen years before an Act of Assembly established the town to be called Charlottesville, in honor of Princess Charlotte of Mecklenburg-Strelitz, the wife of the new king, George III. From the Reese family the house passed into the Maury family.

A rising young lieutenant of only twenty years of age by the name of James Monroe, who had been with General Washington at Trenton, visited the house many times during the early years of the Revolutionary War. It was here on April 21, 1779, that the citizens of Albemarle County signed their own "Declaration of Independence." In 1787 the house passed into the hands of Mr. and Mrs. Hudson Martin, probably the first citizens of Charlottesville, except for Thomas Jefferson and the leaders of the Revolutionary War. Martin was George Washington's nephew and Mrs. Martin the daughter of Colonel Nicholas Merriweather Lewis, owner of The Farm in town. Later the house attracted the attention of James Monroe's brother, Joseph Jones Monroe, who purchased it in 1797. Fortunately, James Dinsmore, the famous architect, was then at work at Monticello, the home of Thomas Jefferson, and he was persuaded to design the mantelpiece of the fireplace at Carrsgrove as well.

In 1799 James Monroe was elected governor of Virginia, and the following year he decided to buy Carrsgrove from his brother. For the next nine years Carrsgrove was the home of James Monroe, who was later to become President of the United States. His granite bust done from life now stands in the garden of Carrsgrove.

But Monroe was not the only great American who left his imprint in the atmosphere of Carrsgrove. In 1824, when Lafayette visited Charlottesville, a party was given in his honor at the house. During the War between the States, the infamous General George A. Custer made the house his headquarters, renaming it Piedmont, the name often given to that part of Virginia. Some alterations were made in 1896 by the then owner, Price Maury, who united the original stone house with two other buildings which were already standing in 1790. The Burrs acquired the house in 1955.

It had been decided to spend the late morning of our second day in Charlottesville at the Burr house, culminating in luncheon.

Naturally, Ingrid knew nothing whatsoever about the house, and during the television interview I gave to the crew from Richmond I made sure that she did not have a chance to speak to anyone about it. Horace Burr thought we should try the library first, since the downstairs front portion of the house was in the oldest section. He was curious to see what Ingrid might discover in the beautifully appointed library, which would have done any English manor house proud.

It was quiet all around us when we entered the library. As I did so, I felt a strange chill traveling down my spine for which there seemed to be no rational explanation. I had no foreknowledge of any ghostly manifestations in that part of the house, and to the best of my knowledge, the library was simply that. When I remarked upon it, Ingrid cut in to say that she too felt an unusual chill. "There is a lot of malice here, not toward anyone in this house, but there is a plan to execute someone."

I requested that she seat herself in a comfortable chair in the library and try for the semitrance state in which the deeper layers of consciousness might be contacted. After a few moments, Ingrid continued. "I think there are three men, and they are making plans to kill one person in an ambush. This has to do with politics, and we are somewhere in the 1730s or 1740s. *I can hear them talk around the fireplace.* The room is very tiny, not too much furniture in it. The floor is bare. I have a feeling they are killing this person unjustly."

I noticed how Horace Burr was hanging on every word coming from her lips. "Why do they want to kill him?" I asked.

"He is a landowner. It has something to do with importing. They have a private grudge against him."

"Where is this ambush to take place?"

"About five or six miles from here. They're going to shoot him on his way home."

"Do they succeed?"

"Yes."

"Are they ever found out?"

"No." She added that the body was later discovered; it was not a presence she felt, but an imprint from the past.

"What was the explanation given for his death?"

"They said it was a robbery."

"Is there anything else you can find out about this man or the plot?"

"The man is a tradesman, but he is also interested in political office. Like a representative or a seat in the government."

"Can you catch his name?"

"He belongs to a prominent family. Something beginning with A."

Since Ingrid indicated that she could not get any more about the room, I turned to Horace Burr for verification of the material we had just heard.

"I know the family this concerns," he replied, "and since I have the invoice of what was in the house at that time, I know she is correct about the furniture."

"What about this ambush?"

"The builder of this house, David Reese, died only three years after he had moved in. It was a sudden and seemingly unexplained death. Just what happened to this man and why he died after such a short time, all these things make you kind of wonder."

"What about his running for the Assembly?"

"Not to my knowledge. However, a somewhat later owner, Joseph Jones Monroe, did sit in the House of Burgesses."

We decided to go to the upper floor. Walking up the narrow staircase, Ingrid found her way directly to a small bedroom on the other side of the house. I had written about this room in 1965, but Ingrid had no idea where she was or what the room meant to anyone. In addition to a beautiful sixteenth-century bed, there was a hand-carved wooden chair in a prominent position—so prominent, in fact, that Ingrid could not help but sit down in it. I asked Ingrid to tell us about any impressions she might have about the room or the chair. Immediately she said, "I sense a tragedy here, and I think it involves a child."

"Oh, God," Burr exclaimed involuntarily. "Please go on."

"I think that someone may have sat in this chair and watched a child die or that something awful happened. I think it was a boy not older than seven. A disease that couldn't be treated. A lingering death. Something awful, like scarlet fever or cholera."

"What happened to the mother?"

"I sense that it is a woman's presence here trying to hold on to the life of a young child. She is alone somehow. The child is all she has. I think this was her home."

"Do you feel her presence here too?"

"Yes, but I sense the child very strongly. I think this was a child's room. The woman does everything she can with doctors, but nothing can be done. The child is delirious for a long time."

Since I knew from my own recollections of Carrsgrove and from the look Horace Burr gave me while Ingrid was speaking that she had accurately retold the story of the haunting in the room, I decided to test her in relation to the chair in which she was sitting. I pointed out a similar chair on the other side of the room. Evidently, they were a pair, both extremely well carved and at least two hundred or two hundred fifty years old. Ingrid insisted that her feelings concerned not an imprint from the past but an actual presence, something we usually call a ghost. As she was speaking, we all noticed a chandelier move considerably of its own volition. Later, after we had completed the session, we tried unsuccessfully to cause it to move by walking up and down the stairs, walking around the room itself, or doing whatever we could to create vibrations. The chandelier remained immobile.

But Ingrid could not get anything further about the chair. Somehow the overwhelming presence of the woman and the child canceled out any less potent impressions the chair might have carried. I turned to Horace Burr and asked him, as usual, for comments.

"Ingrid was very close to the tragedy which occurred here," he began. "The woman was sitting in this chair, and three feet from it is the spot where she killed herself. It was about her child, which she thought was hopelessly sick. As you know, Hans, we heard her sobbing voice many years after her death and thus discovered the tragedy which had occurred here many years before. But these could not be the chairs she sat in; they came later. The area, however, is correct. Incidentally, these are the oldest documented man-made things in America; they came over from Wales, first to Jamestown, and then to this area. These are the chairs that used to be in The Farm, and in one of them General Banastre Tarleton spent the night wrapped in his cloak in 1781. Incidentally, the unfortunate woman whose presence Ingrid felt here took poison because she felt the child would be deformed. Her dying gasps were heard at the other end of the hall, across the stairwell into the master bedroom, where her father was sleeping, and as he stepped out into the hall and heard her gasps, she died. The child however, grew up to be a perfectly normal and beautiful young woman."

Which proves that a powerful ghostly manifestation from this century can very well overcome the rambling, though pungent, thoughts of an eighteenth-century British general, especially if he, as Tarleton did, enjoyed the hospitality of his Revolutionary "enemies" far more than was customary under the circumstances.

Down in Florida

Dr. Rebekah Parker is a long-time resident of Fort Myers. She has taken the occult matter-of-factly all her life, neither being afraid nor shying away from it because of her position. That is because she has had experiences herself. Experiences that can't be explained on so-called rational grounds. Many years ago she was in charge of a children's home in another state. When she took the position she was assigned a certain room. The room seemed cheerful enough at first. Soon, however, she realized that there was something terribly wrong with it. Almost from the start of her residence there she would awake around three o'clock in the morning with the definite impression that someone was trying to choke her. The strange sensation was not of her own doing, she realized; there was nothing physically wrong with her. While she considered asking for another room and at the same time dismissing such a request as outlandish and probably out of place, she also realized that something had to be done about the situation.

One day the grandmother of one of the children under her care called on her and engaged her in conversation. Although the doctor had not brought up the subject, somehow the conversation veered toward the occult. The lady avowed freely that she was psychic. Dr. Parker decided she should test the lady's abilities and she asked her whether she could tell her anything about the room they were in. The lady nodded and closed her eyes and leaned back in the chair. Almost instantly the woman went through the movements of someone being choked to death. In front of the doctor's surprised eyes the woman turned purple in the face and had all she could do to break the spell which had suddenly come on her for no apparent physical or logical reason. As soon as she had regained control over herself she explained what had happened. A bride of six months had been choked to death by her husband in that very room.

Dr. Parker demanded proof and details. Again the lady medium closed her eyes and came up with names and dates. How she could have known so much about the house was a mystery, since she had not been in it before. "What shall I do about this?" the doctor asked. "The husband is earthbound," the lady medium said and suggested that the doctor pray for him. Prayer might very well release him. The doctor nodded and thanked the lady for her help. The following night she prayed in earnest until three o'clock. She had prepared herself for this, determined to rid her room once and for all from its evil connotations. At the stroke of three a figure appeared before her. It was a male wearing what seemed like a long nightshirt and a stocking cap on his head. The doctor did not panic but remained in her bed praying. She observed how the figure passed through the open door and walked down the stairs in his bare feet. She could plainly hear the noise of the feet touching the floor. Then she heard him open the front door and disappear into the rose garden in back of the house. Never again did Dr. Parker have the choking experience from that moment on.

She asked the lady who had given her the key to the psychic experiences in the room to return to the home to inform her of her own experiences. Was the unhappy man really gone? Again the medium leaned back and closed her eyes. She could still see him in the garden at night, she explained, but he was no longer earthbound and could leave at will.

Mrs. Alverna Allender lives at West Panama City Beach, Florida. She is a lady in her middle years with grown children and comes from a family where ESP experiences have been frequent. Probably the most unusual experience she has had happened one day in 1965 when she lived in Kenner, Louisiana. She was waiting for the bus with her four-year-old son when suddenly she felt herself traveling at great speed in the direction of the house of a church member whom she knew and who lived about seven miles away from her. She could see the landscape flying by as if she were traveling on a very fast bus. She was nearly there when she turned around and looked back toward where she had come from. At that point she felt her four-year-old pull her leg, saying, "Mommy, the bus is coming." She found herself back at the bus stop. She did not experience any sensation of riding back to the bus stop. One moment she was near a friend's house, the next moment back at the bus stop. She felt somewhat odd but otherwise all right.

All week long she tried to puzzle out her strange experience. About a week after the occurrence had taken place she ran into a friend by the name of Helen Kenner. Agitated, her friend stopped her on the street. "Hey," she said. "Are you haunting me?" Mrs. Allender demanded to know what this was all about. Patiently Helen Kenner explained that she had been in her trailer home a week before when she had seen her standing outside looking in. Immediately she had told her husband that they were going to have a visitor and to put his shirt back on, for it had been a very warm evening. When she turned around and looked out the window the apparition of her friend was gone. She ran outside to look, assuming that her friend had just wandered off for a moment and would enter the house almost immediately, but there was no one around. Mrs. Allender demanded to know what she had looked like, and what kind of clothes she was wearing at the time. Without a moment's hesitation Helen Kenner answered, "A pink blouse and a blue skirt."

Mrs. Allender blanched. The description of her dress was entirely correct. Moreover, she had made that pink print blouse herself, had never worn it before, and thus her friend could not have seen it on a prior occasion.

Carolyn Manning comes from Miami, Florida, though she now lives in Ohio. She has had ESP experiences all her life, but the experience that shook her up the most happened to her not long ago. For several nights she dreamed an identical dream. In this dream a casual friend of hers whom we shall refer to as Mrs. B. called her and asked her to come to her house. In the dream Carolyn went to her friend's house and looked at a cold spot in the den. Her friend had asked her to come over and help her figure out why a certain spot was always so cold. The spot, her friend explained, was so cold she could not even put a chair into it. Next Carolyn saw herself walking up to a patio with sliding doors and had the feeling of gravel under her feet. Then she stepped up one step into a den and could plainly see the wooden panels. Now her friend showed her the cold spot and she reached out and felt the cold air herself. Suddenly she was drawn into that cold spot and felt herself coming out of her own body as if someone else were trying to take over her body. Immediately she knew that it was a young woman and that she was crying very hard. The entity said that she did not know where she was and kept calling for someone named Capp, over and over calling for Capp to help her. The words Carolyn heard in her dream were "Capp, Capp, please come and help me. I am lost. It is dark and I cannot see any more. Please, Capp. Please come and help me." Still in the dream, she heard herself ask the woman's name and was told that it was Elaine or something close to that.

At that point the dream ended abruptly and Carolyn Manning found herself back in her own bed sitting up shaking and crying. She didn't feel that she had dreamed this but somehow that it had happened to her in reality. The impression was so strong it didn't leave her for days. Finally, after thinking it over, she decided to check on it. She hesitated to call her friend, a casual acquaintance, out of fear of being ridiculed, but she kept on having the same dream over and over. Finally it got to be too much and she decided to telephone the lady in question.

Mrs. B. listened quietly as Carolyn Manning told her, in a haunting voice, what she had dreamed. When she had finished there was a moment of silence on the other end of the line.

Then Mrs. B. said that she did have a cold spot in her den and that the description given by Carolyn was entirely correct, yet Carolyn Manning had never been to Mrs. B.'s house and had no way of knowing what it looked like. As for the sobbing woman Elaine, or something close to that, and for her crying out for Capp, Mrs. B. had an answer for that too. Capp was her husband's uncle. He had been married to a woman named Ellen who had died suddenly two months before.

The ways of the unseen are strange at times. Someone "out there" had evidently decided to have Carolyn serve as a go-between bridging the gulf between a distraught and confused spirit and a husband who would want to know that his wife was still alive in another dimension.

Little Mama

Mary's mother was a special kind of woman. She had lived with the psychic for so long it had become part of her everyday nature and she took her premonitions and psychic hunches in her stride.

Her family got so used to mother's foretelling every major event affecting them, they were surprised to find other families did not have such a mother. On one occasion the family had assembled and decided to ask mother to read cards once again. Although she had done so many times before, this time she agreed very reluctantly. When the cards had been "thrown," both Mary—who knew a thing or two about the cards also—and her mother knew why. Mother's death and the difficulties that would follow it were in the cards. Within a year, all that mother had said about her own demise came to pass, but it wasn't the end of mother.

A week after her funeral, a cousin of Mary's by the name of Carrie, was relaxing on her sofa watching television, when her aunt—Mary's mother—stood before her with a smile. Pointing at herself and her radiant countenance, she said, "I'm not dead, see?"

But far from reassuring cousin Carrie, it threw her into a state of shock. Immediately she telephoned another cousin and inquired if her aunt was really dead.

"Indeed she is," the cousin assured her, "We buried her last week." With that, Carrie went back to her sofa, sure she must have dreamed the whole thing. But a moment later, her aunt reappeared, repeating the same message.

Growing up with that kind of psychic awareness made Mary somewhat more tolerant towards the psychic and unknown than other girls of this day and age, but it did not cause her to be unduly interested in the subject either, and she never looked for the thrills of séances, the occult, and the mystic. This was just as well as she married a doctor who had little use for "such foolishness." They had two children, both girls, but after eighteen years of marriage, they broke up and the doctor moved out, leaving the two girls with their mother. Both were now teen-agers and turned out to be bright, knowledgeable youngsters, well-liked in the neighborhood. Katie, the fifteen-year-old, was in high school, and her sister Boots already went to college.

Mary is a petite, quiet-looking woman with a slight Southern accent, who tends to be conservative in dress and manner. Even her "little talent" of being able to read cards for her friends was an embarrassment to her: her Methodist religion was and is a serious matter with her and she really did not want any truck with the occult.

On the day of Halloween, 1962, she and her girls moved into an attractive eighteen-year-old house in Atlanta. The house is in a quiet, suburban neighborhood, and all around are other small homes in little garden plots of the kind that are the backbone of a residential community all over America these days. Not far from the house run the tracks of the railroad, now used only for freight, and old Fort McPherson is a short walk away. This may or may not be of importance in the story I am about to tell, but one of the bloodier actions of the Civil War was fought in that valley, on the very ground the house now stands on.

The house is actually on two levels; at street level there is a large living room which one enters first when coming in from the front. There are three bedrooms deployed around it, and, on the right side of the house, a den leading into the kitchen. From one of the bedrooms there is a stairwell, secured by an iron railing, leading into the basement. There is a closet underneath the stairs. In back of the house, there is a large patio and outside stairs also leading into the basement.

The lower level is only partially finished. The rear third is left open for an additional room, and the front third is a dirt area containing the furnace, and slanted toward the front of the house. Only the right-hand third of the basement area is actually used by the family. A laundry room occupies most of the space and a wall seals it off from the undeveloped dirt area.

Everything about the house is cozy and warm. The furniture is pleasant and functional and if it weren't for the events following their move, Mary and her daughters would be just another genteel Southern family whose man had left, but who carried on nonetheless properly and adequately. Mary had been a topnotch secretary for many years and was respected in the community.

Immediately after they had moved in and gotten settled, Mary knew there was something odd about the house. She woke up in the middle of the night and sat bolt upright in bed: someone was digging downstairs!

Impossible, she thought, but when the noise persisted night after night, she wondered whether her neighbors weren't perhaps putting in a water pipe. The sound emanated from beneath the stairs in her bedroom, directly underneath which was the basement.

After a while, she decided she had to know what was behind that scraping, digging sound. She left her bed and went downstairs to see if she could find any reason for the sound. There was nothing. No rats or mice. No freshly turned up dirt either inside or outside the house. The neighbors weren't doing any digging, either. Then, just as suddenly as it had started, the digging stopped. Mary was ready to sigh with relief and hoped that her fears of the house had been unfounded.

But her joys were premature. Night after night, at exactly 2 A.M. she and her daughters heard the sound of someone trying to break into the house, but there was never anyone there, and after they had lost a lot of sleep, they called the police. When the police failed to turn up any clues, Mary installed heavy bolts inside the front and rear doors. That very day she returned from an errand to an empty house and found the heavy bolts of the back door ripped away—from the inside!

When Mary moved into the house, she had been on the verge of a nervous breakdown due to her unhappy marriage. When the phenomena started, she was afraid to discuss them with anyone, even her own girls, out of fear that word would get back to her estranged husband and she would be held mentally deficient. Soon her usual afternoon naps were disturbed by an unseen person entering the house, walking through it as if he or she knew it well, and sometimes even running the water or flushing the toilet. Even the bolted doors did not stop this incursion. Often, when she was doing her laundry in the basement, she would clearly hear footsteps over her head, then the sound of drawers being opened and shut, and water being run. She tried to change her hour of rest to thwart the intruder but no matter how she changed it, the unseen presence found her out and disturbed her rest. It was almost as if someone knew what went on in her mind, someone *inside* the house!

Hiding her fears from her daughters did not work, either. Katie, bright girl that she is, seemed unduly frightened and finally her mother questioned her. That was when the two women realized they had both heard and experienced the same unearthly things. Moreover, Katie had felt a pair of hands upon her during the night when she knew she was alone in the room.

On one occasion Mary saw a pair of men's slippers before her, and a pair of feet in them, but no other part of the body. Thinking someone had come in to kill her, she was frozen with fear. After a while, which to her seemed eternity, the materialization faded. As soon as she could, she gathered her things and ran to her mother's house.

In plain daylight, such heavy objects as books began to disappear or reappear at other places and it seemed as if someone were playing a cat and mouse game with them. But who, and why?

When the older girl, now eighteen, came back from school, she did not realize what her mother and sister had gone through. So it was with considerable surprise that she heard someone using a typewriter in the basement when they all knew that there was no one there, and no typewriter.

With a grim sense of humor, Katie explained to her sister that it was "only" a ghost!

Katie had gotten used to the presence in the house. Of course she had no idea that some of the power for the manifestation might come from her, being at the age when poltergeist phenomena are possible. One night she was awakened from heavy sleep by that certain feeling that she was not alone in the room. She was right. There, by her bedside, stood a shadowy figure. Her mother was in the other bedroom, and Katie actually slept in what was before her mother's room, the most haunted part of the house. While the figure vanished, there were other tangible proofs of a presence. Someone was forever pulling Mary's blanket off her as if to rouse her. Katie was luckier. Her blanket was only pulled once in the years they occupied the house. Perhaps the ghost was nonplused by Katie's attitude, which now alternated between contained fear and refusal to be upset by the unseen intruder.

Even Christopher, their cat, became terrified and refused to go outside or to the basement "to do his business," as Katie would call it, unless accompanied by one of them.

Soon Mary and her daughters realized that they weren't dealing with one ghost alone. On several occasions, the quick footsteps of a child were heard by them, along with the heavier footsteps of an adult. Someone seemed to be calling out to them by name. In January of 1968, when they had learned to live with the dreaded powers in the house, Mary awoke to the sound of music, faintly coming from the area of the kitchen ventilator. She investigated but found neither a radio playing nor any reason for this music to be heard. So she returned to bed and tried to ignore it. Just then two sets of footfalls reached her ears through the covers. One set of feet turned toward Katie's room, while the other pair of feet came right toward her bed! There they stopped abruptly. Something icy then seemed to touch her chest. She screamed and jumped from her bed. Apparently this broke the attack and she was able to look into Katie's room. But her daughter was fast asleep.

A peculiar smell now caught her attention, as she returned once more to her own room. It seemed like a mixture of oil, gasoline and dirt and reminded her of some of the filling stations she had bought gas in.

Still critical of her faculties, Mary wanted to make sure she was neither dreaming nor imagining the whole incident.

Prior to her secretarial work, she had been working for a group of psychologists and knew the elementary precautions one must take if one wants to be sure of one's facts. But she was fully awake and had not dreamed it.

About this time Mary began to wonder about the unseen—or, rather, *generally* unseen—presences in the house. How were they, first of all, able to manifest themselves in so forceful a manner. She knew enough about the psychic to realize that someone had to be the medium, but she did not think it was she, at least not alone. Then one night she had her answer. She awakened to the sound of a voice coming from Katie's room. A female voice was saying a phrase over and over again, and Katie was answering by repeating it. As Mary strained her ears, she could clearly hear it. "Golden sand," the voice said in a sweet, kindly voice and "Golden sand," Katie replied in a childish voice totally different from her adult, normal tone. Then she heard Katie clap her hands and say, "Now what can I do?"

By now Mary had tiptoed over to Katie's room and was peeking inside. To her surprise, Katie was fast asleep in bed. She woke the girl and told her to come into her own room. Puzzled and half asleep, Katie obeyed and spent the rest of the night with her mother. The following morning, Mary questioned her about the phrase "Golden sand." Katie did not recall having spoken during the night, but the phrase did seem vaguely familiar to her.

As the days wore on, Katie recalled and finally discussed with her mother an "experiment" she had undertaken a year before, during the Christmas holidays. The two girls and a friend had decided to while away the evening with a homemade ouija board more for fun than because of a desire to stir anything psychic into greater activity. Neither of the two girls particularly "believed in" ouija boards, but they were curious.

What developed was a communication, allegedly from the ghostly intruders.

A girl by the name of Cathy claimed to have been murdered by her own brother, who lived with her mother and herself on the plot of land adjoining the house. There was an insane stepfather, too, and it was his restless ghost that did the walking, the communicator claimed, along with her mother and herself. The date given was 1949. The spot where the communicator claimed to have been buried was indeed the area where most of the noises, such as the nocturnal "digging" had been heard. But can one trust information obtained from a ouija board? Katie was not too convinced and put little stock into the information at first. One day she saw a fortyish woman "out of the corner of her eye" and felt someone fondling her hair. Was the ghostly woman kind to her because she reminded her of her own unfortunate daughter? Or was Katie's imagination running away with her?

But soon Mary also became aware of the "Little Mama" as they came to call her. Her own mediumship had evidently gotten to the surface under the attacks of the psychic around her.

Relaxing finally, in an effort to find out what the ghost wanted with her, Mary was able to "hear" with her inner ear the psychic message sent her from the woman, over and over again.

"I need your help to cross the stream!"

Did she mean she did not know how to cut herself loose from the house and go over to the Other Side? Very likely, Mary thought, but what could she do to help?

Three days later, while she was having her afternoon nap, she heard someone come through the front door. She sat up and yelled at the unseen presence to go away and leave her alone.

A man's gruff voice replied, "She can see me!" But Mary saw no one. A few hours later she heard the now familiar female voice whisper in her ear, "I need your help!"

"Where are you?" Mary said aloud.

"In the basement . . . in the dirt . . ."

Mary went downstairs, unafraid now, and turned on all lights. All was quiet then.

It occurred to her that the evil one, the man, was trying to harass them, while the "Little Mama" was actually attempting to protect them, as best she could.

An almost emotional relationship resulted from this belief on Mary's part, and she was able to summon Little Mama at will now, or so she thought. She felt her presence at times but never got to actually see her. But the friendlier she got with the female ghost the more threatening the male wraith seemed to get. At one point Mary was sure he was trying to kill her and burn the house down while they were asleep.

By now there was no longer any question that their house was indeed haunted—all they wanted to know was how to get rid of their unwanted guests. Had Mary alone experienced these things, perhaps not much would have come of it, but her girls also felt them and especially Katie, who had had physical contact with unseen hands. Something had to be done or their sanity wouldn't be worth a cent. All the while the voices kept getting louder and bolder and the footsteps more frequent.

Mary felt a "man under the bed with a knife" and the ringing in her ears that preceded actual voices kept getting more frequent each day.

If they were hallucinating all this to make themselves suffer, what was the point? Consciously, Mary wanted nothing more than peace and quiet, and unconsciously, at the very worst, she had deep-seated emotional disappointments, but hardly a desire to hurt herself. Katie's exuberant life force was hardly a hideout for repressed hostilities and her level-headed attitude towards the phenomena at this point indicated no hidden motives for attention: someone as beautiful as she was scarcely needed more attention: both adults and her own teen-age friends liked her and made her one of the most popular girls in the community.

And yet, the phenomena in the house were rising in a steady crescendo that could lead only to disaster.

At this point, Mary found her religion once more.

Turning to Jesus Christ as a means of driving out "the demons," she managed to hold on by the sheer willpower of her Biblical faith. Not so for the young girls, but their involvement with the psychic was far less total than their mother's.

"These creatures are trying to get into bed with me," Mary complained with a feeling of horror.

She could take it no longer and voluntarily checked herself into the nearest hospital.

After a week and total rest away from the disturbances, she felt stronger again and was ready to face the problem once more. She returned home, but continued her treatments at the hospital as an outpatient.

Then she invited a group of people interested in psychic research to try to exorcise the presences in her home.

The group, headed by a distinguished metaphysician, came and performed the ancient rituals of "casting out the demons," demons meaning not devils but deranged human spirits.

It didn't help very much or for very long, though. The Little Mama no longer communicated with Mary. Instead, the harsh, male voice commanded her to do things, and she obeyed. It dawned on Mary that her mediumship had opened her up to such incursions and there was little she could do to stop them.

She fought, feebly, but was unable to keep herself from doing the unseen tormentor's bidding.

"Get up," he would command, and the voice resounded loudly in her mind, "Get up and do something." So she finally fought her sleepy condition and washed some dishes.

Sleeping pills made it possible for her to find some rest, but the ghostly presences came back as soon as she opened her eyes again.

"I need you," she heard a female voice plead and realized that Little Mama had finally broken through again, "I need you, come to the basement. . . ."

And then, somehow, the voices faded. Whether the work done by the local psychics had loosened the hold the entities had had over Mary and the house, or whether the ghosts simply got bored with it all, no one can say for sure.

But Mary got her strength back and her reason and Katie turned once more into a good-looking, average youngster more concerned with the next dance than with psychic phenomena.

Perhaps Mary's visits to the basement, her genuine affection for the unfortunate woman spirit, had somehow helped her across that stream she had been unable to cross by herself. Once gone, the man's presence would no longer be emotionally motivated.

As the days grow into weeks and the weeks into months, the whole terrible period of their possession becomes less and less real to Mary and her daughters and perhaps that, too, is as it should be, for the line between reality and fantasy is very faint indeed at times, almost as faint as a ghost finally giving up his hold upon his earthly memories and tragedies.

The little house by the railroad track has been quiet and pleasant ever since.

Louisiana Ghosts

Jean Hatton comes from a family in which the psychic has been in evidence for many generations. Precognitive dreams, clairvoyance, foreknowledge of events or places have been rampant on her mother's side of the family, and even as a pre-teenager Jean had some ESP experiences. Around forty years of age now, she and her husband live in the heart of New Orleans. She was a professional musician for a while and taught music in high school for five years. Her mother's family is Irish, Dutch, and Indian, while her father's side of the family came from Wales, England, and Ireland. Thus a predominance of Celtic elements in her background may be responsible for her readiness to accept the reality of psychic phenomena. At any rate, when she moved from her childhood home in San Antonio, Texas, to New Orleans she made friends with a married couple living on Decatur Street in the French Quarter. The very first time she tried to enter their apartment she almost tripped. She felt a kind of elastic force trying to keep her out as if she were not welcome. The house in which the couple's apartment was located was a very old house. That one and some of the adjoining ones were among the few that hadn't been destroyed in the fires so common in this part of town. At least two hundred years old, the house in question was one of the finest examples of colonial architecture.

Forcing her way through the invisible curtain, Jean then entered the apartment. She saw an old fireplace against one wall facing a bedroom door. The entrance was to the right. To the left were the living room and a long narrow room probably used as a pantry or wardrobe. The owner of the apartment tried to tell her that something very tragic had occurred in the apartment, but before he could do so Jean herself told him the story. How she could know this was as much a mystery to her as it was to her host. But she pointed at a clock and insisted that it would always stop at three o'clock in the morning because it was then that "something had happened." Before she knew what she was doing, Jean found herself standing by the fireplace looking at the clock. Then she turned toward the door, resting her hands on the mantelpiece. She seemed to be wearing a white gown with full sleeves, probably a nightgown. At this moment she clearly heard steps. A door was opened and through it came the "wrong man." The man she saw now clairvoyantly was tall, had unruly gray hair and a deep-set type face. He wore a silk hat and black cape. She knew then that the woman was trying to express herself through her; that she had been stabbed where she stood and had fallen in front of the fireplace.

At this moment she came out of her semi-trance. It was all she could get, but her host assured her that the impression was not fantasy. He explained that he had seen just such a woman walk at night, her bloody hands crossed on her breasts. Both he and his wife had frequently heard the footsteps of someone coming up the stairs to their third-floor apartment. One night when Sheri, the wife, was home alone playing old English folk songs on her guitar, she looked up and saw the two entities standing there in the door. She was not afraid so she kept on looking at them before they faded away.

It became clear to the owner of the apartment that something very drastic had occurred at a previous time. But they could not figure it out and learned to live with their spectral visitors. One day the husband was up in the attic, above their apartment, clearing up some flooring. To his horror he discovered two human skeletons underneath. Hastily closing the door to the attic behind him, he took the two skeletons and quietly buried them. He decided not to report the matter to the police after all since it might have been something that had occurred a long time ago and calling attention to it now might draw unfavorable publicity to himself and the house. From that moment the psychic phenomena stopped abruptly. But the owner of the apartment was not satisfied until he knew what had caused the two skeletons to be buried in so unusual a place as the attic of the apartment. He started to dig into the past of the house and asked questions around the area. As far as he could figure out, this is what happened. The woman in the nightgown had lived in the apartment, and once while she was waiting for her lover the door had opened and instead of her lover her husband had come through it. He had discovered the relationship and had come to kill her. After he had murdered her he in turn waited until the lover arrived and killed him too, then hid the bodies in the attic.

Silently the host handed Jean a knife to touch and psychometrize, that is to say, read from it what could be gleaned of its past. As if she had been handed a glowing piece of coal she dropped it immediately. She could not touch it no matter how often she tried. The knife was an old knife of nondescript appearance, with a discolored blade, and of no particular merit. Almost hysterical, with sobs Jean assured her host that it was the knife that had been used to murder the woman. He nodded. He himself had found the blade among the bricks of the fireplace.

Ghosts in Texas

When Texas joined the union it had the option of becoming five separate states or remaining one large state. As we all know, the new state chose to be one state. If it is larger than states are supposed to be in a federal union it also has a tendency to aim for bigger and better things. Not necessarily to accomplish them, but to try to interest other states and people in them. So it doesn't come as a great surprise that there are comparatively more psychic occurrences in Texas than there are in a smaller state. Also, its colorful history, during which the area changed hands several times, has contributed to the number of psychic incidents from the past. Texas contains at least two major population centers, Dallas and Houston. Thus the psychic occurrences in Texas differ greatly in nature from hauntings in, let us say, the Carolinas or Virginia. In the latter they are frequently connected with homesteads and very old houses. In Texas the phenomena take on a more personal note and seem to be tied in with people rather than locations.

Elaine M. is a pleasant woman in her thirties living about 50 miles from Houston. On my last visit to that city I talked to her about two of the many strange experiences she has had. These two shook her up more than anything else that had happened to her and I began to see why.

The first event happened in the fall of 1957. Elaine and her husband had just received word that their two closest friends, Jack and Linda S., with one of their children, had died of asphyxiation in their home in Florida. Apparently Linda had been slated for brain surgery two weeks later and had not been able to face it. The death by gas of three people so close to her depressed Elaine very much. She and Linda had been very close, cared for each other and worried about each other's children. But after several months she began to come out of her depression. In January of 1958 Texas underwent an unusually hard cold spell. It was therefore necessary to use additional heaters, and it was the custom in Mr. and Mrs. M.'s home to leave the gas heat on all night. In the kitchen there was an ordinary open gas stove, but they kept the flame low, and since the windows were all locked there didn't seem to be any danger of any of the flames going out and causing gas to leak into the apartment.

One night, at two o'clock in the morning, Elaine felt herself waking up. Clearly as if she were standing next to her she heard her good friend Linda speak to her. "Elaine," the voice said, "get up and see about the boys." Elaine was terrified and fully awake now. As she was about to jump out of bed she smelled gas. She ran to the boys' room and found the gas jets wide open. In another five or ten minutes the gas would have caused an explosion from the other heaters. Quickly Elaine turned them off. At this moment she felt a cool moist cloud surround her and clearly heard her late friend Linda laugh and say, "I told you." For several days after this Elaine was upset over what had occurred. She was grateful to her late friend for having warned her but at the same time she did not easily accept the communication from the beyond. A few days had passed when she found herself discussing the entire matter on the telephone with a minister. Somehow the conversation drifted from the psychic occurrence to her late friend's personal life and the difficulties she had encountered in adjusting to the world in which she lived. As she was speaking so freely about Linda, being all by herself in the room, she happened to turn her head and saw the flame in the heater slowly die out as if someone had just turned it off, yet no one had been near it. At that point she felt a sense of acute anger and a presence beyond her own. Elaine started to cry into the telephone. Her minister friend urged her to hang up and run for it, but even that she was completely unable to do. She knew that her late friend had come to listen in on the conversation about her and that she resented it. A few moments later her minister friend and his wife came running into the apartment. At that point Elaine was able to let go of the telephone and fall to the floor. Linda has not returned since. To this day Elaine regrets having gossiped about her late friend in view of that friend's help on the previous occasion. She remembers the old adage "de mortibus nihil nisi bonum," meaning when you speak of the dead speak only of good things.

The other experience which Elaine cannot ever completely forget occurred not long after the first one. She had an increasing feeling that one of her children would pass on soon. This went on for about a year and caused a mental condition which she found hard to cope with. Somehow she managed to live a normal life in spite of it. On April 2, 1958, she happened to be taking a dozen 4-H Club girls to a fabric shop to look for yard goods. It was 5:15 in the afternoon when she suddenly panicked. Without adequate explanation she rushed the giris in her care to the car and drove like a madwoman toward her home. One mile before she reached her home she passed an ambulance going in the opposite direction, and at that instant she knew that her four-year-old son Scott was already dead. She drove into her street, where her neighbors stood in groups crying and talking. Her fears were confirmed. Someone offered to drive her to the hospital. No one had yet told her exactly what had occurred. Later she learned that the boy had been alive but had died shortly after at the hospital. He had drowned. Apparently, she was told by her husband, he had jumped into a creek after their dog to rescue him. When she was told this, Elaine got very angry and did not wish to speak about it. Why were they all lying to her, she wondered, when she knew so much better what had actually happened. For the next three days she stayed in seclusion. Then the evening after her little boy's funeral she gathered up some of his toys and carried them across the street to some of his little friends. As she did so she suddenly knew that a little boy playmate of her son by the name of Warren had pushed her boy into the creek. Returning home, she confronted her husband with the explanation, and he had no choice but to confirm it. Several times later she felt her little boy's presence although she could not see him. She felt no unhappiness with the little spirit yet wondered whether she should tell him that he had passed on in case he was not aware of it. Then a year after his passing, in September, when he was to have started school she felt him very strongly. A school bus was passing the house when she suddenly heard her dead little boy say to her, "I want to go to school."

Without thinking about what she was doing, she heard herself reply, "But you can't, darling, you're dead." Since then all has been quiet around Elaine's house. She hopes her little boy has found another school of his own over there where he now lives.

Jeffrey Oromaner is an electrical engineer by profession and because of his training not easily given to the acceptance of occult phenomena. He and his family moved into a newly built house on Sharp View Avenue in Houston on November 15, 1968. He was the first occupant of the house. His professional connection with a large computer company makes it necessary for Mr. Oromaner to travel frequently. At such times his wife is alone with their two children. The chain of events which made Mr. Oromaner wonder about poltergeists in his new home began with the sudden appearance of two large stuffed animals belonging to his three-year-old daughter. The animals had been missing for two weeks and no amount of searching had turned them up. Suddenly they reappeared in a most conspicuous place where they could not possibly have been overlooked. While the Oromaner family was still debating this phenomenon something else occurred.

Mr. Oromaner was out of town and his wife and a fourteen-year-old baby-sitter spent the night in the downstairs bedroom of the house with the two children. While downstairs they heard a tremendous amount of walking and moving about upstairs. Immediately assuming that someone had entered the house, they called the police. The police came and found nothing amiss. As soon as the police had left, the walking upstairs resumed. Mrs. Oromaner and the sitter were too frightened to do anything about it during the night, but as soon as morning came they went directly into the children's bedroom upstairs. There they discovered that a table with the boy's electric train on it had moved clear across his large walk-in closet. No one had been upstairs during the night, nor had any human agency made these changes in the room. The following day Mr. Oromaner returned from his trip. He took the report less than seriously and teased his family about it, but when he awoke the next morning he was not so sure of the whole thing. In his daughter's room someone had taken a shelf down from among three shelves hanging on the wall. All the small stuffed animals that had been on the shelf were scattered around the room. Needless to add, the girl had not done this, nor had anyone else been in the room during that time. A few days later Mr. Oromaner had to leave town again for a few days. Thoroughly frightened by now, his wife decided to ask two friends, two fourteen-year-old girls, to stay the night with her. Again they were awakened around two o'clock in the morning by the footsteps of someone walking upstairs. They also heard the boy's window being opened. Since they were all downstairs, including the kids, they decided to barricade themselves in the downstairs bedroom, forcing a heavy dresser in front of the door. Then they went to sleep with somewhat mixed feelings. When they awoke the next morning they discovered that the door to the bedroom was cracked about six inches across.

The following day Mr. Oromaner returned. He listened with somewhat more concern to what had happened in his absence. His wife went to bed early because of a cold. He remained downstairs alone watching television until about 11:30 P.M. Everything was in its proper place. He locked up and went to bed. Awakening the next morning, he noticed that two candle holders and a flower arrangement had been taken off the mantel of the fireplace, along with a ceramic leopard from atop the television, and that all these objects were arranged perfectly on the fireplace. He had not done any such thing nor had anyone else been in the room who could have done this. No one, that is, of flesh and blood. He immediately checked every window in the house, every door and every chain lock; nothing had been tampered with. At this point Mr. Oromaner, despite his scientific training, became thoroughly convinced of the reality of the phenomena in his house. As if in response to his open-minded attitude toward the occurrences, they materialized now with greater frequency. An artificial weeping willow four feet high and rather heavy was moved six feet and lifted up to the first stair of the staircase. All without the help of human hands. Mr. Oromaner's pool balls were scattered and hidden all over his poolroom as if they had been Easter eggs. A flower arrangement was removed from a dresser and found on the floor right next to it without natural cause. Their clock radio was switched on by itself three times in a way that was different from the time he and his wife would have set. It was his custom to turn off all lights before going to bed. Nevertheless, more than once did Mr. Oromaner find the upstairs lights on when he was quite sure that he had not turned the switch prior to going to bed.

One Sunday afternoon his wife was taking a nap in the middle of their king-size bed. Mr. Oromaner was about ten feet away in another room when he heard the telephone fall off the table next to the bed. He assumed that the telephone had been close to the edge and had somehow fallen off but on checking realized that this could not have happened by natural means. He replaced the receiver and went back to the other room. Five minutes later he heard the telephone being violently knocked off the table again, and he ran into the bedroom only to find it stretched the length of its cord on the floor. During all this commotion his wife had been asleep.

At that point Mr. Oromaner requested my assistance in clearing up the matter. Unfortunately his company transferred him to California before I could look into the origin of the strange occurrences at his house on Sharp View Avenue. The new occupants of the house have so far not complained about any unusual goings-on. A written request by Mr. Oromaner to the new owners concerning such matters has remained unanswered, so one can only assume that the new owners have nothing to report or do not care to discuss it. What makes the case even more puzzling is the fact that no ghosts have disturbed the peace of the Oromaner family in their new location in California.

The old Howard home on South Main Street in Henderson, Texas, is a southern mansion of the kind that is so numerous throughout the South. In 1851 the mansion was erected by a certain James L. Howard on land he paid $100 for. It is the oldest brick home in town. Today it belongs to the Heritage Association and is being maintained as a museum, with visitors coming not only from other parts of Texas but even from abroad. The house has three stories and six rooms, and each room has a fireplace of its own. Four columns adorn the front of it. Perhaps the most remarkable thing about the house is the fact that every room has a fireplace, some of them very large old-fashioned fireplaces of the kind you rarely see any more. The stairs have banisters made of the highest grade walnut.

When the Howards built this home they stated proudly, to anyone who would hear it, "God Almighty Himself could not tear it down because it was well built." Even the worst storm seemingly could not touch the house. There is the account of a particularly horrifying electrical storm when a streak of lightning hit one of the corner columns, causing only slight damage. One of the Howard brothers ran out into the yard, looked up into the sky and shook his fist and said, "See. I told you that you couldn't tear down my house." With so large and outstanding a mansion in a small town, it is only natural that legends would crop up around it, some of which are true and some are not. One of them making the rounds concerns a murder in the house. The present owners, the Rusk County Heritage Association, have checked into it and found that an accident and not a murder had occurred. The accident concerns a member of the Howards named Pat Howard who lost his life in an accident in the home. In fact the descendants of the Howards went to great length to explain again and again that Pat Howard died of an accident and that the shooting that took his life was not murder in any sense of the word. Of course, where there is smoke there is sometimes fire. Was the family merely trying to kill the story, or were they correcting the facts? I have never been to the Henderson mansion but have talked with people who have been there, so my account must of necessity be second hand. In 1905 Mrs. M. A. Howard and Dore Howard, being alone, decided to sell the house to a certain Mrs. M. A. Dickinson. Mrs. Howard was then in ill health. The sale did not go down well with her children and the rest of the family, who would have preferred to have the house stay family property. It seems incredible today that such an imposing house could be sold for $1500, but, of course, that was a lot more money in 1905 than it is today. Still, even for 1905, $1500 was very little money for a house of this kind. It seems strange therefore that the sale was made in this manner. The sale of the house from the Howard family to an outsider took the town by surprise. No one had surmised that it could be for sale, especially not for such a low price. The house had a reputation as an historical landmark. Sam Houston himself slept there many times, since he was a cousin of the Howards. In 1950 the house passed from the Dickinson family to Hobart Bryce, who in 1961 deeded the property to the

Historical Association. One of the townspeople who had spent much effort in restoring the old house and who had been active on behalf of the fund-raising committee was a certain Carl Jaggers. Partly due to his efforts and those of others, the house is now in excellent condition again and open to visitors as a museum. My attention was drawn to it when I appeared on a television program in nearby Tyler, Texas. The lady who interviewed me, Jane Lassiter, provided me with much of the material about the Henderson house.

While the controversy among the townspeople concerning the restoration of the house was going on and there was some doubt whether the house could be saved or had to be torn down, no one had the time or inclination to look into any possible ghostly manifestations at the house. But as soon as the matter had quieted down and the house was safe from the wreckers' tools and perhaps because of the renewed quiet in the atmosphere, something did occur that had not been observed before. Maia Jaggers was one of those who served as honorary guides around the house, particularly during the weekends, when there were more visitors than during the week. She would act as hostess to those who came to look at the house. One Sunday afternoon in the winter of 1968, she had just finished showing the house to a group of visitors and was quite alone in it for the moment. She found herself downstairs looking toward the stairway leading to the upper stories. At that precise moment she saw a woman materialize before her eyes. Seemingly solid, or almost so, it was clearly a woman of a past age. As she looked closely at the apparition, she realized that it was the ghost of Mrs. Howard herself. As soon as Maia Jaggers and the ghost had come face to face the apparition floated up the stairway and disappeared. She has not been seen since that time. Could it be that a grateful Mrs. Howard wanted the one person directly connected with the salvage of her home made aware of her continued existence in it? Was her presence in what was once her home caused by a belated regret at having sold out to others against the wishes of her family? If you are ever in Henderson, Texas, be sure and drop in on Mrs. Howard's house. Sale or no sale, she seems to be quite at home in it still.

Grace Trotter lives in Dallas and is in her middle thirties. She is the author of several novels for young girls published by leading houses. In recent years, however, she has become more and more interested in the occult, partly because of an experience that opened her eyes to the continuance of life after death. She contacted me after she had read my book of that title to tell me of a visitation that, in a manner of speaking, had changed her outlook entirely. In 1965 Miss Trotter, who writes under the professional name of Nancy Paschal, suffered the loss of her father in July, and in October that of her mother too. The double passing left a deep imprint on Miss Trotter. Her mother had died on a Friday and was buried the following Monday morning.

That afternoon, after her friends had left the house, Miss Trotter lay down to rest in her house and fell asleep. She was awakened from deep slumber about an hour later by something or someone whose presence she felt in the room. She opened her eyes and looked straight into her mother's face. This was no dream but a fully materialized apparition. She noticed that her mother was dressed in white, and while she was observing her in awe her mother came over to her and kissed her. She felt the imprint of her lips quite clearly. At the foot of her bed stood a smaller woman, a brunette, dressed in red. Grace Trotter also recognized the other woman as her mother's mother, her own grandmother, even though she had died many years before Grace was born. She had been familiar with her appearance from a large picture which had been in the house. Not a word was spoken and the entire experience lasted perhaps five or ten minutes. After it was over Miss Trotter wondered whether she had not been asleep after all when it occurred. There was a certain wish to believe and a deep understanding for the need for this occurrence to have taken place, but at the same time her rational and scientific mind wanted to be sure that that which she had experienced was real. She did not have to wait long for additional confirmation. Two weeks later she awoke one morning and saw her mother again coming from the door. Now Grace Trotter realized that her mother did not look her age, that is to say the age she was when she passed on. Again she wore a beautiful dress. The other woman who had been in the first visitation was along this time too. But what amazed Grace Trotter more was the fact that her mother carried in her arms what appeared to be a six-month-old baby. It came to her in a flash that the baby was she, for she had been six months of age when her mother was twenty-four. The picture of her mother holding her own self as a baby was the additional proof of identity Miss Trotter needed. The apparitions faded quickly, but the imprint they left behind has stayed with her ever since. As a professional writer and poet she felt herself impelled to put down on paper what the experience had meant to her, and she has asked me to reproduce that beautiful poem called *Safe Passage* in this account. Here it is:

SAFE PASSAGE

By Nancy Paschal

My mother passed on a Friday
Just twenty minutes after Thursday midnight.
I was alone with her when she drew the breath
That was final. And it was right
That it was free from pain and peaceful, dear Lord.
But grief caught me like blinding light.
I couldn't see my way without her—
My counselor, my friend, my own sweet mother.
She was a real young eighty-nine
And I had loved her all of sixty-five years,

But giving her up was so hard
That I couldn't stop the hurting or the tears.
She was buried Monday morning.
That afternoon, after all my friends had left,
I lay on my bed and fell asleep.
In an hour, when I woke up sad and bereft,
Mother was standing beside me.
She bent over and kissed my lips, quick and deft
And loving, as she always was.
I gazed into her smiling face
And it was young—not more than twenty-four.
Her body looked strong, with beauty and grace.
One morning two weeks later I woke early
And saw her again, coming in at the door.

She had a six-months-old baby in her arms.
I had been six months old when she was twenty-four.
So the baby was me.
She brought my baby-self back for me to see,
To prove that she still lived and cared
And that death is only a passageway.
The spirit of life everlasting dared
To show itself as plain as day.
Death is a safe passageway.

One of the most popular legends in American ghostlore is the "hitchhiking ghost story." It has been told to me many times by people in many states. Carl Carmer has immortalized the hitchhiking girl ghost in one of his books and there is no doubt that the legend is part of traditional American folklore. Consequently I treat further variations of this tale with extreme caution, if not outright skepticism. Basically the story concerns someone driving at night who is flagged down by a stranger in the road. The stranger is always a girl, always beautiful, and she always wears unusual clothes such as an evening gown or other formal attire. She asks for a lift home, and of course the motorist obliges. The girl then gets in and sits in the back, and when the motorist reaches the destination requested by the girl he turns around and lo and behold there is no one in the back seat. His curiosity has been aroused. He rings the doorbell at the house in question, someone opens the door, and when he describes the girl hitchhiker he is told that the lady in question died many years ago and that this has happened before. So much for the traditional hitchhiking ghost.

I am indebted to Chuck Meegan of the Dallas *Morning News* and to a reader by the name of Joanne Darr of Dallas for a story which seems to run in a similar pattern but has the ring of truth to it. Miss Darr moved to Dallas in 1962 and soon after her arrival heard about the ghost of White Rock Lake. Being somewhat interested in the occult, she questioned those who told her of this particular apparition. The lake is man-made and is now in a residential area, part of a city park. The alleged ghost lived in that area. In former years there were some very fine homes close to the water, and in the thirties these homes were famous for garden parties and boating excursions on the lake. According to tradition, during one of these parties a boat tipped over and a young girl and her fiancé were drowned. In other accounts it is only the girl who was drowned and her ghost is now wandering around looking for her fiancé. She wears evening clothes and tries to hitch a ride back home to Gaston Avenue in the Lakewood area, which is about three miles' distance. But according to local tradition she simply disappears before she gets there. According to some other accounts she disappears immediately after she is given the ride to where she wants to go. Her benefactor then goes to that address and meets her grandfather, who explains the situation to him.

All this seemed terribly ridiculous to Miss Darr. She discussed it with a local friend, who didn't find it so amusing as she did. Her grandfather had been fishing just after dark not long before, and as he looked out onto the lake he clearly saw a human shape floating above the water. He didn't catch many fish that night. The story kept bothering Miss Darr and she did some further research. Through material in the Dallas *Morning News* she made contact with a woman who worked for Neiman-Marcus as the head of the advertising department. The lady was quite obliging in recounting her unusual experience. This happened in the late thirties or early forties, she explained, and it was in the early morning when she and her boyfriend, who later became her husband, were driving home and passing the lake. Suddenly they noticed a girl crawling up the embankment next to the road. They stopped the car in order to help her. She was dripping wet and wore a blue evening dress. She explained that she lived on Gaston just past Lakewood and that she had been in an accident on the lake. They offered to drive her home and the girl got into the back seat of the car. Since the woman and her boyfriend were rather tired at the end of a long evening, they didn't feel like talking to the stranger, and the girl also remained quiet in the back seat. When they were nearing the Lakewood area the woman turned around to see if the girl was all right. To her amazement the stranger had completely vanished. The car they were driving was a two-door sedan, and no one could have gotten in or out through the windows.

The address where the girl once lived has since been turned into an apartment house. Nevertheless, every year, especially in the spring or fall during the height of the social season, various people claim to have seen her there. The story appealed to one of Miss Darr's friends, who decided to do a little bit of ghost hunting on his own. He went to the general area where the figure of the girl had been observed in the past and waited. To his surprise he saw a white form standing in the road. When he came closer to her she dissolved. Evidently the girl of White Rock Lake is still trying to hitch a ride home.

Sylvia W. is in her late twenties, has been married twice and has lived a full and normally exciting life. Since the age of eight she has had precognitive experiences, warnings, feelings about impending events, many of which have come true, and psychic dreams. She has always accepted the importance of ESP in her life and never had any fears of the so-called occult. But recently something has happened in her life that has her stumped. She has fallen in love with a widower, Albert, whose wife and infant daughter were killed in a motorcar accident in 1961. Albert's wife herself had had a premonition of the impending accident and had told him so. Moreover, three days after her death she appeared before him and assured him that she would always be with him and take care of him. Before her passing she had requested that should she die he should not remarry. He did not promise this, but she had earnestly requested it.

As soon as Albert had gotten over the shock of his wife's untimely passing he began to mingle socially once again. Despite increased social interest he remained single. However, when he met Sylvia they became involved with each other in a love relationship. They had originally met because her house was rented from his company. They dated for about six months, and the first four months of their relationship were undisturbed and harmonious. But then strange things started to happen and they couldn't help noticing it. Strange noises and movements occurred both in her house and in his house. That was not surprising since they spent time in both. There were knockings on the door and when they opened it there was no one there. This happened mainly late at night. Then there were sounds of someone walking in the next room or heavy objects seemingly dropping to the floor. Upon investigation they found nothing to substantiate the noises. On occasion the blinds would open by themselves or a book would move of its own volition and open by itself to a certain page while the room in which this happened was closed off and no one had access to it. Apparently someone was trying to convey messages to Albert, for the books were marked at different passages. When they read one of the passages in a particular novel that had been left in a conspicuous spot so that they could not overlook it, they realized who was behind the phenomena. The passage in the book dealt with a female competitor who was domineering; about honest love, and about one partner being "from another world." And one passage referred to someone having seen the light.

Fantastic as it seemed at first, they realized that the dead wife was trying to break up their romance from the beyond. When they were together during the night there was a knocking on the window.

Albert got up to investigate outside. After he had left the bedroom Sylvia rose and looked out onto the patio through the blinds. The lights were on in the patio and she assumed that Albert was checking that area of the house. Also, she clearly heard the door to the kitchen open and close and lock itself. After Albert returned she learned that he had not even been in the back of the house where the patio and kitchen are located. He had been to the front only. In the middle of the night they tried to go over the phenomena and make some sense out of them. In listing them they realized that the disturbances had started just about the time Albert had declared his love for Sylvia. Moreover, Sylvia had just borrowed an object that had belonged to Albert's first wife. It was a typewriter. She had left it on the floor only to find it moved the following morning from the floor and back to the shelf where it had originally been. No one had been near it during the night. That is to say, no one of flesh and blood. What were they to do? Pending a visit to me I explained that they must address the deceased woman and explain the facts of life to her or perhaps the facts of "after life." Only by making her understand the error of her ways could they hope to release her from her compulsion and themselves from her interference. I have not heard from Sylvia since then and can only hope that it worked.

I met Mrs. Ann B. the last time I was lecturing in Houston. She is a middle-class housewife. Her husband is an electrician and doesn't put much stock in her occult experiences. He discourages them. Nevertheless, all through the years Ann has had flashes, premonitions and visions, most of which later became objective reality. She is one of those Texans who have the gift of second sight in a very clear way and would like to use it constructively to help others if not herself. Among the most interesting experiences reported by Ann B. is an incident which occurred in 1957. At the time she was living in a small town near Houston. She was having recurrent dreams in which she saw her husband being hurt. Specifically she saw a flash of fire and her husband came rolling out of it across a wooden floor. He seemed to be in terrible pain. Since she had the dream a number of times she decided to discuss it with him, but he would not listen. Then the dream stopped. A few days after she had had this dream for the last time her husband had to go to a nearby town to do some electrical work in a church. While he was doing this, two high-tension wires accidentally touched and her husband was caught by the current. In order to get out of it, he rolled across a wooden floor and his hands and arms were badly burned. On August 1, 1960, in the evening, she had a vision of her brother-in-law, who lived in another city in Texas. They had not been in touch lately and there really wasn't any emotional reason for her to have the vision at this time. Nevertheless, she suddenly saw his head and shoulders and he seemed to be ascending. The strangest part of this vision was that there were pieces of broken metal floating all around him. She noticed that he had a most peaceful look on his face and knew that he had been killed in an accident. She told her husband so, but it wasn't until the next morning that the telephone rang and they were told that the brother-in-law had been killed in a plane crash.

The interest in mind development classes is considerable in the South today. From this a new crop of non-professional mediums will emerge, people who understand that the gift is natural and not to be shunned. Some time ago I wanted to go to the Alamo with a reputable professional medium to do some research on the spot where so much history was made. Although I addressed the current custodians of this shrine twice and my letter was never returned, I was never given permission to do so nor did I receive an answer. Possibly ordinary people are a little ahead of those who fancy themselves representatives of public opinion. I have received many invitations from Texans to come and visit their haunted houses or to listen to the account of their extraordinary experiences with extrasensory perception, so I can forget the Alamo.

The Headless Grandfather

G rover C. was one of those colorful old-timers you hardly see any-more these days, not even in the deep South. It wasn't that Grover had any particular background in anything special, far from it; he was an untutored man who owed his success solely to his own willpower and an insatiable curiosity that led him places his educa-tion—or lack of it—would have prevented him from ever reaching.

He saw the light of day just before the turn of the century in rural North Carolina. At the age of nineteen he married for the first time, but his wife Fannie and the child she bore him both died from what was then called "childbed fever," or lack of proper medical treatment. He had not yet chosen any particular career for himself, but was just "look-ing around" and did odd jobs here and there. A year later he was mar-ried again, to a lady from Georgia who is still living. After their first girl was born, they moved to Columbus, Georgia, and Mr. C. worked in a local mill for a while. This didn't satisfy his drive, however, and shortly afterwards he and his brother Robert opened a grocery store. The store did right well until "the Hoover panic," as they called it, and then they managed to sell out and buy a farm in Harris County.

Life was pretty placid, and after an accident in which he lost his daughter, Mr. C. moved back to Columbus and tried his hand at the grocery business once more. About this time, the restless gentleman met a lady from Alabama, as a result of which he became the father of an "extracurricular" little girl, in addition to his own family, which eventually consisted of a wife and nine children, two of whom are dead, the others still living.

When his second-born child died of an infectious disease, Mr. C. had his long-delayed breakdown, and for several years, he was unable to cope with his life. During those rough years of slow, gradual recuperation, his daughter Agnes ran the store for him and supported the family.

As his health improved and he began to return to a happier and more constructive outlook on life, he developed an interest in real estate. With what money he could spare, he bought and sold property, and before long, he did so well he could dispense with the grocery store.

Soon he added a construction business to his real estate dealings and was considered a fairly well-to-do citizen in his hometown. This status of course attracted a variety of unattached women and even some who were attached, or semi-detached, as the case may have been, and Mr. C. had himself a good time. Knowledge of his interest in other ladies could not fail to get to his wife and eventually he was given a choice by his wife: it was either her or *them.*

He picked them, or, more specifically, a lady next door, and for thirteen years he was reasonably faithful to her. Eventually she disliked living with a man she was not married to, especially when he happened to be married to someone else, even though he had bought her a cute little house of her own in Columbus. Mr. C. was not particularly happy about this state of affairs either, for he developed a penchant for drinking during those years. After they separated, the lady next door left town and got married.

Far from returning to the bosom of his family, now that the Other Woman had given him the gate, Grover looked elsewhere and what he found apparently pleased him. By now he was in his late sixties, but his vigorous personality wasn't about to be slowed down by so silly a reason as advancing age!

About 1962 he met a practical nurse by the name of Madeline, who turned out to be the opposite of what the doctor had ordered. After a particularly heavy argument, she kicked him in the nose. When it did not stop bleeding, she became alarmed and took him to the hospital. The family went to see him there even though his wife had not exactly forgiven him. But at this point it mattered little. Mr. C. also complained of pain in his side and the children firmly believed that the practical nurse had also kicked him in that area. Since he died shortly afterward, it was a moot question whether or not she had done so because Mrs. C's abilities no longer corresponded to her amorous expectations. The old gent certainly did not discuss it with his family. He was seventy when he died and Madeline was a mere sixty. Death was somewhat unexpected despite the fact Mr. C. had suffered from various ailments. During the days he had been alone in his room at the hospital. At first, he shared the room with another older man, but several days later a young man was sent in to be with him. The young man's complaint was that he had a lollipop stick stuck in his throat. There probably aren't too many young men with such a predicament in medical annals, and even fewer in Columbus, Georgia. The family found this mighty peculiar, even more so since the young man was a close relative of Madeline, the very practical nurse.

They complained to the hospital authorities and the young man was moved. It is not known whether the lollipop stick was ever removed from his throat, but chances are it was or we would have heard more of it. Young men with lollipop sticks in their throats either die from them or become sideshow attractions in the circus; the records show neither so it must be assumed that the lollipop stick got unstuck somehow somewhere along the line. At any rate, Mr. C. was now guarded by one of his children each night, the children taking turns.

They are firmly convinced that the practical nurse slipped her erstwhile benefactor some poison and that perhaps the boy with the lollipop stick stuck in his throat might have done her bidding and administered it to the old gent. This is a pretty sticky argument, of course, and hard to prove, especially as no autopsy was ever performed on Mr. C. But it is conceivable that Madeline made a discovery about her friend that could have induced her to speed his failure to recover and do so by any means at her command. She knew her way around the hospital and had ready access to his room. She also had equally ready access to his office and thereby hangs a strange tale.

On one of the infrequent occasions when Mr. C. slept at home, his estranged wife was making up the bed. This was five months before his demise. As she lifted the mattress, she discovered underneath it a heavy envelope, about six by ten inches in size, crammed full with papers. She looked at it and found written on it in Mr. C.'s large lettering, the words:

"This is not to be opened until I am dead. I mean good and dead. Daddy."

She showed the envelope to her daughter, Agnes, but put it back since she did not wish to enter into any kind of controversy with her husband. Evidently the envelope must have been taken by him to his office sometime later, for when she again made his bed two weeks before his passing, when he was still walking around, she found it gone. But there was a second, smaller envelope there, this one not particularly marked or inscribed. She left it there. A short time later Mr. C. was taken to the hospital. When Mrs. C. made the bed she found that the small envelope had also disappeared.

While the C.'s house in Columbus was not exactly a public place, neither was it an impregnable fortress, and anyone wishing to do so could have walked in at various times and quickly removed the envelope. As far as the office was concerned, that was even easier to enter and the family had no doubt whatever that Madeline took both envelopes for reasons best known to herself, although they could not actually prove any of it. At no time did the old gent say an unkind word about his Madeline, at least not to his children, preferring perhaps to take his troubles with him into the Great Beyond.

After his death, which came rather suddenly, the family found a proper will, but as Mr. C. had generously built homes for most of his children during his lifetime, in the 1950s, there was only a modest amount of cash in the bank accounts, and no great inheritance for anyone.

The will named Mrs. C. as executor, and as there was nothing to contest, it was duly probated. But the family did search the office and the late Mr. C.'s effects at the house for these two envelopes that were still missing. Only the wife and daughter Agnes knew of them, even though "nobody and everybody" had access to the house. The servants would not have taken them, and the safe was empty. As the old gent had occasionally slept in his office on a couch, the family looked high and low in his office but with negative results. The only thing that turned up in addition to the will itself was the neatly typed manuscript of a book of Biblical quotations. Mr. C. had been a serious Bible scholar, despite his uneducated status, and the quotes arranged by subject matter and source represented many thousands of man-hours of work. When his daughter Marie had seen him working on this project in 1962, she had suggested he have the scribbled notes typed up and she had prevailed upon her Aunt Catherine to undertake the job, which the latter did. Somewhat forlornly, Marie picked up the manuscript and wondered whether someone might not buy it and put a little cash into the estate *that* way.

The mystery of the disappearing envelopes was never solved. Even greater than the puzzle of their disappearance was the question about their content: what was in them that was so important that the old gent had to hide them under the mattress? So important that someone took them secretly and kept them from being turned over to the family, as they should have been?

Although there is no evidence whatever for this contention, Marie thinks there might have been some valuables left to Grover C.'s love child, the one he had with the lady from Alabama early in his romantic life.

At any rate, after several months of fruitless searches, the family let the matter rest and turned to other things. Grover C. would have gone on to his just reward, especially in the minds of his family, if it weren't for the matter of some peculiar, unfinished business.

About a year after Grover's death, Lewis C., one of the sons of the *deceased*, as they say in the police records, was busy building a brick flower planter in his home in Columbus. This was one of the houses his father had erected for his children, and Mr. C., the son, had been living in it happily without the slightest disturbance. Lewis was thirty years old and the mystery of his father's disappearing envelopes did not concern him very much at this point. Here he was, at four o'clock in the afternoon, on a brisk March day in 1967, working on his planter. Giving him a hand with it, and handing him one brick after another, was a professional Negro bricklayer by the name of Fred, with whom he had worked before. They were in the living room and Lewis was facing the back door, Fred the front door.

"A brick, please" said Lewis, without turning around.

No brick came. He asked again. Still no brick. He then looked up at his helper and saw him frozen to the spot, gazing at the front door.

"What's the matter, Fred?" he inquired. He had never seen Fred so frightened.

Finally, as if awakening from a bad dream, Fred spoke.

"I've just seen Mr. C.," he said, "big as life."

"But Mr. C. has been dead for a year," the son replied.

Fred had worked for Grover for many years and he knew him well.

"What did he look like?" the son inquired.

"White . . . light," Fred replied and then went on to describe the figure in white pants he had seen at the door. Although it was only the bottom half of a man, he had instantly recognized his late employer. Grover was bowlegged and the white pants facing him surely were as bow-legged as old Grover had been. There was no doubt about whose lower half it was that had appeared and then gone up in a puff again.

Lewis shook his head and went on with his work. But a short time later he began to appreciate what Fred had experienced. In the middle of the night he found himself suddenly awake by reason of something in the atmosphere—undefinable, but still very real.

The lights in his bedroom were off, but he could see down the hallway. And what he saw was a man wearing a white shirt, dark pants . . . and . . . with no head. The headless gentleman was tiptoeing down the hallway toward him.

Lewis could only stare at the apparition which he instantly recognized as his late father, head or no head. When the ghost saw that Lewis recognized him, he took three leaps *backward* and disappeared into thin air. Unfortunately, Catherine, Lewis' wife did not believe a word of it. For several months the subject of father's headless ghost could not be mentioned in conversation. Then in December of 1968 Lewis and Catherine were asleep one night, when at about 2:30 A.M. they were both roused by the sound of heavy footsteps walking clown the hall from the bedrooms toward the living room. As they sat up and listened with nary a heartbeat, they could clearly hear how the steps first hit the bare floor and then the carpet, sounding more muffled as they did. Finally, they resounded louder again as they reached the kitchen floor. Lewis jumped out of bed, ready to fight what he was sure must be an intruder. Although he looked the house over from top to bottom he found no trace of a burglar, and all the doors were locked.

In retrospect they decided it was probably Grover paying them a visit. But why? True, he had built them the house. True, they had some of his effects, especially his old pajamas. But what would he want with his old pajamas where he *now* was? Surely he could not be upset by the fact that his son was wearing them. They decided then that Grover was most likely trying to get their attention because of those envelopes that were still missing or some other unfinished business, but they didn't like it, for who would like one's headless father popping in in the middle of the night?

But apparently Grover did not restrict his nocturnal visits to his son Lewis' place. His granddaughter Marie, who lives in Atlanta, had come to visit at her grandfather's house in the spring of 1968. The house had no city water but used water from its own well system. It was therefore necessary to carry water into the house from outside. On one such occasion, when she had just done this and was returning with an *empty* basin, Marie stepped into what looked like a puddle of water. She started to mop up the puddle only to find that the spot was actually totally dry. Moreover, the puddle was ice cold, while the water basin she had just carried was still hot. She found this most unusual but did not tell anyone about it. Within a matter of hours eight-year-old Randy reported seeing a man in a dark suit in the bathroom, when the bathroom was obviously empty.

Apparently the old gent liked children, for little Joel was playing the piano in his Atlanta home in February of 1969, when he heard the sound of shuffling feet approach. Then there was the tinkling of glasses and all this time no one was visible. Grover had always liked a snort and a little music.

Soon Marie began to smell carnations in her house when no one was wearing them or using any perfume. This lingered for a moment and then disappeared, as if someone wearing this scent was just passing through the house.

In 1967, her Aunt Mary came to visit her in Atlanta and the conversation turned to the mysterious scent. "I'm glad you mentioned this," the aunt exclaimed, and reported a similar problem: both she and her husband would smell the same scent repeatedly in their own house, sometimes so strongly they had to leave the house and go out for some fresh air. But the scent followed them, and on one occasion "sat" with them in their car on the way to church on Sunday morning!

They weren't too sure whether it was more like carnations or just a funeral smell, but it surely was a smell that had no rational explanation. Then in 1968, Mary informed her niece that a new perfume had suddenly been added to their list of phenomena: this one was a spicy scent, like a man's after-shave lotion.

Not long after this report, Marie smelled the same sharp, men's perfume in her own house in Atlanta, in her den. This was particularly upsetting, because they had shut off that room for the winter and no perfume or anyone wearing it had been in it for months.

In 1969, she had occasion to visit her grandfather's house in Columbus once again. She found herself wandering into her late grandfather's old bedroom. She stopped at his dresser and opened the drawer. There she found her spicy scent: a bottle of Avon hair lotion he had used. None of her husband's eau de cologne bottles had a similar smell. This was it. But how had it traveled all the way to Atlanta? Unless, of course, Grover was wearing it.

Marie is a thirty-year-old housewife, has worked for years as a secretary to various business firms, and is married to a postal clerk.

She was upset by her grandfather's insistence on continuing to visit his kinfolk and not staying in the cemetery as respectable folk are supposed to do, at least according to the traditional view of the dead.

Evidently Grover was far from finished with this life, and judging from the lively existence he had led prior to his unexpected departure from this vale of tears, he had a lot of energy left over.

That, combined with a genuine grievance over unfinished business—especially the missing two envelopes—must have been the cause for his peripatetic visits. Marie decided not to wait for the next one, and went to see a card reader in Columbus. The card reader could tell her only that she had a restless grandfather who wished her well.

Unfortunately, even if the cause for Grover's continued presence could be ascertained, there was no way in which the missing envelopes could be legally recovered.

Marie tried, in vain, to get a local psychic to make contact with her grandfather. Finally, she turned her attention to the manuscript of Bible quotes. Perhaps it was the book he wanted to see published.

Whatever it was, she must have done the right thing, or perhaps all that talk about the headless grandfather had pleased the old gent's ego enough to pry him loose from the earth plane. At any rate, no further appearances have been reported and it may well be that he has forgotten about those envelopes by now, what with the attractions of his new world absorbing his interest.

Unless, of course, he is merely resting and gathering strength!

Hauntings in Virginia

With one exception no state in the Union is more often concerned with hauntings, in the public mind, than is Virginia. That is so because the rolling hills south of Washington, dotted as they are with magnificent manor houses, many of them dating back to colonial days, seem to be the kind of atmosphere ghosts prefer. The sole exception to this public image are the New England mansions perched perilously atop stormswept cliffs where, usually during storms, the ghosts of sea captains still walk and the unwary traveler is frightened to death. That, at least, is the impression still rampant among the uninstructed, although it is perfectly true that there are sea captains in New England manor houses walking long after their time on earth has expired.

But Virginia, which is primarily horse country and was settled originally by people from the Anglo-Saxon countries, is very much like England in many respects. Even the ghosts, such as they are, that continue a shadowy existence in some of the estates and plantation houses are similar in their habits to those found in English stately homes. Almost "the first state in the Union" because of its early connection with the creation of the country and because it was the home of so many of the leaders of the Revolutionary War, Virginia must be considered the closest to an oligarchic state in America. Divided among a small number of illustrious families, Virginia has for a long time been a feudal barony of sorts, and to this very day the great houses attest to the way this first among the thirteen colonies developed. Even though the plantations that were once the life blood of these houses are no longer in existence, the houses themselves continue to flourish because the Virginians have a keen sense of history and tradition. Many of the houses, of course, have been restored because of decay. Nevertheless, there are still some which have stood the test of time and survived from their seventeenth- or eighteenth-century origins almost intact to this day.

Foremost among such manor houses is the magnificent estate of Westover on the James River. Built originally in 1730 by William Byrd II, the man who founded Richmond, it stands amid an 11,000-acre working farm. The formal gardens surrounding the house are open to the public, but the house itself is not. A magnificent eighteenth-century ceiling in the entrance hall matches the paneling of the walls. Throughout the manor house there is evidence of grandeur. This is not the home of a country squire but of a statesman of great wealth. When William Byrd was killed during the Revolutionary War the widow sold the original furniture in 1813. Eventually the house passed into the hands of Mrs. Bruce Crane Fisher. Her grandfather had bought the house in 1921 and became the eleventh owner since the plantation had been in existence. Mrs. Fisher has furnished the house in recent years with authentic eighteenth-century English and European furniture to restore it as closely as possible to the original appearance. The Georgian house stands amid tall old trees and consists of a central portion and two wings. The central portion has three stories of elegant brickwork and two tall chimneys. The two wings were originally not connected to the center portion of the house, but the right wing had to be restored in 1900 since it had been damaged by fire from a shelling during the Civil War. At that time the two wings were also connected to the house and are now accessible directly from the main portion. The main entrance faces the James River and has the original wrought-iron entrance gate with stone eagles surmounting the gateposts. Thus, with minimal additions and restorations, the house today presents pretty much the same picture it did when it was first built in 1730.

Colonel Byrd took his beautiful daughter Evelyn, pronounced *Eevelyn* in Virginia, to London for the coronation of King George I. That was in 1717 when the great men of the colonies, when they could afford it, would come to the mother country when the occasion arose. Evelyn, at the time, was eighteen years old and her father decided to leave her in England to be educated. Soon he received disquieting news from his confidants at the London court. It appeared that Evelyn had been seen with a certain Charles Mordaunt and that the two young people were hopelessly in love with each other. Normally this would be a matter for rejoicing, but not so in this case. Charles was an ardent Roman Catholic and the grandson of the Earl of Petersborough. Colonel Byrd, on the other hand, was politically and personally a staunch Protestant, and the idea of his daughter marrying into the enemy camp, so to speak, was totally unacceptable to him. Immediately he ordered her to return to Westover and Evelyn had no choice but to obey. As soon as she arrived at the family plantation she went into isolation. She refused to see any other suitors her father sent her or to consider, or even to discuss, the possibility of marriage.

This went on for some time, and Evelyn quite literally "pined away" to death. Some weeks before her death, however, she had a very emotional discussion with her best friend, Anne Harrison. The two girls were walking up a hill when Evelyn, feeling faint, knew that her days were numbered. She turned to her friend and promised her that she would return after her death. Mrs. Harrison did not take this very seriously, but she knew that Evelyn was not well and her death did not come as a shock. The following spring, after Westover had somehow returned to a degree of normalcy and the tragic events of the previous year were not so strongly in evidence, Mrs. Harrison was walking in the garden sadly remembering what had transpired the year before. Suddenly she saw her old friend standing beside her in a dazzling white gown. The vision then drifted forward two steps, waved its hand at her and smiled. An instant later it had vanished. At the time of her untimely death Evelyn Byrd had been twenty-nine years of age, but in the apparition she seemed much younger and lovelier than she had appeared toward the end of her life. The specter has reappeared from time to time to a number of people, both those who live in the area and those who are guests at Westover. A lady who lives nearby who has been there for nearly three decades saw her in the mid 1960s. She had been coming out of the front door one summer and was walking down the path when she looked back toward the house and saw a woman come out behind her. At first she thought it was a friend and stopped at the gate to wait for her. When the woman came closer, however, she didn't recognize her. There was something very strange about the woman coming toward her. There seemed to be a glow all about her person, her black hair, and the white dress. When the woman had arrived close to her she stopped and seemed to sink into the ground.

On December 11, 1929, some guests from Washington were staying at Westover, and on the evening of their arrival the conversation turned to ghosts. The house was then owned by Mr. and Mrs. Richard H. Crane, who explained that they themselves had not seen the ghost during their tenancy. One of the house guests retired to the room assigned to her on the side of the house overlooking the great gates from which one has a fine view into the formal gardens. Sometime that night the guest awoke and went to the window. There was no apparent reason for her behavior. It was quite dark outside and very quiet. As she glanced out the window she saw the figure of Evelyn Byrd. She described the apparition to her hosts as filmy, nebulous and cloudy, so transparent no features could be distinguished, only a gauzy texture of a woman's form. The figure seemed to be floating a little above the lawn and almost on the level of the window itself. As she looked at it almost transfixed, the apparition acknowledged her by raising her hand and motioning to her to go back into the room and away from the window.

The gesture seemed so imperative that the house guest obeyed it.

When I requested permission to investigate the house I was politely denied access. Perhaps the present owners are afraid that I might induce the lovely Evelyn to leave Westover for a better life in paradise, and that would never do, for Westover is, after all, the nearest thing to paradise on earth, at least to an eighteenth-century lass whose lover has gone away. Had I had the opportunity to come into contact with her through some reputable medium perhaps I might have reunited the two in a land and under conditions where her stern father Colonel Byrd could no longer keep them apart.

Another famous Virginia mansion is Blandfield, which has more than one ghost. In the late 1960s the Richmond *Times Dispatch* made a survey of some of the better ghost houses in the area. Tom Howard interviewed a number of people who owned such houses and he also journeyed up to Blandfield to interview the owner. Here is his report. "Blandfield, an eighteenth century mansion in Essex County, has been frequented by a variety of spooks for two centuries. They've come as eerie lights in the night and wispy figures of men and women stalking through the halls.

"Mrs. William Nash Beverley, wife of the owner, related that about five years ago house guests reported apparitions on two occasions. The first was in a long, flowered dress walking across the upstairs hall. Everyone searched the home, but the stranger wasn't found. Two days later, a second guest saw a woman, in a long, dark skirt, cross a downstairs hall, and enter a room. Again an investigation found no one, said Mrs. Beverley.

"The most recent episode came several months before, she said. Mrs. Beverley recounted the experience. She and two dogs were in the downstairs library one afternoon and the only other person in the house was an ill relative who she knew was asleep in an upstairs bedroom. Suddenly, heavy footsteps sounded in the room directly overhead.

Startled, she listened. The dogs sprang to their feet, hair bristling.

"First I thought I would take a shotgun and go up, said Mrs. Beverley. Then I thought how silly that was. But I was uneasy, so I put a leash on each dog and we rushed up the steps. As I went up the steps, the dogs became more excited, their hair stood straight up.

"She went straight to the bedroom of her relative, who was lying quietly in bed, still asleep. The dogs strained at the leash and pulled toward the room where she heard the heavy footsteps. She opened the door and the dogs bounded in fiercely . . . but there was no one there. She explored every hiding place in the room, but found no trace of a living human being. The dogs quieted down and she decided that, at last, she had heard one of the famed Blandfield ghosts."

There is a rocking chair ghost at Shirley plantation in Chase City and another rocking chair ghost at Ash Lawn, once the home of President James Monroe, and the ghost of Governor Kemper is said to still inhabit Walnut Hill, his erstwhile home. I have reported a number of such cases in an earlier book called *Ghosts I've Met*. In fact, the area around Charlottesville, which I investigated personally in 1965, abounds with authentic hauntings.

It is just possible that someone who is psychic and who might have passed the building now housing the Health, Education and Welfare Department in Charlottesville might feel peculiar, perhaps a chill or two, perhaps only a sense of displacement in time.

On that spot there was once a magnificent house built around 1820 in the style of the Roman country houses of Andrea Palladino. James Dinsmore, an architect brought there by Thomas Jefferson, designed the house for Francis B. Dyer, a lawyer. Later it passed into the hands of William B. Fitch, but eventually the house changed hands again and just before the Civil War it belonged to a certain Eugene Davis, a man prominently connected with Episcopal Sunday school work. He was the oldest son of Professor John A. G. Davis, Chairman of the

University of Charlottesville. The professor was killed during one of the student riots of those days. Shortly afterwards, when another son, James Maury Morris Davis, occupied the cottage in the yard, the first uncanny experiences took place. Studying late one night, young Davis heard the gate click and footsteps sound along the hall. He opened the door but saw no one out there. This repeated itself numerous times. When the house passed into the hands of Major Horace Jones, who headed a boys' preparatory school in Charlottesville, the phenomena continued. Some of the students who had been assigned the cottage to live in complained of footsteps in the yard. The gate would click open and shut and there never was anyone there. It was assumed that the murdered professor was checking up on his former home. The phenomena continued until after Major Jones died in 1904. When the cottage was eventually pulled down and replaced by the present structure, the noises stopped, but there is no telling what a psychic person might feel standing on the spot where the hauntings used to be.

There is a quietly elegant old frame house at 6321 Monument Avenue in Richmond which belies its violent history. The Richmond *News Leader* of April 7, 1967, told its story for the first time to a broader public. The owner at the time, Donald B. Wiltshire, had seen the ghost of a little old man with a chin beard as he was going to bed. He was so surprised by the apparition that he fell on the top step. Mr. Wiltshire employed the services of a historian, Mrs. Roger Mann, to dig into the past of his house. Mrs. Mann discovered that nineteen bodies had originally been buried in two graveyards somewhere on the Wiltshire property. Moreover, there was good reason to assume that half a million dollars was buried somewhere on the premises. To date that treasure has not been recovered but it has a basis in fact. In 1821 the house on Monument Avenue belonged to a certain Dan Green who worked in a bank. At the time Mr. Green was accused of absconding with $500,000. Since the money was never found the teller was acquitted. The only things remotely relating to the treasure were some coins found by men excavating for a swimming pool a few years ago, but they didn't add up to $500,000.

Andy Wilkins is a young ghost fancier of southwest Virginia. He has kept me informed of some of the goings on in the area, notably of Berry Hill, a magnificent manor house not far from Westover. In fact, it is built on land once part of the Westover estate. Built and owned by the Bruce family, which is related by marriage to the owners of Westover, the estate is now empty. A few years ago a certain Fred Watkins bought Berry Hill as a wedding gift for his son, but when the young people tried to spend the night in it they were frightened out of it by footsteps and the uncanny presence of something they could not see. Since then the house has been closed. The building is being kept up like a museum, but there is only a caretaker on the grounds. Allegedly the ghost is the son of the original builder, who died childless but resents that the house passed out of the Bruce family to strangers.

White Marsh in Gloucester County is a magnificent plantation house now owned by Mr. and Mrs. William Ingles and a private residence. In 1654, 3200 acres of land were granted to a certain Lewis Burwell whose descendant the present owner is. Today only 2000 acres remain. The house has passed through several hands since the Burwells owned it. The present White Marsh was built in 1798 and enlarged by the Tabb family in 1883. There is a legend that a curse was put on the place at the time when John Tabb bought it, a curse that was to last until the property was returned to its "rightful owners," presumably the sons of Thomas Rootes, who had sold the place to the Tabbs. But apparently the curse was not very effective, for the Tabb family lived at White Marsh undisturbed until 1906, when the place passed into the hands of Willie Buries, who made extensive changes, replacing the Georgian style with Greek revival. When the house passed into the hands of the current owners, the Ingles, they had to re-do the house to bring it back to its original appearance. Constance Ingles moved into the house in 1948. She made extensive inquiries about anything dramatic that might have transpired in the house in its long history. She discovered no murders or suicides, but apparently several infant children of the Tabb family had died there. There was an account of a ghostly apparition, however, according to which mother Tabb was seen entering a certain room, opening a bureau drawer, removing all the child's clothes, shaking them out and folding them and returning them to the drawer. Mrs. Ingles just knew that this concerned the room where their two oldest sons were living at the time and she always knew that it was young Bill's chest of drawers the ghostly mother Tabb was opening. A neighbor had actually seen mother Tabb passing her on the stairs with her swishing taffeta skirts.

Constance Ingles has a long history of ESP and experiences that can only be classed as memories from a previous lifetime. She had seen her first ghost at the age of sixteen when she was a student at Bennington College West. This was at a small inn near Seneca, New York. At White Marsh Mrs. Ingles has not actually seen any ghosts, but she has shared, with her husband and their little daughter, an auditory experience that has left them very much impressed with the fact that there are unseen presences at their home. Three or four weeks after they had moved into the house Mrs. Ingles was awakened by the sound of heavy footsteps in the attic proceeding from the north side of the house to the center. Reluctant to wake up her husband, Mrs. Ingles wondered who was walking about when she heard her little daughter, then four years old, call "Mommy, who is that walking in the attic?" Now sure that she was not hallucinating, she awakened her husband. Together they decided to investigate. The footsteps were directly over their heads then. A moment later they halted again, and then something seemed to land on the roof of the one-story wing, right under their bedroom window. They dashed to the window and heard a loud thud as something seemed to hit the ground. Seconds after that there was heard the sound of horses' hoofs going up the lane. The next morning they investigated and found hoofprints under the window. They checked whether one of their horses had escaped from the barn, but none had. Also, the round window in the attic, on the south side where the footsteps had halted, cannot be opened. Mr. Ingles, who is a firm disbeliever in such matters as psychic phenomena, was impressed.

Although she has not seen this herself, Mrs. Ingles, all the children, and some of their friends have frequently reported the appearance of something filmy-white in the gardens. Marguerite Dupont Lee has reported some of the traditional legends associated with White Marsh in her books. One of them concerns the sound of a party, music, and dancing going on in the house when there is no one there. Another one deals with a woman rocking in a chair in the northeast bedroom, the room once occupied by General Lee during his visit to White Marsh. A year after the Ingleses had moved into White Marsh they employed a black couple from Philadelphia named Henry and Frances Parker. Mrs. Ingles is quite sure the couple were not aware of these traditions when they first came to the house. Shortly after their arrival the butler came to Mrs. Ingles on a Sunday morning wondering if they had come home unexpectedly the afternoon before. They had not and she so informed the butler. He then reported that Saturday afternoon, when the children had been sleeping and he and his wife had been in their room, they had heard someone playing the piano. Assuming that Mrs. Ingles had returned home and was playing the piano, he decided to leave the matter alone, but his wife insisted that it didn't sound like Mrs. Ingles playing. So he decided to go out and look. When he reached the stair landing, within perhaps two or three steps of the piano, the music stopped and there was a whooshing sound that moved toward the door to the back hall. Still shaken by this episode, the butler was even more impressed with the presence of something unseen. A few weeks later when he took Mrs. Ingles her morning coffee he explained that he and his wife had not slept all night because something was rocking in their room. When Mrs. Ingles pointed out that there was no rocking chair in that room, he explained that he knew that very well, but that their straight chair seemed to rock as if it had rockers under it.

Despite Mrs. Ingles's ESP leanings, things have been on the quiet side these past few years. It is conceivable that the ghosts of White Marsh have taken the Ingleses to their heart and do not wish to interfere with their lives by appearing before them. Ghosts have a way of staying dormant for long times, being unaware of the passage of time and content to relive their own most important moments.

Midwest

The Ghost Car

Marlene S. is a thirty-seven-year-old housewife leading a typical American housewife's life—which is to say she is neither given to explorations into the unknown nor particularly involved in anything out of the ordinary. After two years of college, she found that her married life took up most, if not all, of her time, but she is still hoping to get her teacher's degree after which she would like to teach English literature on a secondary level. But with four youngsters—ranging in age from eleven to fifteen—and a husband around the house, time for study is limited. Her husband, Mr. S. is a district manager for a shoe company.

Marlene came from an average Nebraska family and nothing particularly shocking ever happened to her, that is, until she, her husband and children moved into a house in Kansas City that will forever be etched in her memories. The house itself was nothing special: about seven years old, inexpensive looking, with four bedrooms, built ranch-style all on one floor.

They moved into this house in 1958 when the children were still quite young. A few weeks after they had settled down in the house and gotten used to the new surroundings, Marlene was lying awake in bed, waiting to fall asleep.

She never could go to sleep right away, and lying awake trying to sort things out in her mind was her way of inviting the sandman.

Because the children were still young, ranging in age from one to five, she had to be always alert for any moves or noises in case something was wrong. Perhaps this contributed to her light sleep, but at any rate, she was not yet drowsy at this point and was fully cognizant of what might transpire around her.

Suddenly, she felt pressure at the foot of the bed as if one of the children was trying to climb into bed to sleep with the parents.

Marlene sat up quickly but quietly, leaned toward the foot of the bed, made a grab, at the same time saying, "Got you!"—only to find herself grabbing thin air.

She assumed the little culprit had quickly scuttled back to his own bed, and got up and went across the hall to the boys' bedroom. After that, she inspected the girls' room, but all four were sound asleep, tucked in precisely the way she had earlier tucked them in and it was clear that none of her children had caused the pressure at the foot of her bed.

She decided she had imagined the whole thing and went back to bed. But the following night, the pressure was back again and again she grabbed nothing but a fistful of thin air.

It got to be such a common occurrence she quit checking on the children whether or not they were doing it. She then decided that it had to be caused by her husband's moving his foot in a certain way. Somehow she reasoned that his moves gave the feeling the covers were drawn up against her foot, creating the impression of an outside pressure. Far-fetched though this explanation was, she accepted it gladly. But she kept her foot against his for several nights after this to find out what move of his caused all this to happen.

As her husband slept, she observed, but it got her nowhere: the pressure was still present, but there was no connection with her husband's foot or his movements.

She had hardly accepted the strange pressure in her bed when still another phenomenon caused her to wonder about the house. Near the doorway to the bedroom she heard someone breathe deeply and heavily when there was no one but her around. When this recurred several times she decided to tell her husband about it. He shook his head and said he had heard nothing. She did not tell him about the pressure on the bed, thinking it just too absurd to discuss. That night she heard the crackling of what sounded like someone stepping on cellophane just before she felt the pressure at the foot of the bed again.

She knew she had left a cellophane bag at the foot of the bed on the floor and she was sure one of her children had come out and stepped on it. Again she grabbed but again her hands held only air and the children were all soundly asleep in the respective rooms.

By now a little bit of fear crept into her mind when she came to realize that there wasn't really any rational explanation for the strange noises and especially the heavy breathing.

But she pulled her knees up at night and thus avoided coming in contact with whatever was causing the pressure at the foot of the bed.

For a while, nothing untoward happened, and the family was busy getting on with the problems of daily living. The strange occurrences drifted into the background for a while.

Then one night, several weeks later, Marlene was awakened from sleep by a most incredible sound. It was as if a giant vat of water was being poured on the house. The swooshing sound of water cascading down upon them reverberated for several seconds afterward. Her immediate thought, being just awakened from deep sleep, was a logical one—one of the kids had not been able to make it to the bathroom and what she was hearing was the result! But no: they were all fast asleep in their rooms.

The next morning, she examined the floor. In the boys' room she found a strange liquid spot. It was like water, except much thicker and did not ooze out as water would, but lay there on the floor, perfectly cohesive and round. It had neither odor nor color and when she removed it with tissue paper, it left no trace. Her husband explained that probably the liquid had oozed up from the ground or dropped from the ceiling but her logical mind refused to accept what was obviously not likely.

There was absolutely no rational explanation for either the swooshing noise or the presence of the thick liquid in the boys' room. Several months afterward, a similar spot appeared in the girls' room. Since they had no animals in the house, the matter remained a puzzle.

The house was so new that any thoughts of ghosts were furthest from Marlene's mind. But strange things began to occur. One day, a car securely parked across from the house on a slanting driveway, came downhill and crashed into the boys' bedroom. Luckily no one was hurt.

Not much later, another car from across the street did the same thing, only this time the car went into the girls' room. The owner swore he had put the car into parking position on leaving it. Tust as he got out, he saw his car roll down the driveway *by itself!*

This wasn't too reassuring to Marlene. Was some unknown force trying to "get" them? Was there a connection between the spots of liquid in the childrens' bedrooms and the two car crashes?

Somehow the atmosphere in the house was different now from the time they had first moved in. It seemed heavy, as if some sort of tragic pressure was weighing upon it. Her husband did not notice anything unusual, or if he did, he did not discuss it with her. But to her there was an ominous presence in the house and she didn't like it.

One night her husband was working late. She had gone to bed and had just turned the lights out. No sooner had she lain down, than she began to hear the heavy breathing again. Next came the pressure at the foot of the bed. With the breathing so close to her, she was absolutely terrified and did not dare move. Whatever it was, it was very near and she realized now that all her reasoning had not explained a thing. Someone other than herself shared her bed and that someone was not friendly.

But what was she to do? The children were asleep in their beds and her husband was at work. She decided that under the circumstances the best thing was to play possum. She lay there as if asleep, barely breathing and not moving a muscle.

She did not know how much time had passed, when she heard the car drive up to their door. The headlights shone through the bedroom window and she heard the motor being turned off.

"Thank God, Don is home," she managed to say under her breath.

Even though the presence was still close by, she somehow managed to get enough courage to jump out of bed and race to the window. Turning on the lights on the way to the living room as she went by, she reached the window and looked out to the driveway.

Instead of seeing her husband and the family car, she was greeted by the blackness of the night. Nothing. No car.

"This is the last straw!" she almost cried and ran back to her bed. Pulling the covers over her she lay there in terror, not knowing what to do next. When her husband finally returned after what seemed hours upon hours, she managed to sob out her story.

"There, there," he said, soothingly, taking her head in his hands. "You've been having nightmares."

"He doesn't believe a word I've said," she thought, between sobs, but she preferred being consoled by a nonbeliever than not being consoled at all.

The next few weeks passed somehow. They had requested a transfer to another location. When it came, she was a new person. The prospect of moving into another house where nothing would disturb her sleep was just too wonderful.

Her husband had rented a big, old mansion in Wichita, where they were transferred by the company, and it was filled with antiques and fine furniture of a bygone era.

When Marlene first saw the house, she thought, "Oh my God, if any house ought to be haunted, this looks like one!"

But it wasn't and the house in Wichita proved as peaceful and serene as a house can be, if it isn't inhabited by a restless ghost.

The house was full of memories of its past fifty years but none of them intruded upon her and she lived a happy, relaxed life now. The experiences in Kansas receded into her memory and she was sure now that it had all been the fault of the house and not something connected with her—least of all, her imagination, for she knew, no matter what her husband had said, that she had seen and heard that ghost car drive up to the house.

She sometimes wonders who the new owners of that house in Kansas are and whether they can hear the heavy breathing the way she did. But then she realizes that it was her own innate psychic ability that allowed the phenomena to manifest themselves when they did. Another person not so endowed might conceivably not feel anything at all.

What was the horrible accident that was being reenacted—from the sound of the water being poured down, to the rushing up of the ghost car? And whose heavy breathing was disturbing her nights?

Many times her curiosity almost made her inquire but then she decided to let sleeping dogs lie. But in later years while living in California, her psychic ability developed further until she was able to hear and see the dead as clearly and casually as she could commune with the living. It frightened her and she thought at first she was having waking nightmares. All through the night she would be aware of a room full of people while at the same time being able to sleep on. Her observation was on several levels at the same time, as if she had been turned into a radio receiver with several bands.

Clearly, she did not want any of this, least of all the heavy breathing she started to hear again after they had moved to California.

But then it could be the breathing of another restless soul, she decided, and not necessarily something or someone she had brought with her from Kansas. She read as much as she could now on the subject of ESP, and tried her hand at automatic writing. To her surprise, her late father and her grandparents wrote to her through her own hand.

She noticed that the various messages were in different hands and quite clearly differed from her own. Yet her logical mind told her this might all come from her own subconscious mind and she began to reject it. As she closed herself off from the messages, they dwindled away until she no longer received them.

This she regretted, for the presence of her father around her to continue the link of a lifetime and perhaps protect her from the incursions of unwanted entities of both worlds, was welcome and reassuring.

By now she knew of her psychic powers and had learned to live with them, but also to close the psychic door when necessary.

Meanwhile the house in Kansas still stands and very few tenants stay for long.

The House on Plant Avenue

Plant Avenue is a charming suburban boulevard running through one of the better sectors of Webster Groves, Missouri, in itself a better-than-average small town, near St. Louis. Plant Avenue is not known for anything in particular except perhaps that it does have some plants, mainly very old trees that give it a coolness other streets lack, even in the heat of summer when this part of the country can be mighty unpleasant.

Webster Groves wasn't much of a landmark either until *Life* magazine published an article on its high school activities, and then it had a short-lived flurry of excitement as the "typical" American upper-middle-class town with all its vices and virtues. But now the town has settled back to being just one of many such towns and the people along Plant Avenue sigh with relief that the notoriety has ebbed. They are not the kind that enjoy being in the headlines and the less one pays attention to them, the happier they are.

In the three hundred block of Plant Avenue there are mainly large bungalow type houses standing in wide plots and surrounded by shrubbery and trees. One of these houses is a two-story wood and brick structure of uncertain style, but definitely distinguished looking in its own peculiar way. The roof suggests old English influences and the wide windows downstairs are perhaps southern, but the overall impression is that of a home built by an individualist who wanted it his way and only his way. It does not look like any other house on the block, yet fits in perfectly and harmoniously. The house is somewhat set back and there is a garden around it, giving it privacy. From the street one walks up a front lawn, then up a few stairs and into the house. The downstairs contains a large living room, a day room and a kitchen with a rear exit directly into the garden. From the living room, there is a winding staircase to the upper floor where the bedrooms are located.

The house was built in the final years of the last century by a man of strange character. The neighborhood knew little enough about this Mr. Gehm. His business was the circus and he seems to have dealt with various circus performers and represented them in some way. He was not a good mixer and kept mainly to himself and ultimately died in the house he had built for himself.

This much was known around the neighborhood, but to tell the truth, people don't much care what you do so long as you don't bother them, and the real estate agent who took on the house after Mr. Gehm passed away was more concerned with its wiring and condition than Mr. Gehm's unusual occupation. As the house had a certain nobility about it, perhaps due to the German background of its builder, it seemed a good bet for resale and so it turned out to be.

In 1956 the house passed into the hands of Mr. and Mrs. S. L. Furry, who had been married twenty years at the time, and had two young daughters, now long married also.

Mrs. Furry's ancestry was mainly English and she worked for the Washington University Medical school in St. Louis, having been a major in psychology in college.

Thus she found herself more than shaken when she discovered some peculiarities about the house they had moved into—such as being awakened, night after night, at precisely two A.M. with a feeling of having been shaken awake. On one occasion, she clearly heard a heavy hammer hit the headboard of her bed, turned on the lights only to discover everything intact where she was sure she would find splinters and a heavy indentation. Soon this was amplified by the sound of something beating against the windows at night. "It sounds just like a heavy bird," Mrs. Furry thought, and shuddered. There was nothing visible that could have caused the sounds.

One morning she discovered one of the heavy wall sconces, downstairs, on the floor. Yet it had been securely fastened to the wall the night before. On examination she discovered no logical reason for how the piece could have fallen.

By now she also realized that the footsteps she kept hearing weren't simply caused by overwrought nerves due to fatigue or simply her imagination. The footsteps went up and down the stairs, day and night, as if someone were scurrying about looking for something and not finding it. They always ended on the upstairs landing.

At first, she did not wish to discuss these matters with her husband because she knew him to be a practical man who would simply not believe her. And a woman is always vulnerable when it comes to reporting the psychic. But eventually he noticed her concern and the problem was brought out into the open. He readily remarked he had heard nothing to disturb his sleep and advised his wife to forget it.

But shortly after, he sheepishly admitted at the breakfast table that he, too, had heard some odd noises. "Of course, there must be a logical explanation," he added quickly. "It is very likely only the contraction and expansion of the old house. Lots of old houses do that." He seemed satisfied with this explanation, but Mrs. Furry was not. She still heard those scurrying footfalls and they did not sound to her like a house contracting.

Eventually, Mr. Furry did not insist on his explanation, but had no better one to offer and decided to shrug the whole thing off. One night he was awakened in the bedroom adjoining his wife's boudoir because of *something strange:* he then noticed a filmy, white shape *go through the door* into the hall and proceed into their little girl's room. He jumped out of bed and looked into the room, but could see nothing. "Must have been the reflection of car lights from the street," he concluded. But it never happened again, and cars kept passing the house at all hours.

The years went on and the Furrys got somewhat used to their strange house. They had put so much money and work into it, not to say love, that they were reluctant to let a ghost dislodge them. But they did become alarmed when their three-year-old child kept asking at breakfast, "Who is the lady dressed in black who comes into my room at night?" As no lady in black had been to the house at any time, this of course upset the parents.

"What lady?" Mrs. Furry demanded to know.

"The lady," the three-year-old insisted. "She's got a little boy by the hand."

Some time later, the child complained about the lady in black again. "She spanks me with a broom, but it doesn't hurt," she said. Mrs. Furry did not know what to do. Clearly, there was something in the house the real estate people had failed to tell her about. After nine years, they found a better house—one more suitable to their needs—and moved. Again, the house on Plant Avenue was for sale. It wasn't long until a new tenant for the handsome house appeared.

In the middle of November 1965, the Walshes rented the house and moved in with two of their three children, ten-year-old Wendy and twenty-year-old Sandy. They had of course not been told anything about the experiences of the previous owners and they found the house pleasant and quiet, at least at first.

A short time after moving in, Mrs. Walsh was preparing dinner in the kitchen. She was alone except for her dog. The time was six-thirty. Suddenly, she noticed the dog cringe with abject fear. This puzzled her and she wondered what the cause was. Looking up, she noticed a white cloud, roughly the shape and height of a human being, float in through the open door leading into the living room. The whole thing only lasted a moment but she had never seen anything like it.

"A ghost!" she thought immediately, for that was exactly what it looked like. Clare Walsh is not a simple-minded believer in the supernatural. She has a master's degree in biochemistry and did research professionally for five years. But what she saw was, indeed, a ghost! She wasn't frightened. In fact, she felt rather good, for her sneaking suspicions had been confirmed. On the day she first set foot into the house, when they had not yet taken it, she had had a deep feeling that there was a presence there. She dismissed it as being a romantic notion at the time, but evidently her intuition had been correct. With a sigh Mrs. Walsh accepted her psychic talents. This wasn't the first time that they had shown themselves.

At the time her husband's ship was torpedoed, she dreamed the whole incident in detail. When she was a child, her aunt died, and she saw her aunt's apparition before anyone in the family knew she had passed on. Since then she had developed a good deal of telepathy, especially with her daughters.

She dismissed the apparition she had seen in the kitchen, especially since nothing similar followed. But the nights seemed strangely active. At night, the house came to life. Noises of human activity seemed to fill the halls and rooms and in the darkness Mrs. Walsh felt unseen presences roaming about her house at will. It wasn't a pleasant feeling but she decided to brave it out and wait for some kind of opening wedge, whereby she could find out more about the background of her house. In February of 1966, her neighbors next door invited them to dinner.

Over dinner, the question of the house came up and casually Mrs. Walsh was asked how quiet the house was. With that, she confessed her concern and reported what she had seen and heard. The neighbors—a couple named Kurus—nodded to each other with silent understanding.

"There seems to be a pattern to these noises," Mrs. Walsh said, "it's always at 4 A.M. and upstairs."

The Kurus had almost bought the house themselves but were dissuaded from it by the experiences of another neighbor who lived across the street. This man had been a frequent houseguest at the house and while there, had encountered ghostly phenomena sufficient to convince him that the house was indeed haunted. The Kurus then bought the house next door instead. When Mrs. Walsh obtained the name of the man across the street, she called him and asked what he knew about their house.

"The original owner has hidden some valuables in a number of places, niches, all over the house." the gentleman explained, "and now he's looking for his treasures."

One of those secret hiding places apparently was the fireplace downstairs. Upon putting down the receiver, Mrs. Walsh started to examine the fireplace. There was a strange hollow sound in one spot, but unless she took tools to pry it open, there was no way of telling what, if anything, was hidden there.

The vague promise of hidden treasure was not sufficient to outweigh the pride of ownership in a handsome fireplace, so she did not proceed to cut open the fireplace, but instead went to bed.

About midnight she was awakened by a peculiar, musty odor in the room. She got up and walked about the room, but the musty odor lingered on. It reminded her of the smell of death.

The next morning she told her husband about it.

"Ridiculous," he laughed, but the following morning the same odor invaded his bedroom and he, too, smelled it. Since Mr. Walsh works for a large chemical concern, odors are his business, in a manner of speaking. But he could not classify the peculiar odor he was confronted with in his own house.

After that, not much happened beyond the 4 A.M. noises that kept recurring with punctuality—almost of Germanic character.

But Mrs. Walsh noticed that the door to the attic was always open. The stairs leading up to the attic from the second story have a stair whose tread lifts. Underneath the stairs she discovered a hollow space! So the tales of hidden treasure might have some basis of fact after all, she mused. The secret space was once completely closed, but the catch had long disappeared.

On one occasion, when Mr. Walsh was down with the flu, he used an adjoining bedroom. While Mrs. Walsh was resting she heard the attic door open and close again four times, and thought it was her husband going to the bathroom. But he had only been up once that night. The other three times, it was another person, one they could not see.

As time went on, Mrs. Walsh kept notes of all occurrences, more as a sport than from fear. Both she and her husband, and soon the children, kept hearing the footsteps going up to the attic, pausing at the now empty hiding place. Each following morning the attic door, securely closed the night before, was found wide open. It got to be such a routine they stopped looking for *real* people as the possible culprits. They knew by now they wouldn't find anyone.

One morning she went up to the attic and closed the door again, then continued with her breakfast work in the kitchen. Suddenly she had the strange urge to return to the attic once more. Almost as if led by a force outside of herself, she dropped the bread knife and went up the stairs. The door was open again, and she stepped through it into a small room they had never used for anything but storage. It was chock-full of furniture, all of it securely fastened and closed.

To her amazement, when she entered the little room, things were in disorder. The heavy chest of drawers at one side had a drawer opened wide. She stepped up to it and saw it was filled with blueprints. She picked one of them up, again as if led by someone, and at the bottom of the blueprint she saw the name "Henry Gehm."

She had been looking in the attic for a supposedly hidden doorway and had never been able to locate it. Was it after all just gossip and was there no hidden door?

At this moment, as she held the blueprints of the house in her hands, she received the distinct impression she should look in a certain spot in the attic. As she did, she noticed that the furniture against that wall had recently been moved. No one of flesh and blood had been up there for years, of course, and this discovery did not contribute to her sense of comfort. But as she looked closer she saw there was now a door where before a large piece of furniture had blocked the view!

Who had moved the furniture?

She felt a chill run down her back as she stood there. It wasn't the only time she had felt cold. Many times a cold blast of air, seemingly out of nowhere, had enveloped her in the bedroom or in the kitchen. As she thought of it now, she wondered why she had not investigated the source of that air but taken it for granted. Perhaps she did not want to know the results.

The events in the attic occurred on March 1, 1966. The following day, she was awakened quite early by incessant footsteps in the hallway. Someone was walking up and down, someone she could not see.

She got up. At that moment, she was distinctly impressed with the *command* to take out an old music box that had belonged to her mother. The box had not played for years and was in fact out of order. She opened the box and it started to play. It has remained in working order ever since. Who had fixed it and was this a reward for having looked at the blueprints for "someone"?

On March 5, she was roused from deep sleep once more at the "witching hour" of 4 A.M., but the house was quiet, strangely so, and she wondered why she had been awakened. But she decided to have a look downstairs. In the dining room, the breakfront which she had left closed the night before, stood wide open. The teaspoons in one of the drawers had been rearranged by unseen hands! A plant had a shoot broken off and the twig lay on the table nearby. Since the dog had not been in the room, there was no one who could have done this.

The next day, her sleep was interrupted again at 4 o'clock. This time the drawer containing her underclothes was all shaken up. Suddenly it dawned on her that her ten-year-old daughter might have spoken the truth when she reported "someone" in her mother's bedroom opening and closing the dresser when Mrs. Walsh knew for sure she had not been in the room.

She realized now what it was. The bedroom she occupied had been Henry Gehm's room. If he had hidden anything in it, he might be mistaking her dresser for his own furniture and still keep looking.

On March 8 Mrs. Walsh was in the basement, and her ten-year-old girl, Wendy, was in the garden playing. The house was quite empty.

Suddenly, she heard the sound of a child running at a mad pace through the dining room and kitchen. It must be Sandy, she thought, and called out to her. She received no reply. She went upstairs to investigate and found the house empty and quiet. Yet the footsteps had been those of a child, not the same footfalls she had so often heard on the stairs and in the attic. So there were two of them now, she thought, with a shudder.

It was then also that she recalled the baby hair she had found under the couch shortly after they had first moved in. At the time she had dismissed it as unimportant, even though no one with *blond* hair lived in the house. The hair was very fine, clearly blond and seemed like the hair of a very young child.

"Like angel's hair," she thought, and wondered.

Five days later all but Mr. Walsh were out of the house, in church. He was still in bed, but after the family had left for church he came downstairs, and fixed himself breakfast in the kitchen. At that moment, he thought he heard Wendy running upstairs.

He assumed the child was not well and had been left behind, after all. Worried, he went upstairs to see what was the matter. No child. He shook his head and returned to his breakfast, less sure the house didn't have "something strange" in it.

Upon the return of the others, they discussed it and came to the conclusion that the house was haunted by at least two, possibly three, people. It was a large enough house, but to share one's home with people one could not see was not the most practical way to live.

A few days later Mrs. Walsh was again in the basement, doing the laundry. A sweater hanging from the rafters on the opposite side of the basement suddenly jumped down from the rafters, hanger and all, and landed in front of her. The windows were firmly closed and there was no breeze. What amazed Mrs. Walsh even more was the way the sweater came down. Not straight as if pulled by gravity, but in an ark, as if held by unseen hands.

"Mrs. Gehm," she heard herself exclaiming. "What did you do that for?"

There she was, talking to a ghost.

What is your first name, anyway? she heard herself think.

Instantly, a counterthought flashed into her mind. My name is Mary.

On March 16, she woke again early in the morning with the sure sensation of not being alone. Although she could not see anyone, she knew there was someone upstairs again. However she decided to stay in bed this time. First thing in the morning, as soon as it was *light,* she ventured up the stairs to the attic. In the little room the furniture had been completely reshuffled! She then recalled having heard a dull thud during the night.

A trunk had been moved to the center of the room and opened; a doll house had been placed from one shelf to a much lower shelf, and a tool box she had never seen before had suddenly appeared in the room.

There were fresh markings in the old dust of the room. They looked like a child's scrawl . . .

Mrs. Walsh looked at the scrawl. It looked as if someone had made a crude attempt to write a name in the dust. She tried to decipher it, but could not. The next day she returned to the room. No one had been there. The children were by now much too scared to go up there.

The scribbled signature was still there, and not far from it, someone had made a handprint in the dust. *A small child's hand!*

As Mrs. Walsh stared at the print of the child's hand, it came back to her how she had the month before heard a child's voice crying somewhere in the house. None of her children had been the cause of the crying, she knew, and yet the crying persisted. Then on another occasion, a humming sound such as children like to make, had come to her attention, but she could determine no visible source for it.

Two days later, still bewildered by all this, she found herself again alone in the house. It was afternoon, and she clearly heard the muffled sound of several voices talking. She ran up the stairs to the attic—for it seemed to her that most of the phenomena originated here—and sure enough the door to the attic, which she had shut earlier, was wide open again.

Early the next morning Mrs. Walsh heard someone calling a child up in the attic. Who was up there? Not any of the Walshes, she made sure. Slowly it dawned upon her that a family from the past was evidently unaware of the passage of time and that the house was no longer theirs. But how to tell them?

A busy family it was, too. At 5 A.M. one morning a typewriter was being worked. The only typewriter in the house stood in Wendy's room. Had she used it? She hadn't, but that morning she found her typewriter *had* been used by someone. The cover had been put back differently from the way she always did it. A doll she had left next to the machine the night before, was now on top of it.

That night, while the family was having dinner in the kitchen, the lights in the living room were turned on by unseen forces. Pieces of brightly wrapped candy disappeared from a tray and were never seen again.

The dog, too, began to change under the relentless turn of events. She would refuse to sleep in the basement or go near certain spots where most of the psychic phenomena had occurred. The seven-year-old dog, once the very model of a quiet suburban canine, soon turned into a neurotic, fear-ridden shadow of her former self.

It got to be a little too much for the Walshes.

The treasure Mr. Gehm was hunting had no doubt long ago been found and taken away by some earlier tenant or stranger. As for the house itself, the ghosts could have it, if they wanted it that much. The Walshes decided to build a new home of their own, from scratch. No more old homes for them. That way, they would not inherit the ghosts of previous owners.

They notified the owner of their intent to move and as soon as the new home was ready, they moved out.

Even on the last day, the sounds of footsteps scurrying up the stairs could be heard.

Plant Avenue gossips can add another chapter to the lore of the Gehm house, but the sad little girl up in the attic won't have any playmates now. Even if they couldn't see her, the children knew she was *there*.

And that's all a ghost can hope for, really.

West

Dick Turpin, My Love

During the summer of 1973, I received a strangely elaborate and pleading letter from a young woman by the name of Cynthia von Rupprath-Snitily. The name itself was fascinating enough to warrant my further interest, but what the lady had to say concerning her strange experiences with the unknown would have attracted me even if her name had been Smith or Jones.

Cynthia had been born December 31, 1948 in Chicago, and lived in the same house until twenty-one years of age, leaving the area only to attend college at Northern Illinois University in De Kalb, Illinois. Immediately I recalled my own visit to Northern Illinois University, a huge college set in a very small town in the middle of the Illinois plains, a school which seemed forever to battle the narrow-mindedness of the surrounding town, while catering to a very large student body bent on exploring the further reaches of the human mind. Cynthia holds a Bachelor's degree in both history and art, and is an art historian by profession. "I have dealt with both fictitious legend and concrete fact," she stated, "and therefore I have knowledge of the fine lines that sometimes separate these two entities. I have thus carried over the cognizance to my everyday life and have incorporated it into my style of thinking. In truth, I am my own worst critic."

In 1970 she married a man she had met at the University of Notre Dame and moved to his home town of Seattle, Washington, where he was employed at Boeing Aircraft.

With the termination of the SST project, her husband enlisted in the Air Force and at the time of contacting me they were stationed at the Edwards Air Force Base in California, about an hour's drive from Los Angeles.

Cynthia had always been a serious and sensitive person, perhaps because she was an only child of parents forty years older than herself. As a result she felt more at ease with older people, preferring their company to that of her own age. Due to her sensitivity, she was in the habit of becoming rather emotional in matters of impact to her. In order to offset this strong character trait and in view of her profession, she tried very hard to develop a logical and orderly method of approach to things, and to think matters over several times before taking any specific course of action. Thus, when she realized that she had psychic experiences from childhood onward and saw them continue in her life, she decided to analyze and investigate the phenomena in which she was a central element. She soon realized that her psychic ability had been inherited on her mother's side of the family; her maternal grandparents had come to the United States from Croatia. Deeply embedded in the culture of many Croatian people is the belief in witchcraft, and the ability by some countryfolk to do unusual things or experience the uncanny. But Cynthia's attitude towards these phenomena remained critical. "I am not overwilling to accept such phenomena without further investigation," she explained. One case in particular impressed her, since it involved her personally.

"This case is unusual because it has occurred to three successive generations through the years. In the 1910s my grandmother was living in Chicago performing household tasks, when a neighbor dressed entirely in black came to the door. The latter woman was commonly known as a 'strega' and my grandmother naturally was not too happy to see her. The woman wanted to know what my grandmother was cooking in the pot on the stove. My grandmother refused and told the woman to leave, whereupon the latter reported that she would return that night, 'to find that which she was seeking.' That night while my grandparents, my mother, and my Uncle Bill were all sleeping in the same bed, the door suddenly blew open and my mother recalls seeing my grandmother literally struggling with some unseen force on the bed. Mother remembers quite vividly the movement of the mattress, as if something were jumping up and down on it. Certainly the sensation was stronger than a reclining figure could have inflicted. An aura of evil seemed to have invaded the room and left as quickly as did the 'force.' Years later, at the beginning of 1949, a similar event took place. My aunt was sitting in our Chicago home, feeding me a bottle, when this force again entered the scene, causing the two of us to be considerably uplifted from the couch. Again the jumping persisted and the evil presence was felt. The next performance by this "thing" occurred in the early months of 1971 in Seattle. It was around midnight and I was reading a novel, while my husband, Gary, slept. I suddenly sensed something wicked within the confines of our room. I tossed it off, but then there began that jumping motion. I became quite alarmed as I realized neither my sleeping husband nor my own reclined body could attest to such motion. I woke my husband, who is not psychic, and he, too, became aware of the jumping movement. It was now growing in intensity, but when I called out the Lord's name, the bed suddenly ceased pitching. It wasn't until April, 1971, after moving from Seattle, that I learned of the two previous experiences."

On her father's side, Cynthia is descended from a noble German family, originally from Hanover. Her father had no interest or use for anything psychic. When Cynthia was only a few months old, her Aunt Doris came to live with the family as a temporary replacement for her mother, who was then quite ill and in the hospital. The aunt was sleeping on the living room couch, Cynthia's father in the front bedroom, and Cynthia herself in a crib placed in the back bedroom. Everyone was very much concerned with her mother's health, and her aunt, being

Roman Catholic, had been praying almost around the clock. She had only been asleep for a short time, when a cold breeze awakened her and to her amazement, she saw a woman, fairly young and dressed in a nun's habit, walking slightly *above* the floor through the living room and turn down the hall toward Cynthia's room. Concerned for the little girl's safety, the aunt quickly followed the woman into the room. There she saw the nun place her hands on Cynthia's crib, look down at her and smile. She seemed quite unaware of the aunt and, her mission apparently accomplished, turned and walked down the hall. The aunt immediately checked the baby, and seeing that the child was allright, went after the apparition. When she arrived at the living room, the figure had vanished, yet there remained a strong scent of roses in the air which even Cynthia's father noticed the following morning. The scent remained in the house, even though it was winter, until Cynthia's mother came home from the hospital. There were no perfume sachets, fresh flowers, or air fresheners which could have accounted for the strange odor. The unusual scent has returned to the house from time to time and can never be satisfactorily explained; it usually coincides with an illness in the family, and has often served as a kind of telepathic warning to Cynthia's mother, when Cynthia was ill while at college. This particular event, of course, was told Cynthia many years later at a family gathering, but it served to underline Cynthia's own awareness of her unusual faculty.

"Perhaps the most vivid and memorable personal experience occurred to me when I was in grade school," Cynthia explained. 'I had always heard footsteps in the 1950s and 60s, starting in the aforementioned living room, coming into the front bedroom and stopping at my bed, both during the day and at night. My parents always attributed the noises to the creaking of old floors, but the house was only built in 1947. At times, the footfalls backed away from the bed, thus disputing the "last footsteps before going to bed" theory. I occupied a twin bed which faced the hallway when the bedroom door was open. On the left side of the bed, my side, was the wall shared by both the living room and front bedroom; Mother slept in the other twin bed adjacent to the driveway wall.

"During one particular night, I had gotten up to go to the bathroom, and upon returning to my bed, snuggled under the covers and shot a quick glance at my sleeping mother. Suddenly, the room became exceptionally cold and on looking toward the door, which I had forgotten to close, I saw four figures coming from the living room *through* the hallway wall and turn into our bedroom. In order to assert that I hadn't unconsciously fallen asleep since returning to bed, I began pinching myself and looking from time to time to the familiar surrounding room and my mother. Thus I know, I was fully awake and not dreaming. The first figure entering the room was dressed, as were all the others, in 19th century Western American clothing. She was a woman in her forties of average height, very thin and dressed in a brown and white calico dress with high-button collar and long sleeves; her dark brown hair was parted in the middle and tied tightly on top of her head in a bun. There was a prim, austere air about her. She moved to the foot of the bed on my far left. Next came a very tall and lanky man, brown hair parted in the middle, wearing a brown three-piece suit, rather shabby. He took his place in the middle, at the foot of my bed. Following him was a woman whom I felt was out of place, even at the time of the vision. She was dressed in the most outlandish purple satin outfit, tucked up on one side as a barroom girl might have worn in the old West. Her blonde hair was curled in ringlets, which were drawn up on one side of her head and cascaded down on the other. I sensed loneliness and a very gentle nature surrounding her as she took her place next to the tall gentleman to my right. Lastly came a very dapper if somewhat plump gray-haired gentleman. He carried a small three-legged stool and a black bag, telling me he was probably a medical man. Hatted and wearing a gray three-piece suit complete with gold watch chain, he seated himself on his stool on my righthand side of the bed. They all seemed terribly concerned over my health, although I was not ill at the time. When the 'doctor' leaned over the bed and tried to take my hand into his, I decided I had experienced just about all I wanted to with these strangers. My voice quivered as I called out to my mother, who was a very light sleeper, and whose back was facing me, informing her of the unknowns who had invaded our bedroom. 'Mother, there are people in the room!' I called again and again. She reassured me sleepily and without turning over that I was only dreaming, and to go back to sleep. During these implorings on my part, the four strangers began backing away from the bed as if they were alamed by my speaking. Whether they actually spoke or I heard them telepathically, I cannot be certain, but I did 'hear' them repeatedly say, 'No, please, we only want to help you. No, no, don't call out.' My cries increased and with that they turned and exited the same way they had entered, through the wall into the living room."

The house in which this vision took place had only been built in comparatively recent times. The land had formed part of a farm in the early 19th century, but the costumes of the figures, Cynthia felt sure, belonged to an earlier period. She wondered whether perhaps the land had been part of a western wagon trail, and she was reliving a child's death. On the other hand, she began to wonder whether it referred to a previous existence of her own, since she has very strong feelings about the 19th century West.

Cynthia has had a number of precognitive dreams concerning events that later took place. But the dream that impressed itself more than any other upon her consciousness had to do with the past. Actually, it was preceded by what she described as "an insatiable interest in England" she developed in early high school, long before the Beatles became the rage of America. This was not a single dream, easily forgotten, but a series of recurrent dreams, all related one to the

446

other, mounting in intensity as if something within her was trying to come to the surface, informing her of a long-forgotten memory.

"At times I noticed myself speaking in a north country British accent and I caught myself using English spellings, drinking tea with cream, and the first time I heard the song, 'Greensleeves,' I felt very moved and certainly melancholy. There is another song, called 'North Country Maid' which has remained my great favorite. I even went so far as to compose a 200-page term paper on England for my sociology class. But long before this project took place, I began dreaming of a cloaked man mounting a horse in the moonlight and riding out of sight into the English countryside. I was in the dream also, dressed in a blue and tan peasant frock, laced up the front. I knew it was me because I remember looking down at the dress I was wearing. In other words, I was actually a participant, not a sleeping spectator of myself, nor recognizing myself as another person. At any rate, I seemed to be coming out of a stable or barn, in which I had been lying on a large pile of hay. I begin running towards the mounting horseman, as if to beg him not to leave. Then I would awaken, only to dream the same dream several nights later.

"One night when I was particularly tired, I managed to continue my dream state after the wench's running, but not for long. In the dream, I uttered between sobs, the name of Dick, and then awoke. The dream continued in this pattern until I, now exasperatedly curious, forced myself to remain sleeping. Finally, one night, I was able to hear the whole phrase—Dick Turpin, my love, wait! Don't go!' Its mission now seemingly fulfilled by giving me a name I had never heard before, the dream never returned again."

At that time, Cynthia had never heard of Dick Turpin. But the dreams had roused her curiosity and she started to research it. Her Encyclopedia Britannica was of very little help, nor did any of the high school encyclopedias contain the name. But in her parents' library she located a 1940 edition of Nelson's Encyclopedia. In it, she found a brief listing of one Richard Turpin, an English highwayman and associate of Tom King, who lived from 1706 to 1739, when he was executed by hanging.

About a year after the dreams had subsided, she was riding with a girlfriend, when she suddenly felt a strong urge to return home immediately. Still under a kind of compulsion, she immediately turned on the television set and picked a Walt Disney show, very much to her parents' surprise, since they knew her to dislike the program. At that moment, flashed on the screen were the words, "The Legend of Dick Turpin." Cynthia then proceeded to watch the program, her eyes glued to the set, interrupting the proceedings on screen with comments of her own. "No, that wasn't what happened," she would say and proceeded to correct it. What was remarkable was her ability to relate what was about to happen onscreen and to mention characters' names before this information became available to the viewers. Afterwards, she felt dazed and remembered little of what she had said during the program.

I suggested that Cynthia meet me in Los Angeles so that I could attempt to regress her hypnotically and determine whether her reincarnation memory was factual or merely a romantic fantasy. We met just before Christmas, 1973, at my Hollywood hotel, the Continental Hyatt House. We discussed Cynthia's psychic experiences and I discovered that she had had an accident in 1969 resulting in a brain concussion. Did the accident influence her psychic perceptions in any way? No, she replied, she had had them for years prior to the accident, and they continued after the accident. Had she ever been to England or was she of English background? Both questions she answered in the negative. Her interest in English history and literature at college came *after* the recurrent dream had occurred to her. Having established that neither Cynthia nor her family had any English background nor leanings, I proceeded to regress her hypnotically in the usual manner. It took only a short time before she was under, ready to answer my questions while hypnotized.

After describing life as a Victorian gentleman in New York, and giving the name of John Wainscott, and the year 1872 or 1892, she proceeded back into the 18th century and the year 1703, to a man who had something to do with a Delaware Street. The man's name was Dick, and evidently we had gotten to the subject of her recurrent dreams.

"He is mounting a horse, and he's throwing his cape back so he can take hold of the reins. He's got a hat on with a plume on it, I am standing by the barn."

"What is your relationship with this man? What is your name?" I asked.

"A wench . . . my name is Sally."

"What year is this?"

"1732."

"What happens then?"

"He rides away like he always does."

"What happens to you?"

"I cry."

And that was all I could get out of her through hypnotic regression. But somehow it must have settled this recurrent dream and the urgency connected with it within Cynthia, for I heard nothing further from her since then.

Do the Barrymores Still Live Here?

Paula Davidson is a charming, introspective girl from Cleveland, Ohio, who decided that a career in the entertainment field could be best achieved by moving to Los Angeles. In 1969 she arrived in Beverly Hills and took a job with a major advertising agency. The job was fine, but there was something peculiar about the house into which she had moved. In the first place, it was far too large to be a one-family home, and yet she had been told that it once belonged to one family—the family of Lionel Barrymore. Perched high in the Hollywood Hills, the house gives a deceptive impression if one approaches it from the street. From that side it presents only two stories, but the rear of the house looks down into a deep ravine, perhaps as much as five or six stories deep. There is even a private cable car, no longer in use. The once beautiful gardens have long since fallen into disrepair and now present a picture of sad neglect.

On the whole, the house was and is the kind of palatial mansion a Barrymore would have felt at home in. Although the gardens have been neglected for years, the house itself is still bright, having been painted recently, and its Spanish décor adds to the mystique of its background. When Paula Davidson took up residence there, the owner had been forced to sublet part of the house in order to hold on to the house itself. One of the rooms in what used to be the former servants' quarters was rented to Heidi, a composer who wrote musical scores for films. She was in the habit of practicing her music in the music room on the first level. Since the house was quiet during the daytime, everyone having gone off

450

to work, Heidi liked to practice during that part of the day. In the still-ness of the empty house she would frequently hear footsteps approach-ing as if someone unseen were listening to her playing. On one occasion she clearly heard a baby cry when there was no baby in the house.

I promised Paula to look into the matter, and on May 31, 1969, she picked me up at the Continental Hotel to take me to the Barrymore mansion. With us was another friend named Jill Taggart. Jill had worked with me before. A writer and sometime model, Jill had dis-played ESP talents at an early age and shown amazing abilities with clairvoyance and psychometry. It occurred to me that taking her to a place she knew nothing about, without of course telling her where we were going and why, might yield some interesting results. Consequently I avoided discussing anything connected with the purpose of our visit.

When we arrived at the mansion, the owner of the house greeted us cordially. Paula, Heidi, the owner and I started out following Jill around the house as my psychic friend tried to get her bearings. Unfortunately, however, we had picked an evening when some of the other tenants in the house were having a party. What greeted us on our arrival was not the serene stillness of a night in the Hollywood Hills but the overly loud blaring of a jukebox and the stamping of many feet in one of the basement rooms.

I have never worked under worse conditions. Under the circum-stances, however, we had no choice but to try to get whatever we could. Even before we entered the house Jill remarked that she felt two peo-ple, a man and a woman, hanging on in the atmosphere, and she had the feeling that someone was watching us. Then she added, "She died a long time after he did." I questioned her further about the entities she felt present. "She's old; he's young. He must have been in his thirties; she is considerably older. I get the feeling of him as a memory. Perhaps only her memory of him, but whichever one of the entities is here, it is madder than hell at the moment." With the noise of the music going on downstairs I couldn't rightly blame the ghost for being mad. Jill then pointed at a corner of the house and said, "I keep seeing the corner of the house up there."

I later discovered that the top room was a kind of ballroom with a balcony. In it Heidi frequently heard a telephone ring, but that was not the only part of the house where an invisible telephone kept ringing. "I used to be down in the bottom room, the one right next to where the noise is now," Heidi explained, "practicing my music, but I'd constantly have to stop, thinking I heard the telephone ring. Of course there was no telephone." I took Heidi aside so that Jill could not hear her remarks. Jill would not have been interested anyway, for she was engrossed in her study of the house now, walking up and down the stairs, peering into rooms with a quizzical expression on her face.

"Tell me," I asked Heidi, "what else did you experience in this house?"

"Frequently when I was down in that room playing the piano I would hear people walking on the stairs; this happened at all times of the day, and there was never anyone up there."

Jill was passing by us now. "I picked up a name," she said. "Grace—and then there is something that sounds like Hugen." I looked at the owner of the house. Jill was out of earshot again. "The party who had the house before us was Arty Erin," the owner said, shrugging.

"Did anyone ever die of violence in this house?" I asked.

"I've heard rumors, something having to do with the cable car, but I don't know for sure."

We all walked over to the cable car, covered with rust and dirt and long out of commission. Jill placed her hands on it to see if she could get any psychometric impression from it. "This cable car has been much loved, I should say, and much enjoyed." Then her facial expression changed to one of absolute horror. Quickly she took her hands off the cable car.

"What is it, Jill?" I asked.

"Someone came down violently, down the hill in the cable car. Later he wound up here near the pulley."

We walked down to the bottom of the ravine, where there was a magnificent swimming pool. The pool itself was still in operating condition, and there was a pool house on the other side of it. Down here the sound of the music was largely muted, and one could hear one's voice again. Jill obviously had strong impressions now, and I asked her what she felt about the place.

"I feel that a very vicious man lived here once, but I don't think he is connected with the name Grace I got before. This may have been at a different time. Oh, he had some dogs, kind of like mastiffs. I think there were two and possibly three. They were vicious dogs, trained to be vicious."

"What did this man do?"

"I see him as a sportsman, quick with words. There were also two young people connected with this man, a boy and a girl. I see them laughing and romping about and having a wonderful time here as teenagers. He seems not to like it at all but is tolerating it. But the dogs seemed to have played a very big part in his life. Nobody would dare enter his property without his permission because of those dogs. Permission, I feel, was rarely given except with a purpose in mind. He has exerted the strongest influence on this house, but I don't think he was the first owner."

"Do you feel that anyone well-known was connected with this house?"

"Yes. More than one well-known person, in fact." I asked Jill to describe the personality that she felt was strongest in the atmosphere of the house.

"I see this man with a small moustache, dark thinning hair, exceedingly vain, with a hawklike nose. He has brownish eyes; they have dark circles under them. He doesn't look dissipated by an excess of drink or food, but he does look dissipated through his own excesses. That is, his own mind's excesses. He prides himself on having the eye of the eagle and so affects an eagle-eyed look. I also suspect that he is nearsighted. I see him wearing a lot of smoking jackets. One in particular of maroon color."

The description sounded more and more fascinating. What profession did she think the man followed?

"I see him with a microphone in his hand, also a cigarette and a glass. He might be an actor or he might be a director."

I asked Jill whether this man owned the house or was merely a visitor.

The question seemed to puzzle her. "He might be a visitor, but I see him down here so much he might be staying here. The young people I described before might belong to the owner of the house."

I wondered if the man in the maroon jacket was one of the disturbing entities in the house.

Jill nodded. "I think this man is as well aware now of what he does as when he was alive. *I think he is still here.*"

"Can you get an indication of his name?"

"I get the letter *S*, but that's because he reminds me so much of Salvador Dali."

"Anything else?"

"Yes, there is an *L* connected with him. The *L* stands for a name like Lay or Lee or Leigh, something like that. Oh, and there is something else. A Royal typewriter is important. I don't know if it's important to him because he writes letters or what, but *Royal* is important."

I was about to turn to the owner of the house when Jill's arm shot up, pointing to the balcony. "That woman up there—she acts very much the owner of the house. I imagine it's Grace." Since none of us could see the woman, I asked Jill for description of what she saw.

"She's a woman in her sixties, with gray or white hair. And it's very neat. She is very statuesque—slender and tall—and she wears a long

454

flowing dress that has pleats all over. She seems to be raising her hand always, very dramatically, like an actress."

I thanked Jill for her work and turned to Marie, the owner of the house. How did all this information stack up with the knowledge she had of the background of her house—for instance, the business of telephones ringing incessantly when there were no telephones about?

"At one time this house was owned by a group of gamblers. They had a whole bunch of telephones all over the house. This goes back several years."

"What about this Grace?"

"The name rings a bell with me, but I can't place it."

"And the baby Heidi keeps hearing?"

"Well, of course, the house used to belong to actor Lionel Barrymore. He and his wife had two babies who died in a fire, although it was not in this house."

Apparently Lionel Barrymore had owned this house, while his brother John lived not far away on Tower Road. Thus John was in a very good position to visit the house frequently. Jill had spoken of a man she saw clairvoyantly as reminding her of Salvador Dali. That, we all agreed, was a pretty good description of the late John Barrymore. Jill had also mentioned the name Lee or Leigh or something like it. Perhaps she was reaching for Lionel.

The mention of the word *Royal* I found particularly fascinating. On the one hand, the Barrymores were often referred to as the royal family of the theater. On the other hand, if a typewriter was meant, one must keep in mind that John Barrymore had been hard at work on his autobiography in his later years, though he had never completed it. Yet the matter of finishing it had been very much on his mind. As for the teenagers Jill felt around the premises, the two children, Diana and John, Jr., had been at the house a great deal when they were teenagers. John Barrymore, however, didn't like children at all; he merely tolerated them.

I asked Marie (who had been here for more than a year prior to our visit) if she had ever seen or heard anything uncanny.

"No, but I can feel a presence."

The house has twelve rooms altogether, but according to local tradition, the three bottom rooms were added on somewhat later. "Has anything tragic ever occurred in this house, to your knowledge?"

"A man fell down those stairs head first and was killed. But it was an accident."

Obviously the house had been lived in for many years both before and after the Barrymore tenancy. It seems only natural that other emotional events would leave their mark in the atmosphere of the old house. Despite all this, Jill was able to pick up the personalities of both John and Lionel Barrymore and perhaps even of sister Ethel, if she was the lady in the gray robe. We left the house with a firm promise to dig into the Hall of Records for further verification.

Two weeks later I received a letter from Paula Davidson. She was having lunch with a friend of hers, director William Beaudine, Sr., who had been well acquainted with both John and Lionel Barrymore. Paula mentioned her experience at the house with Jill and me and the description given by Jill of the entity she had felt present in the house. When she mentioned the vicious dogs, Mr. Beaudine remarked that he remembered only too well that John had kept some Great Danes. They might very well have been the vicious dogs described by Jill.

Since that time Paula Davidson has moved away from the house on Summit Ridge. Others have moved in, but no further reports have come to me about the goings-on at the house. If the noisy party we witnessed during our visit was any indication of the present mood of the house, it is most unlikely that the Barrymores will put in an appearance. For if there was one thing the royal family of the theatre disliked, it was noisy competition.

456

Hollywood Not-So-Confidential: Even Ordinary Citizens Have Ghostly Experiences

North Beachwood Drive in Hollywood is an average street. Most of the houses on this particular block are two- or four-family houses divided up into apartments. Farther up the street is one of the major motion picture studios, but the block in question is rather quiet and not at all ghostly in appearance. The C. family moved into apartment No. 4 in one of the houses on the 1200 block in 1963. Mr. C. is an artist, and they had a four-year-old daughter at the time. The apartment was the only one at the top of a stairway, and anyone coming up those stairs would be a member of the C. family or someone paying them a visit.

Shortly after the C.'s had moved into their new apartment, they noticed some rather unusual things. After they had settled in the new place and started paying attention to the surroundings, they became aware of a strange phenomenon occurring every night between eight and nine P.M. *Someone was walking up their stairs.* At first only Mrs. C. paid attention to it. Clearly those were the footsteps of a very old person having difficulty ascending the stairs. The footsteps were deliberate and loud, slowing down and then picking up speed again. After a while they stopped, but no one was heard coming *down* the stairs again. This went on for several evenings in succession.

Mrs. C. realized that there was no one actually coming up the stairs, and she wondered if she was hallucinating. She therefore did not mention it to her husband. A few days passed. One evening, again at the same hour, her husband suddenly looked at her and said, "Quiet, I hear something." Both C.'s then clearly heard the same slow footsteps coming up their stairway. This time, however, they jumped up and tore the door open. There was no one there. Mr. C. immediately ran down the stairs as quickly as he could and looked around the corner and up and down the block, but there was no one to be seen. Mrs. C. then confessed that she had heard the same noises several nights in a row.

They decided to lie in wait the following night. Sure enough, between eight and nine P.M. someone unseen tried to come up their stairs, and when they ran out to look, there was no one about. They were puzzling as to what to do about this phenomenon when their neighbor, Peggy V., decided to spend a night with them. Her daughter and the C.'s daughter were playmates. That night, everyone was fast asleep—Mrs. V. on the couch in the living room and the C.'s in their bedroom when an uproar woke them between two and three A.M. What woke Mrs. C. was an incessant scream coming from Mrs. V. As soon as she could be calmed down somewhat, Mrs. V. explained that she had been awakened by the sound of someone brushing his teeth and gargling in the bathroom. Puzzled as to who it might be, Mrs. V. had sat up on the couch. To her horror she clearly heard the dining room chairs in the dark apartment being pulled from the table, people sitting down on them, glasses being used and silverware tinkling, and muffled conversation. Since she knew very well that there was no one but herself and the C.'s in the apartment at the time, she screamed in absolute horror, unable to understand what was happening.

In conversation the following morning, Mrs. C. discovered that her neighbor had some occult interest in the past and was apparently "mediumistic." The C.'s themselves were not hostile to the idea of ghosts. Both of them were slightly interested in the occult and had a few books on the subject in their library. Mr. C. had always felt that ghosts were indeed possible, although he had never thought of having some of his own in the place where he lived.

The next day Mrs. C. went to see the owner of the building. After some hesitation, the landlady, Mrs. S., admitted that the previous tenant of their apartment had committed suicide in it—as a matter of fact, in the very bed in which the C.'s were now sleeping. That was quite enough for the C.'s. They decided to move from the apartment. When Mrs. S. was told of their determination to live elsewhere, she gave them an argument. "The old lady was a wonderful person," she exclaimed. "It is not a shame to commit suicide." Tactfully Mrs. C. explained about the phenomena they had witnessed.

Mrs. C. had had no ESP experiences either before or after living in the apartment on Beachwood. Nor had she any desire to again experience anything like it. One ghost was quite enough for her.

Polly Blaize is a lady in her early fifties, filled with the joy of life and spilling over with the excitement of many experiences with the world of spirits. She comes from a distinguished old New England family; many of her ancestors were either passengers on the *Mayflower* or early colonial dignitaries, and she counts two American presidents, Franklin Pierce and John Tyler, among her near relatives. Of Scottish background, she left New England at an early age to come to Hollywood, where she worked briefly for Warner Brothers. An early marriage proved a failure but left her with two small children. After a succession of various administrative jobs, she eventually remarried in 1965. Her husband is a design engineer working for NASA. Polly—or as she is more formally known, Pauline—lives with her husband in one of the beach communities south of Los Angeles now, but the experiences I am about to relate happened to her when she lived in and around Hollywood.

In 1924, not long after she had moved to California with her parents, Polly became friendly with a young boy named Billy Bennett. They were teenagers together when their families lived across from each other on Highland Avenue in Hollywood. Billy lived in an apartment that was part of a row of one-story apartments of the court type. The apartments have long since been leveled. His mother was then a famous screen star by the name of Belle Bennett, best know for her starring role in the 1925 version of *Stella Dallas*.

Time passed, and Pauline was married. Her marriage did not last very long, and she found herself at age twenty with the responsibility for two small children, a one-year-old daughter and a two-year-old son. One night she was in bed, fully awake, when she heard the shrieking sounds of what seemed to her like a flock of birds. The window was open and she heard the birds coming through it, hovering around her with the sound of beating wings. The sound was so loud she could barely hear the human voice in the midst of this flock of birds. There was nothing to be seen, but the voice was that of Billy Bennett. "Beware of people who can hurt you, I still love you; I am ever near to protect you," the voice said, over and over. All this time she could see absolutely nothing but the darkness of the room.

Only a few days before the incident, Billy had died suddenly at the Presbyterian Hospital in Hollywood. His warning proved to be accurate indeed. For many years Mrs. Blaize lived almost as a recluse, until she met her second husband and married again, this time with happier results.

But the incident that has etched itself most deeply into her memory took place in 1935 when her daughter was five years old. They had just moved into a one-bedroom apartment on Cheremoya Avenue in Hollywood. It consisted of a living room and a bedroom, and between the two was a dressing room large enough to contain a chest of drawers, a counter, and a large dressing mirror. About a week after they had moved into this apartment, Polly was suddenly awakened by the sound of what seemed to her like a heavy thud. It sounded as if a human body had dropped, followed by what sounded like a body pulling itself across the living room floor, from the dressing room area halfway to the kitchen, which was located on the other side of the living room. At first Polly paid no attention to these odd sounds, but when they repeated themselves exactly in the same manner at exactly the same time night after night, she became alarmed. Much later, she learned that her little girl was just as much aware of these sounds as she was.

Polly decided to make some inquiries of the landlady. The latter, named Beatrice Scriver, listened to the account of the nightly disturbances and then turned white. Since everyone in the building, which contained eight apartments, seemed to be familiar with the story, there was nothing for Mrs. Scriver to do but to let Polly in on the secret.

Prior to Polly's moving into the apartment, the place had belonged to a woman and her nineteen-year-old son. The young man was a successful athlete and had high hopes for a professional career. Suddenly he was informed that he would have to lose one of his legs because of severe illness. After he had been given this verdict by his doctors, the young man returned home and in front of his dressing room mirror shot himself to death. He fell to the floor, his body hitting it near the dressing-room door. Not quite dead, he pulled himself into the living room, pushed himself up on one elbow, then dropped again to the floor, only to try to pull himself up again. He did this several times in an effort to reach his mother, who was then in the kitchen. Because she had the water running, she had not heard the shot through the closed door.

Polly shuddered. Mrs. Scriver had described the exact sounds she had heard night after night in her apartment. But there was still another sound she wanted an explanation for. It sounded to her as if a basket were being pulled along the floor. The landlady nodded grimly. The young man's body had been taken out of the apartment in a basket, down the back stairs and to the morgue.

But that was not the end of the story by any means. Being spiritually attuned, Polly realized she had to help release the young man from his sufferings. Quite obviously, she argued, he did not realize what had happened to him. (In the intervening time, the young man's mother had also passed away.)

Polly thanked the landlady for the information and went back to her apartment. Her eyes fixed themselves on the dark rug on her living room floor. Turning the carpet back, she noticed a large brown stain and realized that it was made by the young man's blood. That was all the proof she needed. That night she waited until the sounds started up again. Speaking in a soft voice, she then called him by name.

"Your mother has gone ahead of you and is waiting for you; do not keep her waiting any longer," she said, pleading with the unseen presence. There was only silence.

Several nights in a row she spoke the same words, and finally there was a sound in answer to her pleading. She was seated in a chair near the spot where he had died when she suddenly heard a long, drawn-out voice as if called to her from far away, saying, "Mama—help me." The voice sounded hollow, as if it were coming from some distant place, but she heard it clearly and responded. For a while the sounds continued. Polly did not give up; she kept repeating her plea, asking the young man to reach out to his mother so that he could be free from the unhappy surroundings where he had died. Ultimately the message got through to him, and just as suddenly as the phenomena had entered Polly's life, they stopped. With a sigh of relief Polly Blaize realized that she had successfully freed the ghostly young athlete.

Lise Caron and her husband Leo moved to Los Angeles in 1965. The family had originally lived in Paris, but the two older daughters, named Liliane and Nicole, had decided to strike out on their own and go to the United States. They liked it so much they induced their parents to follow them. Thus Mr. and Mrs. Caron and the third daughter joined the two girls in Los Angeles in a house at El Centro Avenue in the 1200 North block. A cluster of houses in the Spanish style is arranged around a narrow courtyard, open on one side toward the street. The landlord occupies the house at the bottom of this cluster of houses, and the apartment that was to be the home of the Carons is the first one on the right.

Liliane had been married a short time before her parents' arrival in Los Angeles and had moved out, leaving Nicole the sole occupant of the apartment. Nicole had decided that the place was too small for three additional people and had therefore rented a single apartment close by, intending to leave her former apartment to her parents and their youngest daughter.

When Lise Caron arrived at the house, she had a good impression of it. The street was quiet, the house, though old, seemed in good condition, and she felt that they would be happy in it. The apartment itself consisted of a good-sized living room separated from the dining room by a folding door.

At the time of their arrival, the dining room had been transformed into a bedroom for Martine, the youngest daughter. Between the dining room and a short hallway stood a chest of drawers. On top of the chest a candle was burning. Surprised, Mrs. Caron turned to her daughters, asking why they were burning a candle. The answer was an evasive one, but Lise was too tired from the long journey to pay much attention to it. Thus, when Nicole implored her mother to leave the candle in its place, she nodded and went on to other things. To the right side of the hallway was a bedroom in which stood two beds separated by a night table with a lamp on it. To the left of the hallway was the bathroom, and in front of the dining room door was the kitchen door. This kitchen door would swing with a particular noise as it went from one side to the other. In every room there were flowers and green plants helping to create a happy impression. The Carons were so happy to be together again after the long separation that they lingered over their dinner. It was late when they decided to go to bed.

Mr. and Mrs. Caron went to their bedroom, while Martine closed the folding door between bedroom and living room. She then went to bed in her makeshift bedroom in the living room.

Almost as soon as Mr. Caron lay down he was asleep. Mrs. Caron was still in the bathroom when she suddenly received the impression that there was someone observing her. Turning around, she saw no one. She continued with her chores, but again received the distinct impression that someone was standing at the bathroom door staring at her. Turning around again, she said, "Is that you, Leo?" But a look into the bedroom convinced her that her husband was fast asleep. She decided to see whether Martine might have gotten up and come in to see her.

Martine was still up, and when her mother came over to her she seemed to have a strange look on her face. "What is wrong?" Mrs. Caron asked her daughter.

"I don't feel comfortable here," the girl said, and explained that she had a strange feeling of a presence. Mrs. Caron did not wish to upset her youngest daughter, so she made light of this, at the same time opening the folding door to change the atmosphere of the room. The only light came now from the flickering candle, and that too helped to create a somewhat spooky impression. But since everyone was tired, she did not want to make an issue of it and decided to find out about the candle later. Then she returned to bed. As soon as she had lain down, she again had the feeling of another presence.

But the next few days were too exciting to leave room for worry about the impressions of that first night, and in the end she ascribed her strange feelings to the need for adjustment to new surroundings.

Unfortunately, the impressions continued night after night. A few days after their arrival she woke up to the noise of the kitchen door swinging. She thought that her husband had gone to the kitchen to get a drink. But a glance at his bed showed her he had not. A little later, she awoke again to see someone standing between their two beds. She thought her husband had gotten up, but to her surprise saw that he was fast asleep. In fact, she could see right through the strange person standing between the two beds. She sat bolt upright, her heart pounding, looking straight ahead at the apparition. At that moment, the stranger vanished into thin air.

She awakened her husband and told him what had happened. Quickly he put on his coat and ran around to the outside of the house, thinking an intruder had somehow gotten into the apartment. But there was no one about.

The next morning she decided to talk about this with her older daughters. It was then that she received an explanation for the strange goings-on and the flickering candle on the dresser. When the two girls had first rented the apartment, they too had the feeling of a presence with them. At first they had been rather scared by it, but after some time they ignored the unusual impressions, preferring to live with whatever it was that was disturbing in the atmosphere rather than to look for a new apartment. This had gone on for some time, when one night they were aroused by the noise of the kitchen door opening. Both girls woke up simultaneously fastening their eyes upon the darkness of their bedroom. There between the two beds stood a man. Their first thought was that a burglar had gotten into the house. As they jumped from their beds the apparition vanished. A quick check of doors and windows disclosed that none of them was open, nor was there anyone outside. Several days later Liliane heard the same noise again. Bravely she opened her eyes and saw a white apparition close to Nicole's bed. Again she sat up in bed, and the apparition vanished. She was not sure, but the second apparition might have been that of a woman. After that the two girls decided they needed the help of a medium and went to see famed clairvoyant Brenda Crenshaw. Mrs. Crenshaw, wife of newspaper writer James Crenshaw, has been a practicing medium in the Hollywood area for many years and has an impeccable reputation for honesty and accuracy. After a few minutes the two girls were told that the medium saw the problem surrounding them quite clearly.

It appeared that a young couple had committed suicide in the apartment some time before. On checking this they found the information to be correct. From that moment on they decided to place a candle in the apartment and to pray for the unfortunate ones every day, in the hope that they might find peace. With their daily prayer becoming part of the routine, they managed to continue living in the haunted apartment.

Mrs. Caron wasn't exactly ecstatic about the idea of continuing to live with the ghostly couple. On the other hand, she thought that perhaps she might release them. She promised herself to stay calm should anything further occur. Her opportunity came a few nights after her conversation with her daughters. She woke up again to the sound of the kitchen door opening by itself. Slowly Mrs. Caron looked up and saw a young man standing between the two beds, close enough to be touched. He was standing near her husband's feet. Mrs. Caron could see him very clearly. He was a short man, with curly hair, but since his back was turned toward her she could not see his face. She estimated that he was between thirty and thirty-five years old. He stood there without moving, as if transfixed. Mrs. Caron hoped that he would turn around so she could see his face, but he did not. After a while the apparition started slowly to vanish, until it was completely gone. He never returned to the apartment visually, but his influence could still be felt for a long time after this incident.

Continuing their prayers for the release of the unhappy couple, the Carons nevertheless felt that their apartment was not exactly a happy one and decided to move just as soon as they could find another place.

I spoke to Mrs. Caron in 1970 and found that all was well in their new place. She had no idea as to what had happened to the apartment on El Centro Avenue but readily supplied me with additional information about the landlord. In October of 1972 I drove to the house on El Centro Avenue in the company of Paula Davidson and her brother.

Walking about in front of the apartment, Paula felt nothing in particular. As for me, I felt rather depressed at the sight of this cluster of houses, which somehow reminded me of something out of Hollywood's past, but that may have been due to my knowledge of the incidents just described. Bravely I rang the doorbell. A dark-haired middle-aged lady opened the door, peering out at me, wondering what I wanted. I explained that I was writing a book about Hollywood, not saying that I meant *haunted* Hollywood. I asked the lady whether she knew anything about the background of her apartment.

"I am sorry I can't help you," she replied politely. "I have been living here only two years."

"Is there anything special that you might have observed during those years?" I asked.

The lady shook her head and smiled rather wryly. "Nothing really. Except that I've been very unhappy here. I've had nothing but bad luck ever since I moved into this apartment. I haven't the vaguest idea why."

Anyone who thinks that such experiences are rare and happen only to the imaginative or perhaps those who are "believers" just doesn't know his facts. I have hundreds upon hundreds of parallel cases in my files, all of them reported by sane, sensible and rational people from every social and economic level. These incidents occur in new houses as well as in old ones. Take the case of Mrs. Barbara McDuffa, a lady who now lives in West Los Angeles. She had gone through a harrowing and, to her, inexplicable experience which preyed on her mind until she could find some sort of explanation for it. She needed a "rational" explanation, because otherwise there was the suggestion that she had per-haps imagined the whole thing or that there was something wrong with her powers of perception. Eventually she heard of my work and tele-phoned me while I was on the Gil Henry radio program in the area. We talked about the matter, and I assured Mrs. McDuffa that there was nothing wrong with her mind, her eyes or her hearing. It just happened that she had moved into a haunted apartment.

In the late sixties, Mrs. McDuffa, her mother, and her son David moved into a brand-new, never before-lived-in apartment on Roscoe Boulevard in Panorama City, a community at the end of Van Nuys, which in turn borders on North Hollywood. At that time Mrs. McDuffa scoffed at the supernatural or the notion that there might be ghosts or haunted apartments. If anyone had mentioned such possibil-ities to her, she would have thought him insane or jesting.

The first night after they had moved into the new apartment, they went to bed fairly early, because there remained much work to be done in the morning. It was a warm night and Mrs. McDuffa couldn't sleep. She decided to get up and open the bedroom window. As she started for the window, she suddenly perceived a tall figure of a man, wearing an overcoat and hat, standing in the closet doorway at the foot of the bed. Mrs. McDuffa had left the closet door open, but there wasn't any-thing in it as yet since they hadn't unpacked their things. When she saw the figure she rushed for the light switch. As soon as the light went on the figure disappeared. For a moment Mrs. McDuffa was stunned, but then she assumed that she had had an hallucination and went back to bed.

The following night she was awakened from a deep sleep by the sound of footsteps on the carpet. As she was trying to get her bearings, she noticed that her mother had been awakened by the same noises. It sounded as if someone were walking on the carpet, shuffling his feet, yet there was no one to be seen. The two women exchanged experiences but eventually put them out of their minds, since there was a great deal of work to be done in the apartment, and no one had much time to think about such matters as the supernatural.

The footsteps, however, continued for several nights. They were now joined by a tapping sound on the window of the bedroom. Since there weren't any shutters or trees or bushes or anything else near the window that could have caused this noise, they were puzzled. Worried that the unseen phenomena might upset the little boy, the ladies then put the boy's bed into their room and shut the door of the other room at night. Still thinking that it might be a prowler or some other physical force, they pulled a dresser up in front of the door so that no one could enter. The door of the bedroom opened into a little corridor. There was no direct access to either the windows or the entrance door of the apartment. That night, as if in response to their new security measures, the closed bedroom door started to rattle. The doorknob moved as if someone were trying to get in. The force rattling the door was so strong that only a wind of hurricane force could have caused it. Nevertheless, it was totally quiet outside the house; none of the windows were open, and there was no natural explanation for the rattling sound or the movement of the doorknob. The women had to conclude that they had been "blessed" by a ghost.

One day Mrs. McDuffa was combing her hair in her bedroom. Suddenly she felt a pressure on her shoulder and then felt something brushing her cheek as if an unseen person had passed very close by her. She turned around, but again there was no one to be seen. Shortly after this experience she heard the noise of a glass being put down as if someone had taken a drink of water in the kitchen. There was no one in the kitchen at the time. Several days after this experience, Mrs. McDuffa, now fully aware that there was something strange going on in their apartment, went to bed, turning on the bedside lamp in order to read. The moment she had turned it on, the lamp went out by itself. Three

times Mrs. McDuffa turned it on, only to see it go out of its own volition. She checked the bulb, but it worked perfectly in other lamps. The
next day she called in an electrician and had the switch examined as
well as the lamp. He could find nothing wrong with either. That night
she turned the lamp on again and nothing went wrong with it.
Apparently her unseen visitor had decided to leave things well enough
alone for that night.

Several days after this experience, Mrs. McDuffa was getting ready
to go to work. It was a dark, rainy morning, and as she shut the door
she looked back toward the apartment. A bright light shone across the
living room as if the sun were shining in. Both her mother and her son
saw the same thing and looked at her in amazement. There was no way
such a light could have appeared in her living room.

One evening everyone had gone to bed; the hall light was left on
and the door between the two bedrooms stood open. Mrs. McDuffa
was looking toward the open bedroom door when she suddenly became
aware of two roundish shapes made of a white, cloud-like substance. It
seemed to her to resemble in a vague way the outlines of a human figure, but no details could be seen. As she observed this apparition in a
state of shock mingled with fascination, the whitish shape slowly drifted into the second bedroom and disappeared.

But that was the end of the trail as far as Mrs. McDuffa was concerned. The following day she made arrangements to move. They had
lived at the apartment for less than three months. Since she had lived
in many places before without encountering anything unusual, Mrs.
McDuffa became convinced that she had somehow stumbled upon a
very haunted apartment. She has no idea who the apparition might be,
nor did she make any inquiries with the landlord. All she wanted was
to get out of the place, and fast.

John K. is twenty-six years old, lives in Hollywood and works as a freight cashier at a steamship company. "I don't quite know where to begin," he said when he contacted me in May of 1971. He explained that he felt he was being harassed by reincarnation memories or by someone he thought was in some mysterious way connected with his personality. Since I am always on the lookout' for "evidential" reincarnation cases, I was naturally interested. In October of the same year we met at the Continental Hotel in Hollywood. Mr. K. turned out to be a slight, quiet-spoken young man far from hysterical and not particularly involved with the occult. Gradually I pieced his amazing story together and discovered what lay at the base of his strange and terrifying experiences.

John K. was born in a small town in the Ozarks with a population of only forty-two people. The house he was born and raised in was quite old, built before the Civil War. His family lived there until he reached the age of twelve, when they moved to another small town in southwestern Arizona. There his father was employed by the government on a nearby Army base. At the age of twenty, Mr. K. dropped out of college after his junior year and headed straight for Los Angeles, where he has lived ever since.

His first twelve years in the Ozarks were spent on a farm with five brothers and two sisters. The family lived a very primitive life. There was no indoor plumbing; heat was provided by a coal stove, and each Saturday night the entire family would take turns bathing in the same tub of water. At first there was no electricity in the house. For the first three grades, Mr. K. went to a one-room schoolhouse. "Our teacher was very young and had not yet finished her college education but was permitted to teach us anyway."

Mr. K. explained, "The reason I am relating all of my earlier surroundings to you is to point out the fact that the first twelve years of my life I lived a very isolated existence." Until he reached the age of ten, Mr. K. had not seen a television set; entertainment in his family consisted mainly of playing cards and talking. He attended the local Southern Baptist Church, into which he was duly baptized; however, after the family left the farm they dropped out of organized religion.

From an early age John K. received the impression of a presence which no one else could see. None of his immediate family had ever been out of the country, yet he was aware of the presence of a French lady whose name, he came to know, as Jacqueline. When he mentioned the presence of this woman to his family he was laughed at and told that he had a fantastic imagination, so he stopped talking about it. At an early age he also developed the ability to dream of events that later happened *exactly* as seen in his dreams. These prophetic dreams did not forecast great events but concerned themselves with everyday matters. Nevertheless, they were upsetting to the boy. He never remembered his dreams, but when the event became objective reality he started to shiver and realized he had seen it all before. This, of course, is called *deja vu* and is a fairly common ESP phenomenon. He could not discuss his dreams with his family, since psychic experiences were not the kind of thing one could talk about in the Ozarks in the early fifties. But he hated to stay in the house alone; he had a terrible fear of darkness and of the house itself.

One afternoon when he was ten years old, he happened to be in the house alone, upstairs in the back bedroom. All of a sudden he knew there was a presence there, and the most horrifying fear swept through him, as if he were being choked to death. The walls seemed to vibrate, and he heard a loud sound for which there did not seem to be any natural explanation. Eventually he was able to break out of his terror and flee down the stairs.

There was something else that seemed strange about John K. from an early age on. He could never relate to men and felt completely at ease only with women—his grandmother, his mother, and his older sister. When he was very young, he began playing with his older sister, six years his senior, and enjoyed playing girls' games tremendously. He would never join his brothers in boys' games. He loved wearing long flowing dresses, fashions of an earlier time that he had found in the attic. Whenever he wore these dresses, he felt completely at ease and seemed to have a rather sophisticated air about him. The strange thing was that he insisted on wearing only those dresses of an earlier period of history; the shorter dresses of the current era interested him not at all. At those times he felt as though he were another person.

It was during those early childhood days that he first became aware of Jacqueline. Especially when he played with his sister, he felt that he was sexually just like her. He continued to wear dresses around the house until the time he started to school. Often when he came home from school he would go upstairs and put on his dresses. Finally, his father became aware of the boy's tendency and threatened to send him to school wearing a dress if he didn't stop, so John stopped. However, the impression of a female life inside him and the desire to wear long dresses persisted.

"Needless to say," Mr. K. explained in complete frankness, "I was not the average run-of-the-mill boy, and I turned out to be very effeminate and was teased constantly by my schoolmates." Rejected by the other boys, he began to turn within himself and did not bother to explain his ideas to others. Although he had never traveled outside the four southern states surrounding his native village, he began to feel very emotional about France, particularly Paris. "I somehow seemed to have fond memories of a life of many human pleasures, a life of a woman who was very aware and felt a need to express herself totally," John K. explained, adding that he knew by that time that Jacqueline, whoever she might have been, had led the life of a prostitute. He thus had a sense of heavy religious condemnation, of being a wicked sinner with the threat of hell hanging over him.

When the family finally moved to Arizona, he thought that perhaps some of his agonies would subside. But the conflict between his present surroundings and the world of Jacqueline increased almost daily. At the age of fourteen he felt that since he could not belong to this world he might as well kill himself and return to where he really belonged. He wrote a farewell note to his mother, the only one to whom he could relate at the time, his sister having married and his grandmother having grown old and feeble. In the note he told his mother that he was going to return to where he belonged, that he felt he had come from another planet and it was time for him to go back. He then ran a rope over one of the rafters in his room, put a chair under it, and placed the noose around his neck, ready to jump. Then fate intervened in the person of one of his mother's friends who had stopped by unexpectedly. Since his mother was asleep, John had to answer the door. The visit lasted a long time, and by the time the lady had left he was no longer in the mood to take his own life.

From then on he did rather well in school, although most people thought him too shy and introverted. He never dated girls, since he felt himself female. But he did make friends with one particular boy and remained close friends with him for ten years. Later, the boy moved to Los Angeles. When John K. dropped out of school in his junior year of college, he came to Los Angeles and moved in with his friend. At the time he was twenty years old. He still felt like a female and was still continually aware of Jacqueline.

It was then that John became involved in the homosexual world and had the first sexual experience of his life. Whenever he had sexual relations, he felt strongly that he was fulfilling the part of the woman.

About six months after he came to Los Angeles, he started to have terrible dreams. One night when he was totally awake he suddenly saw a woman standing at the foot of his bed. She was wearing a long nightgown and had long hair and was smiling at him. She seemed to float just above the floor. At first John thought that it was his imagination and passed it off as a silly dream. The next night the same thing happened. He realized the apparition wanted to tell him something. Strangely enough, he wasn't particularly frightened. The third night the apparition returned, and her smile had turned into a frown of deep sorrow. She returned the following night, and this time her face showed utter terror. Deep veins stood out on her face, her eyes were bloodshot, and her mouth grinned hideously.

She returned once again the following night, and this time her entire head had been torn off, and blood was spilled all over her beautiful flowing gown. John was fully aware of the utter torment of her soul. That same night something grabbed hold of his arm and forcibly yanked him out of bed and onto the floor. He screamed for help from his roommate, who was in the next room, but the young man had no compassion for his condition and yelled out for John to shut up or he would have him committed.

After this incident John thought he was going mad and wondered to whom he could turn for advice.

A few months passed. He was still living in Hollywood with the same roommate but by this time was a prostitute himself. He had gone to college and found himself a good job, but he had had a strong urge to become a prostitute, and so followed it. Whenever he engaged in these activities he felt a very deep satisfaction. Also at this time he resumed wearing female clothes, and since his roommate was a make-up artist by profession, he would do the make-up for him. John would never go into the streets in this array; he would wear these clothes only at home. His friends began to call him Jackie, for Jacqueline.

Whenever he put on the clothes, John became another person. The first time he saw himself in complete make-up and female clothing he felt that Jacqueline had won at last. He now felt that she had taken total possession of him and that he was cursed for life.

"It was not a simple case of transvestitism or going in female drag,"

John explained, "It was a complete soul satisfaction on my part, and when Jacqueline came out she controlled me completely. She was very strong and I was very weak."

It finally reached the point that when John came home at night he would dress up in female clothing and spend the entire evening in this manner. He even slept in evening gowns. He removed all the hair from his body and delighted in taking baths and dousing himself with perfumes. This went on for two years, until John felt that something had to be done about it. He realized something was wrong with him.

About that time another friend introduced him to Buddhism. For three years he practiced the Buddhist religion, and through it was able to find many answers for himself that had eluded him before. Because of his devotion to Buddhism, Jacqueline finally left, never to return again. A new male image began to emerge slowly but surely as a result of his Buddhist practices, and once again he was able to relate to the environment around him and find a reason for living.

Through a friend, John received my address. He contacted me in the hope I might hypnotize him and regress him to an earlier life in which he might encounter Jacqueline. John was firmly convinced that his predicament had been due to an unfulfilled reincarnation problem, and that perhaps through hypnosis I might put him further on the road to recovery.

"I never felt fulfillment during my pre-Buddhist sexual contacts while portraying Jacqueline," he told me, "but it did satisfy my Jacqueline personality completely. But she is totally gone now and a new John is emerging—one who is not afraid of the dark anymore and who can live alone and stand on his own two feet, and who will someday marry a girl and have a family. I am very optimistic about the future."

Although neither John nor his immediate family had had any interest in or knowledge of occult practices, this was not entirely true of others in his background. An Aunt Mary had been a practicing witch, had owned many books dealing with witchcraft of the fifteenth and six-teenth centuries, and had been a sore subject in the family. Nobody dared talk about her. But she had died before John was born, and all knowledge John had of his Aunt Mary was necessarily secondhand. Nevertheless, there had been ESP talents in the family on his father's side, mainly messages from dead relatives, though John was never able to obtain any details. In his family the occult was something not suit-able for family conversation.

After Jacqueline had left John, he kept having ESP experiences unrelated to his ordeal. They were not world-shaking experiences, but they did convince him that his ESP faculty had remained unimpaired by the hold Jacqueline had exercised upon him for so many years. A short time before our meeting there had been a steamship strike and he was laid off. He was wondering if he should get another job outside the steamship industry when he had a strange dream. In the dream he saw his boss at the steamship company coming out of his office and saying to someone, "Call John K. back to work." At the same time he saw the number 7 flash through the dream. Upon awakening he remembered every detail. On September 7 his boss came out of his office and told an aide, "Call John K. back to work," and, as foreseen in the dream, he returned to his former position.

I was rather interested in his continuing ESP experiences since I had begun to wonder whether Jacqueline was indeed a reincarnation memory or perhaps something else. We proceeded to begin hypnotic regression. I first took John K. down to age twenty, when he remem-bered every detail of his life. He even remembered the names of his best friends and what was on his desk at the time. I then took him back to age twelve and his life in Missouri. In each case he even knew his exact height at the time. He knew the names of the nearest neighbors, how many children they had and even the name of their dog. Satisfied that he was deeply in the third stage of hypnotic regression, I then took him back beyond the threshold of birth into an alleged earlier life. I worked very hard and very gradually to see whether we could locate some other personality that had been John K. in a previous lifetime, but he saw nothing. I then asked him to look specifically for Jacqueline.

"Do you know who she is?" I asked.

"She is someone who doesn't like me."

"Is she a real person?"

"Yes."

"Have you ever lived in France?"

"No."

I then took him as far back as the Middle Ages, fifty years at a time, in case there were other incarnations. When we got to the year 1350, he said he felt very strange and put his hands upon his chest in a gesture I interpreted as religious. But there was no recognition of another person. I then took him, step by step, back into the present, finally awakening him, and then inquiring how he felt. Since John was a good hypnotic subject, he remembered absolutely nothing of what he had said during hypnosis.

"Do you feel different from the way you felt fifteen minutes ago?" I inquired.

"Well, I had a headache before I came; I don't have a headache now."

He felt well-rested and satisfied with himself. Jacqueline had not put in an appearance, as she would have if she had been part of John K. I then explained to the young man that his ordeal had not been caused by reincarnation memories or an unfulfilled earlier lifetime. To the contrary, he had been victimized by an independent entity, not related to him in any way, who had somehow sought him out to serve as her medium of expression in the physical world. Jacqueline, the French prostitute, whose choice of clothes indicated that she had lived in the nineteenth century, wanted to live in this century through another body. For reasons of her own she had chosen a male body for her experiment.

If there was any reincarnation connection between the two, it remained obscure. There is, of course, the possibility that John K. had been in another life someone close to Jacqueline, in her time, and had since reincarnated while Jacqueline had not, and that the woman attached herself to John K. just as soon as she could after his birth into the present life. I myself tend to favor this theory. It is unfortunate that this earlier John K. could not be rediscovered either consciously or in hypnosis. But if this earlier incarnation had led a fully satisfactory life, the need to retain traces of memory would not be there.

In the case of Jacqueline, her inner conflict between what she was doing and the religious pressure exerted upon her must have been the compelling factor in keeping her in a time slot, or, rather, suspended in time, preventing her from reincarnating herself. In her predicament and frustration she needed to express herself through someone in the present, since she could not herself go on and be someone else. Deprived of her medium, Jacqueline perhaps will have found an avenue of escape into the next stage of existence and hopefully will not be heard from again.

When it comes to seeing the ghosts of celebrities, all sorts of people are likely to imagine they are in touch with their favorite movie star, when in fact they are merely expressing a wish fulfillment. In such cases, however, there exists a real attachment, an admiration for the personality involved. Frequently the people who have such fantasies are fans who have never met the star in question but wish they had.

Not so with attractive Doris Danielson, a Texas divorcee whom I met in Houston, after she had requested my help in clearing up the mystery of her psychic experiences. Now in her thirties, she works as a secretary.

"Miss Danielson, have you ever had any interest in psychic phenomena since you have grown up?" I began my questioning.

"No, I haven't."

"Have you had any experiences whatever that you might classify as psychic besides the one we are about to discuss?"

"No."

"When did this phenomenon take place?"

"It was in March of 1957. I was about to be discharged from the Air Force and was staying with a friend, Roger Smith, overnight. His house was in Trenton, New Jersey. I had been a stewardess, and I was planning to leave for New York to try to get into modeling. This happened the night before I left.

"I woke up for some reason in the middle of the night and crawled to the edge of the bed on my hands and knees. I asked myself, why did I wake up? I couldn't think of any reason. Then I looked at the door— it appeared to be getting brighter! Then a circle formed in the middle of the door. It was red. The circle started coming toward me. And inside the circle was *James Dean's head.*"

"Had you seen his face before?"

"I'd seen him in the movies, but I had no particular interest in James Dean; I simply thought he was a good actor. But I never thought about him. The only parallel in my life was that my boyfriend at the time resembled James Dean somewhat in his likes and dislikes, such as motorcycles, speed, and all that."

"Did he *look* like him?"

"Not really."

"How long did the image last?"

"I don't know, but I kept thinking if I stared at it long enough it might disappear. I did, but instead it floated across the room, and only then did it disappear. It came from the door and floated toward me as I was sitting on the bed. Just a head in a circle."

"Did it speak?"

"No."

"Was there any form of movement?"

"I can't remember any form of movement. His hair was very curly. Suddenly, it was gone. I sat there and pinched myself to make sure I was awake. When it was gone I really became scared, and I prayed."

"Have you had any similar experiences before or after?"

"No. The only other experience I had was after I had moved to Houston. I was married then, and my husband had gone on guard duty and was to be away for two weeks. Two days after he was gone, this happened. I had just turned out all the lights and gone to bed. I heard somebody come down the hallway. I thought it was my husband coming back, although I wasn't expecting him. He was the only one who had a key. I said, 'Bob, is that you?' But there was no answer. Then I felt someone come right into the bedroom and stand by my bed. The springs of the bed creaked as if someone were sitting on it. I shot out of the bed on the other side and ran to the bathroom, where I turned on the lights. There was nobody in the bedroom."

"Was the house in any way connected with a tragedy?"

"No. It was a brand-new house when we moved in."

"Did the footsteps sound like a man's or a woman's?"

"I had thought it was my husband coming home, but I don't know how I *could* have heard footsteps, because there was a rug on the floor."

"Had you seen any James Dean movies since the first incident?"

"No."

One can only surmise that the late actor recognized Doris as a potential communicator, but somehow never got his message across the veil.

Pipeline to the Beyond

A s I have said in my previous books, ghost hunting is fruitless without a good medium to serve as spokesman for the unhappy ones
in the in-between world.

Genuine mediums are few and far between. By that I don't mean to
imply that the majority of psychics are fraudulent. They are not. But
there are a good number of people who are neither frauds nor really
efficient mediums; they are gifted with a degree of ESP or with psychic
powers, but are not able to channel them properly and constantly into
directions where their abilities can be used for the obtaining of scientific evidence.

Some spiritualists are genuine and some are not, and only a handful of those who are not genuine are dishonest. In most cases known to
me, the medium who fails to give evidence is merely incapable of doing
so and does not realize it. Occasionally, a medium will build up what he
or she obtains through psychic means, to make it sound better than it
is. And a few are genuinely great instruments between the physical and
psychic worlds.

Dealing with hauntings as I do, I naturally place the highest value
on trance mediumship, since it gives me an immediate, clear-cut entry
into the world of the ghost. When the ghost speaks to me through the
entranced medium, I can pose questions and get answers directly and
under my own control.

On the other hand, I have always worked with creditable clairvoy-
ants, people who sense events and things and are able to describe them

often very precisely. My aim is information, regardless of the manner in which it is obtained, but it is information that is unknown to me, the medium, or those present at the time it is given to me that I desire. I want information I can check out. By obeying simple safety rules of evidence, I am able to dismiss any unfriendly allegations of coincidence, mind-picking, previous knowledge and other forms of alternate explanations for what I have come to accept as genuine psychic material.

California teems with metaphysics and its practitioners of various persuasions. I give them all a wide berth, for the realm of religious philosophy is incapable of objective proof by reasonable scientific standards. Then there are the psychic readers and professional mediums, none of whom has attained a world reputation to date, except perhaps Sophia Williams, the great voice medium, and she is no longer working, I am told.

I found a man named Zenor well spoken of in Hollywood, although I could not get to see him. The "church directory" of any spiritualistic magazine is full of advertisements of psychics, some of which may indeed be talented people.

I had occasion, however, to meet a few of the non-professional mediums who had not seen fit to commercialize their gifts—not that doing so is necessarily bad. Everybody has a right to choose the way in which to make a living, and if the charge for a psychic reading is modest, it seems to me a fitting way to work for a livelihood and yet do something of value—provided one is scrupulously honest in one's readings and does not allow interpretations or the desire to please to interfere with the results!

One of those who impressed me particularly by her sincerity was an unassuming middle-aged lady by the name of Maureen Petersen. I first heard of her in 1960 and met her in person three years later, when she drove all the way from her home in Turlock, California, to meet us.

What had made her come forward was a haunted house she once

lived in; like so many others who reach me, she thought her instance might be of interest to me in my quest for ghosts.

Mrs. Petersen's stay at the old house in Healdsburg, about two hours north of San Francisco, took place back in 1920, but her memory was remarkably fresh about it.

When she was fifteen years old, her family moved into this ordinary-looking house on Tucker Street, a house without either attic or basement, with all rooms being on one level. Immediately both her mother and Maureen became aware of strange goings-on in the house. Being psychic had been handed down in the family for the third generation then, and they took it all in their stride.

Night after night, they heard the sounds of running water in the kitchen sink, although the faucets were off; the sound of light switches being turned, of dishes rattling in the cupboard, chairs being pushed around, and finally a sound resembling that of the crash of a heavy object falling. This was accompanied by heavy, masculine footsteps of one or more men, and lasted several hours, always starting and ending at the same time each night!

At first it was only her mother who awoke because of the disturbances and Maureen often slept through them. Her father never heard anything unusual, not being psychic. Whenever she was awakened by the noises, Maureen's mother investigated all rooms, only to find everything dark and nothing amiss.

Soon the young girl also heard it. The first time she thought her father had gotten up for some reason and was causing the disturbances in the kitchen. But he was fast asleep all that time.

Maureen shared a bedroom with her sister and it adjoined the dining room where the activities seemed to center. She decided to brave it out and usually the noises ceased after a while.

One night the heavy footfalls came toward her bedroom door, however, and her heart almost stopped beating. Then they stopped abruptly at the threshold.

At this point Maureen's father decided to make some inquiries about the background of the house. It was then that the family discovered their home had been a meeting place for a group of men who used it, as Mrs. Petersen so delicately puts it, "to drink and carouse in."

They decided to move out and kept their mouths shut. But the next tenant was no luckier. When they returned to the house sometime later, their successors complained about the very same phenomena that had driven them away.

Although her parents have long passed away, Maureen's sister Rose still lives in Santa Rosa and her brother Myron is in San Francisco. Both were witnesses to the unearthly phenomena at the time, and her sister, now Mrs. Rose Hatch, recalled the incidents quite clearly.

But what interested me in the case of Mrs. Petersen was not just another haunted house, of which I know a large number already, but her mediumship. We chatted about her experiences when she met with me in Hollywood.

A native of Colorado, Maureen grew up with the belief in the supernatural all around her, for both her mother and maternal grandmother had been gifted psychics. As a matter of fact, her own daughter also has the gift, apparently passed down through the female line of the family.

While still in her teens, Maureen acquired the ability to foretell the future, and on one such occasion informed her astonished family that she would marry a poor farmer and move back to Colorado with him. The family at this time was living in California. Then she turned to her sister Rose and predicted that she would marry a professional man and live well. Many years later, both predictions came true. Maureen married a poor farmer and moved to Colorado with him, and Rose settled down with a dentist.

After her first husband passed on, Mrs. Peterson married her present husband and returned to California.

The incidents of paranormal nature in her life were numerous during those years. Take, for instance, the time she was walking to a neighbor's house with her little girl, Mardelle.

"Something's happened at home, we must go back," she suddenly screamed, and they retraced their steps at once. At home they found her little boy Melvin had been attacked by a neighbor's dog.

Or the time she needed some dental work done and found herself unusually reluctant to enter the dentist's office. The treatment was painful and she ascribed her foreboding to her fear of pain. But when she returned for additional treatment the next day, she found that the ceiling had collapsed over the dentist's chair.

Soon Maureen developed the gift of automatic writing, that is, letting a psychic force use her arm and send messages through her in this manner. Voices which she feels are spirit friends guide and protect her and often warn her of impending danger. Often she has been able to heed these warnings and prevent the worst.

I asked Mrs. Petersen to tell me of some of the more remarkable incidents of this kind.

"Once, my second husband, Gilbert, and I were hundreds of miles away on a trip when I was told to turn back, as one of my children needed me. We started home and, as soon as we arrived, went to the home of my daughter, Mardelle Adams. She was alone with her children. She was in premature labor and had been unable to locate her physician. Phoning from a neighbor's house, I was able to engage another, and we took her to the hospital an hour before the birth of her child.

"One day I had a dream which was not a dream but a warning.

"I saw my sister, Rose Hatch, in a car in great danger. Very upset, I told my family but didn't write my sister, fearing to frighten her. A card arrived telling me she was on vacation. When I saw her, she said that on this trip her foot had accidentally jammed against the accelerator and the car came within inches of going over a bridge into a deep canyon with the whole family in it. This same day her husband barely saved her from drowning in a whirlpool in a strange river."

But Mrs. Petersen's traffic with the netherworld did not confine itself to such dreary things as warnings of impending doom or dangers. Many of her ESP experiences show the close contact she was apparently able to maintain with the non-physical world for all these years.

Having a gifted medium as an outlet, a person to manifest through, must evidently mean a great deal to discarnates, for they seem to show their gratitude for this service by giving Mrs. Petersen "a hand" in many mundane matters as well as spiritual counsel.

Again I requested that she select some of these experiences and tell me about them in her own words, as she recalled them. There was no hesitancy in her voice as she related her brushes with the uncanny.

"Six years after my first husband passed away, a relative, Joyce M., received a message by automatic writing that he would appear to me within three days. Three days later I awoke and noted, through closed lids, that it was light. Then I saw a book with open pages appear above the foot of my bed. As I tried to make out the printing in it, it disappeared and my husband appeared. He looked young and handsome and very real. He soon disappeared, and right afterward I felt his kiss on my lips as plainly as I ever felt it in life. I was definitely awake.

"After losing my husband, I was grieving and felt a great need to visit my sister, but lacked the money for a bus ticket. One morning I was walking to town, and, before leaving, remarked to my mother that if I found the money on the sidewalk I would visit my sister. I found just a little more than the needed amount on the sidewalk. It hardly seems a coincidence, since I have never found money on a sidewalk before or since.

"I have seen apparitions or thought forms quite often. On a number of occasions, I have seen my husband returning home, when he was nowhere near and didn't return for some time. I used to see my first husband the same way. Once I saw my husband Gilbert on his bicycle. I was in the yard and only a few feet from him. He turned his head and looked at me but said nothing. I went inside and he disappeared, and didn't arrive until some time later. He wasn't near the house when I saw him.

"My mother and I were shopping and went on separate errands, agreeing to meet at the car. Returning, I saw her in the back seat. I glanced away a moment as I stepped to the front of the car. My mother had disappeared. When she did come she said she had been wanting very much to return to the car at the time I saw her there.

"While writing a friend in England, a spirit came to me. He identified himself as John Bennet and gave other identification. He named a son and said he wanted to get in touch with his relatives in England. I had never heard of this man but my English friend had mentioned the son in letters. I wrote her, Mrs. Arnold W., and her letter verified the information in the message, including the name, and confirmed that this man had recently died."

I made a note to take Mrs. Petersen to a haunted house sometime—not the one she knew so well, perhaps, but one about which she knew nothing whatever. That way, her mediumistic powers could be tested to a larger degree.

One of the difficulties with mediums is the reception they get from their families or friends when their peculiarities are discovered. Until we can educate the "non-believers" that being psychic is not so bad as having a dreaded disease, we cannot very well expect people to come forward and talk about these experiences as freely as they should.

Anatomy of a ghost? Many people have questioned me about the apparent inconsistencies between the various forms in which ghosts make themselves known.

Sometimes, the form is merely a light or ball of light moving about. This in my opinion is the concentrated life force within the personality when that personality does not wish to make itself known or be identified as someone who has lived in the body. Sort of a lazy type of ghost!

White mists, whitish outlines of bodies or amorphous white clouds, sometimes almost human in shape, sometimes not, also occur. But most apparitions are of people wearing clothes and appearing very much "alive" in the physical sense. They are two-dimensional generally in that you can walk through them and they will dissolve instantly when challenged.

But occasionally the dead appear as solid bodies, so solid they are mistaken for the living. In my estimation they can accomplish this amazing feat by surrounding their thought forms with a plastic matter drawn from the living in the house and/or built up by concentration of their own energies to the required densities. This plastic substance, sometimes referred to as ectoplasm, and in an earlier period as teleplasm, varies in density from smoke to solid "flesh." It is equally capable of instant dissolution. All the personality inside this "mantle" has to do is interrupt the thought and suggest dissolution. I have come to these seemingly outlandish conclusions of what the dead can do only after many years of careful study and thousands of cases involving apparitions.

There is no real inconsistency between these ghosts—merely a difference in method and intensity of desire to make oneself known to the physical world!

Perhaps a good case in point is the psychic world of a twenty-three-year-old housewife in Ontario, California.

Mrs. Walter W—— her name is long and practically unpronounceable—hesitates to discuss her gifts with the neighbors for fear of being ridiculed or considered odd. With me she knew she would find understanding, so she communicated freely.

At 21, she had left home and had struck out on her own. Her parting from her mother had not been without emotional upsets and she found herself rather under a strain at the time she rented an apartment. Immediately she felt "bad vibrations" at the place. She explained her feelings by her general mood, but in her heart she knew that this would not hold water. Especially not as an explanation for the sound of footsteps and of the front door opening and closing by itself, without any visible visitor around!

Soon she heard footfalls also on her porch at night and felt herself being watched. One night she could not ignore it any longer and looked up. There in the doorway of the bedroom, leading in from the living room, was a fog-like translucent substance hanging in the upper portion of the doorway. Not believing her eyes, Mrs. W. assured herself it was all in her head and tried to sleep. But the feeling of the presence grew stronger. She felt sure "it" was very close to her now. Finally, she opened her eyes again. The substance was hanging directly over her head a few feet from her face! She screamed and buried her head in the pillows.

The next morning she was calmer, but the "mist" reappeared again and again. She left the lights on at night, but the feeling of a presence persisted. The rent was low and she hated giving up such a convenient flat.

Then another apartment directly across from hers became available and she moved into it. No more white mist, no more presence. Whatever it was had stayed in the haunted flat.

In old houses such as this, where people come and go frequently and few questions are asked, tragedies can remain undiscovered for long periods, or even forever. Mrs. W. was sure the ghost merely wanted to confide in her, but she just was not ready to be the channel for his plea.

The Ghost in the Closet

It all started in 1964 when I was lecturing for the American Society for Psychic Research in Los Angeles, and a good many people came forward to tell of their own psychic experiences, especially those involving ghosts and apparitions. In fact, so many people attended this lecture, and so many more got in touch with me afterwards about their own experiences, that the Society got worried about it, and I haven't spoken for them since. Small wonder, for I never mince words and I don't send my audience home wondering if the speaker really believes what he is telling his public. My cases are well documented and I call a spade a spade—er, a ghost a ghost!

One of the people who could not get to hear me speak was a lady named Verna Kunze. She had seen a ghost and I asked her to make a written statement about her experience. A practical and factual woman, Mrs. Kunze did not hesitate to do so.

"I had purchased an apartment building in San Bernardino, California, on G Street, which had formerly been a nun's home on E Street closer in town. Undoubtedly it had been a single dwelling mansion at one time.

"The upper right hand apartment was more suited to my needs and the one I was occupying during the time—September 1957 to October 1960.

"After I had lived there for some months I came in from a shopping trip and, going to the closet in the front bedroom, opened the door to hang up my coat. There I saw very clearly, standing inside the closet in front of the door, a man of medium height (about 5' 8"), round face, fair complexion, dressed in clothing about the style of the early 1900s, pink and white striped shirt, no coat, high stiff turned-over collar, sailor straw hat on his head, nondescript tan trousers and button shoes—I think they were brown with white trim. Garters to hold up his sleeves were on his arms.

"At first I was so startled (not scared) that I couldn't say anything but while I was staring at him, the picture faded from sight.

"I saw him again in the same position, same clothing, in exactly the same manner on three other occasions.

"Being rather psychic but not a medium, I asked the Supreme Deity for protection and thought nothing of it. After about the third appearance, I asked that he depart, asked God's blessing on him and saw him no more. However, on the last impression, it seemed to me that he might have been murdered and stood in the closet to be hidden—or had committed a murder and was hiding in the closet. He was as clear in picture as though he were real. I told a medium friend about it who visited me a short time later but no one else.

"Later I sold the apartment and returned to Santa Ana to live. I do not know who owns the apartment building now as it has changed hands since."

I travel a great deal and it was not until the fall of 1966 that I finally got around to the ghost in San Bernardino. I got in touch with Mrs. Kunze to see if anything had happened, or at any rate if she could arrange for us to visit her old apartment.

Mrs. Kunze went to see the current owners of the house and found them somewhat hesitant about the whole business. They had not received any complaints from anyone about ghosts and would just as well let sleeping ghosts lie. But Mrs. Kunze is a persuasive person, having spent many years working for the immigration service. She promised not to divulge the exact address of the house or the name of the current owners, and finally an appointment was made for us to have a look at the house in October 1966. Fortunately, the tenant of the corner apartment we were interested in had just vacated and the new owner had not yet moved in—so we would find an empty flat.

In return for so much spade work, I promised Mrs. Kunze to address the Psynetics Foundation in nearby Santa Ana, a group in which she was active. The visit to their headquarters was a most pleasurable experience.

After we arrived in Los Angeles, I phoned Mrs. Kunze again to make sure we had access to the apartment, for the drive to San Bernardino takes two hours and it was one of the periodic hot spells the area suffers—so I wanted to be sure we were welcome. All was in readiness, and we arrived at the house on schedule, at four in the afternoon on a hot October day.

The house sat back from the street, a modest yellow stucco building of two stories which belied its age, which was, I later discovered, considerable for this part of the world.

A dark-haired lady received me at the door, while Catherine and Sybil Leek remained in the car, out of earshot. Mrs. Kunze also came out to greet me. I then fetched the others, and without saying anything pertaining to the house, we left the dark-haired lady, who was the landlady, downstairs and walked up to the second floor where we followed Sybil into the "right" apartment. She knew just where to go.

Mrs. Kunze sat down in one of the chairs, Sybil stretched out on the bed and we waited for what might happen now. We did not have to wait long, for Sybil instantly got the scent of things.

"Death and destruction," she said, "comparatively recent. This is an absolutely horrible place."

She shivered, though the temperature outside was above 90 degrees. I, too, felt a chill and it wasn't the power of suggestion, either.

"I think death has hung over this place for some time,"

Sybil elaborated now. "If there was anyone in it I would warn them not to be here."

"Is any entity present?" I asked casually, for I already knew the place was haunted. What I did not know of course was the story behind the haunting or anything more than what Mrs. Kunze had originally written me. And Sybil had no knowledge of that, either.

"I seem to be attracted to the bathroom and that little door there," Sybil commented. "The bathroom has some significance in this. Stomach feels irritated."

"What about any structural changes ?" I interjected.

"I haven't paid attention to that, for the overwhelming influence is of terribly brooding, resentful . . . death. Like having my head in a piece of *black velvet*. Something hanging right over me."

"Does it involve violent death ?"

"Yes. Suffocation. But then again, I have this sickness of the stomach, but that may be associated with someone here. . . ."

"Is it murder, suicide, or accidental death?"

"*Two people* are involved. A murder, because of the resentfulness. Connection with the door. Not clear yet. An usurper, a person who should not be here."

"How far back do we go here?"

"It could be now . . . it seems very close. Recent."

"Describe the person you feel present here."

"A slightly round-faced lady . . . funny, I keep getting another house!"

Sybil interrupted herself. She knew nothing of the fact that this house had been moved to its present site from another place.

"Where is the other house?" I asked.

"The person who is here was involved with *another* house. Tall, thin trees nearby. Two houses . . . the other is a pleasant house . . . light colored car. . . ."

I asked Sybil to look at the woman again, if she could.

"Hair short in neck. . . ." Sybil said, gradually becoming more and more in trance, "I can't find the body, though . . . one part of her is here and one part of her is there . . ."

"Is she present now?"

"I follow her. . . ."

"Is she in this room?"

"Yes . . . and then she goes . . . D . . . Don . . ."

"What is her occupation?"

"The voice . . . voice . . . she runs away . . . somebody mustn't know, she says . . . she is very vain . . ."

"How is she dressed?"

"Black head," Sybil said. It struck me suddenly that Sybil might be describing a nun's habit.

"Why is the black head here?" Sybil now demanded to know.

But Sybil was speaking of a black *face.*

"Light car, black face," she mumbled.

"Why is she here?" I wanted to know.

"Waiting for . . . this isn't her home. Waiting for relief. Somebody came to take her away from here. A woman. Because she did not live here."

"How did she get here then?"

"She needed to stay here to wait for things . . . to come to her."

"Whose place is this?"

"Don't know . . . knew someone here. The little car, light car. D-o-n."

"What happened to her here?"

"She—was—suffocating—sick to stomach—head and neck——"

"Did she commit suicide?"

"No."

"Was she murdered?"

"Don't say that!"

"Was she killed?"

"Yes . . ."

"By whom?"

"D-o-n."

"Why did he kill her?"

"From the house . . . somebody made her come here . . ."

I explained, via Sybil, that she must not stay on here. But it did not go down well with the elusive ghost.

"Wants to be alone here," Sybil reported.

"What is troubling her?"

"Mistaken identity. She was . . . misjudged . . . the *other house.* . . ."

Had someone accused this woman of something she did not do? Was she a nun?

"Verraco," Sybil said, clearly. It did not ring a bell with Mrs. Kunze, who was observing the proceedings closely. Nor, of course, with me.

"I don't know what it means . . . Verraco," Sybil said.

"Does she realize she is dead?"

"No, she thinks she is sick."

"Can she hear you?"

"She understands, but then she goes away again. I have to go after her."

I asked Sybil to instruct the ghost about her true status.

"Man . . . doesn't trust him," Sybil reported. Had the ghost woman been hurt by a man and did she therefore not trust any other man?

Sybil nodded, that was it. But it was of no avail.

"Go away, she says," Sybil continued, "people upset her, nobody understands what she feels like. Very unhappy woman."

There was a moment of interruption, when I changed tapes. Meanwhile, Sybil startled us with an expression that did not seem to fit in.

"Sing to me," she said, in a drowsy tone, "she was singing . . . she likes music . . . she was misjudged . . . two people, two lives . . . *she was two people* . . ."

496

I kept coaxing her to confess.

"Suppose he comes back again. . . ." There was terror in Sybil's voice now.

I promised to protect her. She remained doubtful. How did I know?

"I have the power to send him away," I assured her.

"What is the truth about her?"

"The truth is that she did nothing to hurt the woman; that was a misunderstanding."

"Who is the other woman?"

"E.K."

"Where does she live?"

"Verracho." It had been "Verraco" before.

"And Don?"

"Man with light car and dark face."

"Does he know the woman, E.K.?"

"Yes."

"Did she send him here?"

"She knew."

"Was she behind it?"

"She organized it . . . to destroy."

"What is her name . . . the one who is here?"

With ghosts, if you don't succeed at first, try again.

"A.D.," Sybil said softly.

"What year are we in?" I asked.

"Today . . . September . . . 16 . . . '63 . . . lot of people round the house, strange people . . . just looking around . . . she is here watching . . . body in the bathroom. . . ."

Was the ghost re-living the discovery of her body?

"Tell her the world knows that she is innocent," I intoned.

Sybil, still under the spell of the entity, reacted almost violently.

"She *is* innocent!"

I kept reassuring her. Finally, Sybil said: "She will sing . . . A.D. . . . Must not return here ever . . . She is gone now. . . ."

Deeply breathing now, Sybil was completely "out" for a few moments, prior to taking over her own body once again.

I then brought Sybil quickly to herself, but for some time after, she kept feeling quite uncomfortable and sighed with relief when we left the place.

Mrs. Kunze, who had witnessed all this, had nodded several times during the hour. I now wanted to find out if there was anything she could add to the brief testimony she had given me originally.

"Did this apparition you told me about ever look at you?" I inquired. The man with "the German face" in the straw hat must have been quite a sight greeting her from the open closet door—very dead.

"No, he did not," Mrs. Kunze replied. "I immediately got the impression that he was dead. His eyes did not move. A minute later he was gone and I hung up my coat."

A month later, when he reappeared to her, he did not stay as long, she explained, but the view was the same.

The third time she started to pray for him, and instead of fading away as on the previous occasions, he disappeared like a flash.

"Weren't you curious about the apartment? I mean, didn't you make some inquiries about its previous occupants?"

"I did not. I knew when I bought the place that it had been the home of nuns, and moved here after some years from another location—where now the Junior High School stands. The building is at least sixty years old. There may have been two or three other owners before I purchased it. It was remodeled around 1953 or '54. Until then it belonged to the nuns."

Again I questioned her about the appearance of the ghost. She stuck to her story. The man was more 1903 than 1953.

"At that time there were certainly nuns here," she commented.

Had she had other uncanny experiences in this haunted apartment?

"Only this," Mrs. Kunze replied. "In my inspirational work, I found I could not work here. My guides told me this was an evil house. But I haven't heard anything."

"How long have you yourself been psychic?"

"When I was about thirteen, I was invited to a Sunday school party, and I was a stranger in the neighborhood, not knowing anyone there. That was in Columbus, Ohio. About a week before the party I told my mother that I had dreamt of and had seen this party, the girls there and even the pictures on the wall—in great detail. A week later I went and recognized it all."

"Have you had any other premonitions?"

"A number of them. I do automatic writing, and a lot of predictions have thus been dictated to me by what I call my masters, my spiritual guides."

I decided we should leave metaphysics alone, and turn to the business at hand.

"About the material obtained just now through Sybil Leek," I said, "does any of it ring a bell with you?"

"Well, she certainly got the business with the two houses," Mrs. Kunze commented. "This house was in two locations, as you know."

"What about the trees surrounding the house?" In this part of California, trees are not common and would naturally be a landmark.

"Probably so," Mrs. Kunze said, "and she mentioned a face covered with black velvet—could that not be a nun covered with a coif?"

"Could be," I agreed. "It seems strange, though, that you haven't felt a female influence here, or have you?"

"Not at all," Mrs. Kunze confirmed, "but I felt from the looks of the *man* that he had either committed a murder or done something very wrong. I just felt it as I saw him there in the closet. I suppose he had jumped in there to avoid detection."

Evidently Mrs. Kunze had seen the ghost of the murderer while Sybil found the ghost of the victim. Now if Mrs. Kunze's prayer had indeed freed the ghost from the spot where his crime had been committed, then it was only natural that Sybil did not feel him any longer there.

At the same time, if Mrs. Kunze felt the overpowering tragedy of the murderer tied to the spot of the crime, it would have blotted out the comparatively weaker presence of the victim, who after all, was not guilty of *anything!*

I discovered that the building in its original site faced a Catholic school and that San Bernardino has a high percentage of Catholics among its inhabitants. Thus a convent would not have been out of place here.

On November 5, 1960, Mrs. Kunze moved out of the haunted apartment to a new house in nearby Santa Ana. The ghost, of course, did not move along with her, for the new apartment was free from any and all psychic influences, pleasant, in fact, in every sense of the word.

While she lived at the San Bernardino address, the evil atmosphere of the place seemed to have taken its toll of her day-to-day life. Everything she seemed to touch went wrong; her personal life was a shambles—apparently for no logical reason. The moment she moved away from the apartment, all went well. Suggestion? Not really. The facts were quite solid.

As for the empty apartment in San Bernardino, it is all ready for the new tenant to move in.

"I wouldn't take this place for nothing," Sybil mumbled, as she rushed past me down the stairs and into the street.

Considering the fact that Sybil had been apartment-shopping with a vengeance at the time, the victim of the ghost in the closet must have made quite an impression on her.

At any rate, the restless nun doesn't live there any more.

The Ghost Who Refused to Leave

One of the most spectacular cases I reported in *Ghosts I've Met* concerned the hauntings at a house on Ardmore Boulevard, Los Angeles.

The house itself, barely thirty years old, was being plagued by the noises of a wild party going on at night, during which apparently someone was killed, by footsteps where nobody was seen walking and by other uncanny noises, including voices resounding in the dark, telling the current owners to get out of *their* house!

I had been to this house several times and brought Maxine Bell, a local psychic, on one occasion. That visit proved memorable not only because of material obtained by Miss Bell, in semi-trance, which proved accurate to a large degree, but because of my own photographic work.

Left alone in the most haunted part of the house, I took at random a number of black and white pictures of a particular bedroom which of course was empty, at least to my eyes.

On one of the pictures, taken under existing daylight conditions and from a firm surface, the figure of a young girl dressed in a kind of negligée appears standing near the window. As my camera is double exposure proof and both film and developing beyond reproach, there is no other rational explanation for this picture. Since that time, I have succeeded in taking other psychic photographs, but the "girl at the window" will always rank as one of my most astounding ones.

The whistling noises, the popping of a champagne bottle in the dark of night followed by laughter, the doors opening by themselves, and all the other psychic phenomena that had been endured by the owner of the house, Helen L., for a long time would not yield to my usual approach: trance session and order to the ghost to go away. There were complications in that Miss L. herself had mediumistic talents, although unsought and undeveloped, and there was present in the household a retarded sister, often the source of energies with which poltergeist phenomena are made possible.

Nevertheless, when we left the house on Ardmore Boulevard I had high hopes for a more peaceful atmosphere in the future. For one thing, I explained matters to Miss L., and for another, I suggested that the garden be searched for the body of that murder victim. We had already established that a fight had actually occurred some years ago in the house, observed by neighbors. It was entirely possible that the body of one of the victims was still on the grounds.

In July of 1964 the noises resumed, and thuds of falling bodies, footfalls and other noises started up again in the unfortunate house. Quite rightly Helen L. asked me to continue the case. But it was not until the spring of 1965 that I could devote my energies toward this matter again.

All I had accomplished in the interim was a certain lessening of the phenomena, but not their elimination.

On March 14, 1965, Helen L. communicated with me in a matter of great urgency. For the first time, the ghost had been seen! At 3 A.M. on March 13, her mother had been awakened by strange noises, and looking up from the bed, she saw the figure of a man beside the bed. The noise sounded to her as if someone were tearing up bedsheets. Frightened, the old lady pulled the covers over her head and went back to sleep. Helen L. also heard heavy footsteps all over the house that same night. Needless to say, they had no visitors from the flesh-and-blood world.

"Are you going to be here in April? Help!!" Helen L. wrote. I answered I would indeed come and bring Sybil Leek with me to have another and, hopefully, final go at this ghost. But it would have to be in June, not April. During the first week of May, Helen awoke on Sunday morning to hear a man's voice shushing her inches away from her pillow. She could hardly wait for our arrival after that. Finally, on June 28, I arrived at the little house with Sybil to see what she might pick up.

"I know there is a presence here," Sybil said immediately as we seated ourselves in the little office that is situated in back of the bedroom where most of the disturbances had occurred. I turned the light out to give Sybil a better chance to concentrate, or rather, to relax, and immediately she felt the intruder.

"It is mostly in the bedroom," she continued. "There are two people; the man dominates in the bedroom area, and there is also a woman, a young girl."

I decided Sybil should attempt trance at this point, and invited the ghost to make himself known. After a few moments, Sybil slipped into a state bordering on trance, but continued to be fully conscious.

"Morton," she mumbled now, "there is something terribly intense . . . have a desire to *break* something . . . Morton is the last name."

I repeated my invitation for him to come forward and tell his story.

"The girl goes away," Sybil intoned, "and he says he comes back to find her. And she isn't here. He was going to celebrate. He must find her. Wedding party, celebration . . . for the girl. She wasn't happy here; she had to go away. This man is a foreigner."

"You're right." The booming voice of Helen L. spoke up in the dark across the room. Evidently Sybil had described someone she recognized.

"Jane Morton," Sybil said now, flatly, "something to do with building, perhaps he had something to do with building this house . . . he's an older man. Jane . . . is young . . . I'm trying to find out where Jane is . . . that's what *he* wants to know . . . I will tell him it didn't matter about the party . . . she would have gone anyway . . . she hated the old man . . . this man fell . . . head's bad . . . fell against the stable . . ."

"Did he die here?" I pressed.

"1837," Sybil said, somewhat incongruously, "1837. Came back . . . went out again, came back with people, was drunk, hurt his head, left hand side. . . ."

Despite my urging, the entity refused to speak through Sybil in trance. I continued to question her nevertheless.

The ghost's name was Howell Morton, Sybil reported, although I was not sure of the spelling of the first name, which might have been Hawall rather than Howell.

"He came here to do some building, someone was accidentally killed and buried in the garden . . ."

"Who buried this person?"

"Boyd Johnson . . . Raymond McClure . . . Dell . . . Persilla . . ." The voice was faltering now and the names not too clear.

"Is the girl dead too?"

"Girl's alive. . . ."

"Is there anyone dead in this house outside of Morton?"

"Morton died here."

"Who was the figure I photographed here?"

"Jane . . . he wants to draw her back here . . . but I think she's alive . . . yet there are things of hers buried . . ."

Sybil seemed confused at this point.

"Meri . . . Meredith. . . ." she said, or she could have said. "Married her." It just was not clear enough to be sure. Morton and some of his friends were doing the disturbing in the house, Sybil explained. He died at the party.

"There was violence outside," Sybil added and Helen L. nodded emphatically. There was indeed.

"Drunk . . . four o'clock . . . he died accidentally . . ." Where is he buried in the garden, Helen L. wanted to know, anxiously.

"Straight down by the next building," Sybil replied. "It wasn't built completely when he died."

Later we all went into the garden and identified the building as the garage in back of the house.

But Helen was not yet ready to start digging. What would the neighbors think if we found a body? Or, for that matter, what would they think if we didn't? There we left it, for her to think over whether to dig or not to dig—that was the question.

I returned to New York in the hope that I would not hear anything further from Helen L. But I was mistaken. On July 5 I heard again from the lady on Ardmore Boulevard.

Her other sister, Alma, who lives in Hollywood but has stayed at the house on Ardmore on occasion, called the morning after our visit. It was then that she volunteered information she had been holding back from Helen L. for two years for fear of further upsetting her, in view of events at the house. But she had had a dream-like impression at the house in which she "saw" a man in his middle years, who had lived in a lean-to shack attached to the garage.

She knew this man was dead and got the impression that he was a most stubborn person, difficult to dislodge or reason with. What made this dream impression of interest to us, Miss L. thought, was the fact that her sister could not have known of Sybil Leek's insistence that a man lay buried at that very spot next to the garage! No shack ever stood there to the best of Helen L.'s knowledge, but of course it may have stood there before the present house was built.

Also, Helen reminded me that on those occasions when her mother and sister slept in the garage, when they had company in the main house, both had heard heavy footsteps coming up to the garage and stopping dead upon reaching the wall. Helen L.'s mother had for years insisted that there was "a body buried there in the garden" but nobody had ever tried to find it.

Nothing more happened until May 8, 1966, when Sybil Leek and I again went to the house because Helen L. had implored us to finish the case for her. The disturbances had been continuing on and off.

With us this time was Eugene Lundholm, librarian and psychic researcher. Trance came quickly. Perhaps Sybil was in a more relaxed state than during our last visit, but whatever the reason, things seemed to be more congenial this time around.

"I'm falling," her voice whispered, barely audible, "I'm hungry . . ."

Was someone reliving moments of anguish?

"Who are you?" I demanded.

"Can't breathe. . . ."

"What is your name?"

"Ha . . . Harold . . ."

He had great difficulties with his breathing and I suggested he relax.

"Kill her . . ." he now panted, "kill her, kill the woman . . ."

"Did you kill her?"

"NO!"

"I've come to help you. I'm your friend."

"Kill her before she goes away. . . ."

"Why?"

"No good here . . . where's he taken her? Where is she?" The voice became more intelligible now.

"What is her name?"

"Where is she . . . I'll kill her."

"Who's with her?"

"Porter."

"Is he a friend of yours?"

"NO!"

"Who are you?"

"Harold Howard."

"Is this your house?"

"My house."

"Did you build it?"

"No."

"Did you buy it?"

Evidently my questioning got on his nerves, for he shouted, "Who are *you?*" I explained, but it didn't help.

"Too many people here . . . I throw them out . . . take those people out of here!"

Strangely enough, the voice did not sound like Sybil's at all; it had lost all trace of a British flavor and was full of anger. Evidently the ghost was speaking of the revelers he had found at his house and wanted them out.

"His friends . . . take them away . . . she brought them . . .

"While you were away?" He was somewhat calmer now.

"Yes," he confirmed.

"Where were you?"

"Working."

"What do you do?"

"Miner."

"Where do you work?"

"Purdy Town." He may have said Purgory Town, or something like it.

"What happened when you came home?"

Again he became upset about the people in his house and I asked that he name some of them.

"Margaret . . ." he said, more excited now. "Mine . . . twenty-five . . . I came home . . . they were here . . . too many people . . . party here. . . ."

"Did you hurt anyone?"

"I'm going to kill her," he insisted. Evidently he had not done so.

"Why?"

"Because of him." Jealousy, the great ghost-maker.

"Who is he?"

"Porter."

"Who is he?"

"He took my place. Eric Porter."

"What year is this?"

It was high time we got a "fix" on the period we were in.

"Forty-eight."

"What happened to you . . . afterwards?"

"People went away . . . Porter . . . outside . . . I want to go away now . . ."

It became clear to me that the girl must have been killed but that a shock condition at the time of the crime had prevented this man from realizing what he had done, thus forcing him to continue his quest for the girl. I told him as much and found him amazed at the idea of his deed.

"Why did he follow me . . . he followed me . . . then I hit him in the guts . . ."

"What did you do with him then?"

"Put him away."

He became cagey after that, evidently thinking I was some sort of policeman interrogating him.

"I watch him," he finally said. "I look after him . . . in the garden. I won't let him in the house."

I asked him further about himself, but he seemed confused.

"Where am I?"

He asked me to leave the other man in the garden, in the ground. He would never go away because he had to watch this other man.

"Margaret comes back," he said now. Was there a foursome or were we dealing with more than one level of consciousness?

"Keep him away from her," the ghost admonished me.

"I will," I promised and meant it.

I then told him about his death and that of the others, hoping I could finally rid the house of them all.

"She'll come back," his one-track mind made him say. "I'll wait till she is in bed and then I'll kill her."

I explained again that killing the other man wouldn't do any good since he was already dead.

"My head's bad," the ghost complained.

"You cannot stay at this house," I insisted firmly now.

"Not leaving," he shot back just as firmly. "My house!"

I continued my efforts, explaining also about the passage of time.

"Forty-eight . . ." he insisted, "I fight . . . I fight . . ."

"You've been forgiven," I said and began the words that amount to a kind of exorcism. "You are no longer guilty. You may go."

"Carry him," he mumbled and his voice weakened somewhat. "Where is she? Who'll clean up?"

Then he slipped away.

I awakened Sybil. She felt fine and recalled nothing. But I recalled plenty.

For one thing, it occurred to me that the ghost had spoken of the year 'forty-eight, but not indicated whether it was 1948 or 1848, and there was something in the general tone of the voice that made me wonder if perhaps we were not in the wrong century. Certainly no miner worked in Los Angeles in 1948, but plenty did in 1848. Eugene Lundholm checked the records for me.

In the 'forties mines sprang up all over the territory. In 1842 Francisco Lopez had discovered gold near the San Fernando Mission, and in 1848 a much larger gold deposit was found near Sacramento.

In 1848 also was the famous gold strike at Sutter's Mill. But already in the early 1840's mining existed in Southern California, although not much came of it.

After we went back to New York, Helen L. reached me again the last week of July 1966.

Her mother refused to leave the house, regardless of the disturbances. Thus a sale at this time was out of the question, Miss L. explained.

Something or someone was throwing rocks against the outside of the house and on the roof of their patio—but no living person was seen doing it. This, of course, is par for the poltergeist course. Just another attention-getter. Loud crashes on the patio roof and nobody there to cause them. Even the neighbors now heard the noises. Things were getting worse. I wrote back, offering to have another look at the haunted house provided she was willing to dig. No sense leaving the corpus delicti there.

But on September 18 Miss L. had some more to tell me. Rocks falling on the driveway behind the house brought out the neighbors in force, with flashlights, looking for the "culprits." Who could not be found. Nor could the rocks, for that matter. They were invisible rocks, it would seem.

This took place on numerous occasions between 6:15 and 7:30 P.M. and only at that time. To top it off, a half ripe lemon flew off their lemon tree at Miss L. with such force that it cracked wide open when it landed on the grass beside her. It could not have fallen by itself and there was no one in the tree to throw it.

I promised to get rid of the lemon-throwing ghost if I could, when we came to Los Angeles again in October. But when I did, Miss L.'s mother was ill and the visit had to be called off.

I have not heard anything further about this stubborn ghost. But the area was populated in 1848 and it could be that another house or camp stood on this site before the present house was erected. There is a brook not far away. So far, neither Mr. Morton nor Mr. Howard has been located and Jane and Margaret are only ghostly facts. A lot of people passed through the house when Miss L.'s family did not own it, and of course we know nothing whatever about the house that preceded it.

One more note came to me which helped dispel any notion that Helen L. was the only one bothered by the unseen in the house on Ardmore.

It was signed by Margaret H. Jones and addressed *To Whom It May Concern*. It *concerned* the ghost.

"Some years ago, when I was a guest in Miss L.'s home at———— Ardmore Boulevard, in Los Angeles, I heard what seemed to be very heavy footsteps in a room which I *knew* to be empty. Miss L. was with me at the time and I told her that I heard this sound. The footsteps seemed to advance and to recede, and this kept up for several minutes, and though we investigated we saw no one. They ceased with the same abruptness with which they began."

I fondly hoped the manifestations would behave in a similar manner. Go away quietly.

But on October 6,1967, Helen L. telephoned me in New York. She had spent a sleepless night—part of a night, that is.

Up to 4 A.M. she had been sleeping peacefully. At that hour she was awakened by her cat. Putting the animal down, she noticed a strange light on her patio, which is located outside her bedroom windows. She hurriedly threw on a robe and went outside.

In the flower bed on her left, toward the rear of the garden, she noticed something white. Despite her dislike for the phenomena which had for so long disturbed her home, Helen L. advanced toward the flower bed.

Now she could clearly make out the figure of a woman, all in white. The figure was not very tall and could have been that of a young girl. It seemed to watch her intently, and looked somewhat like the conventional white bedsheet type of fictional ghost.

At this point Miss L.'s courage left her and she ran back to her room.

The next morning, her eyes red with exhaustion, she discussed her experience with her aged mother. Until now she had been reluctant to draw her mother into these matters, but the impression had been so overpowering that she just had to tell *someone.*

To her surprise, her mother was not very upset. Instead, she added her own account of the "White Lady" to the record. The night before, the same figure had apparently appeared to the mother in a dream, telling her to pack, for she would soon be taking her away!

When Helen L. had concluded her report, I calmed her as best I could and reminded her that *some* dreams are merely expressions of unconscious fears. I promised to pay the house still another visit, although I am frankly weary of the prospect: I know full well that you can't persuade a ghost to go away when there may be a body, once the property of said ghost, buried in a flower bed in the garden.

After all, a ghost's got rights, too!

The Ghostly Lady of Newbury Park

In some of my books I have reported on lady ghosts that roam the realms of the ethereal here and there in the world, but this chapter deals with a phenomenon of a different density: the *ghost lady* is very much flesh and blood, and her nickname, bestowed upon her for very good reasons as we shall see presently, merely indicates that she is prone to hauntings.

Some people are psychic and see ghosts and all's well; some even see them in more than one place; but my friend in Newbury Park sees them practically everywhere.

I should hasten to add that her ghost experiences are genuine, not the kind produced by an overactive imagination. How do I know this? Because I have met the ghost lady and visited the places where she has partaken of the uncanny, with no less a perceiver in matters psychic than Sybil Leek, trance medium extraordinary who never misses a ghost if there is one about, or minces words if there isn't!

It all started around the beginning of January 1966, when I received a letter from Mrs. Gwen Hinzie of Newbury Park, California. She wished to contribute some material to my research efforts.

"In 1946 I was 26 years old," she wrote. "I spent about four months in New York City working as a secretary. I lived in Brooklyn Heights—at different times in two different rooming houses—and there (in both) was conscious of ghosts.

"One of these old brownstone houses was in the next block south of the St. George Hotel in Brooklyn Heights and the other about a half block distant. It has been so long ago I cannot remember the street names now.

"In the first house mentioned I lived on the ground floor. It was an old firetrap really and even had rats. It was a four-story building in poor repair.

"I lived in a room off the furnace room that had a door leading out to the side of the building. My only heat was from the furnace room itself and there was a small opening in the wall (covered with coarse wire screening) through which the heat was supposed to pass. I lived there for about one month (November 1946).

"My experiences took place over about a two-week period. The first thing that happened was hearing a woman crying in the night. Then another woman spoke to her sharply and she stopped crying. This seemed to be on the other side of the wall in the room or apartment occupied by the only other tenant on that floor. When I asked her later about this, she denied that anyone ever stayed with her!

"Later, one evening I came into the furnace room to go to my room and passed through what seemed to be a pall of black smoke. There was no smoke odor but the furnace was burning. When I told my landlady about it she said she was sure there was nothing wrong with the furnace.

"Another evening, through the wall opening I previously mentioned, there appeared a *thick white mist*—but it looked more like smoke than mist. I got out of my chair and went to the bed to pick up something to flap away this 'smoke' (it was only halfway through the opening) and when I turned back again it was gone.

"At another later time during the day I found *this thick white mist materializing before my eyes.* Then it disappeared. There was also a black mist that had materialized while my back was turned another time—but this was one that frightened me. The other had not. I spoke to 'it' and said to go away but it was several seconds before it did.

"After I had been there about a week I found it necessary to buy a small electric heater since it was becoming cold in there, and I found I had to sit before my little stove with my coat on. It did not even warm my feet. The heat seemed to radiate only about two and a half to three inches from the stove. I became ill while living in that room with a respiratory infection and was so cold that I found by the time I had been there about three weeks that I could not warm up until I had been in our (too) warm office about two hours!

"By that time I believed there were ghosts there and upon inquiring of the landlady found that she had nothing to say. She merely suggested I find another place to live.

"About the first of December I moved into another brownstone. (I should explain here that when I had first arrived in Brooklyn Heights I was visiting friends and stayed in *their* apartment. I had not been there a week before I *occasionally saw strangely dressed people on the street.* I thought this was my imagination as I seemed to get carried away thinking of what the old place must have been like in its heyday. I thought at first there might have been a theatre nearby and that these were actors but later found out this was not the case.)

"I soon was busy going back and forth to work and did not see strange people on the street. One of these people that I did remember was a woman—in her twenties or possibly a little older—who was tall, thin and looked about six months pregnant. She wore a dress that was long and had long sleeves or three-quarter-length sleeves and a bustle. The bodice was very snug and the waist very tight but the bulge below the waist suggested pregnancy. She walked rapidly down the street (across the street) away from me.

"Imagine my shock when I entered my new boarding house and saw *the same woman,* dressed the same, standing in the doorway leading from the foyer to the hallway in the rear of the building! She was standing facing the wall, so was sideways to my view, and when I unlocked the door she distinctly jumped and looked with fear on her face toward

515

the door. *Then she calmly walked into the wall.* I never saw her again there or anywhere else.

"We (my husband and children and I) now live in a small town in Ventura County and are renting a house on farm land. We have a barn—not in sight of the house—and there is some peculiar phenomenon here. There is a road from the house—to the left—that curves around a small hill, at the bottom of which is the barn. You cannot see it until you turn the bend in the road but this barn has a very peculiar atmosphere. It was built no more, I'm pretty sure, than 30 years ago. We have there some rabbits and there is a horse stall though the old horse rarely uses it. Our dog is not afraid to go in there nor are the cats. Yet just before you reach the bend in the road you become aware of this peculiar atmosphere. It is a quiet and solitary feeling in this area and in the barn. The atmosphere is almost the same as you feel in a cemetery but not as peaceful. It is not especially depressing or terrifying—but it is, to me, an uncomfortable place to be. I call it a feeling of discomfiture as *I feel like an intruder.* My husband does not feel it and says I fill my head with all kinds of spooky ideas. I wonder, though, if this might be due to a grave being nearby—*I don't know* that there is one so this may not be it; or could it be the old buggies in the barn, or is it really my imagination? So peculiar—what do you think?"

Well, I thought enough of Mrs. Hinzie's letter to communicate with her further. In the first place, her longhand showed no sign of imbalance, something I can often tell from a person's handwriting or signature. To the contrary, Mrs. Hinzie sounded to me like a pretty level-headed person and her description of the uncanny had clarity and depth. I decided I was going to like the lady and wrote back for more details. For one thing, I detected a peculiar discrepancy between her avowed position of a simple housewife in a small farming community, and the way she expressed herself, so I asked for her background and Mrs. Hinzie was glad to oblige.

"I was born in Los Angeles in 1920 and am of Irish-English descent. I was raised in that city and Beverly Hills, where I attended both public and Catholic schools. I attended the University of Los Angeles and was graduated in 1943 with a Bachelor of Arts degree. I have three sisters and our life was fairly ordinary, I think. We were never poor but not rich. After I was graduated from the University I worked for several years and married in 1952 and now have three children—one of whom is also sensitive.

"I have had clairvoyant experiences many times in my life and until recently did not mention them, as paranormal experiences were considered too 'far out' for ordinary people. Now, of course, there is much interest in the subject.

"When I was 12, in 1932, we rented a house at 3rd Avenue and 12th Street in Los Angeles—the only house on the north side of that short block. When I first went into the house I walked with my mother from the front hall to the breakfast room and looked in while talking to her. I saw (her back was to the door) what I thought was a colored woman bending over a box in that room and, believing mother had hired her to help with the unpacking, greeted her. Then this dark form spread itself over the cardboard box like a coat. As I stared it pulled itself up and became a tall dark form—it appeared hooded but had no face. I called my mother's attention to it and she screamed. It backed out of the room into the kitchen, so tall it bumped its head against the top of the door and went around the corner. We did move in, but never, to my knowledge, did anyone see it again. I cannot explain it at all but it was very loathsome and frightening.

"Across from the breakfast room was a small closet with a door leading to the basement. I and others also did, from time to time, hear footsteps coming up those stairs, but no one had the courage to investigate, as far as I know.

We lived there about five months and then moved away.

"My husband, Don Hinzie, has suggested that I tell you the following, but I believe it is a fairly common experience.

"When I was 21 years old my father passed away from a heart attack. I was in the room at the time of his death. He had been in great pain and was lying on the bed. Emergency hospital attendants were there giving oxygen but he lay with his hands clenched. When he stopped breathing, his hand relaxed, and within seconds a white vapor ascended from his opening hand and disappeared. This I have been given to understand as being the release of the soul from the body and have heard of it before.

"When I was about 18, our dog Rowdy, then 13 years old, died. He simply disappeared from our home and I did not at first believe he was dead although a body looking like his had been found, and I continued for a few days to put his food out by the back door for him. Then one *evening I saw him come up* toward the food. He would not let me touch him and would not touch the food. He then walked away toward the side of the house. In a few minutes I followed him but he had disappeared. Later on a few occasions I saw him on the front lawn, where he had been accustomed to sit, and once heard him barking out there. I told my parents about it but I don't believe they ever saw him.

"This clairvoyance can be less than a blessing. When I was about eight or nine there was a child in our neighborhood who had died of an illness, and one day about a month after his death (I knew him but he was not a friend of mine) I was with some children near his home when I saw him standing on the driveway and I said so. I was called a liar and lost at least one friend as a result of it. After that, I stopped mentioning things I saw. At the time I did not know I saw a ghost. I thought they were not telling me the truth about the boy being dead!

"I also saw another ghost in San Francisco in 1947. Until about 1961 or 1962 I did not know whom I had seen. It was *not until then* that I read about her. Her name I do not have but can find out. Her story is in a book called, I think, *American Ghosts*. It was while my roommate and I, vacationing in San Francisco, were riding on a cable car up to Nob Hill. We both saw her.

"The cable car had stopped at a cross street. There were other people on the street and she caught my attention because of her filmy white dress. It seemed inappropriate on the street. She was a young girl, not pretty, but smiling and apparently nodding to people on the street. She seemed substantial enough until she started to pass a couple of girls on the sidewalk, when her full skirt and part of her body *passed part way through one of the girls*. Just before she passed these girls the side of her gown suddenly appeared spangled with water drops or brilliants, but it seemed as if water had suddenly been sprayed on her gown. Knowing then that she was a ghost, and having caught her eye, I tried to tell her in my mind to go to heaven, but she looked frightened and disappeared. My roommate and others saw her and she has been seen many times walking along the street on Nob Hill.

"In my first letter to you I mentioned the peculiar atmosphere near our barn. There was something I forgot to mention and it did not come to my mind until about five days ago when *I heard the voice again*.

"After we had been here about six weeks or so one day I heard a child's voice say 'Hi!' very cheerfully. It seemed to come from across the yard. I did not see anyone and it was during school hours and I didn't understand it but felt, my vision being so poor at the time due to temporary eye trouble, that I had simply not seen the child. Also, one day at the clothesline, I thought I saw, directly in front of me but on the hill about 40 feet away and partly obscured by a tree, a human being, male, not very old. As I watched through my misty eyes, I saw him walk away, I thought, over the brow of the hill. Now that I can see better I know the hill doesn't slope away abruptly there. You would have to walk at least another 50 feet.

"The children and I have heard the cheery little 'Hi' a few other times but after the summer was over we did not hear it again until a few days ago when our only dog and I were home. I had just walked away from the door about six steps when I heard a cheery little 'Hi.' I turned quickly but saw no one (it sounded about six or eight feet away from me). The dog heard it too and got up—not frightened or suspicious (he is half German shepherd and quite alert), but only curious. He went around to the side of the house, apparently saw nothing and ran across the drive to the side of the hill and looked down. Not seeing anything he came back to the front of the house and lay down, unperturbed. Today, when my little daughter, aged 8, came home from school she told me her little friend that she walks home with thought he saw a boy running across the lawn when there was no one here. I have been saying rosaries for the repose of the soul of this person if that's what it is and also for a nullifying of the uncomfortable atmosphere on the road leading to the barn and the barn itself and believe this is helping. At least, the last time I was at the barn, a few days ago, it had a pleasant, peaceful country air.

"So much for my experiences."

No wonder Mrs. Hinzie sounded well educated—she was! I had not bargained for the San Francisco story and welcomed it of course, especially as I seemed to recall it in an indefinite way from James Reynolds' *Ghosts in American Houses*.

I decided to go after the story immediately, as it seemed so unusual by ghostly standards: after all, a ghost in the middle of the street seen by several people is out of the ordinary. I requested the testimony of the friend who Mrs. Hinzie claimed was with her at the time she had the experience in San Francisco. The friend, now Mrs. William Mace but at the time named Peggy O'Conner, was Gwen Hinzie's roommate for about a year and a half. Since Miss O'Conner's marriage in 1948 they had not kept up the contact, however, except for an occasional Christmas card.

"She saw the ghost and was very upset about it," Mrs. Hinzie explained. "Other people on the cable car I was in also saw the ghost, as I heard a couple of women comment on it."

Imagine riding up a hill in a cable car, looking out the window and seeing a ghost!

I suggested Mrs. Hinzie meet me in San Francisco so we could locate the exact spot where the incident took place. She readily agreed, and offered to come with her close friend Sharon Bettin, with whom she shared many interests; also, Mrs. Bettin's parents had a house at Santa Cruz, and the two ladies could stay there.

It sounded fine to me, but Mrs. Hinzie warned that there might be a hindrance. If her husband, who is the custodian at the local school, should not be able to arrange to take care of the children, she would not be able to go. As it turned out, the powers-that-be made her trip possible exactly as planned.

At the time of the incident, Mrs. Hinzie recalled, she was staying at the Fairmount Hotel, atop the hill, and the ride was no more than three or four blocks up the hill. She was reasonably sure she could find the spot again. I, of course, was going to bring Sybil Leek with me, not telling her the reasons.

The story, as reported by James Reynolds in *Ghosts in American Houses,* is quite a shocker, considering the period it occurred in. It was of course unknown to Mrs. Hinzie at the time she saw the ghost.

The disappearance of Flora Sommerton a few hours before her debut was a great mystery for many years. Flora was the only child of Charles Benfow Sommerton, originally from Kansas City, Kansas, who had built a mansion on Nob Hill, San Francisco. Sommerton was rich, his wife was ambitious, and the debut of their daughter on her eighteenth birthday in 1876 was to be an affair of splendor. Moreover, Flora's parents had wedding plans for Flora. They insisted that she should marry in due course a young dissolute snob named Hugh

521

Partridge whom she despised.

On the afternoon of the day of the debut, Mrs. Sommerton urged Flora to take a long nap in order to be fresh for the party at ten that evening. Instead Flora insisted on going out, and she disappeared. She was last seen by a grocer's delivery boy to whom she gave a written message for her mother. The boy delivered the note to the Sommerton residence, which was in a great flurry of preparations for the party; in the excitement the maid who received it promptly mislaid it.

Came early evening and no debutante. Also missing was the beautiful white gown covered with crystal beads that had been ordered from Paris for the debut. A family conference was called. A maid finally found the misplaced note. The family decided to carry off the party anyway. The domineering Mrs. Sommerton would not permit her husband to notify the police. Guests were told that Flora had had a sudden illness and had been sent to the country. In spite of all this, the ball was a great success.

In the morning Mr. Sommerton called in the police and put up a huge reward—$250,000—for the return of his daughter. That money was to lie unclaimed in a San Francisco bank for many years, even after the death of Charles Benfow Sommerton, which occurred shortly after the fire in 1906 which destroyed the Sommerton mansion.

Throughout the decades many tips and clues were offered, but Flora was elusive. Mrs. Sommerton finally called off the search although there was a little evidence that Flora was still alive. Mrs. Carrie Sommerton died in 1916.

The evidence was an undated letter written to the police by an Adele LaBlanche in Los Angeles. Miss LaBlanche was the prima donna of a touring company that was presenting *The Prince of Pilsen* in Los Angeles. But her letter referred to an incident in Chicago. Miss LaBlanche had sprained her ankle and had been obliged to call upon her understudy, Miss Jarvis. Her costume, however, did not fit the smaller Miss Jarvis. Whereupon the wardrobe mistress, described by Miss LaBlanche as "a quiet, faded, middle-aged woman," fished out a dress she said might do in this emergency. It was out of fashion but beautiful, a creation of white tulle "sprinkled like the heavens on a starry night with crystal beads." Miss Jarvis wore it and then tried to buy it. Said the wardrobe mistress: "No, I cannot sell it. It is my only link with the past. It is Nob Hill and what I might have been." Then, Miss LaBlanche wrote, "a startled look came into her eyes, and she took her dress and fled, again leaving no trace."

The mystery was finally solved in 1926. Flora Sommerton was at last located, dead, in Butte, Montana. Here she had been known as Mrs. Butler, housekeeper for ten years in the Butte Central Hotel. Coroner's verdict: death from heart disease. But the police were skeptical about her name, Butler.

In her valise was found a nest of clippings dating back from 1876 to 1891 that referred to the search for Flora Sommerton, daughter of a multi-millionaire nabob. The clippings came from all over the United States. When Mrs. Butler died, she was dressed in a white ball gown conjectured to be of the 1880s which was entirely covered with crystal beads. Her age was given as about 57, but she must have been 68 when she was found dead in a hotel room by a housemaid.

The Reynolds account ends with a rumor.

"Now people report seeing a girl in a shimmering dress strolling in streets and gardens in the Nob Hill section of the city. She seems to be returning from a late party. The figure smiles at passers-by and moves in a leisurely manner. As in her life, Flora is still walking alone."

The time had come for me to fly to California and follow up on the story so vividly told by Reynolds, and, of course, to check up on Mrs. Hinzie's experiences. It was a warm day in May of 1966 when I met Mrs. Hinzie and her friend Mrs. Bettin at the Hilton Hotel in San Francisco.

I had decided to discuss the case once more with the ladies prior to proceeding to the spot. Present during our conversation was my good friend Lori Clerf, a social worker living in the city. Sybil Leek was to join us downstairs about an hour later, just in time for the ride. She could not overhear any of our earlier conversation.

We established once again that the cable car was the California Street line, and that the girl in the party dress had walked down one of the streets crossing California Street.

"You were looking out the window of the cable car when this happened?" I asked.

"No, there was no glass—just the open side of the cable car, where you step up."

No reflection then, on glass. That alternative explanation was out.

"When she walked through two other people, did you think it was unusual?"

"Well, she was also improperly dressed for the street—that's how I noticed her in the first place."

A woman would, of course.

"Coming home from a party in the middle of the afternoon," Mrs. Hinzie added. Even in San Francisco that might be considered unusual. "As I was looking at her, the dress seemed diaphanous, but you could not see through it. All white, no other colors. And as I was watching her it looked as if there were water suddenly sprayed on her side; it clung there, shining as water does in the sun."

There was some time still before we would meet Sybil, so I went over my previous notes and questioned Mrs. Hinzie about other psychic experiences she might have had and not told me about. For it was already plain to me that the most interesting part of the case was not the ghost but the lady who saw her. It is not often that a person observes with such wealth of detail psychic events that are later checked out and substantiated, and I wanted to make sure I had all the incidents right. Had Mrs. Hinzie told me all?

She had not. In 1941, when she was 21 years old, she had gone with her mother and sister to be house guests of W.A. Winnipeg, Canada.

"In January of that same year," Mrs. Hinzie began her stor father had passed away and in March of that year Mr. A lost his wife, so he and my mother were both widowed, been friends since 1924. The house had over thirty rooms, time the only people living in it were Mr. Anderson, his daughter Bett Jane, and three servants.

"The day we arrived and drove up the gravel in front of the house I saw what I thought was someone at the window upstairs that tur out to belong to Mrs. Anderson's sewing room. But ther up there at the time. We entered the big hallway, and Mr. standing there to receive us. At this moment, my hair went up I don't know why, for I had met him a number of times befor comed us and we were taken into the living room. It was a hot day and I had a headache, so I sat in a chair in the living room, facing the hal while someone went to get an aspirin. At this moment, as I sat ther heard a car pull up on the gravel outside, then a door slam, hear the front door open. But a moment later I heard some steps come across the hall, and a young girl crossed the hall in front of my vision, and she was wearing a white dress with silver slippers with rhinestones on them, and one of the straps was broken. I thought ther her stockings and shoes, and that her skirt was torn; her hair was blo and her eyes were very pale blue. *She had a dark spot right up on the cr of her head.* That was all—she just went out of my field of vision."

"How did she get in?"

"She was just there."

"What did it all mean?"

"Well, the Andersons had a daughter who committed suicide in

1936. Her name was Martha, and she had married a man against her parents' wishes."

"Did you tell Mr. Anderson what you had witnessed?"

"Yes. I had at first thought it was his other daughter, Betty Jane. But Betty Jane only arrived later that afternoon. We were in the house for ten days, and I saw the girl several times more."

"Can you elaborate on these experiences?"

"When I got to the top of the stairs I would see her going to her bedroom, and on one occasion I was standing in the hallway just about to go into a room my mother was occupying on the second floor when I saw this girl cross by me and go into that room; but the room, which was decorated in orange and beige, seemed to be all white, white draperies all over—and she just vanished into the white draperies!"

"Anything more about the girl with the dark spot on her head?"

"Once she walked into the room and faded into the white of the draperies. Then I could see a man standing on the other side of the bed behind these curtains. She walked in and went 'Hah,' like that, and they started to talk, but I could not make out the conversation. I stood there mesmerized, just watching. Then it sounded as if someone had just broken a stick, I mean the noise I heard, and she came out from behind the curtains, with her arms up behind her head, walked about three steps, then she fell, right in front of me. Her eyes seemed crossed as if she had been hit on the head. A little trickle of blood came down her forehead. Then her eyes half-closed, and at that point I felt a terrific blow on the back of my own head—it felt as though I were being driven through the floor . . . and my sister was standing in the hallway screaming at me . . . . saying, 'Bunny, Bunny' . . . which is my nickname . . . and I felt very peculiar. My mother of course insisted I had imagined the whole thing."

"Remarkable," I said. "Then you actually saw the entire traumatic scene just as it happened. You are indeed psychic."

Mrs. Hinzie nodded with a wan smile.

"The following year my mother married our host. Two years later, she came to see me in Los Angeles, and referring to the incident finally admitted—'I saw it too . . . it was horrible!'"

"What happened to the house?"

"Mr. Anderson and my mother later rented it and finally took an apartment where they lived until his death. The house is still standing but I have no idea as to who owns it now."

"What about the scene you witnessed?"

"Mother asked me never to tell Mr. Anderson and I didn't. But I had still another experience in this house, on the day we left.

"I was sleeping in Martha's bedroom—she was the daughter who died—and I slept very badly that night. I woke up early, when I heard someone working the door handle. Now I had locked the room from the inside on retiring. But a woman came in, nevertheless, and I said, 'Oh, Mother . . .' but she did not look like my mother— she wore a silken long dressing gown . . . she had her hands up over her head . . . I was still kind of sleepy . . . I must have dozed off again, and when I woke up a little later she was still in my room, only now she wore a cotton dress, and I thought it was Mother and said, 'Oh, Mother, what time is it?' But she said, 'I'm Em . . .' and I said, 'When are we leaving?' and she replied, 'Ten minutes of nine.'"

"What happened then?"

"She moved the clock on the dresser, and walked out. I got up—it was just eight o'clock—and I put on my clothes fast. I realized then who Em was. The late Mrs. Anderson."

"What about this ten minutes to nine remark? Any significance?"

"I don't know, but we actually did leave exactly at that time. Ten minutes to nine."

"Was that the last time a dead member of the Anderson family appeared to you?"

"In 1953, when my husband and I returned to Los Angeles from

Omaha where we lived for a while, we stayed at the house shared by my mother and Mr. Anderson for several days. That particular night I am about to mention, a son of Mr. Anderson's by the name of Gordon and his fiancée were also staying in the house, which was at Ninth and Western Avenue. At this moment, my husband was lying down, for he was not feeling well after an operation; Mother and the fiancée were out of the room to look at some jewelry. Gordon was in the kitchen and Mr. Anderson was out of the house, so I was sitting in the living room all alone.

"I got up and walked into the adjoining dining room where I found Gordon, whom I had thought in the kitchen, mixing drinks. There was always bad blood between us, and for one reason or another he grabbed my arm. The others now came back in, just as a voice was heard seemingly from outside saying, 'Gordon, stop that!' Mr. Anderson seemed taken aback. 'Why,' he said, 'that was Em's voice.'"

"Two ghosts then," I said, "mother and daughter, but mother evidently is free to travel."

"She died naturally," Mrs. Hinzie explained. "No reason she should be earthbound."

"Quite so." I nodded and looked at my watch. It was time to meet Sybil and go to California Avenue where the ghost of the girl in the party dress might be waiting—if we were lucky.

The important point of the incident was Mrs. Hinzie's total ignorance of the story or tradition about this ghostly girl at the time she saw her. It was fifteen years later that she accidentally came across the account in James Reynolds' book in the Public Library. Thus we must rule out unconscious hallucination of a known event.

When we arrived atop Nob Hill, it was about four in the afternoon, and traffic was heavy. Lori parked her shining white car carefully—that's the only way you can park a car in San Francisco if you don't want it to roll downhill—and we walked a few steps to the street intersection of California where Mrs. Hinzie remembered the incident. What did Sybil feel at this spot? Did the noises of the onrushing traffic blot out all psychic impressions, or did she feel something other than flesh-and-blood and gasoline?

"Yes, I do," Sybil intoned immediately. "I feel fear . . . someone is afraid . . . more than one person involved . . . fear . . . someone wants to run away . . ."

How right she was!

"What sort of person is it wants to run away?" I prodded.

"A young person," she replied, while trying hard to get an impression above the din of the traffic. No medium ever worked under more trying conditions, but then the experiment was unique.

"Man or woman?"

"Young . . . feeling of panic . . . I feel cold . . . despite this hot day . . . look at the goosepimples on my arms. . . ."

"Why is this person running away?"

"I think there is a link with the house I just pointed out to you."

The house, though old, was not the house belonging to the girl's family, though the spot might have been the same site.

"It's someone who runs away from a house," Sybil continued, "she ran this way. . . ."

"She?"

"I don't know . . . but suddenly I felt 'she.' I have 1830 in my mind. '30 is very clear. Several people are involved in this . . . this chase. A hounding."

"Any unhappiness involved?"

"The girl . . . she is panic-stricken."

"Why?"

"I have a feeling of terrible disease, horror."

Later I realized that Sybil might have picked up the girl's death. She had died of heart disease.

"Is she still here?"

"Yes, definitely."

We left the crowded spot none too soon, for people began to recognize us—Sybil, in her purple dress and stockings, and me, the Ghost Hunter—from our television appearances, and I never like to answer questions on busy street corners.

Sybil had no way of "guessing" the connection of the spot we took her to with the ghostly girl. Nor could she have picked the unconscious mind of Mrs. Hinzie, who was distant from Sybil, nor mine, for I, too, let Sybil go around the area by herself.

Mrs. Hinzie had indeed impressed me with her experiences and I decided to follow up on what had originally brought us together, courtesy U.S. mail: the haunted house and barn at Newbury Park, California.

Mrs. Hinzie wanted my opinion on her "problem," but I had been so intrigued with the San Francisco case, I had put the question aside.

"I have been disappointed that you have not yet commented on our situation here," she wrote me—"the uncomfortable atmosphere around the barn and the voice I've heard saying 'Hi,' but I do have, I believe, additional information on that which we think is interesting."

"First I will tell you about our town, Newbury Park. It *is* on the map and up to five years ago had a population of about 5,000 or less. We now have about 11,000 people, I believe. My husband and I have lived here since June 1961 but in another part of town 'til last February. The town's only claim to fame is its stagecoach inn, a hostelry which, I understand from Mrs. Michael Hagopejion, the president of the Conejo Valley Historical Society, was used as a hotel and stop-over for the stagecoach travelling between Santa Barbara and Los Angeles from 1876 to 1915. The inn is now being moved from its location, the equivalent of about two city blocks from us, to another location a few hundred feet away, as the freeway overpass will pass through the original

530

site of the inn. It is a two-story frame building of 19 rooms.

"Up to 1960 Newbury Park, except for a very small residential section, was all ranch land. These ranches were in size from hundreds to thousands of acres. Many of the owners were related to each other, and so for the past 90 years it has been a small ranching community.

"I have learned from our friend Martin Bettin that sometime in the late 1800's there was a boy staying at the inn who, probably in exploring the hilly country close by, became lost. The boy was never found. I cannot help wondering if the child's voice we have heard, and it *is* the voice of a young boy, could be the ghost of this lost child?

"Martin Bettin got his information from a fireman at the Lake Sherwood fire station. His name is Simeon Dyke and he got the story from his father, an old-timer in the Conejo Valley.

"Another thing of interest to the barn area (which I find uncomfortable): This property, belonging to Allen Hays, our landlord, was purchased by his father sometime between 1910 and 1920, I understand. We live on about 21/2 acres of land, but the Hays ranch consisted of hundreds of acres and, after old Mr. Hays' death, was divided between his children, Allen Hays and Reba Jeffries.

"Through Simeon Dyke, Martin learned that in about 1920 there were a house and barn in the pasture adjacent to our present barn. They were torn down years ago. But at that time the people who lived in that house had a little girl, aged two or three, who fell into an open well or cesspool and was drowned. Could this, I wonder, have anything to do with my feeling about the barn area? Actually, however, my feeling is not around the pasture but the barn itself, outside that fenced pasture and also the road—part of it— above the barn closer to the house.

"I overheard a conversation between Martin and Sharon Bettin and Sharon's mother, Mrs. Davies, while I was at Mrs. Davies' house, and asked them about it. Apparently they didn't want to say anything in front of me, but Martin and Sharon have admitted to Mrs. Davies they have an uncomfortable feeling in our barn. I had always felt myself *like a trespasser there,* and seldom visit the barn, but Martin has about 100 rabbits there and he is there frequently. He says he feels as if someone might come around the corner at any time. He says it's almost as if you expect someone to suddenly come up from nowhere and tap you on the shoulder—and Martin isn't timid. Sharon said she felt uncomfortable there, too."

By now I thought I knew Newbury Park pretty well without ever having set foot on this little speck of land. Mrs. Hinzie had a way of describing her world that had authenticity, and I decided to let her be our guide if and when we could go there in person.

Meanwhile I asked her to report further unusual happenings to me when they took place. Mrs. Hinzie was a bit worried about my postponing our visit to the fall of 1966.

"We expect to move from here in about a year, and it is unlikely that the place will be tenanted again after that, as Mr. Hays, our landlord, wants to sell this property for commercial use and undoubtedly this little house will be torn down. It is 10 years old and made of cement blocks.

"There have been three occurrences that I have not mentioned, over the past two months. The most recent was a weird 'singing' or 'whistling' noise which I heard a few nights ago. I am reasonably sure this was not my imagination, as my son, David, has told me of hearing such a noise about two months ago while he was in the bathroom. He was frightened, but no one else heard it and I could not imagine what it could be other than a little air in the pipes. But when I heard what I assume was the same noise it was while I sat up alone in our living room-kitchen.

"The other thing that happened was the day I saw the ghost. I knew from the voice that it was a boy of about 10 or 12. But this day (in late January) while I was washing the windows, I saw through the window pane clearly standing by the fence a young boy *and you could see the fence through him!* It was in the morning and that side of the house was shaded but the yard behind it was in brilliant sunlight. I wasn't sure I could believe my eyes and when I turned around he was gone.

"Another hard-to-explain thing that happened was one evening at least a month ago—maybe more—when my husband and I were sitting in the living room and the room was fairly quiet. We both heard a sound that could only be called a whimpering near the door. I had heard this several months before but no one else had."

The experiences of young children are generally considered unworthy of belief when one investigates scientifically phenomena of this kind, and yet no one dares say that all children make up stories and that there are not keen observers among the very young.

I did not attach importance to the testimony of the Hinzie children by itself, but coming on the heels of so much *adult* evidence, it seemed to reinforce the whole case and therefore I am reporting it. Mrs. Hinzie carefully wrote down what her children reported seeing in the house.

"David told me about some misty shapes he had seen, and said the other kids also saw them some time ago in their bedroom. He said it was dark in the room and these 'things' were light.

"Near the ceiling he saw three misty shapes and they seemed to be looking down at the children. They were vague but he thought they were people. He called me and when I came in and opened the door they disappeared.

"Until June of 1965 (that is, in reference to our staying in this house), my husband, Don, worked nights (2 P.M. to 10:30 P.M.). It was during that period (between late February and mid-June) that one night there was an uproar in the bedroom and the children all called me and I rushed in, after removing books, etc., from my lap in the living room and opened the door and the kids pointed to the *ceiling* near the end of the bedroom partition and said, 'See it, mom'—'see it.' But I saw nothing.

"I turned around to turn on the light and it was gone.

"The kids said, that night, they 'saw something' in that spot. They said it was 'horrible' and could not describe it. Said it was not misty and had, according to them, no definite shape. They asked me to leave the door open, which I did after first closing it and telling them it was nonsense. But they were nearly hysterical when I closed the door, so I immediately reopened it. They settled down almost immediately after that and slept. There was no reoccurrence of that particular night.

"The children sleep in a room that is on the north side of the house and has two windows on that side. There are no windows in the east wall or the south or west wall and the two bedrooms I mentioned are really one room partitioned to within about three feet of the door.

"The 'shapeless, horrible' thing the kids saw was on my mind for a while after that, and when I saw something in there later on, I was not sure it was not subconscious suggestion on my part and never mentioned it to anyone, but it was about three weeks later that it happened. The children were insisting upon the door being left open and I allowed it for several weeks after they saw this thing.

"The night I saw *something,* the door was, therefore, open. I was sitting across from the door by the windows and looked up to see a *misty, whitish shape in the doorway* next to the partition and partly over it— above floor level some six feet, I would say. It seemed to move slightly and I really thought the kids must have seen something. I went in but all was silence. There was no odor of smoke, and the thing must have gone farther up on the wall because it seemed higher. Also, it did not move now as I looked at it. I left the door open and went back to my chair, but when I had sat down again it was no longer visible.

"At least once, after we had been in the house about a month, my son John asked me if fog could come in the house and into the bedroom. He was in bed at the time and asked me if I could see the 'fog in the room.' I told him that if fog came in (we had much rain and fog at the time) it would not be visible, as the house is warm and would make this vapor disappear. However, he insisted there was fog in the room. I could not see it.

"John, too, has been subject to nightmares in the past 5 to 6 years and I am beginning to wonder about them. He is not a particularly fearful child when awake—is, as a matter of fact, braver than our other two children and very matter-of-fact. He is highly intelligent and is always seeking answers to things. He will be 10 in June. Many times my husband or I have had to call out loudly and sharply to John during the night when he has been shouting in his sleep—sometimes sitting up— to jolt him out of his dream, as he doesn't hear you when you speak to him in a normal tone and are beside his bed while he is having one of these nightmares. I have found he is not as bad lately but have also found touching him or being by his side will often frighten him greatly even with the light on. I sometimes find, though, that calling out to him only half awakens him, and I have to go into the room, turn on the light and go up to his bed talking all the time before he knows who spoke to him. Then he settles down. But children do have nightmares, and I did not give it really serious thought until about Christmas time last year (1965) when one night, after I had gone to bed and all the family was asleep, I heard John start talking as if he were awake, making comments and talking (apparently) to David.

"Then I thought I heard a patient voice answering him *and* calling him by name saying to the effect 'no, John,' then John began to get excited and I, thinking it was David, heard finally an irritable 'Oh, John, go to sleep, shut up!' There was just a moment or two of silence and then John started very excitedly: 'What? *What?* Who's there? Who *are* you?' I called to John, 'It's Dave,' and then went into the bedroom and turned on the light. John was as close to hysterics as I've ever seen him, huddled in his bed, alternately covering his head and pulling out. He began to relax when he saw me, and Dave was sprawled out on the bed looking very much asleep—and I'm sure he was, as he was face up and made no effort to shield his eyes from the light when I came in. I went up to John's bed and said to him, 'John, you're dreaming,' but am sure he was not asleep because he looked at me, *seeing me,* and said he wasn't. He said he thought someone was asking him questions but he didn't know who it was. I told him it must have been Dave, but he said it didn't sound like Dave and I must admit it really didn't—the voice was somewhat slurred at times and different from Dave's. John insisted there was someone else in the room, but I told him this could not be. He was sure it was a boy.

"There hasn't been much else happening around here recently other than my hearing outdoors, apparently on the hill behind the clothes line, a whimpering sound, quite loud, that lasted for several minutes at a time.

"Also, yesterday afternoon, my daughter and I were sitting on the patio and we both heard distinctly two car doors slam on the other side of the house. She went to see if the truck doors had slammed shut, but they were both open and there were no cars out there. On many occasions, particularly after we had lived here only about a month or so, when I was here alone in the afternoon, I would hear a car stop on the gravel by the carport and a door slam shut—not very loud but distinct—and not so loudly as we heard them outside yesterday. Yesterday, however, I heard no crunching of gravel.

"At first, when I heard the car pull up and the door slam I would get up and go look out the kids' bedroom window, but I never saw anything.

"I forgot to mention that one day, three months after we had moved in here, I was sitting at the table in the living room-dining room-kitchen area and *saw the door open.* The handle was turned gently. I heard a little sound and it opened—about six inches. I went and closed it and that was all."

The incidents in the little house at Newbury Park seemed to point out some pretty curious things: for one thing, the white form was seen well above ground level, near the ceiling, as it were. After we looked over the house in person, I realized *why*. The house had been built onto the hillside, artificially terracing it, so that the ceiling level coincided with what was formerly the ground level. Any ghosts appearing at the ceiling were really walking on what was *to them*, at least, still ground level!

I had not yet been to the house when the children's report was sent to me by Mrs. Hinzie, although we had met in San Francisco. But at that time I specifically asked Mrs. Hinzie not to talk of the events in her house at Newbury Park so that Sybil could not "tune in" on them, and nothing pertaining to Newbury Park was discussed. When we finally did go there in October of 1966, it came as a great surprise to Sybil to meet the ghost lady from San Francisco again—in her own surroundings this time!

On May 18th, Mrs. Hinzie was further disturbed by occurrences of a paranormal nature.

"Last week I walked into the house from outdoors and closed the door behind me. There was no one in the house and no animals in the house, but I distinctly heard a few feet from me a cat hiss sharply. I looked around to be sure that no cats were in the house. This had also happened last summer.

"Twice in the past month—only a few days apart—I thought I *was touched by someone*. The first time I was washing dishes at the sink and felt, I thought, two small hands lightly on my back at the waistline. I turned around thinking John had sneaked up on me (the children were in bed) but there was no one there. A few days later I walked outside in front of the front window, to the door. There is a bench in front of the window. As I walked by the bench I distinctly felt the *back of my skirt and my slip being pulled firmly*. I reached down to touch my clothes but they were in place and the pressure immediately stopped.

"Perhaps I should have known there was something odd about this place when we moved.

"The day my husband brought me to the house to see the place I had a strange experience. Don, my husband, had just painted the house inside and it was clean and when he asked me what I thought of it, I said, 'Well, it's all right, but don't you think Mr. Hays ought to fix *that hole in the wall?*' To me it looked as if, above the stove, there was a cement block neatly removed from the wall. He said, 'Where?' and I said, 'Why, right there where that red light is coming through.' He said there wasn't one and yet I thought there was a red light glowing there, not fire but more like an electric light. It faded out and the block was, of course, in place. My family laughed at me, so I thought I had imagined it, but last week as I sat with my back to the window, facing the stove, I was watching television. For some reason I looked up and saw the calendar on the wall to the left of the stove lighted up as if someone had thrown a beam of red light on it. The curtains were opened behind the couch where I sat but no one could have stood outside and played a beam of light on the calendar. It encompassed only the calendar."

The skirt-pulling incident reminded me of similar attention-getters in other cases of hauntings, except that I felt a certain pathetic helplessness here, as we were apparently dealing with the ghost of a child, and there is nothing sadder.

On May 31, Mrs. Hinzie had further developments to report, for as so often happens, the nearer one gets to visit a haunted place, the more frantic do the restless ones become, to make sure, perhaps, that you don't overlook them!

"The last occurrence—which I had not told you about—happened within a few days of my return home from San Francisco. I walked between the dining table and the fireplace and felt small gentle tugs at the side of my skirt. There was nothing there to catch the skirt on and

I was, for once, *not* alone in the room. But I didn't mention it to any-one then. *It would seem that someone wants to get my attention.*

"The night after I returned from seeing you (Tuesday, May 17) I was sitting alone in the living room and the children and my husband were all asleep in bed. I heard a *loud* slam of a door in the bedroom (there is only one leading outside) and went in. Everyone was still asleep, apparently undisturbed, and I found the door ajar—I mean by that closed but not firmly latched—a slight push would have opened it. Yet a slam as hard as I heard would surely have latched the door firm-ly, as there is nothing wrong with the catch.

"The last thing that happened was day before yesterday when my son John, who was reading in the bedroom, heard a car pull up on the gravel. There was no one there, but there was a distinct crunching sound as tires passed over gravel. This, strangely enough, is the only really consistent thing that happens here. I have heard a car's tires on the gravel so many times since we moved in that I usually simply ignore it. Only when it is *very* distinct (I mean really loud) do I look outside. When I hear it, I am not aware of the sound of a motor—just the sound of the tires as the car comes to a stop.

"The first time I ever noticed this house, I felt a Model T Ford car, open sedan type, coming up the front road to the house. This makes no sense as the road has been here only about four years.

"That particular day I was sitting in the car with the children at the foot of the hill, in the parking lot there, and one of the children brought the house to my attentlon. Few people notice it—although we are not isolated—possibly because you can see only the roof top from the park-ing lot below.

"The house was built 10 years ago. The hill was excavated to make room for the house and no one else had ever lived on the spot. There was another road, now not in use, on the other side of the house from the road now used near the front of the house, but it was closed off by part of the hill being excavated only about four years ago. The road generally used now goes through the parking lot at the foot of the hill. There is also another road connected to the road not now in use which goes to the barn."

The business about the Model T Ford puzzled me, of course. But there are cases on record where ghost cars have been observed by psychically gifted people. Anything touched by human emotions may have an etheric double, and if such a car had been part of an emotional experience, a ghost of that car might very well still be part of the atmosphere around the house!

It was plain to me that Mrs. Hinzie was able to see simultaneously into both halves of our world, and that events impressed upon the psychic ether around us were just as clear to her as events in the physical world.

On recollection, Mrs. Hinzie admitted to still another incident involving clairvoyance, which seemed to me particularly relevant because it concerned another ghost car.

"This happened about 1945 or 1946. Fremont Place is a small walled section of Los Angeles—a few blocks only in size, on the south of Olympic Boulevard opposite Los Angeles High School. It was an affluent district in the 20's and the early 30's.

"My mother and her husband, W.A. Anderson, were on a visit to Los Angeles and they had rented a house for a month on a street in the area.

"I sat in the back seat of the car—my brother-in-law drove and my sister and mother and W.A. Anderson were all present. As we drove up the street, I looked into the rear view mirror and saw behind us and gaining on us (we were going slowly) an old sedan (1920's), very high and narrow—a closed car. I could clearly see a woman sitting in the back seat. It looked a little dusty and muddy as I recall but not particularly worn out, or shiny and well-cared-for either. As my brother-in-law eased the car toward the curb, this old sedan passed us *very* closely on the left side and turned closely in front of us in to the curb. It stopped or had almost stopped—that was more my impression (there was no sound of a motor, by the way)—and the door in the rear right side opened immediately and a woman got out. Her face I did not see but she wore a black dress, the 30's hemline, rather long, and a widow's veil on her head. It was thrown back from her face in front and hung over her arms and back to about her elbows. She was walking quickly up toward a house—I think it was the house we entered—when my attention was called away from her by someone in the car. I did not see her again. As my brother-in-law rolled to a stop he hit the old car and we *felt a jar.* I told him what we had hit, but apparently *no one else had seen the car* as they all laughed.

"We then walked up to the house and opened the door. My hair, I was told, stood on end all the time we were there, which was less than 10 minutes.

"There was a large entry hall and lounge room to the right which we went into. I kept feeling as if someone were going to rush out of the butler's pantry behind the dining room to the left all the time I was there, but never really saw that part of the house so I don't even know if there *was* a pantry!

"Mother and W.A. Anderson had been there since the day before—rented the house sight unseen. They had, mother said, quarreled the night before in the house and her husband slapped her—this I think was significant—the place had such an air of tension as if suddenly a fist fight would start. I asked if it was the house in which a man had committed suicide in the 30's; he was a well-known business and society figure, as I recall."

When I was in Hollywood in October 1966, I passed through the area. It is indeed an aristocratic looking "compound," where the politically great and movie stars had made their homes. It still has an air of mystery around it.

On October 5th, shortly before our planned visit, Mrs. Hinzie had had another brush with the uncanny.

"The thing I'm about to tell you happened about 2 to 4 weeks ago. I was outside. The children were just out of school (about 3:30 P.M.) but none had come up the hill. Our dog, Penny, was with me. I heard a child's voice; it sounded like a little girl 5 to 6 years old. She called out something very clearly but I do not remember what. It sounded as if she were not exactly on the road but *above it* near the trees at the bend of the road. The dog heard it, too, and went over near the road and then came back.

"The other thing that happened was a week ago Saturday about 6 P.M. I was standing at the sink fixing something for dinner. The kids were down at the school and Don, my husband, was at the barn. The bedroom and bathroom doors were open but the front door was closed. I heard the front door close—*not open*—not loudly but not stealthily— and saw from the corner of my eye a child, *a boy wearing a white shirt,* go from the direction of the door toward the bedrooms or bathroom. I was so certain I had seen and heard someone I went in search of him because I knew it was not one of my boys. They don't ever wear white shirts, except on Sunday. But there was no one there. That same night I saw a streak of light on our bedroom partition—about two feet long and about four inches at one end, two inches at the other—a pointed thing like an arrow.

"It was very white and low on the wall—about three and one-half feet up—I don't know where it could have come from; it was quickly gone."

Finally, the great day arrived. Everything had been prepared for our coming by Mrs. Hinzie—by everything I mean not only her own house and "case," but two other hauntings not far away which she had brought to my attention and which we intended to look into on the same day prior to returning to Los Angeles.

It was an unusually warm day in October 1966 when we started out from Sybil Leek's apartment near Western Avenue. My wife, Catherine, was driving, I was doing the piloting with a map, and Sybil was snoozing in the back seat, tired out from an avalanche of radio and TV appearances in connection with her latest book.

Thanks to Mrs. Hinzie's exact instructions, we made the trip over sundry freeways in about an hour, going toward Ventura and finally veering off the freeway when we reached the little town of Newbury Park. With some maneuvering we managed to find the parking lot through which we were to drive in search of the dirt road leading up to the knoll on which the house stood.

It was the kind of road perfectly suited to a Model T, and not really to a modern no-shift car, but we made it and arrived at the Hinzie house around noon, with the sun blazing down at us at something like 95 degrees Fahrenheit. Our hostess came out to greet us, and we quickly entered the neatly kept little house. The children were still at school and only Mrs. Hinzie and her friend Mrs. Bettin were in the house. Sybil took a chair near the window and I started to work with her almost immediately.

As always, I first asked Sybil if she had any feelings about the house as she came upon it for the first time.

"Not about the house," Sybil replied, "but about the ground . . . the side of the house. I don't think it is a road now. The land is more important than any building here. There is a spot outside the house. . . ."

She did not feel particularly restless *inside* the house, however.

"Outside, there must have been a great deal of coming and going," Sybil continued. "More than one person is connected with it, a communal feeling. This, I am sure, was a meeting place."

She felt that the spot went back three hundred years, and that more than a single restless personality was in evidence. With that, she began to relax and her state of trance became more pronounced.

"Two different periods," Sybil mumbled now. "Sixty years ago, beginning of the century, and then . . . two different nationalities. . . ."

"Who is present here now?"

"Daniel . . . Walker . . ."

For a few minutes there was heavy breathing, and then another personality appeared to be in command of Sybil's lips. At first, the voice was faint, and I had to strain to hear at all, but gradually, as we paid attention, it became stronger until it was heard clearly for all of us to understand—except that it was in Spanish, a language Sybil did not speak fluently; she knows only a few phrases and words, about as much as a tourist might pick up on a casual visit to Spain.

It was a man's voice that came through her now.

"No gusta," it said, and repeated, as if to impress us with the fact that there was something he did not like, *"no gusta."*

"What is your name?"

"Rafael."

"What?"

"Rafe. . . ."

"Why are you here?"

"Wait."

"Whom are you waiting for?"

"Man . . . Pietro . . . *frater.* . . ."

"What is your brother's name?"

"My—brother—Darshee—Darshin——"

"Where does he live?"

"Valley. . . ." He pronounced it *"Valle,"* the Spanish way.

Then he seemed to become cognizant of my presence.

"Who are you?"

"I'm a friend," I replied softly, "who would like to help you."

"I shall kill you. Go away quickly!"

"Is this your property?"

"Mine."

"How long have you been here?"

"Don't know."

"What year is this?"

"Eighteen-eighty-two," he said haltingly.

"What day?"

"Day?"

"What is your birthday?"

"June . . . birthday. . . ."

"What is your father's name?"

"Daschee." I could not be sure if he said Darshee, Dashee, Dasche, or something sounding like it.

"First name?"

"Dashee Hermanos." Did he perhaps mean "Taje" pronounced in the Spanish way?

"Your mother's name?"

"Maria Garcia . . . Graciella."

"Where did you go to school?"

"School . . . *escuela.* . . ."

"Do you understand English? What I am asking you?"

A moment of silence.

"No . . . I am married . . . Melita. . . ."

"What was her maiden name before she married you?"

"Doran."

"Where was she from?"

"Escuela. . . hablo . . . escula. . . ."

I decided to try to get the information, which had been very confusing up to now, by using what Spanish I knew.

"Do you understand English?" I said in Spanish.

No reaction.

"¿Estan Vd. Espanol?" I tried.

"Si . . ."

"*Por que razòn està Vd. acqui?*" I inquired again. (Why was he here?)

"*Me . . . hermano . . . muerte . . .*"

How old was his brother who died? "Ten," he said in Spanish, becoming very emotional now.

What was his brother's name? "Dan . . . Dana . . . Dajo. . . ."

What could we do to help? "Where is my son?"

Evidently he was looking for his son. I asked where he would like to go now.

"*No gusta,*" he repeated, and we were back where we started, not much wiser.

"*¿Que desira Vd. ?*"

"*Mi hijo,*" he pleaded, "I want my son."

The son, it seemed, was only two years old.

I asked him now what was his profession, what did he do. But I did not get an answer. He slipped away before I could get him to tell me, and Sybil returned to her own body—and senses. But before she was entirely "out," I sent her back, this time to observe while entranced, and to describe to me, still in trance, what she saw in the nonphysical world around her.

"Four people . . . child and two men . . . little child, not baby, died suddenly here . . . two men are digging . . . for the child is dead . . . also a woman . . . she is watching me . . . disturbance here . . children play . . . I don't think she likes the men . . . very uneasy feeling between the people here . . . children playing will disturb the little one . . . this is a bad spot for children . . . child can't move . . . hot, no water . . . spirits in the mountains . . . spirits protect this ground, this is not for people to live on . . . should respect the land . . . this land belongs to the spirits . . . sacred to the great . . . from the mountain. . . ."

"Are the four people still here?"

"Feathers and food . . . for spirits . . . lot of people here . . . dancing quietly . . . dark hair . . . nothing at the top and trousers . . . Homayo is the name . . . spirit . . . from the mountains to this spot . . . Homayo the great one . . . eagle feathers. . . ."

I promised we would "sacrifice" in their honor.

"No animals here . . ." Sybil continued, "this is Homayo's place. Do not disturb. Children should not be here."

I assured the Indian spirit that his memory would be respected and then I recalled Sybil to the year 1966. But Sybil stayed "with it" awhile longer, it appeared.

Homayo was still on her mind. Nothing would grow here, she felt. There was a plague here, and the child was a victim of it.

"The child is buried under the tree," she now said. The only tree, we later found, was in back of the house, an ancient tree indeed.

"By the little road," the entranced Sybil added. That, too, was correct. The little road in back of the house did go by the tree. There was a house there once which no longer exists.

What did the parents want done about their child?

"Don't disturb it," Sybil reported, "leave the tree."

"What are they looking for in the house?"

"Digging. . . ."

"What was here before?"

"Wooden house. Child died here. No water."

The men were fighting over the land, she added. "Too many people coming here, Homayo strikes them down. Thirst."

"What does the child look like?"

"Thin, brown child."

"Male or female?"

"Can't tell. Perhaps ten, nine, ten. Walking, riding. Has a cloth over it. On the ground. Long hair."

"What is its name?"

"Raffi. . . ."

Evidently the two layers confused Sybil, for she was not sure which was which—the Indians or the later settlers.

Finally, Sybil came back to her own self. While she rested up from all that had come through her the past hour, I turned to Gwen Hinzie and asked for her comments concerning the material that had now been added to our knowledge of the case.

"Well, of course, we've seen a ten-year-old boy several times here, and yesterday I saw a man, too, outside this window, in his middle fifties, with kind of a humped back—and there were Spanish-speaking settlers here and it is a fact that the Chumash Indians lived here . . . also, there was a house behind the school over there, where people lived until about 1920. They had a child, a little girl, who fell into a well and died. There certainly were people out here in 1882, and many of them spoke Spanish."

"What about the name Daniel that was mentioned early in the session?"

Mrs. Hinzie nodded.

"A family named Borchardt owned much of the land here for many years . . . and Daniel was Mr. Borchardt's first name, I think. But I'm not sure."

"What about the child being buried under the tree?"

"Well, there is this big tree behind the house, and I did see a child—a ghost child, that is, about a year and a half ago, behind that tree."

"Was it male or female?"

"Male, but it looked older than the one I had seen on the lawn at the house. I thought at first it had gone down the hill, but it could not have disappeared from view at that spot—unless it had sunk into the ground. There just is no way to go."

I agreed that this would have been impossible, after inspecting the spot.

"About those Indians," Mrs. Hinzie said, as an afterthought, "it sounds like a ceremonial ground rather than a burial ground. Women would never do in a ceremonial area."

Mr. Hinzie, who had come in at the onset of the trance session and had sat quietly watching it all, now spoke up.

"There is an Indian burial ground being excavated right now nearby."

I then talked to the three children, ranging in age from 9 to 12, and they reiterated their stories substantially as told to me by their mother. They seemed like bright, normal youngsters, no more imaginative than ordinary children and not too eager to talk about it all.

When they pointed to the ceiling of their room as the haunted spot, Sybil, who had stepped into the room now, nodded assent.

"That would be the original land level," she remarked, "and *they* would walk on that level."

We then went outside, as Sybil felt an urge to "putter around" despite the great heat.

Sybil insisted that there was an Indian trail leading from the hills to the sea directly through the house—in fact, over the spot where the children had seen the apparitions. Mr. Hinzie confirmed that there was such a trail although he did not know its exact location.

We returned to the car now, as Mrs. Hinzie had other points of psychic interest in store for us.

Since then, Mrs. Hinzie has tried to check up on some of the Indian doings in the area. In nearby Agoura, in the San Fernando Valley, archaeologists from the University of California were busy digging up a Chumash Indian burial ground. These Indians, Mrs. Hinzie discovered, had been converted to Christianity by Spanish Franciscan priests. This area was within the ground covered by the mission at San Buenaventura, now Ventura. The Indians have disappeared and there is but one survivor living in Newbury Park now who is half Chumash and half Mexican.

I haven't heard anything further about any disturbances at the Hinzie house since our return from California. With so many layers of psychic consciousness in the spot, it seems a little difficult to sort out the ghosts. But the fact remains that Mrs. Gwen Hinzie has a prolific talent for seeing and hearing them, and our own Sybil was able to give information that dovetails with the earlier testimony. Indian ceremonial grounds are a little hard to pin down, as there is no written literature among the Indians, but the little lost boy, between two states of being, as it were, must surely be guided across the threshold. Perhaps as the flesh-and-blood children in the Hinzie house grow older and their available energies cannot be drawn upon any longer for some of these psychic manifestations, the ghost of the boy will also fade away into the "land of the great spirit" where red or white skins no longer matter.

A few days before, as we were flying toward Los Angeles, Sybil had suddenly turned to me with a puzzled expression.

"What a strange occupation," she said, "to be a worm rancher!"

I was nonplused. What had brought on that remark? Sybil was not sure. It had just entered her mind.

I dismissed the strange thought, but when we met Mr. Hinzie, he took us to the back of the house where the barn stood.

"I've got a little business on the side going in there," he explained lightly. *"I'm a worm rancher!"*

I had never heard of anyone raising worms for fishermen, but apparently this occupation was not unique, though admittedly rare.

Sybil evidently had a premonition of all this. It makes me feel that our mission to Newbury Park was indeed "in the cards" long before we set foot there.

Mrs. Hinzie kept looking for possible confirmations of some of the things that had come through in trance. For one thing, the business about Indians at her house wanted further elucidation.

In January of 1967, Mrs. Hinzie was able to send excerpts from proper sources on the local Indians, the tribes Sybil had referred to in trance.

"I have researched the Chumash Indians out here to some extent and have found out a little bit bearing out Sybil's description of religious rites, which I'll quote here. This information comes from a book called *San Buenaventura, The Mission by the Sea,* by Father Zephyrin Engelhardt, O.F.M., printed in 1930 for the author by the Schauer Printing Studio, Inc., Santa Barbara, California.

"The following (pp. 33-40) was written by Father José Senan between 1812 and 1823 during his term of office as Presidente at Mission San Buenaventura, in Ventura. It was in answer to a list of questions proposed by the Spanish Government and sent to the priests at each mission with regard to the Indians of their area who lived and worked at the particular mission. They were called *neophytes* and all were of the Chumash tribe. The quotes are numbered apparently as they were in Fr. Seilan's *Requesta* (reply).

"'12. No inclination to idolatry is observed in our neophytes; nor can it be said that in savagery they practiced any formal idolatry. In the vicinity of their rancherias (small villages) *and on the mountain,* they used to have some places which they kept very clean, swept, and adorned *with beautiful plumage* put on poles. To these places they would go as to their sacred places. Here they would *assemble* in time of need and conduct a sort of pilgrimage. One of their number, in the name of all the rest, who observed profound silence would pray for rain, offering an abundance of acorns, seeds, and wild fruits which constituted their daily sustenance. They would catch fish or kill deer in order that no bear might catch them or the bite of a rattlesnake might not afflict them. They would pray also for health and other good things. At the end of the supplication, they would in their simplicity and crude veneration offer beads, acorns and various seeds, in order that they might be regarded with favor by the invisible one, whom they pictured to themselves according to their rude notions as the author and giver of rains, seeds, fruits, and other good things. The first part of this petition was always uniform. It was preceded by a salutation which in our language (Spanish) means as much as "Grand Captain or Captain of Captains, behold us and hear what we say."

" '19. The gentiles (pagans) of this vicinity have not adored the sun nor the moon.

" '28. They never offered human sacrifices to gods.

" '33. . . . in paganism they used only a flute-like thing made of elderwood, as also a bone *whistle,* with which the players produce a shriek and violent trill, at the same time making strange and ridiculous contortions of the body. Their songs are weird, more adapted to arouse sadness than gladness.

" '36. The dress of the male neophytes consists of a short overall, called cotón, or a breechcloth, in place of breeches, and of a blanket. All this clothing is made at the mission. The pagans know nothing of dress, except that women wear the hide of a deer or fringes of grass to meet the demands of natural decency.'

"This, above, is shown to have been written August 11, 1816, at Mission San Buenaventura, by Father José Senan."

"As to our own house, all is peaceful and serene, except that twice in the past month I've heard someone humming (kind of tunelessly) outside the door or at least close to it. It is the voice of either a child or a woman. We have no more lights or opening of doors and cars arriving on the gravel or slamming of car doors.

"There is no longer the feeling of little cat feet on our bed. My husband used to feel a cat walk across his feet whether he was sleeping on his lunch hour or at night. I had always felt it walking up toward me on my side of the bed but until he told me he felt the little feet I really thought it must be my imagination. It never walked ON me, just beside me. This was true almost from the time we moved in here. It is a very light step, almost weightless but not quite."

To sum it all up: Sybil, a stranger to those parts, had correctly described the ghost of a young child, the presence of Indians on the very spot where I had taken her, and a number of small but significant details, such as the ridiculous bit of information concerning Mr. Hinzie's worm-ranching activities. More important even, Mrs. Gwen Hinzie's own place in our psychically oriented world of study and knowledge seems pretty secure to me. She is, to borrow from Gilbert and Sullivan, the very model of a modern amateur medium!

In July 1967 Mrs. Hinzie contacted me again. All had been serene at the house for several months, except for a couple of gentle reminders that perhaps one of the ghosts, the child, had not yet left, even though the father had gone on.

A door opened by itself on one occasion; then a small white cloud appeared next to Mrs. Hinzie's bed which she at first mistook for cigarette smoke, until she convinced herself that the ashtray was cold. But the clincher came a few days after, when she was awakened in bed by the touch of a hand taking hers! The unseen hand felt soft and warm, but very firm. When it clasped Mrs. Hinzie's own hand, she naturally tried to withdraw it. The ghost hand tightened, and at the same time Mrs. Hinzie felt a strong pain in her armpits, as if fingers were pressing there.

In desperation, Mrs. Hinzie moved her own hand, with the ghost hand holding on to it, to her face and *bit into it*.

"It felt as though I had bitten into foam rubber," she said, but the ghost hand let go now and soon sleep returned to the "ghost lady of Newbury Park."

I advised Mrs. Hinzie to speak to the little ghost, should it ever return, as a mother would—to have the little one join his father out there in the great beyond.

But then some children, even ghostly ones, are notoriously bad at taking orders.

The Haunted Barn

Mrs. Hinzie had really done some useful spadework for us. There were two sites where uncanny goings-on had been reported and she wanted us to see them firsthand. In a country like California, where so much violence has taken place not only during the 19th century pioneer days but in comparatively recent times, psychic occurrences are not at all unlikely, and I only asked that there be some specific "complaint" in these cases. There was.

Our first stop was the Stagecoach Inn, a handsome mid-19th century building originally erected as a way station when this spot was a major factor in the stagecoach route to and from California. Later, it had deteriorated into an inn, the kind that takes on all comers and does not ask too many questions just so long as they can pay their bills.

According to Guy Runnion, editor of the *Conejo News*, who is the unofficial historian of this landmark, there had been killings here, and as far back as the 1930s, reports of hauntings at the Inn were prevalent.

A Mr. Dyke of nearby Thousand Oaks confirmed that his own father, a well-driller during those years, had spoken to him of such goings-on.

At present, the Inn is a museum, and it has just been moved on its foundations to a new location a few yards farther back from the original site to allow the freeway to pass. Whether the alleged ghost or ghosts would resent the move, or move out themselves, was a moot point—for me to find out.

The historical society in the person of Dr. Cyril Anderson has charge of the buildings now.

From 1952 to 1965, however, it had been used as a giftshop by a couple named McIntyre who spoke of a female ghost there; however, when questioned, Mrs. Kenneth McIntyre passed the matter off as "just a story" without substance.

When Gwen Hinzie was doing newspaper work in the area in 1962, she had occasion to visit the Inn frequently since it is only a few blocks away from the Hinzie house, and the land, in fact, is really one and the same parcel, connected with both the hill on which the Hinzie house now stands and the entire Hays family holdings around it. That this was of some significance we were to learn a little later.

But when Mrs. Hinzie first entered the 19-room mansion, Mrs. McIntyre remarked how odd it was that Mrs. Hinzie's hair should suddenly stand on end. Evidently hair raising is to Mrs. Hinzie what goose pimples are to Sybil Leek: an indicator of pyschic energies in the area.

At this moment, Mrs. Hinzie heard a crash upstairs, but she was assured by the proprietor of the giftshop that there was nobody above stairs. But her curiosity was aroused and she next talked to Donna Fargo, of the famous Wells Fargo family, regarding the Inn. Bandits, it seems, were roving in this area during stagecoach days, and only twenty miles away at Colahasas, things were truly "wild west."

The Inn had been built in the expectancy of a great deal of business because of the Butterfield mail route which was supposed to have gone through the Conejo Valley on the way to St. Louis; and there was already a post office at Newbury Park in 1875. But the Civil War interfered and the Butterfield line declined in importance, as the main route went through the Santa Clara Valley instead.

We arrived at the house while the sun was blazing, and the coolness of the inside was a welcome relief from its unremitting rays. The work of restoration was in full progress, but one could see that the house had had some stature at one time; it reminded one of the typical Western gambling inn movie set, complete with stairway leading to the rooms upstairs.

Sybil had started to "putter around" and I took great care to point out the various pitfalls where she might have landed in the basement without benefit of stairs. But Sybil is agile, and her five senses, not to mention her sixth, kept her out of trouble.

I found her in a room to the left of the stairs, a room that undoubtedly was once a guest room when the Inn was a hotel.

"This room interests me," Sybil explained, "more than the rest of the house. Before we arrived I had a feeling of something very unstable. Well, it is. The foundations are not ready. The house has been moved. Also, I feel a connection with the other place as if this were in line with it."

I realized that the land was of one piece. Was Sybil picking up the Indian trail again?

"What sort of place do you feel this is?" As always, I had not told Sybil anything about the place we were in at the moment. It could be a private house, a manor, anything; there was nothing to indicate that it was an inn, especially a stagecoach inn. And yet Sybil got the scent.

"A meeting place . . . not just a residence. Too many people come and go and leave disturbances . . . food and drink place. . . ."

Meanwhile, Leighton Field, a photographer with the Historical Society, and Kathy Berg, a young lady reporter from the *News-Chronicle,* had arrived and followed us around in the hope of catching, if not a ghost, at least some interesting conversation.

"I'm very depressed," Sybil now said, "especially in this room . . . tragedy . . . perhaps the room above also. . . ."

We entered the upstairs room and Sybil picked up something stronger now.

"Think of the name Pierre Devon," Sybil suggested, "that is the name that is there . . . 1882 to 1889 . . . violent headache . . . right hand side of head . . . died here . . . still present in this part of the house . . . short, dirty, not a farmer, mountains . . . passing through . . . passing through before Los Angeles . . . *hidalgo* . . . what does it mean?"

"That means gentleman," said the curator, who had come up to us. "The house was built in in 1876, so it was here in 1882."

But despite a careful search of the fragmentary records still extant about the period in question, no Pierre Devon could be pinned down. If this man was merely a transient passenger, spending a night here en route to Los Angeles, there hardly would be any. And if some local murderers had relieved him of his gold, there would be even less reason to let the world know.

Thus it appears that Pierre Devon, whoever he was, has taken the secret of his demise with him. I only hope that seeing Sybil, and being briefly aware of the outside world through her, will have sufficiently shaken him to allow him to leave the place of his death. Now that the Inn has been moved back from the original site, he really has no reason to stay on. Who ever heard of a ghost sitting on the freeway? He'd get himself killed all over again!

Our main objective that afternoon, however, was a *haunted barn* not far away in Thousand Oaks. What I had gathered through Mrs. Hinzie was that there were two local theaters: an old one no longer used as such, and a new one just opened, and that both, strangely enough, were haunted. As we were in direct line to the new playhouse first, I decided to have a look at the Conejo Valley players' spanking new theatre and talk to those who had experienced the uncanny.

The new theatre turned out to be a tastefully constructed auditorium with modern stage facilities, seats graduated for excellent viewing, and an overall feeling of newness belying anything ghostly. I had been told by Mrs. Hinzie that the original site of the haunting was the "old theatre," a barn at Thousand Oaks which is now a Baptist Church, but that somehow the ghost had travelled with the actors and taken up residence in the new house. This I had to see, for ghosts, to my mind, do not leave the spot of their passing.

To greet us, several members of the community theatre—an amateur endeavor, of course—were on hand. The auditorium, I noticed, was built into the hillside, very much like Mrs. Hinzie's house. In fact, it partook of the same piece of land as the Hinzie house and the Stagecoach Inn; thus I would not have been surprised, I thought, if Sybil felt Indian influences here, too. She was walking around somewhat restlessly, examining her feelings in the place. But she felt nothing here.

I turned to Mrs. Beverly Adams, one of the principals of the Conejo players, who had experienced some of the phenomena connected with this theatre.

"The first time anything happened," she began, "was when my husband and Herman Detering were here with me after rehearsals, one night about a year ago. We were closing up and we were all standing in the control booth, and I walked to the doors looking into the auditorium, on to the stage, and I heard voices and walking around in the back dressing room. I mentioned it, saying, evidently everyone isn't out of the theatre yet, so my husband and Mr. Detering went backstage to get them out—but they found nobody there. They, too, had heard the footsteps and voices. The dressing rooms are to the left of the stage and I was in back of the theatre, but I heard it. It sounded like a couple of people talking back there. A man and a woman."

"Could there have been someone there who left before you got to the dressing room?"

"Impossible. We would have seen them leave. The rear door is locked. That was around 11:00 at night."

"Only once?"

"No, I have heard unexplained noises around here two or three times. One night I was sitting in the first row watching rehearsals of *Finian's Rainbow* when I heard someone at the door trying to get in. The doorknob was rattling, so I went over, for we keep the door locked

558

so you can't open it from the outside, but only from the inside. There was nobody there. I sat down again when I heard footsteps going up onto the stage from the other side, and I thought, well, they must have gone through the other door. Then it dawned on me that the steps outside were concrete and that the steps I heard being walked on were wooden! Then I heard walking back and forth in the wings, so I asked Laverne Kaufman, who was sitting next to me, and she had heard it too."

"Have you had any psychic impressions here other than the noises you heard?"

"Yes," Mrs. Adams replied, "I've had cold, clammy feelings both here and in the old place, here in the first row where we are now and backstage in the wings also, at various times."

"How old is this theatre—was there anything here before?"

"Two years and there was nothing here before."

I turned to dark-haired Laverne Kaufman, who had joined us now, and asked what she had experienced here during the time she had been active in the community theatre.

"As my friend has told you, when we were watching the rehearsal of *Finian's Rainbow*, I, too felt the cold—strangely enough she felt it on her left leg, and I on my right leg; she got up to leave and get some coffee, and the sensation left me—but when she returned, the chill was back. At one time I have heard the piano give off a run which I recognized as a piece of music from a show. My son also heard it and it went through twice, yet there was nobody at the piano at that moment!"

I'm sure the musicians' union would not have liked this.

At this point Sybil reported that the left-hand side of the stage was a haunted area.

"Let us now find out what occurred in the *old theatre*, the one that is now a Baptist Church," I said, and turned to Mrs. Adams. "What happened to you there?"

"Shortly after I entered the theatre for the first time—that's the old barn—I was helping on the sets for one of the plays when I heard directly above us some footsteps. *Someone was pacing back and forth above us in the loft!*"

"A man?"

"A man's footsteps, heavy, long strides. This was about three years ago. I was with another player, a gentleman, and I turned to him, saying, 'I thought we were alone here—who's up there?' Instead of an answer, he took me outside the building. The only entrance to the loft was from outside the building. The loft was much too low for a man to stand, much less to walk back and forth in. Moreover the door was locked, and the lock looked as if it had been in place for quite a while. We unlocked the padlock and entered the loft. There was nobody to be seen. We looked in every nook and corner but the loft was empty. So we locked it up again and went downstairs to resume work. No sooner had we done so, when the pacing above started up again. I've heard this same pacing many times since, sometimes during the day, sometimes at night, even during performances. And there is never anyone there—visible, that is."

"Didn't the audiences notice it?"

"If they did, they must have thought it part of the performance, or crew."

"But you knew?"

"Yes, we knew the difference. We had the key and the loft was securely locked at all times. We never found out about any tragedy in this place, but I, being somehow psychic, have always felt a tragedy there—a triangle involving two men and a woman."

"You say you are psychic—have you had other impressions?"

"On one occasion I was in the theatre and commented on my belief that a murder had been committed as part of a triangle, and at this point I had a cold, clammy feeling surrounding me—and I felt this one man was trying to get through to me and that his name was something like Byron."

"Byron?"

"Yes. I started to check up on the name, but every time I was in the theatre I had this horribly oppressive feeling so that I became afraid to check any further."

"Have you had any psychic experiences before the ones at the theatre?"

"I've always been able to sense if there was going to be a death in the family . . . or trouble . . . even as a child, but people made fun of me. . . ."

"Is there any similarity between the ghostly noises heard by you at the haunted barn and at the new theatre?"

"Yes, I seem to sense that this Byron is at the other theatre also. He always liked music at the barn and does so here, too. One night we were rehearsing *A Thurber Carnival* over at the barn, and when we played some taped music and then stopped it to go home, we heard four loud bangs on the ceiling as if to tell us to continue. When we sang the same song, to see if 'he' would react, we instantly heard the ghost pacing above us. I've even had someone pull my covers *at home,* scratch the underside of my pillow and pull at my mattress, so I am wondering if he isn't following me home, too!"

"More human than ghostly!" I interjected.

"I guess he wanted my attention at home, to keep him company," Mrs. Adams replied, "or something . . . I would hear pebbles hit the roof, bumps against the wall—and I have the same cold, clammy feeling here as I had in the old theatre. I think he's attached himself to me because I'm sympathetic."

"Did you ever have any visual impression of what your friend looked like?" I asked. Evidently this was not an ordinary ghost but a lost soul looking for an explanation to his confusion.

"At the time I sensed the name Byron," Mrs. Adams recalled, "I had the impression of this man standing at my left, about five ten, a husky man, like a construction worker or logger, wearing jeans, boots, and a pale blue plaid shirt, sleeves rolled up to his elbows."

"And his face?"

"Heavy features. . . ."

"Did you feel any unfinished business around him?"

"Yes . . . he was trying to tell me about some tragedy, something he wanted to have found out—he was almost begging me to check further into that location, that area—*things that happened there at the old barn.*"

"Then it is there that we may find a solution," I conjectured, hoping that Sybil might pick up a clue where the tragedy originated.

"One time here at the new theatre, after we had heard him make noises, I said, 'Goodnight, Byron, we will see you again'; and as we were riding home in the car—I felt him sitting in the backseat. It felt so cold and clammy I was greatly relieved to get out of the car when we arrived at my house. I put my purse down in the bedroom and walked back into the living room and sat down to read; and all of a sudden that same cold, clammy feeling was with me, and my dog started to set up a howl and bark frantically, just sitting at my feet staring into the hallway!"

"Was that the last time the ghost tried to reach you?"

"Yes, I moved shortly after."

Herman Detering, one of the men active in the running of this community theatre, seemed like a quiet, soft-spoken realist to me, not the sort of flamboyant actor one might conceivably accuse of imagining things. I questioned him about his own experiences.

"Nothing special here in the new theatre, but at the old barn, I recall one early morning, I was working alone in the control booth when I heard footsteps overhead and got the distinct impression of someone looking over my shoulder, to see what I was doing. I was recording some music at the time. I shone the light on the loft, which had been locked, but there was nothing in the area where I had heard the footsteps except so many seats stacked that nobody could possibly have walked there."

"What did you do?"

"I locked the door and went home."

"Could anyone have walked in the area of the loft where you heard the steps?"

"Impossible. It is only three feet high, not counting the seats stacked there. Nothing of flesh and blood could walk there."

We proceeded to the church now called the Missionary Baptist Church which stood on a bluff overlooking the freeway access road. We had been told that our visit was not welcome when Mrs. Hinzie had requested permission from the minister, one Elder Wayne Ivett, to have a quiet sitting in the church that would not interfere with worship. He intimated that the Bible (his version, anyway) said there were no ghosts, and if there were any in his church they'd be the work of the devil and nobody in his congregation believed in ghosts.

Under the circumstances I decided not to bedevil the poor man, and to have a look at the outside of the building and see if Sybil would pick something up by being close to it. Since the minister did not own the public road, that would be legitimate.

Well, the church looked exactly like an old dairy barn, which it was originally, when a Mr. Goebel owned it. However, none of the current flock were around, so we approached and looked at it through windows. There was a big padlock on the door, so if the devil was inside, he must have gotten in through the rear entrance. Since I was not about to have any ol' devil best us, we walked around that way, too, which was not easy as the road around the barn was more fit for small animal traffic than human feet.

Sybil abruptly halted when we passed the entrance to the loft, which was a small wooden door atop three small steps. It, too, was locked.

"Someone is escaping . . . running away . . . thirty, forty years ago . . . a man is escaping after committing some crime . . . an element of violence. . . ."

"Do you feel he is still here?" I asked. The others had grouped themselves around us now, hanging on Sybil's lips.

"Yes," Sybil replied emphatically, "because he did not escape in his real life. I *think he was stabbed.* But *his* crime was not stabbing somebody else. Perhaps theft. . . ."

Mrs. Beverly Adams reacted at this moment as if something of importance had just struck her.

"That's what I felt all along," she said excitedly, "and I had the impression that the man who was stabbed was the lover of the wife of the man who did the stabbing."

As we passed the rear of the building, one of the party noticed that the back door was open. I hesitated to enter, for the welcome mat was certainly not out for us; on the other hand, any tourist visiting the area would have walked in and not have committed a sin, for a church is the house of God and should be open to all, no matter who they are.

We decided to have a look at the inside of the barn church, since fate had obviously so arranged it. The inside was plain and uninspiring. A small room to the right of the stage and a washroom were all that the building contained in addition to the stage, on which the pulpit stood, and the seventy-five seats. But then faith does not require fancy trappings.

I turned to Sybil for her impressions.

"Same thing here . . . the man trying to escape . . . I think he was connected with some crime connected with the earth . . . stealing . . . he was killed upstairs. . . ."

We went outside again, for the atmosphere suddenly seemed very heavy.

"I wonder if any of the congregation has heard the footsteps," I wondered out loud, and Gwen Hinzie took me up on that.

"When we were here in August—just two months ago—a lady and her 14-year-old daughter, members of this church, came in while we were here, looking at the church. I questioned them about the phenomena and the girl looked at her mother and said—'Shall I tell them?'

"It seems that she and a young friend had clearly heard footsteps overhead especially while music was being played. On one occasion the two girls were alone in the barn church, and one of them tried the piano.

"Suddenly, both of them heard footsteps in the loft over their heads. They were quite alone in the building, or so they thought, and they went to check the door to the loft. It was tightly locked."

"In other words," I said, "the haunted barn is still *active?*"

Mrs. Hinzie nodded. "I'm afraid so."

I asked both Sybil Leek and Beverly Adams to send mental messages to the unfortunate young man who thought he had to stay on because of his tragic death, that he need not do so, but that, in effect, all was well for him now.

He seemed to have found a measure of joy in watching the theatricals underneath his self-imposed prison. When the barn ceased to be a theatre and became a church, he stayed on. Perhaps he does not even know the difference. That's how it is sometimes with ghosts.

The Restless Dead

Not only houses can be haunted, but people as well. There are literally thousands of cases where people have seen or heard the ghost of a dead person, usually a person with unfinished business on his mind at the time death overtook him.

Let me set down my criteria for such experience, so that we understand what we are dealing with. When a person dreams of a dead relative this may or may not have significance. When the dream includes specific details unknown to the dreamer at the time and later found correct, then the dreamer is getting a psychic message in the dream state when his unconscious is free from the conscious mind and thus easier to reach.

I have examined hundreds upon hundreds of recent cases and carefully eliminated the doubtful or hallucinatory. What remains is hardcore evidence.

California, land of sunshine and pleasant living, has a great many such incidents, perhaps because death here is something alien, something that does not quite fit with the warmth and serenity of climate and outlook.

Take the case of Mrs. G.A., in Santa Susana, for instance. Mrs. A. is not a person given to belief in the supernatural. In fact, her total disbelief that the events that shook her up in 1958 were in any way psychic caused her to contact me. Somehow the "rational" explanation—grief over the passing of her husband—did not satisfy her eager mind and ultimately she wanted to know.

Her husband and Mrs. A. were working on their boat in the back-yard on a warm California day. Suddenly, she heard him cry out "Honey," as if in pain. He had been working with an electric sander at the time. Alarmed, Mrs. A. turned around in time to see him clutching the sander to his chest. He had been accidentally electrocuted. Quickly she pulled the electric plug out and tried to hold him up, all the while screaming for help; but it was too late.

The ironical part was that A. had had nightmares and waking fears about just such an accident—death from electrocution.

Two months went by and Mrs. A. tried to adjust to her widow-hood. One night she was roused from deep sleep by "something" in the room. As soon as she was fully awake she perceived an apparition of her late husband, suspended in the air of their room!

He did not make any sound or say anything. Strangely enough, the apparition wore no shirt; he was bare-chested, as he would not have been in life.

In a moment he was gone, and Mrs. A. went back to sleep. In the morning she convinced herself that it was just a case of nerves. The day wore on. It was 4:30 in the afternoon and Mrs. A. was seated on her liv-ing room couch, relaxing and waiting for a telephone call from her mother. All of a sudden, she heard her car drive up to the door. She realized at once that this could not be the case, since she was not driv-ing it, but it struck her also that this was the precise time her husband always drove up to the door, every afternoon!

Before she could fully gather her wits, he was there in the room with her. He looked as he had always looked, not transparent or any-thing as ethereal as that. Mrs. A. was literally frozen with fear. Her late husband knelt before her seemingly in great emotion, exclaiming, "Honey, what's wrong ?"

At this point, Mrs. A. found her tongue again and quietly, as qui-etly as she was able to, told her late husband what had happened to him.

"There has been an accident, and you were killed."

When she had said those words, he uttered the same sound he did at the time of the accident—"Honey!" as if remembering it—and instantly he vanished.

Mrs. A. has never felt him around her again since. Evidently, her husband has adjusted to his new state.

Sometimes the ghostly denizens drive the living out—only to find themselves without a home in the end. Such was the strange case recently of a house in Paso Robles owned by the Adams family. I heard about their predicament when I appeared on the Art Linkletter Show.

Mrs. Adams has three children, aged 11, 10, and 9. Their problem: the house they bought used to be a "red light house," as she put it. Before they bought it, two girls lived there with an old man as a kind of chaperon. After the police forced the girls out of business, the old man remained behind until his death.

Shortly after moving in, the Adams family noticed that all was not well with their home. The husband worked nights, and at the time he went to work between the hours of midnight and three A.M., strange noises were heard outside the house, such as banging on the wall—only nobody human was doing it. This was in December of 1957. Gradually, the noises changed from a slight rattle to a big, loud bang on the walls. Occasionally it sounded as if someone were ripping the window screens off the house.

Mrs. Adams called the police repeatedly, but they could not find anything or anyone causing the disturbances. Her husband, who worked in a bakery, also heard the noises one night when he stayed home. Always at the same time, in the early morning hours.

Soon Mrs. Adams also distinguished footsteps and human voices when nobody was walking or talking. On one occasion she could clearly hear two men talking, one saying he would try to get into the house. Then there were knocks on the walls as if someone were trying to communicate.

It got so bad that the Adamses started to make inquiries about the past of their property, and it was then, two years after they had moved in, that they finally learned the truth about the house and its former use.

They decided to let the ghosts have the house and moved out, to another house which has always been free from any disturbances. The haunted red light house they rented out to people not particular about ghosts. But they did not do too well at that. Nobody liked to stay in the house for long.

That was in 1964. When I checked up on Mrs. Adams in 1966, things had changed quite a lot.

"They tore it up repeatedly," Mrs. Adams explained, and since it was an old house, the owners did not feel like putting a lot of money into it to fix the damage done by the nightly "party."

It got to be under standard and the city council stepped in. Thus it was that the ghost house of Paso Robles was torn down by official order. The Adams family now owns an empty lot on which they can't afford to build a new house. And the ghosts? They have no place to go to, either. Serves them right!

Ralph Madison is a man who lives life and has enjoyed every moment of it. He is a great-grandfather four times over and not a young man, but he was still working in 1965, when I heard his strange story, as a part-time security guard in the museum at Stanford University.

He makes his home in Palo Alto, and has been married to the same woman since 1916. Not boasting much formal education, Madison considers himself a self-made man. Perhaps the only thing unusual about him is a penchant to send people tape recordings instead of letters. But perhaps Madison is only being practical. In another ten years' time we may all correspond in that way.

I would not be interested in Mr. Madison if it weren't for one particular incident in his life, an incident that made him wonder about his sanity—and, after having reassured himself about it—about the meaning of such psychic experiences.

It happened in 1928 in Palo Alto, on Emerson Street. Ralph Madison was minding his own business, walking in the vicinity of the five-hundred block, when he noticed a man he knew slightly, by the name of Knight. Mr. Knight operated a cleaning establishment nearby. The two men stopped to talk and Madison shook hands with his acquaintance.

It struck him as peculiar, however, that the man's voice seemed unusually wispy. Moreover, Knight's hands were clammy and cold!

They exchanged some words of no particular significance, and then they parted. Madison started out again and then quickly glanced around at his friend. The man he had just shaken hands with had disappeared into thin air. At this moment it came to him with shocking suddenness that Mr. Knight had been dead and buried for five years.

In a high state of excitement, Madison ran into a real estate office operated nearby by a Mr. Vandervoort whom he knew well. Quickly relating what had happened to him, Madison was assured that Knight had indeed been dead for five years and that he, Madison, was seeing things.

But Ralph Madison knows in his heart he shook hands with a dead man on a street corner in Palo Alto, in plain daylight.

A strange case came to my attention recently, strange among strange experiences in that it involves a kind of possession against which orthodox medicine seems to be powerless.

At least Mrs. B. of Burlingame went to six doctors for help, took countless nerve tonics and calming agents—but to no avail. When she heard of my work in ESP, she contacted me with a cry for help. This was in March of 1966 and I finally talked to her in October of the same year. Her voice was firm and there was no sign of panic in it. Still, what had happened to her would cause a lot of stronger people to throw in the towel in a struggle against insanity.

A widow now, Mrs. B. originally came from the Middle West where her father had been a physician, as were his father and grandfather before him. Her mother before her marriage was a high school teacher and she herself was the daughter of a Senator.

Mrs. B. taught school also and later took up nursing as a profession. She was married from 1949 to 1960 and considers her marriage a most happy one. No emotional turmoils followed her widowhood, since Mrs. B. was an avid reader and musician and had surrounded herself with congenial friends. One could safely say that her life was serene and well ordered.

But it took her three letters, before she could commit to paper the shocking experiences that had suddenly entered her life. I always insist on written statements from those reporting seemingly paranormal cases, and Mrs. B. reluctantly complied. It was her feeling of shame that prompted me to omit her full name from this account.

It started with a presence in the room with her, when she knew that she was quite alone. Before long, she felt the intimacies of another person on her body—a person she could not see!

She thought she had cancer and consulted every conceivable specialist, but got a clean bill of health. Yet, the attacks continued. Was she imagining the unspeakable? She began to question her own sanity. The physicians she consulted knew no answer except to reassure her that she had no physical ailment to account for the strange sensations.

Now I have heard similar stories about "attacks" by sex-minded ghosts before and sometimes they are the imagination of a frustrated middle-aged woman. No doubt about it, a change of life can produce some pretty wild symptoms in a woman, or for that matter in a man. Thus it was with extreme caution that I accepted the testimony of this lady. I wanted to be sure the case was psychic, not psychiatric.

I questioned her along ESP lines. Had she ever had psychic experiences—other than the very graphically described invasions of her privacy—in the house she lived in, or elsewhere?

Apparently, the answer was affirmative. Some months before her contacting me, she was doing housework on a Sunday, when she heard a voice speak to her, apparently out of thin air, a voice she did not recognize but which sounded rather low and was speaking in a whisper.

"The G.'s are coming today." Now the G.'s were friends of Mrs. B.'s living at some distance. She had not seen or heard from them for months, thus was not expecting their visit in any way. Consequently, Mrs. B. refused to believe the strange "voice." But the voice insisted, repeating the sentence once more!

Mrs. B. continued with her work, when around 1 P.M. she decided to take a rest. At 2 o'clock, the doorbell rang. Since she was not expecting any visitors, she was slow in answering it. It was the G.'s, just as the voice had said!

Since then, the ghostly voice has been heard by Mrs. B. many times, always announcing someone's coming. The voice has never erred. The name, day and exact hour are given and each time it comes to pass.

The presence of an unseen person continued to trouble Mrs. B. but in addition she heard a voice speak two words, "my wife," several times, and on another occasion, "her husband," as if someone were trying to tell her something she should know.

Mrs. B., of course, rejected the idea that it might be her own late husband who was haunting her, for he never believed in anything psychic while in the flesh. Shortly after this line of thought, she clearly heard the voice say, "She just does not understand."

When I was ready to see Mrs. B. in Burlingame, which is near San Francisco, she had already moved to another house in Santa Monica. It was there that I finally talked to her.

The situation was much the same, it appeared, ruling out any possibility that the ghost or invader was somehow tied up with the house in Burlingame.

The voice, which she still did not recognize, was very insistent now.

"Her husband . . . she just does not understand" was followed on another occasion by a statement, "I would do anything in the world . . . I wonder what she would do if she knew."

Then the words "sweetheart" and "my wife" were added and repeated on many occasions. All this happened to Mrs. B. in a house in which she was quite alone at the time.

Still, Mrs. B. refused to face the possibility that her husband, skeptic though he might have been in the physical state, had learned the truth about psychic communications and was now trying to reach her—in the way *a husband might!*

Sometimes the tragedies that make people of flesh and blood into non-physical ghosts are less horrifying than the ghosts that continue a kind of forlorn existence in the world in between—or rather I should say the ghosts are not the comparatively benign apparitions of people as we knew them, but something far more terrible, far more sinister.

Wayne Barber is a young ambulance driver who used to run the service out of Baker, California, one of the worst stretches of road because of the many automobile accidents that have happened on it. Now it is my personal opinion that half the people driving cars should not, and, furthermore, that licenses should be renewed only after annual examinations of those who qualify for them. What happened to Mr. Barber is only one case in point.

Aged 29 years, six feet tall and married, Wayne Barber is a rough and tough man who, as he put it, "can eat a ham sandwich in complete comfort with dead bodies all over the highway." It's part of his business and he isn't the least bit sentimental about it.

Until February 1966 he had absolutely no belief in anything resembling the human soul, anything beyond death. But then something pretty terrible happened.

On Washington's Birthday there was a wreck about five miles east of Baker, California, in which seven people died. A group of three drunks was heading down the freeway in the wrong direction and had a head-on collision with a carload of people going to Las Vegas. In this car a mother and father were taking their daughter and her fiancé to be married!

The car headed in the wrong direction burned before the bodies could be removed. The others, mother and father, were pinned in their car and the two children that were to be married were thrown clear. All seven were dead.

"Any wreck involving the living is worse than handling the dead," Barber explained, "and this was not the worst wreck my attendant and I had ever handled. I am mentioning this so you don't think we had a case of nerves."

After making certain there were no survivors, they cleared the bodies off the highway and started to check them for identification. Removing the bodies is part of an ambulance crew's work, and Barber and his aide did just that—or what was left of the bodies—in order to clear the road for traffic.

A day later a sandstorm came up, and five women travellers in the area could not proceed because of poor visibility on the road. They appealed to Barber to put them up overnight at the ambulance station, and he readily agreed. He then went to the rear of the building to put together five cots for them from his supplies of standby equipment.

It was around 10 :30 P.M. and the yard lights failed to work. He could see only about five feet, but he carried a small flashlight. As he busied himself on the standby rig near the corner of the building, he suddenly felt himself *watched*. Who would be standing there watching him in the driving storm?

He spun around and faced something he had never faced before.

There at arm's length was what he later described as "a thing," a terribly mutilated figure of a human being, a boy, with legs hanging crookedly, just as they had been compounded in the accident, the body twisted at the waist and the head hanging at a weird angle, indicating a broken neck. But the eyes were watching him, looking straight into his—living, human eyes!

Barber was frozen to the spot long enough to observe every detail of the horrible apparition.

"There was a sad longing in the eyes, and a gratitude," Barber said afterwards. "In those eyes there was no intention to harm me."

Suddenly, his reactions returned and he tore into the ghost with his flashlight as if it were a knife. But he was thrashing thin air, and nothing but sand hit his face!

At this point his German shepherd, a very rugged animal, came out of the darkness howling, out of his senses with fear. Barber continued on back to the house with the stretchers for the cots. It was then that he saw what he calls "the other thing." This one was a girl. He did not see as many details of this ghost as he had observed of the male apparition, but he saw her outline clearly. It was enough for him to take a day off immediately.

But the dog was not the same for weeks, becoming a complete nervous wreck until he had to be given away to a sympathetic lady. Soon after he was run over and killed.

Barber married after this experience and he had no intention of ever talking about it to his new bride. But the dog he had acquired to take the place of the shepherd soon behaved in the most extraordinary fashion also, precisely the same as the shepherd. What was the dog seeing around the place? Barber then told his wife about the two ghosts.

The second dog had to be given away, too, when he became unmanageable in the place. Now Barber has a pug dog and he seems to

be able to tolerate the influences that still pervade the spot a little better than his two predecessors.

"Something here is protecting me," Wayne Barber explains, and he
and his wife refer to the ghosts somewhat bravely as "the little people."

Had the spirits of those two who never lived out their normal lives
attached themselves to their rescuer?

Mrs. Daphne R. lives in Malibu, California, with her husband and
children. Her second husband is a Navy man and they have moved frequently. Originally English, Mrs. R. has had a number of psychic experiences and is unquestionably mediumistic. But the incident I found
most fascinating had to do with a ghost her little daughter encountered.
It interested me because not all the restless dead are hopeless, pathetic
human beings in trouble, unable to help themselves. This ghost even
helped another person. It happened in 1952.

"I was working in Heidelberg as a secretary, and I had a little three-
year-old daughter from a broken marriage, who lived with my parents
in England. I got awfully lonely, and increasingly sure that I ought to
bring her over to Germany to live with me. So one day I flew over to
England, and rode the train down to Folkestone, collected the child and
her belongings and took her back to London. I had to wait a few days
for her papers, so I stayed at the private home of a rather well-known
photographer.

"He was most kind, and offered to put my daughter and me up for
the time we had to spend in London. He was a widower. I hardly saw
him, as he was out all the time on assignments. He had a small boy of
around four or five, and an English nanny. They lived in a rather posh
narrow house.

"One night I wanted to go to the theatre, and asked the nanny if
she would baby-sit for me and keep an eye on my little girl. I should
add here that the child was in a terrible emotional state about leaving

my parents (I was almost like a stranger to her), and she wept all the time, and seemed calmer with the nanny than with me.

"Anyway, I went out, and left the little girl in the double bed we were sharing, and the nanny promised to pop in and out of the bedroom to watch her, as the little boy had also gone to bed nearby. I wore a black suit—which is an item of importance. When I got back around 11:00 P.M., the nanny was in the kitchen, and she said Kitty had cried quite a bit (not for me, but for my parents, whom she missed), and that suddenly she had been quiet, so the nanny had run up to take a peek at her, and she was fast asleep and smiling in her sleep. The next morning I awakened, and the child was in a very happy mood, so much so that I said to her that I was so happy to see her smiling for the first time in about two days, and that perhaps she was a bit happier about going to live with Mummy in Germany. She replied that yes, she was very happy. Then she said, 'I was unhappy last night, and I cried, because I wanted my Nana (she referred to my mother), but then the LADY came over to my bed and stroked my head and told me you were out and would be back soon, and that she would stay with me until you got back.' I merely thought she was referring to the 'nanny' in the house, and said 'Yes, nanny is a nice lady,' and my daughter said, 'Oh no, it wasn't the nanny, it was a pretty lady with long red hair, and she was beautiful.' Then she went on to prattle about how the 'Lady' had told her how much Mummy loved her, and how unhappy it made Mummy to see the child cry, and that really it was much better for her to be with her mother than with her grandparents, and the child ended up saying 'I realized she is right, Mummy.'

"Later that day, I asked the nanny if she had had a guest, and when she said no, I told her about the above incident, and she was quite aghast, and related to me that her master's late wife had long red hair, and was a beautiful woman, but had been very unhappy, and I suppose nowadays we would think she was mentally unbalanced; apparently she threw herself from the balcony of the room in which my daughter and I had been sleeping. She was so interested in this—the nanny, I mean—that she asked my daughter what the 'lovely lady' had been wearing, and Kitty, my daughter, said, 'A lovely long blue satin nightie,' and later the nanny said that the late lady of the house had committed suicide in a blue satin evening house-gown."

Maureen B. is a San Francisco housewife now, but in 1959, when her first brush with the uncanny took place, she was attending college summer school and living by herself in the old house her parents, Mr. and Mrs. John F., had bought recently on Toravel Street.

Records showed the house to date back to 1907, which is pretty old for the area. The parents had gone away on vacation and Maureen should have had the place to herself—but she didn't.

Sometimes she would stay awake all night because she had the feeling of not being alone in the house. There was *something* or *someone* staring at her—someone she could not see!

The tension made her ill, but nothing further happened until the summer of 1960 when she found herself studying late one night in the breakfast room downstairs.

Although physically tired, she was mentally quite alert. The door leading to the back porch, where the pantry was situated, was locked from the inside, and the key was in the lock. The door leading from this back porch into the yard outside was double-locked and the key was hidden away. None of the windows in the old house would open.

Nevertheless Maureen suddenly heard, in the still of the night, a swishing sound from the other side of the door, followed by footsteps and the clinking of a chain. Her heart pounded with fear as she sat there frozen, staring at the door. The key in it was turning and a voice outside the door was moaning.

For a couple of moments Maureen sat still. Then she gathered up

578

her wits and ran up the stairs and roused her father. Quickly he came down and unlocked the door, and searched the back porch and the yard. There was nobody to be seen.

The next day the family decided that Maureen "must have heard" streetcar noises from the street. As for the key turning in the lock, why, that was just her overtired eyes playing tricks on her.

Maureen knew differently, for she had lived with the noises of streetcars for a long time and the moan she had heard outside the door was no streetcar. And the key moved back and forth in the lock before her eyes. It did not make a clicking sound, however, as it does when it engages the lock to unlock the door. Since the rest of the family had not experienced anything out of the ordinary in the house and did not accept the possibility of the psychic, Maureen found it convenient to let the matter drop, even though she found out a few things about the house her folks had acquired back in 1957.

It had been an antique shop previously, and prior to that an old invalid had lived there. His bed was near the front window giving onto the street, so that he could watch the goings-on outside in the way old people often want to—it gives them a feeling of not being shut-ins, but still part of the active world. By the time he died, the house was in deplorable condition and a real estate firm bought it and fixed it up.

For many years the old man had called this house his home, gradually becoming more and more invalided until death had taken him away from it. But had it?

When I appeared on a special television program with Regis Philbin in Los Angeles in the fall of 1966, on which we discussed ghosts and psychic experiences and illustrated them with some of the evidential photographs I had taken of such apparitions, many people wrote or called with psychic adventures of their own or houses they wanted me to investigate.

One of the most interesting cases involved a man not particularly friendly toward the possibility of personal survival or mediumship who had been forced by his experiences to re-evaluate his views.

Earle Burney is an ex-Marine who lives in San Diego. He was discharged from the Marine Corps in June 1945 and went to work for the Navy as a guard at a Navy Electronics Laboratory installed since World War II in an old mansion at Loma Portal, California. The work was highly classified, and security at the place was pretty strict as a consequence.

At first Burney's job was to guard the mansion during the night, coming in at 11:15 P.M. He knew nothing about the place, and the man he relieved, for some strange reason, never talked to him about the work—seconds after Burney got there, his predecessor was out the door, as if he could not get away fast enough to suit himself.

Burney then inspected the place from top to bottom, which was part of his routine. He locked the door he had come through and put a pot of coffee or the fire in the kitchen. The house had retained much of its ancient glory, with mahogany paneling and a big, winding stairway leading up to the second story. He was puzzled, though, by a bullet hole someone had put in one of the wall ventilators.

One morning not long after he had started his job, he was sitting at his watchman's desk drinking coffee, when he heard footsteps upstairs. It was just two o'clock and there was no one in the building besides himself.

Naturally, Burney jumped up immediately. The footsteps were heavy and were coming down the hallway toward the head of the stairs. Burney started up the stairs, but when he reached the top, the footsteps had stopped dead and there was nobody within sight.

He searched every inch of the house but could not find any human being who could have caused the footsteps.

After that, he heard the steps again a few more times, but by now he was not so excited over it. He decided to ascribe it to "the house settling or cooling off," although he could not really explain how such a noise could sound like human footsteps.

Then another phenomenon puzzled him even more. He would be sitting by his desk with only a small light burning, and the rest of the house as dark as could be. Still, he would hear music. The first time this happened, he thought that perhaps someone had left a radio on somewhere. But he found no radio anywhere. Then he discovered, as he searched the dark recesses of the old mansion, that the music was heard everywhere exactly the same way—no louder, no softer. It was faint, but then it would stop, and Burney realized he had not imagined it but really heard "something."

Burney decided to take his little spaniel dog Amber with him. The dog was friendly and fun-loving, about as normal as a dog can be.

That night, he took her with him and made her lie down by his desk. No sooner had he done so than he noticed a strange change in the behavior of the animal. Suddenly very nervous, the dog would not go near the stairs, and just lay there near the desk, whining.

At two A.M. the ghostly footsteps came. The dog let out a blood-curdling scream and headed for the door. Burney let her out and she shot out into the dark, hitting an iron statue across the yard. Although not physically hurt, the dog was never the same after this incident. The slightest noise would frighten her and her fun-loving nature had given way to a pitiful existence full of neurotic fears.

Burney was very much puzzled by all this and decided to ask some questions at last.

He discovered that others had heard those nighttime footsteps too. In fact, there was a big turnover of guards at the mansion and the reason he, an ex-Marine, had been hired was primarily because of the strange events. They figured he would not be scared of a ghost. He wasn't, but the job was hard on him, nevertheless. Especially after he found out about the bullet hole in the wall ventilator. A frightened guard had put it there. But bullets don't stop ghosts.

The Restless Dead walk on, walk on. Some of them are lucky because someone *cares* and brings a medium to the house or calls me to help. But for every restless one who gets help, there are a thousand who don't. I have come to the conclusion that there are literally thousands and thousands of houses where someone died unhappily in one way or another—not necessarily violently, but not peacefully—and still walks the floors. I wish I could help them all.